PUBLICATIONS
OF THE
ARMY RECORDS SOCIETY
VOL. 25

LORD KITCHENER
AND THE
WAR IN SOUTH AFRICA
1899–1902

W0007271

The Army Records Society was founded in 1984 in order to publish original records describing the development, organisation, administration and activities of the British Army from early times.

Any person wishing to become a member of the Society is requested to apply to the Hon. Secretary, c/o the National Army Museum, Royal Hospital Road, London, SW3 4HT. The annual subscription entitles the member to receive a copy of each volume issued by the Society in that year, and to purchase back volumes at reduced prices. Current subscription details, whether for individuals living within the British Isles, for individuals living overseas, or for institutions, will be furnished on request.

The Council of the Army Records Society wish it to be clearly understood that they are not answerable for opinions or observations that may appear in the Society's publications. For these the responsibility rests entirely with the Editors of the several works.

The Society's website can be found at www.armyrecordssociety.org.uk

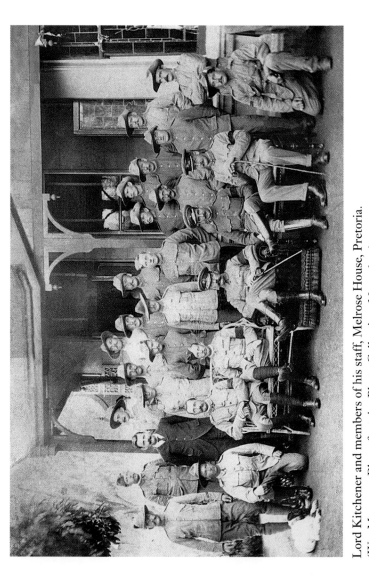

Lord Kitchener and members of his staff, Melrose House, Pretoria. (War Museum, Bloemfontein, Photo Collection, No 15609.)

Lord Kitchener and the War in South Africa 1899–1902

Edited by
André Wessels

Published by
SUTTON PUBLISHING LIMITED
for the
ARMY RECORDS SOCIETY
2006

First published in the United Kingdom in 2006 by
Sutton Publishing Limited · Phoenix Mill · Thrupp · Stroud
Gloucestershire · GL5 2BU

Copyright © The Army Records Society, 2006

All rights reserved. No part of this publication may be reproduced,
stored in a retrieval system, or transmitted, in any form, or by any means,
electronic, mechanical, photocopying, recording or otherwise, without
the prior permission of the publisher and copyright holders.

British Library Cataloguing in Publication Data
A catalogue record for this book is available from the British Library.

Lord Kitchener and the War in South Africa 1899–1902
Wessels, André
(Department of History, University of the Free State)

ISBN 0-7509-4557-5

Typeset in Ehrhardt.
Typesetting and origination by
Sutton Publishing Limited.
Printed in Great Britain by
J.H. Haynes & Co. Ltd, Sparkford.

ARMY RECORDS SOCIETY
Charity Registration No. 326484

COUNCIL FOR 2005–2006

PRESIDENT
Professor Sir Michael Howard CH CBE MC DLitt FBA FRHistS

VICE-PRESIDENTS
Field Marshal Sir John Chapple GCB CBE DL MA FSA FRSA
Professor John Gooch BA PhD FRHistS

COUNCILLORS
Chairman: Professor Ian Beckett BA PhD FRHistS
Colonel Hugh Boscawen BA
Mark Connelly BA PhD
Professor David French BA PhD FRHistS
Nikolas Gardner BA MA PhD
Lieutenant-General Sir Alistair Irwin CBE MA
John Lee BA MA
Brigadier Allan Mallinson BA
Patricia Methven BA Dip Arch FKC
Major-General Jonathan Riley BA MA DSO
Major-General Sebastian Roberts OBE
Professor Peter Simkins MBE MA
Roderick Suddaby MA
Major-General Julian Thompson CB OBE
Dan Todman BA MPhil PhD

HONORARY SECRETARY
Nikolas Gardner BA MA PhD

HONORARY TREASURER
Mike Singh Esq

MEMBERSHIP SECRETARY
Chris Mann BA PhD

Contents

CONTENTS

Map

Editorial Acknowledgements

The vast majority of the extant papers of Lord Kitchener are in the National Archives (TNA), formerly known as the Public Record Office (PRO), Kew, and in the National Army Museum (NAM), London. I gratefully acknowledge the kind assistance, generously given, of Dr Peter Boyden of the NAM, as well as the staff of the Reading Room of the NAM, and of Mr John Carr and Mr James Guthrie (both of TNA), and also the staff of TNA's Reading Room. I am also grateful to TNA and the NAM for providing access to the documents in its possession. Documents from the NAM have been included by kind permission of the Director of the NAM. Dr Peter Boyden has to be mentioned once again for all his time and assistance with regard to copyright matters, not only with regard to documents kept by the NAM.

I also gratefully acknowledge the generosity of the following in enabling me to consult and, where requested, to publish documents in their possession and/or copyright: Ms Pamela Clark of the Royal Archives, Windsor; Ms Kate O'Brien (Archives Services Manager, King's College, London) and Ms Patricia J. Methven (Director of Archives Services, King's College, London), as well as the other staff members of the Liddell Hart Centre for Military Archives; Dr William Frame and the late Mr Robert Smith of the British Library's Manuscript Room, as well as the staff members of the old Manuscript Reading Room in the British Museum building; Ms Jane Hogan of the University of Durham's Archives and Special Collections; Ms Natalie Adams and other staff members of the University of Cambridge's Churchill Archives Centre; Ms Zoe Lubowiecka of the Hove Reference Library; Ms Helen Wakely of the Lambeth Palace Library, London; the Bodleian Library, Oxford; the Killie Campbell Africana Library, Durban; Ms Diana Madden of the Brenthurst Library, Johannesburg; Mr Stephen Walton of the Imperial War Museum, London, and the Public Record Office of Northern Ireland, Belfast.

Documents in the Royal Archives are reproduced here by the gracious permission of Her Majesty Queen Elizabeth II. Material in Crown copyright is reproduced with the permission of the Controller of Her

Majesty's Stationery Office. Other material is reproduced with the kind permission of the Rt Hon The Third Earl Kitchener; the Rt Hon The Viscount Midleton; the Warden and Fellows of New College, Oxford; the Trustees of the Liddell Hart Centre for Military Archives; the Hamilton family; the Rt Hon The Lord Baden-Powell; Mr Peter B. Blood; the Deputy Keeper of the Records, Public Record Office of Northern Ireland, and the Trustees of the Imperial War Museum. If anyone's copyright has been inadvertently infringed, I hope my sincere apologies will be accepted.

Among other individuals – and I am sorry if I have not named them all – I am indebted to Dr William Philpott, Honorary Secretary of the Army Records Society; Colonel Frik Jacobs, Director of the War Museum, Bloemfontein; Professor M.C.E. van Schoor; Mr Johan Loock; Professor Naòmi Morgan; Ms Elria Wessels; Dr Dirk van der Bank; Ms Marianna Botes; Rev. Dr Fanus Erasmus; Dr Keith Surridge; Dr Mark Curthoys; Rev. Dr Stowell Kessler; Dr Arnold van Dyk; Professor Kay de Villiers; Adv. Jaco de Bruin, and to my parents and sister for their encourage-ment. I owe a particular debt to Professor Ian Beckett, Chairman of the Army Records Society, who first raised this project with me, for his wise guidance and all his help so generously given.

I would also like to mention the kind assistance given to me by staff members of the following archives, libraries, organisations and institutions: the National Archives of South Africa, Pretoria; the Free State Archives Repository, Bloemfontein; the Library of the University of the Free State, Bloemfontein (in particular Ms Jean Prophet); the Bodleian Library and the Rhodes House Library, Oxford; the Imperial War Museum, London; the House of Lords Record Office, London; the Gloucestershire Record Office; the Devon Record Office, Exeter; the Scottish Record Office (both at the General Register House and at the West Register House), Edinburgh; the Churchill Archives Centre, University of Cambridge; the Royal Artillery Institution Library, Woolwich, and the Royal Commission on Historical Manuscripts, London.

Marizanne Janse van Vuuren did most of the basic transcriptions of the sometimes hardly legible documents. Without her assistance, this publication would not have been completed on schedule. The following assistants in the Department of History also contributed in one way or other: Anna-Karin Evaldsson, Kobie-Mari van der Walt and Tshitso Challa.

Most of the typing was done by Mrs Ansie Olivier, whose patience and diligence I gratefully acknowledge. Typing assistance was also provided by Mrs Christa Mitchell, Mrs Christine van Zyl, Mrs Miemie de Vries and Mrs Liska Engelbrecht. Eventually the final draft of the manuscript was produced with great skill and patience by Mrs Ansie Olivier. The language editing of the introductions was done with great care by Ms Alice de Jager.

André Wessels
Department of History
University of the Free State
Bloemfontein
Republic of South Africa
31 May 2002

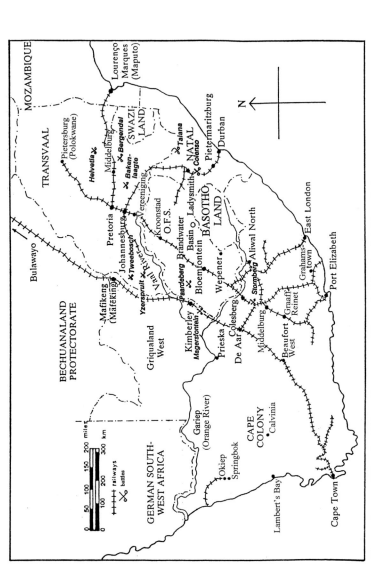

General map of South Africa 1899–1902. (Compiled by André Wessels.)

Introduction

Horatio Herbert Kitchener was born on 24 June 1850 at a shooting lodge called Gunsborough House (or Villa), today known as Coolbeha House, some 5 km from Listowel in County Kerry, Ireland (today the Republic of Ireland). Herbert (as he was known)[1] was the second son of Lieutenant-Colonel Henry Horatio Kitchener (originally from Cossington, Leicestershire) and Anne Frances[2] ('Fanny'), daughter of Rev. John Chevallier, vicar of Aspall Hall, Suffolk. Henry was the first in his line who followed a career in the British Army. Frances Chevallier was of Huguenot origin. She married Henry on 24 July 1845, when she was nineteen and he 39. They went to India, where Henry served in the 9th Foot (Norfolk Regiment), but Frances began to suffer from bad health, and the couple returned to England in 1847, together with their first son, Henry Elliott Chevallier. In London, Frances Emily Jane ('Millie') was born in 1848. Lieutenant-Colonel Kitchener could not find a military appointment in England, and consequently sold his commission in 1849. That same year he moved his family to Ireland to begin a new career as a farmer.[3]

Herbert had a squint. His eyesight was defective, which meant that he was not good at sport, and he was also very shy. When he was thirteen years old, the Kitcheners (whose family now also included two more sons, namely Arthur, born in 1852, and Frederick Walter, born in 1858) moved to Switzerland, where it was hoped Mrs Kitchener's health would improve (she had problems with her lungs), but she died on 27 October 1864, leaving Herbert devastated. In Switzerland, the young Herbert went to an English boarding-school at the Château du Grand Clos in Renaz, and he learnt to understand, speak and write the French language – skills he never lost. In February 1868 he entered the Royal Military Academy, Woolwich, and passed out in December 1870. He was now qualified to take up a commission (as Lieutenant, on 4 January 1871) in the Royal Engineers – but not before he had briefly served as a volunteer on the side of the French in the Franco-Prussian War, from 27 December 1870, just for a few days. As a Royal Engineer, Kitchener initially did routine service at home, but in 1874 he was seconded to the Palestine Exploration Fund.

After Britain acquired Cyprus in 1878, Kitchener was sent to that island to do survey work. This work was stopped because of a lack of funds, and Kitchener was sent as vice-consul to Kastamuni in Asia Minor, until March 1880, when he was able to continue his survey work on Cyprus.[4]

In 1882 Kitchener obtained short leave and went to Alexandria to take part (in an unofficial capacity) in the campaign against Arabi Pasha. He then returned to Cyprus to continue his survey work, but at the end of 1882 accepted the post of second in command of the Egyptian Cavalry. On 4 January 1883 Kitchener was promoted to Captain. In that year he did survey work in the Sinai Peninsula, and in 1884 he took part in the campaign against the Mahdi in the Sudan. On 8 October 1884 Kitchener was promoted to the brevet rank of Major. In 1884–5, during the abortive efforts to save Major-General Charles Gordon and his force in Khartoum, Kitchener served in Sir Garnet Wolseley's Intelligence Department. On 15 June 1885 Kitchener was promoted to the brevet rank of Lieutenant-Colonel, but about a month later he resigned from the Egyptian Army and returned to Britain, having established his reputation as an able and hard-working officer, and as an authority with regard to the customs and habits of the Arabs, Egyptians and Sudanese.[5]

At the end of December 1885 Kitchener went to Zanzibar as the British member of a joint British-French-German Commission (the Zanzibar Boundary Commission) that had to delimit the territory of the local sultan. The next year he was appointed Governor-General of the Eastern Sudan and the Red Sea Littoral. There he was in almost constant conflict with the local leader of the Dervishes, Osman Digna. On 17 January 1888, during a raid on Osman Digna's headquarters, Kitchener was severely wounded in the lower right jaw, but he fully recovered. For his good work in the Eastern Sudan, Kitchener was made a Brevet Colonel on 11 April 1888, and aide-de-camp to Queen Victoria, and in September 1888 he was appointed as Adjutant-General of the Egyptian Army. When in 1889 the Dervishes threatened to advance northwards all along the Nile and invade Egypt, Kitchener was given command of the cavalry in that part of the Egyptian Army that was deployed in order to repulse the invaders. As cavalry commander, Kitchener took part in the battle at Toski (3 August), where the Dervishes were severely beaten. For outstanding services rendered in this campaign, Kitchener received the CB.[6]

In 1891 Kitchener reorganized the Egyptian Police, and on 13 April 1892 he became the new Sirdar (i.e. Commander-in-Chief) of the Egyptian Army. He was convinced that the only way to establish full control over the Nile Valley was to advance into the Sudan and defeat the Mahdi and his Dervishes once and for all. He devoted most of his time to preparing for such a campaign, reorganising the Egyptian Army, appointing young and energetic British officers in key posts, and improving training and combat-readiness. While still busy with all these preparations, Kitchener was created KCMG in 1894.[7]

The River War started in 1896 with an advance on Dongola. A Dervish force was defeated at Firket on 7 June 1896, and on 24 September Dongola was occupied. On 25 September 1896 Kitchener was promoted to Major-General, and created KCB. For approximately a year thereafter, Kitchener consolidated his army's position and prepared for the next stage of his campaign. In August 1897 the British forces went on the offensive again, occupying several towns and driving the Dervishes southwards. On 8 April 1898 Kitchener defeated a large Dervish force on the Atbara, and in due course the British Cabinet ordered him to continue his advance. On 2 September 1898 Kitchener fought his most famous battle near Omdurman, when his force of about 8,200 British and 17,600 Egyptian soldiers defeated the Dervish army of some 50,000 warriors, led by Khalifa Abdullahi. The battle lasted from about 06.00 to about midday, and left approximately 11,000 Dervishes dead, at least as many wounded, and at least 5,000 taken prisoner. Kitchener's force only lost about 50 killed and 400 wounded. On 4 September Kitchener entered the ruins of Gordon's palace in Khartoum.[8]

In the meantime, Major Jean-Baptiste Marchand led a small force from the Congo in the direction of the White Nile. He reached Fashoda, whither Kitchener rushed with an escort. Kitchener negotiated with Marchand, and in due course the Egyptian flag was hoisted. Kitchener then returned to Britain (arriving on 27 October 1898) to receive a hero's welcome. He received the thanks of both houses in the British parliament (and £30,000), was fêted all across the United Kingdom and was raised to the peerage as Baron Kitchener of Khartoum (hence 'K of K') and of Aspall in the County of Suffolk. Without detracting from Kitchener's achievements in Egypt and the Sudan, it has to be noted that he was a brilliant improviser rather than a traditional successful commander-in-the-field or a true student of war. Although he was present at the most important clashes, he left most of the fighting to subordinates. But Kitchener had drive, a profound firmness of purpose, courage, character, and good judgement, and was able to win the support of and persuade the British government to authorize the steps necessary to defeat the Dervishes.[9]

Kitchener returned to the Sudan as Governor-General (19 January 1899). In the course of 1899 he successfully effected the pacification of the Sudan, and hunted down the Khalifa, who was eventually killed on 22 November.[10] Shortly afterwards, on 18 December 1899, Kitchener was informed that he had to go to Gibraltar to meet up with Lord Roberts, the new Commander-in-Chief of the British forces in South Africa, and to accompany 'Bobs' to South Africa as Chief of Staff.[11]

By the time Kitchener left Egypt to go to South Africa, he had cemented his reputation as a distinguished general, first-class administrator and organiser, and an excellent negotiator and diplomat – although in practice he did not always live up to this reputation. He was at the same time an enigmatic, complicated and controversial person. He was a workaholic and had an overpowering personality; was ambitious, ruthless and obstinate; firm, resolute, stern and strong – and yet often showed signs of insecurity; sometimes he was garrulous and self-revealing, and at other times introspective, silent, reserved, aloof, austere, and secretive. He hated new people around him,[12] hated state dinners[13] – and hated to be photographed.[14] He valued friendship, but had few real friends, and rarely made any declaration of affection.[15] These traits had led to speculation with regard to his sexual orientation. On the one hand there are those, like Frank Richardson, who regarded Kitchener as being homosexual,[16] while others, like John Pollock, refute this claim.[17] The fact of the matter is, Kitchener was a loner, a shy and lonely bachelor, probably asexual, preferring to expand the British Empire, and to further his own career.

While there are those who state that Kitchener's sympathies always remained with the high church party of the Church of England, and that he was always a convinced and professing Christian,[18] others believed him to be a free-thinker.[19] Like King Edward VII, King George V and many senior British officers, Kitchener was a Freemason.[20]

Kitchener cared for beautiful things (objects) – for example his collection of porcelain, antique furniture, and art – rather than for fellow human beings.[21] He was a grim, iron conqueror,[22] who did not have much (if any) sympathy for the wounded, not even in his own armies.[23] He definitely did not have a charming personality, being cold, capricious, abrupt, with a tendency to be unreceptive to well-intended advice, inconsiderate and tactless – without doubt a difficult officer to serve under, and as a consequence unpopular with his fellow officers of equal or lower rank. He found it difficult to delegate authority, and tended to interfere with his subordinates in the performance of their duties. Men, including fellow officers, feared rather than liked him. And yet he could also be pleasant and even genial, and was protective of those who served him faithfully, and his few intimate friends could even attest to his keen sense of humour.[24]

But, first and foremost, Herbert Kitchener was a soldier who had fought his way to the top and who (like most of his fellow Britons in the nineteenth century) believed in the progressive expansion of the British Empire. By the end of the nineteenth century his success in the Sudan had gripped the imagination of the British public – almost to the same extent as the Duke of Wellington had done after Waterloo.[25] Kitchener was his own man, a military outsider who belonged to neither Lord Roberts' nor Lord Wolseley's 'ring' of officers. This then, was the man who, on 18 December 1899, was informed that the British government had decided that he had to accompany Lord Roberts, the new Commander-in-Chief of all the British forces in South Africa, in the war against the Boers, as Chief of Staff.

Sources and Editorial Method

From about 1884, when he was 34 years old and taking part in the Nile expedition, the then Captain Horatio Herbert Kitchener diligently preserved what he regarded as important documents, including copies of telegrams and reports that he sent, as well as those he received. When he was at the War Office from 1914 as Secretary of State for War, he removed certain documents which would now be regarded as official papers. However, with regard to his personal documents (for example letters), Kitchener was very chaotic, and chance played a major role in determining what survived and what did not.[1]

After the Anglo-Boer War, Kitchener returned to England, and then sailed to India to take up his new post as Commander-in-Chief. En route to India, while sailing through the Red Sea, he threw overboard the private correspondence that he had accumulated since about 1875.[2]

Lord Kitchener's action was not the only occasion when important documents relating to the Anglo-Boer War were destroyed. As a matter of fact, it is not clear exactly what percentage of Anglo-Boer War documents have in fact survived. Up to 1939 the official papers in connection with the war were kept in a basement room (measuring some 5 metres by 5 metres) of the War Office Library in Whitehall, London, together with documents relating to the First World War. Shortly after the outbreak of the Second World War, the military authorities requisitioned this room, and all the documents were removed to wooden huts in a small square at Arnside Street in Walworth, London. On 9 September 1940, during the Blitz, incendiary bombs struck the square, totally destroying the huts. Of more than 1,000 tons of documents, only about 250 tons were saved. Much of this material was damaged by water from fire engines. It is impossible to say how much Anglo-Boer War material was lost, because the lists were amongst the documents destroyed. More than half the monthly staff diaries which give details of military operations and of the movements of the various columns, could not be traced. Documents collected by the Intelligence Division (40 large boxes full of documents) are also lost, as well as certain documents of Lord Roberts and Lord Kitchener. These include many operation reports as well as miscellaneous reports and correspondence produced by Kitchener.[3] These losses are particularly serious in the light of the fact that most of the destroyed documents deal with the history of the guerrilla phase of the Anglo-Boer War.[4]

Notwithstanding the above-mentioned unfortunate incidents, thousands of documents relating directly or indirectly to Lord Kitchener's conduct of the war in South Africa are preserved in repositories in the United Kingdom, with a large volume of copies that are available in South Africa. In the 1950s the South African historian Dr W.J. de Kock copied a vast number of documents concerning the Anglo-Boer War in British collections. The microfilms and photocopies were deposited in what is today the National Archives of South Africa in Pretoria. However, the National Army Museum's Roberts Papers, as well as the British Library's Lansdowne Papers, are among the collections not available in South Africa.

If all the surviving documents (for example letters, telegrams, despatches, memoranda, minutes and proclamations) created by Kitchener during the war, as well as all the letters that were written to him or in which there are references to him were to be published, they would fill several volumes. The correspondence between Kitchener and Roberts alone consists of nearly 900 letters. It is significant to note that in the surviving Kitchener documents there are very few references to the role played by blacks and coloureds, or to the internment camps (the term that will, instead of the emotionally charged term 'concentration camps', be used in this study).

For a single volume such as this, it has inevitably been necessary to make a most rigorous selection according to a number of criteria, for example, unpublished letters have received priority; an attempt has been made to avoid repetition of information; and with a few exceptions, only documents written or dictated by Kitchener himself, or letters directed to him personally, have been included. As far as possible, documents have been included that shed light on Kitchener's military strategy; on the nature and extent of his role as Lord Roberts' Chief of Staff, and later as Commander-in-Chief in South Africa, and the effect this role had on the course of the war; and on his relationship with Roberts and his other senior officers. The reader will hopefully obtain a first-hand view of Kitchener's interpretation of events.

For the purpose of this study, the Kitchener Papers at the National Archives (TNA), formerly known as the Public Record Office (PRO) and Lord Kitchener's letters to Lord Roberts (which are kept by the National

Army Museum, NAM), were of great importance. Consequently 73 of the 115 documents published here are from TNA and 22 from the NAM. Another collection of particular value for this publication is that kept by the Royal Archives, Windsor (correspondence between Lord Kitchener and Queen Victoria).

It was decided not automatically to exclude documents merely because they have appeared in print elsewhere, because such documents sometimes fill gaps to ensure a coherent narrative (see, for example, documents 1, 26 and 51). However, these were kept to a minimum. None of Kitchener's despatches, proclamations or hundreds of telegrams were reproduced, but where necessary cross-references to those sources will be found in the notes.

When the Anglo-Boer War broke out at 17.00 on Wednesday 11 October 1899, Lord Kitchener was Commander-in-Chief of the Egyptian Army and it was only from 18 December 1899, when he was appointed as Lord Roberts' Chief of Staff for the war in South Africa, that he became involved in the conflict. Consequently, two documents have been included in the brief Prologue. In Part 1, which covers the period from 11 January to 28 November 1900 (i.e. from just after the arrival of Roberts and Kitchener in South Africa to just before Kitchener took over as Commander-in-Chief of Her Majesty's forces in South Africa), the correspondence between Kitchener and Queen Victoria (kept by the Royal Archives, Windsor) is of great importance. It is particularly significant to note what Kitchener conveys (usually very briefly) to his Queen, and what he conveniently omits. This part of the publication not only gives a review of Kitchener's role as Roberts' Chief of Staff, but also sheds light on Roberts as Commander-in-Chief in South Africa, his great flank march via Paardeberg to Bloemfontein, his march northwards via Kroonstad and Johannesburg to Pretoria, and the outbreak of the guerrilla war. This section also includes the only letter (of importance for this volume) that was written many years after the war (see document 15), because it sheds light on the relationship between Kitchener and Roberts.

From 4 December 1900 onwards, Kitchener and Roberts wrote letters to one another on a weekly basis, as did Kitchener and Mr St John Brodrick, the Secretary of State for War. These letters form the basis and backbone of the rest of this publication. So, from December 1900 onwards, there are many more documents to choose from. Kitchener's weekly letters to Roberts and Brodrick are sometimes very similar. To indicate similarities and differences, both Kitchener's letters of

13 December 1901 have been included, viz. document 83 (to Roberts) and document 84 (to Brodrick). In Part 2 (December 1900 to March 1901) the first few months of Kitchener's command in South Africa are discussed; i.e. up to and including the Middelburg peace negotiations. When these talks failed, the war became more bitter than ever before, as Kitchener desperately tried to corner and destroy the mobile Boer commandos, resorting out of sheer necessity to unconventional, harsher and more controversial methods to end the war. These measures, and Kitchener's mood swings with regard to the conflict, come to the fore in Part 3 (April to December 1901).

Part 4 deals with the so-called New Model Drives in the Orange River Colony (January to April 1902), as well as operations during that period in other parts of the war zone, in particular the Western Transvaal. By this time Kitchener had the support of Lieutenant-General Ian Hamilton as Chief of Staff, and consequently two of Hamilton's letters (one to Brodrick and the other to Winston Churchill) are included in this section. Hamilton's comments on Kitchener's conduct of the military operations during the last few war months are elucidative, but Kitchener's correspondence with Roberts and Brodrick still forms the core of this section, although no letters of Kitchener to Roberts dating from 10 March to 8 June 1902 could be traced. In Part 5 (April and May 1902), which deals with the peace negotiations, all the letters are (with two exceptions) written by Kitchener to Brodrick, as the Commander-in-Chief kept his political master, the Secretary of State for War, informed about the progress of the talks at Klerksdorp, Vereeniging and Pretoria. The two exceptions are a letter by Brodrick to Kitchener (document 104), and an illuminating letter of Ian Hamilton to Churchill (document 105). This section also includes one letter (document 97) written by Kitchener to Brodrick at the end of March 1902, which refers, inter alia, to the coming April peace negotiations.

In the Epilogue the termination of hostilities (31 May 1902) and the end of the fighting are described briefly, as well as Kitchener's return to England. As this volume deals primarily with the military course of the Anglo–Boer War, not much attention is paid to political questions. For this reason not much of the correspondence between Kitchener and Milner was included. A lack of space obviously also played a role.

In 2000 the Army Records Society published their 17th volume, namely A. Wessels (ed.), *Lord Roberts and the War in South Africa 1899–1902*. In that Anglo–Boer War centennial publication the emphasis fell on Lord Roberts' command in South Africa (January–November

1900), albeit that his views on and influence with regard to the Kitchener phase of the conflict (December 1900–May 1902) were also portrayed and evaluated. This new publication on Kitchener and the war should be regarded as a companion volume to the Roberts book. Consequently the emphasis here is on the period of Kitchener's command (29 November 1900 onwards). In the Roberts volume a fairly elaborate background history with regard to the Anglo-Boer War was supplied in the introductions, especially for the period up to the end of November 1900. This will not be repeated in detail in this Kitchener volume, although the guerrilla phase and Kitchener's anti-guerrilla strategy will be discussed in some detail. In some instances, portions of the background history supplied in the introductions in the Roberts book will of necessity be repeated in this Kitchener book. In the light of the fact that the Kitchener volume must be able to stand on its own as an independent publication, although it is actually intended as a companion to the Roberts book, there will thus be some overlapping with the latter; and several Biographical Notes and other Notes have had to be repeated, albeit that the contexts are sometimes different; after all, many of the people who played an important role while Roberts was Commander-in-Chief in South Africa, continued do so under Kitchener. Thus, the Roberts and Kitchener publications complement one another and should ideally be studied together.

This publication is neither a biography of Kitchener, nor a day-to-day account of the Anglo-Boer War. The documents that were selected for inclusion will not necessarily provide a connected career narrative or refer to all the battles or events of the war, but will as far as possible illustrate the main issues and events and perhaps provide signposts for other historians and other interested persons. The publication aims to be a military campaign study on the role played by Kitchener with regard to the Anglo-Boer War, illustrated by 115 archival manuscripts, most of them never published before.

All the documents have been reproduced in full, but opening and closing salutations have been omitted. In some cases, a printed version of an original document exists, in which cases the two versions have been compared. Usually the printed version only differs with regard to minor aspects of punctuation. Where possible, the texts have been altered to conform with the original manuscripts.

Punctuation, grammar and spelling of the published documents have not been changed, although where a particularly extraordinary phrase or word appears, this has been emphasised by the addition of [sic]. Where a common mis-spelling occurs often, only the first instance thereof is, if deemed necessary, indicated to draw attention to the fault. A wide range of spellings are encountered when studying 'colonial wars'. As far as possible the philologically correct version is used in the introductions and notes, but alternative (and sometimes more familiar) versions are given in parentheses when the correct versions are used for the first time, for example Thukela (Tugela) River and Mafikeng (Mafeking). Where there are no full stops at the end of a sentence, two blank spaces have been left in an effort to enhance the readability of the text.

The following signs have been used in editing the text:

[   ]   indicate comment on the text or additions to the original text to make sense

…..   indicate that it was not possible to decipher a word in the manuscript

(   )   are brackets used by the authors of the original manuscripts.

The source of each document is given at the end of the document. (See also the list of abbreviations.) Within each section or part, documents run in strict chronological sequence (with one exception – see document 15). Nearly 250 persons are referred to in the 115 documents selected for publication, most of them on more than one occasion. Biographical information on most of those to whom there are two or more references in the documents, is to be found in the Biographical Notes. The following are the main sources that were used in writing the Biographical Notes: the *Dictionary of South African Biography*, *Dictionary of National Biography*, *Who Was Who*, *The Official Army List for the Quarter Ending 21st December 1899*, *Standard Encyclopaedia of Southern Africa*, and the *Boer War Services of Military Officers of the British and Colonial Armies, Imperial Yeomanry, Mounted Infantry, Local Units &cc 1899–1902*, as well as some of the biographical notes in the Army Records Society's volumes 2, 8, 9 and 17. Short biographical details of those mentioned only in passing, or about persons who either did not play a very important role or about whom not much biographical information could be obtained, are supplied in the Notes. Once again, the above-mentioned sources were used. The Notes also include brief annotations of the main events referred to in the documents, as well as references to sources in which some of the telegrams and other material referred to in the documents have been published.

Since the volume on the role played by Lord Roberts was completed, the Anglo-Boer War centennial has led to the publication of several hundred new books and articles. Some of the new information and interpretations have been included in this volume on the role played by Lord Kitchener in the war, and references to several of the new publications will be found in the Notes and Bibliography. The Bibliography also includes references to the archival collections that were consulted, as well as the secondary sources used in writing the background history (introductions) to the different sections, and in writing the Notes and Biographical Notes. Included among the sources are some of the large number of books and theses written in Afrikaans, Dutch and German in the course of the past century. However, these sources are only a fraction of the total number of publications on the war, estimated at about 2,700 books, more than 2,000 journal articles, more than 100 dissertations and theses, and nearly 1,000 smaller publications such as pamphlets.

Abbreviations

Military

AAG	Assistant Adjutant-General
ADC	Aide-de-Camp
AG	Adjutant-General
AQMG	Assistant Quartermaster-General
AG	Adjutant-General
BEF	British Expeditionary Force
CB	Companion of the Order of the Bath
CGS	Chief of the General Staff
C-in-C	Commander-in-Chief
CIGS	Chief of the Imperial General Staff
CIV	City [of London] Imperial Volunteers
CMG	Companion of the Order of St Michael and St George
CO	Commanding Officer
COO	Chief Ordnance Officer
CRA	Commander, Royal Artillery
CRE	Commander, Royal Engineers
DAAG	Deputy Assistant Adjutant-General
DAG	Deputy Adjutant-General
DAQMG	Deputy Assistant Quartermaster-General
DC	District Commander
DSO	Distinguished Service Order
FM	Field Marshal
GCMG	Grand Cross of the Order of St Michael and St George
GOC	General Officer Commanding
GOC-in-C	General Officer Commander-in-Chief
GSO	General Staff Officer
HMG	His (or Her) Majesty's Government
HQ	Headquarters
IG	Inspector-General
IGS	Imperial General Staff
ILH	Imperial Light Horse

IY	Imperial Yeomanry
KCB	Knight Commander of the Order of the Bath
KG	Knight of the Garter
MD	Military District
MI	Mounted Infantry
MS	Military Secretary
NCO(s)	Non-commissioned officer(s)
OC	Officer Commanding
PMO	Principal Medical Officer
POW	Prisoner of War
QMG	Quartermaster-General
RA	Royal Artillery
RAMC	Royal Army Medical Corps
RCA	Royal Canadian Artillery
RE	Royal Engineers
RFA	Royal Field Artillery
RHA	Royal Horse Artillery
SAC	South African Constabulary
VC	Victoria Cross
WO	War Office

General (official and unofficial abbreviations)

CC	Cape Colony
dep(t)(s)	department(s)
Gov(n)t	Government
HM	His (or Her) Majesty('s)
inst	*instante*, i.e. of this month
JA	Judge Advocate
MP	Member of Parliament
ms	manuscript
NW	North-West(ern)
OFS	Orange Free State
ORC	Orange River Colony
SA	South Africa
s.a.	*sine anno*, i.e. no date of publication indicated
sic	an indication that the preceding word(s), etc. is correctly quoted, even though it seems unlikely or is clearly incorrect
s.l.	*sine loco*, i.e. no place of publication indicated

UK	United Kingdom
wh	which
ZAR	Zuid-Afrikaansche Republiek (i.e. South African/ Transvaal Republic)

Archives and Publications

BL MS Room	British Library Manuscript Room, London
DNB	*Dictionary of National Biography*
DSAB	*Dictionary of South African Biography*
IWM	Imperial War Museum
LHCMA	Liddell Hart Centre for Military Archives, King's College, London
NAM	National Army Museum, London
PRO	Public Record Office, Kew – since 2003 known as the National Archives (TNA)
PRONI	Public Record Office of Northern Ireland, Belfast
RA	Royal Archives, Windsor
SESA	*Standard Encyclopaedia of Southern Africa*
TAD	Transvaal Archives Depot, now part of the National Archives of South Africa, Pretoria
TNA	The National Archives, Kew

Glossary

Afri(c)ka(nd)er(s)	descendant(s) (mostly white) of those Dutchmen (and/or Germans and/or French Huguenots) who settled in the Cape from 1652 onwards, and in due course also in other parts of what is today South Africa.
berg	mountain.
Boer (boer)	literally: farmer; a Dutch-speaking armed burgher of the Transvaal or Orange Free State republics who fought against Britain.
bult	knoll; hill(ock); ridge; rising ground.
burgher	literally: citizen; male (usually of age 16–60 years) in the Transvaal and Orange Free State republics who was eligible for military service.
donga	gully.
dorp	town; village.
drif(t)	ford; shallow fordable point in a river.
fontein	spring; literally a fountain.
modder	mud.
kaffir	mode of reference to a black person, now regarded as offensive.
kop(pie)	hill; peak; kopje.
kraal	enclosure for livestock, or cluster of black African huts.
krantz (krans)	overhanging sheer cliff-face or crag, often above a river.
laager (laer)	camp; defensive encampment of parked wagons and/or carts, but also any defensive enclosure, whether of barricades, masonry, etc.
nek	saddle or pass between two hills.
poort	gap or pass through a mountain range; literally: gate.
riet	reed.
spruit	a tributary watercourse feeding a larger stream or river, sometimes dry.

Uitlanders	foreigners; strangers, i.e. those people not of Dutch/Afrikaner origin who came to the Transvaal to seek their fortune on the gold-fields.
veld(t)	open space; open country.
vlei	hollow in which water collects; marsh.
Volksraad	Legislative Assembly of the Transvaal, the Orange Free State, and later also of the Union (1910–1961) and Republic of South Africa; literally: People's Council.

Prologue
11 October 1899 to 10 January 1900
From the Commencement of
Hostilities to Kitchener's Arrival in
South Africa
Introduction

The Anglo-Boer War broke out at 17.00 on Wednesday 11 October 1899. At that stage there were only 22,104 British soldiers inside or on their way to South Africa, with an additional number of approximately 5,000 local colonial troops immediately available for action.[1] Although the Boer republics (the Zuid-Afrikaansche Republiek, ZAR, i.e. South African Republic, or Transvaal, and the Oranje-Vrijstaat, OVS, i.e. Orange Free State, OFS) could mobilize a total of at least 50,000 burghers (ZAR 30,000 and OFS 20,000), only approximately 35,000 were deployed at the various fronts when the war broke out.[2]

The British forces in South Africa were unable to defend all the borders between the two British colonies (Natal and the Cape Colony) and the Boer republics. The main Boer invasion was expected to take place in Natal, and consequently the largest number of British troops were deployed in that colony: more than 10,000 men with 30 guns, under the command of General Sir George White, at Ladysmith; more than 4,000 men with eighteen guns, under the command of Major-General William Penn Symons, at Glencoe; and some 2,500 men (mostly local volunteers) at places such as Colenso, Estcourt, Acton Homes and Helpmekaar. In the Cape Colony Lieutenant-Colonel R.G. Kekewich had to defend Kimberley (the 'Diamond City') with some 2,500 men and twelve guns; Colonel R.S.S. Baden-Powell had approximately 1,000 men to defend Mafikeng (Mafeking); there were some 1,250 soldiers stationed in Cape Town, 400 at Orange River

1

Station, 500 at Molteno, 600 at Naauwpoort, 1,400 at De Aar (probably at that stage the most important railway junction to the British in South Africa), and 700 other soldiers scattered in small garrisons across the vast Cape Colony, with some 1,450 soldiers deployed in Rhodesia (present-day Zimbabwe) and Bechuanaland (present-day Botswana), in close proximity to the ZAR.[3]

The British hoped to protect Natal and the Cape Colony as best they could against Boer incursions, until an expeditionary force, consisting of an army corps of approximately 46,000 men, could be sent to South Africa. This force was sent out under the command of General Sir Redvers Buller. Queen Victoria would have preferred Lord Kitchener as the overall commander, and in November 1899 Kitchener was indeed considered as a candidate to go to South Africa as a potential second-in-command to Buller. Buller planned to invade the OFS from the Cape Colony, capture Bloemfontein (the OFS capital), then march northwards along the main railway line to Johannesburg, and then to Pretoria (the ZAR capital), after which the war – as some British commanders claimed, the politicians hoped, and the public believed – would be over.[4]

The Boers deployed the largest part (approximately 17,500 men) of their forces on the Natal border – under the command of General Piet Joubert (the Commandant-General, i.e. C-in-C) of the ZAR, and Chief Commandant Marthinus Prinsloo of the OFS. In the Western Transvaal, General Piet Cronjé commanded a force of some 6,000 men; on the Northern Transvaal border, General F.A. Grobler commanded 1,700 men, and in the Eastern Transvaal, General Schalk Burger had some 1,750 men. In the Western OFS, Chief Commandant C.J. Wessels and Commandant J. Prinsloo commanded 4,800 men; in the Eastern OFS there were approximately 1,000 burghers, and on the Southern OFS border there were initially some 2,500 men under the command of Chief Commandant E.R. Grobler, Chief Commandant J.H. Olivier and Commandant J.J. Swanepoel.[5]

Although the Boers initially had more men in the field than the British, they did not immediately take the initiative, and neither did they invade the British colonies at as many places as possible, nor try to capture vast British-held areas or disrupt the British infrastructure. During the first phase of the war (i.e. the Boers' limited offensive, from 11 October–mid-November 1899),[6] the republican forces took up defensive positions inside the British territories, whence it was hoped they would be able to fend off the attacking British forces. Thus, their improvised strategy was basically defensive in nature, and they hoped that – as had happened during the Transvaal War of Independence (1880–1) – they would soon be able to force the British government back to the negotiating table.[7] The lack of decisive action on the part of the Boers during the first few months of the war had a highly negative impact on the Boers' war effort as time progressed, and was one of the reasons why in due course the conflict degenerated into a regional total war (with elements of a civil war) which led to the destruction of vast areas of the war zone, and the deaths of tens of thousands of civilians, both white and black.

On the Kimberley front (the Boers' western front) the republican forces invested Mafikeng (14 October 1899–17 May 1900),[8] also lay siege to Kimberley (15 October 1899–15 February 1900),[9] and occupied a number of towns unopposed (Taung, Veertienstrome, Warrenton and Vryburg, 16–21 October 1899), which led to the outbreak of a rebellion in the area, with several hundred local Dutch (Afrikaans)-speaking inhabitants joining the Boer commandos.[10] In due course Lord Kitchener would be sent to the North-Western Cape Colony to co-ordinate the putting down of the rebellion.

On 11 October 1899 the Boers invaded Natal, took Newcastle (14 October), and defeated Penn Symons' force at the battle of Talana (20 October),[11] but suffered a serious defeat themselves at Elandslaagte (21 October).[12] The British forces in Northern Natal fell back to Ladysmith. In an effort to break the pincer-like hold of the Boers on the town, White launched simultaneous attacks on the Boer forces at Modderspruit (Lombardskop) and Nicholsonsnek – together also referred to as the battle of Ladysmith (28 October) – but the British suffered defeats on both fronts.[13] At Nicholsonsnek a fairly unknown Acting Commandant, Christiaan Rudolph de Wet, led the daring charge against the British forces. In due course De Wet would cause first Lord Roberts, and later Lord Kitchener, great problems and frustration.

On 2 November 1899 the siege of Ladysmith formally commenced,[14] but not before Major-General J.D.P. French had escaped on the last train to leave the town, to subsequently cause much annoyance to the Boers on the Colesberg front, relieve Kimberley, and serve as GOC, Cape Colony, under Lord Kitchener, 1901–2. With approximately 75 per cent of all the British troops in Natal trapped in Ladysmith, the rest of the British colony was extremely vulnerable, but Joubert (who was a pacifist at heart!) as usual was hesitant to take forceful action. Only on 14 November 1899 did he move southwards with 2,100 men, two

3

guns and a pom-pom (i.e. a one-pounder quick-firing gun), on what was not much more than an extensive reconnaissance operation. On 15 November the Boer task-force captured an armoured train to the north of Frere Station. Amongst the British prisoners of war was the later well-known statesman, Winston Churchill, who at that stage was the war correspondent for the *Morning Post*. Earlier on, he had fought as an officer in the 21st Lancers under Kitchener in the Sudan, and had taken part in the charge of the 21st Lancers at Omdurman. After a battle near Willow Grange Station on the stormy night of 22–23 November, Joubert decided to fall back on the Thukela (Tugela) River, from where he hoped to beat back any British attacks.[15]

Until the middle of November 1899, a phoney war situation prevailed on the North-Eastern Cape front. President M.T. Steyn of the OFS naïvely gave his assurance to W.P. Schreiner, the Cape Colony's Prime Minister, that the Boers would not invade that colony, provided that the colony was not used by the British as a springboard for attacks against the Boer republics.[16] Had the Boers invaded the Cape Colony at several places with large mobile units at the outbreak of hostilities, they would probably have captured vast areas of the colony and precipitated a large-scale rebellion. In practice they waited until 13 November 1899 before crossing the Gariep (the Big River, i.e. the Orange River). In the course of the next ten days, the Boers occupied the towns of Aliwal North, Colesberg, Burgersdorp, Jamestown, Lady Grey, Venterstad and Barkly East, and on 26 November, Stormberg was captured. Although many of the local Dutch (Afrikaans)-speaking inhabitants welcomed the invading Boers with great enthusiasm, no full-scale rebellion occurred, and fewer Cape colonists rebelled than the Boers had hoped and anticipated. In this regard Major-General French played an important role, because through continual manoeuvres and mock attacks he created the impression that he had many more soldiers at his disposal than was really the case, and he also created the impression that a major British attack would be launched from the North-Eastern Cape against the OFS.[17]

In the meantime, on 31 October 1899, General Buller had arrived in Cape Town on board the passenger and mail ship *Dunottar Castle* to take up his post as Commander-in-Chief of all the British forces in South Africa. Although on the surface it seemed as if the Boers had, by November 1899, achieved a fair amount of success, this was strictly speaking not the case. The Boers did not follow up the possibilities at their disposal, and preferred for the most part to besiege the passive

British garrison instead of launching incursions deeper into the Cape Colony and Natal. They allowed the British to consolidate their position and to land and deploy reinforcements in the war zone. Nevertheless, Buller thought it advisable to re-evaluate his original strategy (which was to invade the OFS with his whole army corps) and make adjustments. In the light of the apparently precarious position in which the British defenders found themselves in Kimberley, but even more so in Ladysmith, Buller decided to divide his army corps of 46,000 men, 114 guns and 47 machine-guns into four contingents. Buller would take the largest component (approximately 22,000 soldiers) to Natal in an attempt to relieve the siege of Ladysmith. Lord Methuen would take about 15,000 soldiers to Orange River Station, from where he had to attempt to relieve the siege of Kimberley. Major-General W.F. Gatacre (who had served under Lord Kitchener in the Sudan, and who had fought at Omdurman) and some 4,000 soldiers were sent to the Stormberg front in the North-Eastern Cape with a view to defending the Cape Colony against further Boer incursions, and French (to whom references have already been made) received some 5,000 soldiers to do the same at the Colesberg front. As soon as the objectives on the various fronts had been achieved, Buller intended to revert back to his original strategy.[18] What followed was the second main phase of the war, also called the Buller phase, which lasted from the middle of November 1899 to 10 February 1900.

As has already been pointed out, French succeeded in keeping the Boers in check on the Colesberg front, but on the Stormberg front Gatacre did not have the patience to play cat and mouse with the Boers. His advance on Stormberg met with disaster when he was defeated on 10 December 1899,[19] during the first of three serious setbacks suffered by the British in one week, in what became known as 'Black Week'. In the meantime, on 21 November, Methuen started his advance from Orange River Station in the direction of Kimberley. At Belmont (23 November), between Graspan and Enslin (25 November), and at the confluence of the Riet River and Modder River (28 November), sharp clashes took place, and although the Boers on all three occasions suffered fewer casualties than the British, the republican forces always decided to withdraw and take up better defensive positions to fight another day. On 9 and 10 December 1899 the Boers' latest line of defence, stretching for approximately 7 km from Langeberg south-eastwards across Magersfontein and further south-eastwards to Mossdrif on the Modder River, was subjected to heavy British artillery fire – the heaviest British bombardment since the one at Sebastopol during the Crimean War (1854–6). However, the Boers had dug in at the foot of the hills, and suffered negligible losses. When, on 11 December, the British army advanced on the Boers' left flank, it came under heavy fire from the trenches, and on the afternoon of 12 December fell back to its camp on the Modder River.[20] The second 'Black Week' battle was, like Stormberg, a comprehensive tactical defeat for the British, but once again the Boers did not follow up their success, giving the British time to consolidate their position.

In the meantime, Buller had amassed his portion of the army corps just south of the Thukela River, in preparation for an onslaught against the Boer defensive positions in the hills just north of the river. On 15 December 1899 he launched the attack at Colenso that was meant to achieve a breakthrough to the besieged Ladysmith garrison, but poor reconnaissance resulted in the left flank of the attack force coming up against an impenetrable part of the Thukela River, while other sections of the British force also faltered in the attack. Buller lost his nerve and called off the attack.[21]

Once again the Boers did not follow up their tactical success, but the third of the 'Black Week' defeats had a devastating effect on the British Army in South Africa, as well as on the British government and politicians – and in due course changed the course of events in the war. On 16 December 1899 Buller sent a telegram to the besieged White in Ladysmith, mentioning surrendering the town as an option.[22] If Buller's dividing of his army corps had led to reservations with regard to his position as Commander-in-Chief, his defeat at Colenso and his notorious telegram to White made it clear that he was not competent to deal with the demands of his post. Buller and his force were, of course, in an untenable position. Whoever had gone to South Africa first would have experienced serious problems, because Britain was not prepared for war; there were too few troops, and they and their officers lacked experience. At the end of the nineteenth century British military training was also not conducive to intelligent initiative, while the Boers, in contrast, were not hampered by traditional military doctrines.

Lord Lansdowne, the Secretary of State for War, decided to appoint Field Marshal Lord Roberts in Buller's place, and with the support of Arthur Balfour (First Lord of the Treasury) turned to Prime Minister Lord Salisbury for assistance.[23] Even before the war had broken out, Roberts had requested Lansdowne to appoint him as supreme commander in South Africa in a war against the Boers, and in a letter written to Lansdowne on 8 December 1899, he repeated his request.[24] Roberts, who at this stage was Commander-in-Chief in Ireland, was summoned to London. On 17 December, Lansdowne, on behalf of the British government, offered Roberts the post of Commander-in-Chief in South Africa, and Roberts accepted, shortly before being informed that his only surviving son, Freddy, had died of the wounds he received at Colenso.[25]

Objections that the 67-year-old Roberts was too old for the post were overcome by appointing Lord Kitchener as his Chief of Staff, albeit that in practice Kitchener was Roberts' understudy and right-hand man rather than his Chief of Staff. Roberts accepted Kitchener on the grounds of his reputation. As has already been pointed out in the earlier introduction, Kitchener was at this stage Sirdar of the Egyptian Army. He was very flattered to be sent to South Africa as Chief of Staff and looked forward to serving under Roberts [1]. Notwithstanding his success in the Sudan, Kitchener was only a Major-General. He asked to be given a local rank senior to that of the other officers in South Africa, but this request was apparently not granted.[26]

Roberts departed from Southampton on 23 December 1899 on board the passenger and mail ship *Dunottar Castle*. In the meantime, Kitchener received a cipher telegram at Khartoum on 18 December, ordering him to join Roberts at Gibraltar. Kitchener travelled by river and rail to Alexandria, and departed on board the light cruiser HMS *Isis* at midnight, 21–22 December, reaching Malta on Christmas Eve. (His appointment as Chief of Staff became official from 23 December 1899.) On Christmas Day he sailed further, now on board the light cruiser HMS *Dido*, arriving in pouring rain at Gibraltar on 27 December, where he joined Lord Roberts [2]. Later that same day they sailed together from Gibralter, on their way to South Africa, on board the *Dunottar Castle*.[27]

Roberts' appointment as Commander-in-Chief, with Kitchener at his side, introduced a new chapter in the strategic course of the Anglo-Boer War. Provisionally, Buller would for the time being still act as Commander-in-Chief, but he had to obtain Roberts' permission before he could make any strategic moves. As early as 1897 Roberts had come to the conclusion that the best method of attack against the Boer republics would be to use the western (i.e. Kimberley) railway line to place the British Army in a position to undertake a flank march on Bloemfontein, the OFS capital. En route to South Africa Roberts, together with Kitchener and his other staff officers, held long discussions with regard to the campaign in South Africa. By the time they arrived in Cape Town on Wednesday 10 January 1900, the plans had been finalised. Roberts hoped to end the war quickly and return to England before the end of the year. In practice he indeed departed back home before the year was over, but little did Kitchener – who for some time had already hoped to go to India as Commander-in-Chief – know that two and a half years would pass before he himself would leave the shores of South Africa again.

I
Lord Kitchener to Queen Victoria

[Holograph]   Dunottar Castle
off Madeira
28th Decber 1899

Lord Kitchener presents his humble duty to Your Majesty and begs to express his very grateful thanks for the gracious letter he received from Your Majesty at Khartoum just before leaving as well as for one delivered to him by Lord Roberts. Lord Kitchener feels greatly honoured by his selection for the important post on the staff in South Africa which Your Majesty has been graciously pleased to confide to him and he begs to assure Your Majesty that no possible effort on his part shall be spared to overcome the present difficulties and to ensure a successful issue to the campaign against the Boers –

It gives Lord Kitchener the greatest pleasure to serve under Lord Roberts for whom he has the highest admiration –

Lord Kitchener left the Sudan in complete peace. The force under Lt Colonel Mahon had reoccupied el Obeid and the whole of Kordofan had willingly come under the government.[1] The rumours of strained relations with the emperor Menelik,[2] started by the enemies of England, were entirely without foundation as Lord Kitchener's relations with the Emperor were most friendly when he left –

The college at Khartoum was progressing well   the building being above the first floor windows   it was hoped to complete the building by next August or September – The teaching staff and students will be then collected[3] –

RA VIC/P4/221[4]

2
Lord Kitchener to Lady Ilchester[5]

[Holograph]   R.M.S. "Dunottar Castle"
                                                                  Madeira
                                                        28th Decbr. [1899]

Many thanks for your letter   I was very sorry to see in the papers
you had lost your brother   I remember you told me about him &
how very ill he had been. I was surprised by a wire to say I had to
go to South Africa with Lord Roberts   I had to get off sharp and
travel fast to catch him at Gib[raltar]   I reached them in just a
week from Khartoum and five hours before Ld Roberts arrived[6] –
We shall have a pretty hard time to get things right at the Cape as
it seems to me things have got a good deal mixed up but Ld
Roberts is the right man and when we have got things square I
hope we shall be able to show the Boers a somewhat different war
game to that they have been having lately –

I was so sorry to hear of Lady Cranburies[7] very serious illness
but I hope she is now getting strong again

We ought to reach the Cape about 11th   I wonder what will
happen out there before then – We shall want a lot of men to
defeat the boers properly – Please remember me to Lady
Londonderry[8]

BL MS Room, Holland House Papers, Add MS 51370, ff. 165–166

Part 1
11 January to 28 November 1900
Kitchener as Roberts' Chief of Staff
in South Africa
Introduction

The diminutive Lord Roberts and tall Lord Kitchener had only met once before (in the summer of 1899, in Ireland, when Kitchener visited Roberts, and Kitchener indicated that should war in South Africa break out, he would be prepared to serve under him as Chief of Staff),[1] had radically different personalities, and Kitchener was reputed to be 'difficult', but they did not clash; as a matter of fact, they bonded very quickly and their abilities complemented each other to a remarkable degree. Together these two distinguished gentlemen formed a formidable team.[2]

After his arrival in Cape Town on 10 January 1900, Roberts' first strategic aim was to position his force in such a way that the Boers would have to fight at a disadvantage. But Roberts' first big challenge in South Africa was to maintain the existing British positions on all fronts until the logistical and other preparations for his offensive had been completed. These preparations entailed matters of organisation such as centralising the complex transport arrangements (to enable Roberts to march across the OFS without the support of a railway line) – a task with which Kitchener assisted; and forming more detachments of mounted infantry – once again, Kitchener's responsibility – although the scarcity of horses hampered those efforts. Roberts advocated good scouting, the optimal use of cover, and flank movements instead of frontal attacks against well-entrenched Boer positions. Thousands of reinforcements were sent to South Africa, including volunteers from the colonies [3]. On 6 February 1900 Roberts and Kitchener left Cape Town for the operational base on the Modder River, where they arrived on 8 February.[3]

In the meantime, in Natal, General Buller continued his efforts to relieve Ladysmith. After his defeat at Colenso (15 December 1899) he moved the bulk of his force to the Upper Thukela. On three occasions he tried unsuccessfully to destroy the Boer line of defence: first at iNtabamnyama (20–23 January 1900), then at Spioenkop (24 January 1900) and finally at Vaalkrans (5–7 February 1900).[4] Buller's campaign on the Upper Thukela exacted more than 2,000 British casualties compared to approximately 400 on the Boer side. Although the campaign unsettled the Boers and left them exhausted, it was nonetheless a complete failure for the British. By the end of the second main phase of the war in Natal, Buller was back at his old headquarters at Frere, south of Colenso, and no closer to Ladysmith at all. In due course, he would try to break through on the Lower Thukela.

Right from the outbreak of hostilities both the British [7] and the Boers relied on black people to assist them in their war efforts – notwithstanding the fact that both parties declared the war to be a white man's war. Both the British and the Boers were aware of the underlying racial tensions in the war zone [4], and Roberts – and later Kitchener – had to keep this matter in mind when planning how to defeat the republican forces.

In the meantime, on the Kimberley front, Roberts had amassed, under his direct command, a total of at least 49,500 soldiers and 110 guns, and on Sunday 11 February 1900, he went on the offensive, with Kitchener at his side. This was the start of the third main phase of the war (11 February–28 November 1900), also known as the Roberts phase. As part of his deception plan, Roberts first took his force southwards to Enslin Station, then eastwards via Ramdam to Watervalsdrif and De Kielsdrif on the Modder River. When General Piet Cronjé, still entrenched at his Magersfontein positions, realised that he was being outflanked and could be surrounded, he gave the order that his force of more than 4,000 men, plus about 60 women and children, as well as all his wagons, were to move eastwards, all along the Modder River, in a desperate effort to escape. Meanwhile, Major-General J.D.P. French – who had been transferred from the Colesberg front in the first week of February 1900 – and his cavalry advanced from Rondawelsdrif in a northerly direction, and then in a north-westerly direction, lifting the Boer siege of Kimberley on 15 February 1900.[5]

Cronjé's slow-moving wagon laager was cornered and surrounded by the British forces on 17 February in the vicinity of Vendusiedrif, close to Paardeberg. Kitchener, who most of the time rode ahead with the mounted infantry, played an important role in checking Cronjé's flight eastwards. At Paardeberg the Boers dug themselves in on both banks of the Modder River. In the meantime, Roberts had caught a chill and was recovering at Jacobsdal. He placed Kitchener in command of the forces concentrated around Cronjé's army at Paardeberg – on the surface a somewhat controversial decision, because Kitchener was apparently only a Major-General and therefore strictly speaking junior to Lieutenant-General Thomas Kelly-Kenny who was in command of the 6th Infantry Division at Paardeberg. But was Kitchener in fact only a Major-General? Over the years this is the view that has been generally held, and most of the Kitchener biographies also hold this view, but according to the *Army Lists* of 1901 and onwards, Kitchener had been promoted to Lieutenant-General on 23 December 1899, i.e. on the day when his position as Roberts' Chief of Staff became official. There is therefore the possibility that, for whatever reason, Kitchener was promoted in secret (?) to Lieutenant-General, but not gazetted as such. If that was the case, it explains why Kitchener was confident that he was in fact the senior officer present at Paardeberg.[6]

Kitchener wanted to defeat Cronjé (the first white general whom he encountered in battle) as quickly as possible, fearing a break-out and/or attacks from the other Boer forces that were on their way to the scene of the siege. Consequently, on Sunday 18 February 1900, after a short bombardment, he threw caution overboard (as well as the lessons learnt thus far in the war) and ordered simultaneous direct frontal attacks from various directions to be launched against the well-entrenched burghers in the Boer laager. His plan of action and orders were not very clear, and the senior officers were not very enthusiastic about the attack. The result was a disaster for the British forces: they were forced back on all fronts, losing a total of at least 303 dead (more than on any other day during the Anglo-Boer War, and more than the approximately 260 fatal casualties the Anglo-Egyptian forces had suffered during the whole of the River War in the Sudan, 1896–8, under Kitchener's command), 906 wounded and 61 captured. The Boers lost no more than about 70 killed and wounded.[7] It is true that Kitchener had few staff to assist him, but he also did not learn from the 'Black Week' defeats. Tactics that worked in the Sudan against Dervishes would seldom – if ever – work against Boers armed and skilful with modern rifles, and fighting from well-chosen defensive positions. Kitchener – who had never lost a battle before – was furious. To add insult to injury, there were allegations that he did not look after the wounded [9]. Kitchener tried his best to create the impression that he did in fact care for the ill and the wounded [7].

Several Boer commandos were sent to Cronjé's assistance, including that of General Christiaan de Wet, who nearly broke the British investment. De Wet took Oskoppies (also known as Kitchener's Kopje) on 18 February in an attempt to create an opportunity for Cronjé to break out, but Cronjé declined and on 21 February British forces recaptured Oskoppies. After Roberts took over command again from Kitchener on the morning of 19 February, the Boer laager was bombarded incessantly with artillery fire. This bombardment did not result in serious loss of life in the Boer ranks, but nonetheless had an extremely demoralising effect on the Boer defenders. On 27 February 1900, the nineteenth anniversary of the Boer victory over the British at Amajuba, Cronjé and his entire force surrendered[8] [5]. Kitchener was not present to witness the surrender, having been sent away to Naauwpoort on 22 February by Roberts to open up the railway communications across the Gariep towards Bloemfontein. Kitchener went to Naauwpoort Junction, and from there to De Aar (on the Cape Town – Kimberley railway line).[9] Although there is no clear evidence that Roberts sent Kitchener away from Paardeberg because of what happened on 18 February 1900, Roberts never again put Kitchener in command of a pitched battle situation.

Through his great flank march, Roberts surprised the Boers and dislocated them both physically and psychologically. Cronjé's surrender at Paardeberg had a very negative effect on the morale of the republican forces on all fronts and they never fully recovered. In due course the Boers would, in desperation, resort to guerrilla warfare, but after their Paardeberg defeat they could hardly win the war any longer – they could merely try to prolong it. Ironically, however, the events at Paardeberg and on the following days soon also affected the British Army in South Africa negatively, because – as shall shortly be pointed out – thousands of British soldiers became ill from drinking contaminated water at or near the Paardeberg battlefield. The question can in fact be asked whether Roberts' strategy should be judged by his success at Paardeberg, or whether it should rather be judged by the fact that eventually he was forced to halt for seven weeks in Bloemfontein, thereby affording the Boers the opportunity to rethink their strategy and regroup (for guerrilla warfare).

In the meantime, in Natal, Buller was ready by the middle of February 1900 to renew his efforts to break through to the beleaguered Ladysmith, where the garrison's position deteriorated by the day. With more than 25,000 soldiers and 70 guns, Buller launched his Lower Thukela campaign. The strategically situated hill of Cingolo was captured on 17

February, and the British forces then captured Monte Cristo, Groenkop and Hlangwane (18–19 February). Fierce battles followed at Rooikop, Hedge Hill, Horseshoe Hill and Terrace Hill (21–24 February), without success for the British forces, but on 27 February (encouraged by the news of Cronjé's surrender at the other side of the war zone) Buller's army broke through the Boer lines at Pietershoogte. The Boers then left their positions on the rest of the Thukela line, as well as those that they occupied around Ladysmith, and retreated northwards. On the evening of 28 February, Ladysmith was officially relieved of the Boer siege.[10]

Glad to hear that Buller had at long last been successful in Natal, Roberts advanced eastwards from Paardeberg in the direction of Bloemfontein. On 7 March, at Modder River Pass, near Poplar Grove Drift, Roberts defeated a Boer force of 5,000 men under De Wet [6], and on 10 March, at Boschrand, in the vicinity of Abrahamskraal and Driefontein, he defeated a force of 3,000 men under De Wet and the ZAR's General Koos de la Rey. On Tuesday 13 March 1900 Roberts entered Bloemfontein, the OFS capital, without any opposition.[11] Within the space of four weeks, Roberts had dramatically changed the entire strategic situation in South Africa, and had placed the Boers in a position from which they never fully recovered.

In the meantime, the rebellion in the North-Western Cape Colony had spread, threatening to become uncontrollable. Roberts sent Kitchener from De Aar to assist in suppressing the rebellion. As has already been mentioned earlier, Kitchener travelled from Naauwpoort to De Aar. There he met Major-General H.H. Settle on 28 February 1900, and they decided to send three small columns to the affected area. Kitchener then returned to rejoin Roberts and accompanied the Commander-in-Chief on a visit to Lord Methuen in Kimberley (1 March 1900) where the relief of Mafikeng was discussed. Kitchener then accompanied Roberts' army from Paardeberg eastwards to Poplar Grove, but left the main army again on 8 March to return to the North-Western Cape Colony when the forces referred to earlier were unable to defeat the rebels. Kitchener then led a reinforced column of 3,000 men, occupying Prieska on 18 March. Kitchener rejoined Roberts in Bloemfontein on Wednesday 28 March 1900, and returned to do staff work[12] [6].

With Bloemfontein in British hands, the OFS government moved their seat of government temporarily to Kroonstad, half-way between Bloemfontein and Johannesburg. In the meantime, De Wet gave the OFS burghers the opportunity to return to their farms. Those who wanted to continue with the war had to assemble at the Sand River railway bridge on 25 March 1900. At a 'krijgsraad' (war council) meeting held at Kroonstad on 17 March 1900, at which both republican presidents, i.e. Steyn of the OFS and Kruger of the ZAR, were present, it was decided, among other things, that the Boers would henceforth change their tactics, and instead of trying to halt the British advance through taking up defensive positions, they would in future concentrate on destroying enemy communication lines; furthermore, the Boer forces had to be organised into smaller units, and had to abandon the use of wagon laagers.[13] It is ironic that it took a serious defeat at Paardeberg, and the loss of Bloemfontein, to force the Boers to exploit what was in all probability their strongest weapon against a conventionally-trained foe, namely their mobility. In the two years that followed, this mobility caused Roberts, and later Kitchener, immense problems.

The Kroonstad meeting was the theoretical starting point of the guerrilla phase of the war, i.e. the fourth main phase, which to some extent overlapped with the third main phase. The meeting can therefore also, without doubt, be regarded as a watershed with regard to the Boer strategy and tactics during the war. In practice the guerrilla phase commenced on 31 March 1900 when, at Sannaspos, just east of Bloemfontein, De Wet surprised and defeated a British force under the command of Brigadier-General R.G. Broadwood.[14] De Wet followed up this success by forcing a British unit under Captain W.J. McWinnie to surrender after a brief siege at Mostertshoek, east of Reddersburg (3–4 April 1900). De Wet was subsequently unsuccessful in laying siege to a British garrison at Jammerbergdrif, just north-west of Wepener. Roberts sent Kitchener away to supervise the Jammerbergdrif relief operation.[15]

As a result of their drinking contaminated water from the Modder River in the vicinity of the Paardeberg battlefield, coupled with the gross neglect of elementary sanitary precautions in the military camps, several thousand British soldiers contracted typhoid (then called enteric fever), and more than a thousand of them died in Bloemfontein alone. As a consequence, Roberts was forced to remain in Bloemfontein for seven weeks to give his soldiers time to recover. He also used this time to consolidate his position, clear the Southern OFS of Boer commandos, and refine his war strategy.

On Thursday 3 May 1900 Roberts – with Kitchener at his side – and more than 20,000 soldiers, with 80 guns and 49 machine-guns, resumed their advance from Bloemfontein, this time all along the main railway line northwards in the direction of the ZAR. The main railway line became the central source of supply to the British Army, and consequently the Army became bound to it to a large extent. The Boers would henceforth try their best to destroy the railway, with the result that repairing the railway as quickly as possible was the biggest challenge facing the Royal Engineers – a feat that they carried out with great skill and speed. In this regard Colonel E.P.C. Girouard (who had served under Kitchener in the Sudan, 1896–8) and his Royal Engineers played a very important role. Roberts' advance was co-ordinated with that of Buller from Natal; with Methuen's advance which had to follow the route from south of the Vaal River over Boshof, Hoopstad and Bothaville in a northerly direction; that of Lieutenant-General Archibald Hunter (who had also served under Kitchener in the Sudan, 1896–8) who had to cross the Vaal River and advance on a route including Christiana, Bloemhof, Klerksdorp and Potchefstroom; and that of Lieutenant-General Ian Hamilton who had to advance east of, but parallel to, the main railway line in a northerly direction – an enormous sweeping action in which a total of 150,000 soldiers, with approximately 300 guns, would participate, and who were supposed to drive all Boer commandos systematically ahead of them. Against Roberts' formidable main force, the Boers were initially only able to deploy approximately 1,700 men along the main railway line, although this force grew in size as time passed. It was no wonder, therefore, that the Boers did not achieve much success in their attempts to halt Roberts' advance. At Brandfort (3 May 1900), the Vet River (5 May) and the Sand River (7 and 10 May), the Boers tried in vain to stop the British advance, and on 12 May Kroonstad was captured by the British [8]. Here the British force had to stay for ten days in order to rest, wait for supplies and more horses, and try to shake off the typhoid that had once again taken its toll. On 28 May they reached the Vaal River, whereupon Roberts formally annexed the OFS. Henceforth it would be known as the Orange River Colony (ORC). The annexation was made retrospective in force from 24 May so that it would coincide with Queen Victoria's birthday. For the duration of the march from Bloemfontein to Pretoria, Kitchener remained with Roberts.[16]

Although his Natal Army was not as badly plagued by illness as was Roberts' force in Bloemfontein, Buller did not, after the relief of Ladysmith on 28 February 1900, pursue the retreating Boer forces; indeed, he remained in Ladysmith for two months, after which – as part of Roberts' wide-ranging strategy – he first advanced eastwards to Helpmekaar, and then marched northwards to Dundee, which was taken on 15 May. On the way, a number of skirmishes took place. On 18 May Buller entered Newcastle, but his northward route of advance was blocked by Boer forces who had dug themselves in at Lang's Nek – the site of a battle (28 January 1881) that had taken place during the Transvaal War of Independence, 1880–1. Buller remained in Newcastle until the beginning of June 1900 to consolidate his position.[17]

Meanwhile, on the western front, the siege of Mafikeng took its slow course. The Boers maintained their siege half-heartedly, while Baden-Powell suceeded in keeping his small garrison's morale high, although conditions in the town deteriorated and food shortages increased. Baden-Powell sent Roberts a message which stated that the garrison could not last beyond 22 May 1900. This message compelled Roberts to order Lieutenant-General Archibald Hunter to mobilise a relief force. This force, under command of Colonel B.T. Mahon, advanced from Barkly West in a northerly direction and on 15 May this force combined with Colonel H.C.O. Plumer's southward-moving force. Meanwhile, Commandant S.J. Eloff, a grandson of President Kruger, attempted on 12 May to take Mafikeng through a direct frontal assault. After a battle that lasted for the entire day, Eloff and 97 other Boers were captured. Apparently ten Boers were killed. After a number of men from the relief force had arrived in the town on the evening of 16 May, Mahon officially lifted the siege of the town the next day.[18]

Roberts hoped in vain that the various British units' advance over a broad front would drive all the commandos ahead of them. The failure to achieve this, however, did not deter him from advancing northwards as fast as possible. After a battle that lasted for longer than a day in Klipriviersberg and its surroundings, south of Johannesburg (28–29 May 1900), the British forces entered the city on Thursday 31 May, without experiencing any resistance. However, the Boers were allowed to withdraw northwards. This was a serious strategic mistake by Roberts. On the Sesmylspruit, just south of Pretoria, the Boers once again tried to halt the British advance, but they were repelled, and the capital of the ZAR was taken on Tuesday 5 June, once again without any Boer resistance [11]. Roberts, with Kitchener at his side, arrived at Church Square, in the centre of the capital, at 14.15 on 5 June. The Union Jack was hoisted, and there was a march past of British troops. The Transvaal government and president fled eastwards.[19]

According to Roberts, the war was now almost over. In reality, however, the war was far from over; as a matter of fact, it would in due course escalate all over the war zone, and would once again include the Cape Colony. The capture of both the republican capitals did not have the envisaged psychological effect on the Boers, and Roberts erred in not dealing decisively with the commandos of De Wet and others who were allowed to operate behind the main British line of advance. Roberts was so anxious to end the war as quickly as possible that he made a serious strategic mistake, which in due course caused many and serious problems for Kitchener.

Roberts initially believed that with the fall of the Boers' capitals, their resistance would crumble.[20] He was mistaken. The Boer armies did not come in to surrender, and Roberts lost the strategic momentum. He lost sight of the grave dangers that a guerrilla war could pose to an army trained and equipped for conventional warfare. Roberts' strategy, which initially delivered excellent results during the first four weeks of its implementation (i.e. 11 February to 13 March 1900), was mistakenly directed at occupying the republican capitals, and not so much at destroying the Boer forces in the field. If Roberts had ensured that all the areas in the rear of his advancing forces were subjugated and properly under British military control, the later need for drives, farm-burning and internment camps would have been eliminated.

Compelled by necessity, Roberts had to launch a large-scale advance and campaign in the Eastern Transvaal. A Boer force was driven from Diamond Hill (Donkerhoek) east of Pretoria (11–13 June 1900), and French was then tasked to lead the British advance eastwards, along the Delagoa Bay railway line, all the way to Komatipoort. This advance was co-ordinated with Buller's advance from Ladysmith.[21]

In the meantime, guerrilla activities (or 'unrest' as Roberts sometimes euphemistically preferred to call them) increased. Although the British succeeded in suppressing the rebellion in the North-Western Cape, De Wet and others continued their successful guerrilla action in the OFS [10]. On 7 June 1900 Roberts sent Kitchener back to the ORC in an effort to put an end to De Wet's activities. Kitchener supervised the repair of the main railway line, but was unable to corner De Wet. En route back to Pretoria, Kitchener's train stood at Vredefort Road[22] for the night of 12–13 June. Kitchener and his staff were settled for the night in tents near the train when De Wet overwhelmed a portion of the troops who accompanied and guarded Kitchener. Kitchener (still wearing his pyjamas) and his staff were barely able to escape and rode off in great haste to the safety of a nearby Yeomanry camp.[23] Shortly afterwards, on 24 June 1900, Kitchener celebrated his fiftieth birthday without much fanfare.

It is interesting to note that as early as 30 June 1900, Kitchener identified President M.T. Steyn and the OFS burghers as the main opponents in the war – he claimed that if they were to be dealt with by the British, the Transvaalers would surrender [13]. However, guerrilla warfare was now also being implemented with success in the Transvaal. On 11 July 1900, the guerrilla phase was started in the Transvaal when four attacks were launched on British units, including De la Rey's attack at Silkaatsnek when Colonel H.R. Crompton-Roberts was defeated and forced to surrender.[24]

In an effort to curb the guerrilla activities, Roberts resorted to stern measures. On 16 June 1900 he issued his controversial Proclamation No 5 of 1900 (and three days later the even harsher Proclamation No 6 of 1900), warning the Boers that if they destroyed railway bridges and culverts, the houses in the vicinity would be burnt.[25] The aim was strictly military, i.e. to make an example of certain culprits in an effort to deter others from aiding the Boer guerrillas. Roberts realised that it would be very difficult for his forces to corner and destroy all the mobile Boer commandos in the field. Some of the British officers applied the proclamations with discretion; others did not, and consequently many farms were burnt unnecessarily. By taking stern measures against the Boer civilian population, Roberts hoped to dislocate the Boers psychologically and undermine their will to continue the struggle. These tactics were similar to those which he had employed in Afghanistan and India, and there they had been successful. In South Africa, however, the measures backfired in due course. To some extent they motivated the Boers to invade the Cape Colony (with the aim of taking the war to the British areas and population, while relieving the pressure on the former Boer republics), and later led to much bitterness. These tactics also caused misery to thousands of black civilians.

In the Eastern ORC the Boers suffered a major setback in July 1900. After Roberts occupied Pretoria, he had to take urgent action to eliminate Boer commandos operating to the rear of the British forces. While some British units were advancing in a northerly direction along the Basotholand border, other British forces advanced from the north-west in the direction of the Brandwater Basin with Fouriesburg as the centre. By the middle of 1900, large portions of the OFS commandos were trapped in this basin. While the Boer officers argued about the overall leadership of the Boer forces in the basin, the British captured one pass after another. Chief Commandant Marthinus Prinsloo engaged in negotiations with Lieutenant-General Archibald Hunter, and after the Boers agreed on 29 July 1900 to submit to the British demand for surrender, Prinsloo formally surrendered the next day. Some Boer commanders did not heed the surrender and escaped with their burghers. Nevertheless, 4,314 burghers, as well as three generals and nine commandants, had lain down their arms by 9 August. The British also captured three guns, approximately 2,800 head of cattle, 4,000 sheep, 5,500 horses and approximately two million rounds of rifle ammunition. Already on 15 July, De Wet, along with President Steyn and approximately 2,000 men and five guns, escaped from the British forces' lines across Slabbertsnek, at that stage the only remaining escape route out of the Brandwater Basin. They were pursued by various British columns, under the overall command of Lord Kitchener [14, 16], as far as behind the Magaliesberg in what became known as the first De Wet hunt. Kitchener drove De Wet's commando relentlessly with a semicircle of columns that were formed behind him. The idea was to drive De Wet against the Magaliesberg, but Ian Hamilton was too late to occupy the Olifants's Nek pass, and De Wet crossed the mountain range on 14 August 1900. In due course, De Wet returned to the ORC to continue the guerrilla war with even more vigour.[26]

Kitchener was very disappointed that he was unable to corner and eliminate De Wet as a factor in the war. At the end of the first De Wet hunt, Kitchener raced to Brakfontein on the Elands River, where Lieutenant-Colonel C.O. Hore and just more than 500 soldiers (with a muzzle-loading 7-pounder gun and two machine guns) were besieged by General Koos de la Rey and at least 500 Boers (with at least four guns, one pom-pom and two machine-guns). Kitchener succeeded in lifting the eleven-day siege on 16 August 1900[27] [16]. Kitchener then returned to Pretoria, where he stayed for most of the rest of 1900.

Meanwhile, French led the British advance further eastwards from Pretoria – an advance which was co-ordinated with Buller's from Natal. On 27 July 1900 French took Middelburg, but he was subsequently required to remain in the region for about a month so that Buller could be given the opportunity to advance further. When the British advance was resumed, Botha and 5,000 Boers blocked the British forces' advance at Bergendal and in its vicinity, to the north-west of Dalmanutha Station. From 21 August, British forces under the command of Buller attacked the Boer positions. During the main attack on 27 August, the British forces succeeded in driving the Boers eastwards. British casualties in this battle came to about thirteen dead and 103 wounded, while on the Boer side there were at least 50 casualties. Five days later, on 1 September 1900, Roberts annexed the ZAR, henceforth known as the Transvaal Colony.[28]

Although General Louis Botha and other Boer commanders persisted in their efforts to check the British advance, the British reached

Komatipoort on 24 September 1900. Meanwhile President Kruger arrived in Lourenço Marques (the present-day Maputo) on 11 September, whence he departed for Europe on board the Dutch cruiser *De Gelderland* on 19 October.[29] On 28 October 1900 Prince Christian Victor, grandson of Queen Victoria, died of typhoid in Pretoria [19]. Earlier, in 1898, he had served under Kitchener in the Sudan.

In September 1900, Kitchener supervised the repair of the Delagoa Bay railway line, i.e. the line running eastwards from Pretoria via Middelburg and Komatipoort to Lourenço Marques. At the end of September and in the course of October 1900, Kitchener reorganised the rail and other traffic at Komatipoort. In November 1900, Roberts sent Kitchener on inspection tours to Natal and the North-Eastern ORC. Kitchener was back in Pretoria on 20 November 1900.[30]

In the last week of September 1900 Roberts was offered the post of Commander-in-Chief of the British Army in succession to Lord Wolseley, and he accepted.[31] Roberts was prepared to leave South Africa because he was (once again!) of the opinion that the war was over for all practical purposes – an opinion shared by Kitchener [17]. Both British officers neither fully appreciated the nature of the continued Boer resistance, nor realised what remained to be done by the British in order to win the war. At midnight on 28 November 1900 Lord Roberts laid down his command in South Africa, and as from Thursday 29 November 1900 Lord Kitchener was the new British Commander-in-Chief in South Africa.[32] As has been pointed out earlier, there is a possibility that by the time Kitchener took over as Commander-in-Chief, he was already a Lieutenant-General, or alternatively, that he was promoted to Lieutenant-General on 29 November 1900, with the temporary (or local) rank of General.[33]

In the course of 1900, Roberts and Kitchener – before the war both already famous and distinguished generals, although Roberts of Kandahar was some eighteen years older than Kitchener of Khartoum – learnt to work together excellently in South Africa. They respected one another and they had an excellent working relationship. Roberts used Kitchener neither as a Chief of Staff nor as a second in command, but rather as his right-hand man and as an understudy to himself, and delegated a large amount of work and authority to Kitchener [15]. Now Kitchener was left alone to deal with the 'dreadful people' [14] who continued their resistance.

3
Major-General Edward Hutton[1] to Lord Kitchener

[Copy]   Ottowa, Jan. 18th, 1900

I have written officially to the Filed [Field] Marshall Comdg the Army in S.A., but as the letter will no doubt come to you, perhaps you will allow me to supplement my official introduction to this Second Canadian Contingent.[2]

I enclose for simple reference a schedule of the troops concerned and a list of the officers personnel.

The Field Batteries are composed for the most part of Militia but with a good necleus [sic] of our regular Field Artillery. the officers are similarly composed. All three batteries have been specially raised, horsed and equipped, and will undoubtedly require at least three weeks of quiet in camp before they will be really fit to take the filed [field]. I have already cabled, on the 4th inst. asking that Lt.Col. Drury[3] and Capt. Panet,[4] both R.C.A. and now on service in S.A. may be permitted to meet those Batteries on arrival, and be relieved from whatever other duty they may have been allotted to / Lt-Col Drury is a first rate Officer and his Batteries will acquit themselves right well under him, I am quite satisfied.

The Second Battn C.M.R. arriving on the Pomeranian should be a very useful Corps.[5] It is composed for the most part of members or ex members of the N.W.M.P.[6] with a certain extra sprinkling of ranchmen and cowboys from the North West. The Officers and men are thoroughly hard seasoned men, who know prairie life and have experience of Indian warfare.

The 1st Bn Mounted Rifles will follow in about a fortnight. they have been raised from the Dominion Military Cavalry with a strong necleus [sic] of our solitary regular Cavalry regiment – Royal Canadian Dragoons. The men are good and of a really good class, and will do good work.

The 2nd Battn. is mounted entirely upon Prairie bred horses, hardy but ugly. The 1st Bn. mounted upon large, better bred and better looking horses bought in Ontario, and Eastern Canada.

The former should do well on the veldt as like the riders they are accustomed to do for themselves in summer and winter. It is impossible however to say what effect the sudden change in climate may have from 40 below zero in the N.W. to the sub-tropical heat of the Cape.

The 2nd Bn. will require about a fortnight and the 1st Bn / about three weeks before they are ready for the Field.

The whole force goes from here complete in all details of transport, camp equipment and ammunition. I sincerely trust that they may do credit to Canada, and merit the honour of having the luck to take part in the campaign.

Orders have been given for raising a 3rd contingent in the shape of an additional battalion of Mounted Scouts at the expense of Lord Strathcona,[7] with an establishnebt [establishment] similar to the two first named Battns.[8] This corps could not, however, leave for another three weeks or a month at the very earliest. It will be at best of "irregular" type as we have pretty well skimmed our milk.

Canada thinks and talks of nothing but war, and public opinion will be very quick to appreciate any honour which our Canadian representatives may win for themselves.

Allow me to congratulate you by on being again employed, and to wish you every success. It is a ..... which keeps me here at the present crisis, but so far Mr Chamberlain has been obdurate.

BL MS Room, Hutton Papers, Add MS 50086, ff. 308–9

4
Colonel R.S.S. Baden-Powell to Lord Kitchener
[Holograph]   Mafeking: 2 March 1900

As a question may arise as to the extent to which I am making use of armed natives – for which I believe the Boers are very upset at my threat to utilize the proferred [sic] assistance of the Protectorate Chiefs – the following is a short resumé of the situation:[9]

At the beginning of the war all natives were warned, on this border, to keep quiet and not to take up arms except in defence of their homes & property.

The Boers invaded our territory. The natives in outlying villages in this district took refuge in Mafeking with such of their property as they were able to bring away. Their villages were burned and cattle taken by the enemy.

On the approach of the Boers the Barolongs[10] took up arms for the defence of their suburb of the town, and the Afrikanders[11] and Fingoes[12] took up arms in defence of their location near the Brickfields.

As the enemy raided our cattle I armed and paid about 200 natives to act as cattle-guards and as guards over our commissariat food and forage stores about the place.

That is the extent to which we used armed natives here.

Up north Khama[13] and Linchwe[14] have given us assistance by protecting the railway where it ran through their territory, and in watching the border with scouts. When the country was threatened with invasion they took up arms in self-defence, and we sent part of our white force to help them.

The Boers brought a force to Sequani on the border, with a view to attacking Linchwe's main town which lies within a mile of the border.

As far as I have learned their attack was planned for 24: Jany.

Col. Holdsworth took a party of whites to assist Linchwe in his defence – but Linchwe took matters into his own hands & anticipated the Boer attack by attacking them on 22nd and beat them.[15] Col Holdsworth refusing to assist him because he was exceeding his orders. – though it seems to be a fine point as to whether Linchwe was not to a great extent justified.

Of this incident, however, the Boers have made capital, saying that we employed natives under white direction to attack them, and they are therefore justified in taking similar measures.

Consequently they have organized, and armed natives, and are using them against us here not only as outposts, and for digging trenches, destroying railway, etc, but also for manning their forts and entrenchments.[16]

They have also taken away a local chief, Saani, who had remained quiet in his own district near, because he had been told that the war was a white mans quarrel.[17] I accordingly demanded Saani's release and the withdrawal, within four days, of the armed natives around us, and threatened that if this were not done I might carry out a plan of invading the northern districts of the Transvaal with Khama, Linchwe and Bathoen.[18]

Genl. Snyman[19] has written declining to withdraw them on the alone plea that we use[d] armed natives first. This, in the absence of full report regarding Col. Holdsworth's and Linchwe's proceeding is what I believe to be the state of the case.

I have declined to organize a native force though the Barolongs wished to form one –

Chief Bathoen maintained a neutral attitude for a time but warned the Boers not to come into his country: But they are now setting him against them as they have not only stopped some of his people who are here from escaping – but yesterday they sent word to them that they might go – and when they had a good crowd of several hundred half-starved women and children in the open – in broad daylight – they fired into them and drove them back into Mafeking – several being wounded though none killed.

It is unsatisfactory work having to deal with such [d]evils as though they were civilized beings –

We hope soon to hear of good progress below and only wish we could be doing more to assist it. But it was most gratifying to all of us to get your kind message, when Lord Roberts just landed, to show that we are doing what was wanted.

Army orders that you send us we will do our best to carry out.

NAM. 1971-01-23-6-2

5
Lord Kitchener to Queen Victoria

[Holograph]   Osfontein[20]
4th March 1900

Lord Kitchener presents his humble duty to Your Majesty, and begs to express his gratitude for Your Majesty's letter of the 2nd Febry[21] –

The troops have all been much elated by capturing Cronjé and his army,[22] and the relief of Ladysmith[23] and Kimberley,[24] which have placed the campaign on a far better footing – We are now arranging for the march to Bloemfontein which I hope will be equally successful – our difficulty regarding transport for so large a force of mounted men is very great, but though we may have to go with short rations and forage no one will grumble, and once at Bloemfontein by opening the Midland railway lines we shall soon be quite comfortable again –

The enemy are as far as I have seen at present not very enterprising, and when mounted troops get behind them, like all undisciplined men, they suffer from panic – Cronjé would have done better not to have attempted his flight across our front, it was however very fortunate that we saw him, as we should hardly have done so had not the advanced division been luckily moving out at 4 a.m. to support Genl French at Kimberley – Just as dawn broke we caught sight of the end wagons of Cronjé's convoy which had passed us in the night, of course we at once went after them and soon engaged their rear guard, and by directing General French to head the enemy off here, we were able to bring them to a stand still; the result was then certain –

We are also organizing a column for the relief of the gallant defenders of Mafeking – Lord Roberts has approved of Lt-Col. Mahon who has served many years in the Soudan taking command of the mounted troops detailed for the purpose. I am sure if anyone can get through successfully he will[25] –

Lord Roberts is very well indeed and is the most delightful chief to work under – the day before yesterday he rode 30 miles into Kimberley and back the next day[26] –

There is certainly a good deal of ill feeling between the Orange Free Staters and the Transvaalers but I think they will fight stubbornly together until after some decisive battle – Genl Cronjé was a coarse looking stout farmer of about fifty[27] without much signs of intelligence but with plenty of determination. his wife accompanied him[28] she looked rather worn out and was evidently frightened, they were both treated with every consideration –

27

The whole force received Your Majesty's gracious message with enthusiasm and we all pray Your Majesty may have perfect health and assure Your Majesty no effort will be spared to bring the war to a satisfactory termination –

RA VIC/P7/38

6
Lord Kitchener to Queen Victoria

[Holograph]   Bloemfontein
30th March. oo

I have the honour to acknowledge the receipt of Your Majesty's gracious letter of the 23rd Febr[29] I gave General M[a]cDonald Your Majesty's message and he has begged me to express how deeply he feels the solicitude Your Majesty has shown on his behalf – He has made a very good recovery and though still lame when walking, is able to ride,[30] and takes the keenest interest in his Highland Brigade –

Lord Roberts was also much pleased in receiving Your Majesty's kind message, he is very well   I do not know when I have seen him looking better – He lives in President Steyns official residence which is a large and comfortable house very well furnished[31] – Bloemfontien is a nice clean little town with broad streets, mostly red brick houses with corrugated iron roofs, a few fairly good shops, most of the houses have gardens and trees round them – To the East West and South there is an extensive grassy plain, on which the troops are now camped, to the north there are some hills about 400 feet high under which the town nestles – The notices and advertisements are almost all in English and the people all talk English well,[32] they seem to be quite pleased at the change and the surrounding farmers freely bring in their produce to market – There is no appearance of a conquered country and everything is quite quiet – I think the people of the Orange State would be very glad if they could get out of the war and I daresay after next engagement they will all break with the Transvaalers who are forcing them on, and desert President Steyn who has deceived them –

The hospitals here are very comfortably established in good buildings,[33] they are well attended to, and the patients are doing well. the climate is excellent –

The Engineers have worked very well at the railway bridges at Norvals Pont and Bethulie, which were completely destroyed, and I hope before long we shall be able to get up a good supply of clothing, boots, and comforts, for the troops which are much wanted. Sir Alfred Milner is here he is looking better and is evidently much relieved at the enemy having left Cape Colony the rebels who joined them are everywhere laying down their arms –

The last letter I had the honour to write to Your Majesty was from Osfontein just before the action at Poplar Grove – Though we did not know it at the time it appears that Presidents Kruger and Steyn were both present at the fight, at a safe distance, and found themselves obliged to retire very hurriedly in a cart with six horses[34] – On his way from here to Poplar Grove President Kruger had promised a commando stationed about half way, that he would inspect them on his way back – They were therefore all drawn up to receive him, but he only put his head out of the covered cart and shouted, Drive faster, and passed without stopping –

The day after the fight we heard that Lt Col Adye had had an unsuccessful encounter with the rebels in the Prieska district[35] – Lord Roberts thought it necessary for me to go at once to take charge of the operations there so I had to travel rapidly to De Aar and organise a small column with which I marched to Prieska via Britstown – I had some of the newly arrived Imperial Yeomanry with me and if they are all as good as those I had, I think they will be most useful, of course they had a great deal to learn but they showed much more intelligence and quickness in learning than the ordinary soldier – They were very keen for active service, very well mounted, and when they have had some practice in shooting, will be I am sure a very satisfactory force – I also had with me a detachment of Lord Iveagh's Irish hospital which did excellent work[36] – Owing to very wet weather we had many cases of dysent[sic]ry and the medical officers and attendants under Dr Stoker[37] were hard pressed but worked splendidly –

On our approaching Prieska the Transvaal Boers deserted the rebels of Prieska district and crossed the Orange River, and on our arrival the local rebels laid down their arms – Six of the ringleaders were put in prison for subsequent trial, but the others were allowed to return to their farms on the understanding that they should come up for judgement when called on[38] –

The district of Prieska had been formally annexed to the Orange Free State by a proclamation issued by President Steyn[39] –

A garrison has now been left there and the country is rapidly settling down –

At the action Lt Col Adye had with the rebels before I arrived, Lieut Harvey[40] of the Warwickshire Regt was badly wounded and had to have his right arm amputated close to the shoulder, he was most carefully looked after in the magistrate's house at Britstown and nothing could exceed the attention and kindness shown him by Mr Acheson and his wife –

When I passed through on my way out he was very well and quite cheerful but a few days later at night the bandages got disarranged, and he almost bled to death before assistance arrived – The local doctor of Britstown Dr. Hopkins at the last moment injected salt and water and saved his life, this is I believe a somewhat difficult operation and it was extraordinary to find in so small a village such a thoroughly capable local doctor – I cannot speak too lightly of the devotion of Mr Acheson his wife and Dr. Hopkins to Lt. Harvey and other sick and wounded soldiers

On my return from Prieska I rejoined Lord Roberts here on the 28th there is a good deal of work in concentrating troops, and reorganising the force here preparatory to a further advance I hope we may be ready about the 16th April – The enemy are reported in strength at Kro[o]nstadt, and are recovering from the panic caused by the capture of this place[41] – Yesterday they occupied some hills a little over 20 miles north, but were driven out by Generals French and Tucker after a sharp engagement[42] –

I have received Your Majesty's telegram and will not fail to write often –

RA VIC/P7/242

7
Lord Kitchener to Queen Victoria
[Holograph]   Government House,
                                          Bloemfontein,
                                          26th April 1900

The advance of the Army has been delayed longer than was expected owing to the great difficulty experienced in getting up sufficient supplies from the base,[43] as well as the very large number of horses and mules required to replace sick and to supply the wants of the increased number of troops that we now have.

With only one narrow gauge line of railway and a limited amount of rolling stock it is not easy to arrange to get up the vast amount that is required – The Army here eat more than two train loads a day so Your Majesty can realize how difficult it is in a short time to accumulate the necessary reserves here –

I am glad to say that we have now got almost all that we require including warm clothing for the men and I hope the advance will soon take place –

Lord Roberts has not been very well lately but he is all right again now; it was nothing serious and a few days rest cured him – Lady Roberts and his two daughters are now with him[44] –

The enemy have shown a great want of enterprise in not attempting to cut our line of railway – They are really more like mounted Franc-Tireurs[45] than anything else – One day they are simple farmers ploughing their land and supplying the army with eggs, milk, or grain, and within a few hours they dig up their rifles and ammunition and mounting rough ponies from the farm, become boers – We are doing all we can to disarm them; but though we get information of some buried rifles from the natives there must be a great number undiscovered in the country –

General Hunter has gone to Kimberley and will I hope soon send a relief column to Mafeking[46] – I had hoped a force would have started earlier but Lord Methuen had been out at Boshof most of the time with all the available mounted troops[47] –

The sick and wounded are doing well, there is a good deal of enteric fever; but the proportion of sick to the number of troops is not great – Nursing in the hospitals is well looked after with the result that the enteric cases mostly recover[48]

We had a sad loss in Capt R. Peel[49] 2nd Life Guards who died of enteric I was with him before he died but he had unfortunately made up his mind that he could not live and would not make an effort, he was a most devoted son and I fear his poor mother will suffer dreadfully.

I do not think the enemy will make a very determined stand until we reach Kro[o]nstad[50] which is a strong position and will probably be held as long as possible – I hear there are a large number of foreigners in Kronstad principally french and German – The boers do not apparently think much of the foreign element in their ranks, and from our experience of them they are much easier to deal with than the boers[51] –

RA VIC/P8/123

8
Lord Kitchener to Queen Victoria

[Holograph]   Kro[o]nstadt
                                                   14[th] May 1900

I have the honour to tender to Your Majesty my most grateful thanks for the souvenir Your Majesty has so graciously sent me which I shall always greatly prize –

Your Majesty's letter reached me while we were on the march to this place and was a source of great pleasure –

The troops are all very cheerful and in very good order, they are most keen to get on and are marching wonderfully well –

I am glad to say that now we are on the move again we have no more cases of enteric fever amongst the troops – Transport and supplies are working much better than they formerly did so that men and horses are now well fed – The weather has been excellent a bright warm sun all day and though the nights and mornings are cold it has been quite dry –

The enemy have not shown, up to the present, any great resistance to our advance,[52] they appear to be much demoralized and their retreat through this town was a route. I hear that President Steyn stood at the ford at the entrance to the town and tried to flog the retreating burghers back to the front, but they would not listen to him – many of them abusing him for bringing about the war – A large number of the Free Staters have given up their arms and returned to their farms –

I am sorry to say on two occasions lately our men have been shot down by Boers firing on them from under cover of the white flag[53] – Our men have been warned so often on this subject that I cannot imagine how they get taken in – On one occasion they put the white flag up over some farm buildings and when a squadron rode up they fired on them at close range – It is very sad but it is a good deal the fault of our men for not taking proper precautions –

Lord Roberts is very well indeed and stands the fatigue of marching and the hard work in a wonderful way –

The railway is being pushed on rapidly behind us – All the bridges have been blown up and a great deal of damage has been done to the line – The Railway Engineers are however doing very well and making excellent progress[54] –

RA VIC/P9/73

9
Mr St John Brodrick to Lord Lansdowne[55]

[Holograph] Moor Park,
Private Rickmansworth.
June 3. 1900

I am afraid that in the recent rapid advances the men in the Field Hospitals have suffered a good deal. Two or three correspondents at the Cape have told me that Kitchener no doubt from transport experiences had cut down the Hospitals at the front unduly, and today I got a cable saying the 'condition of up country hospitals deplorable men dying for want of nursing and perishable [?] comforts' – It is not required, but as my only correspondents at the front are very reliable I though[t] it best to let you know.

You are probably aware that K. is credited with a good deal of harshness about the Paardeberg wounded & it ought [to] be worth while to send a wire to suggest that no expense should be spared to provide comforts to mitigate the inevitable suffering of sick and wounded in these forced marches.

Forgive my troubling you and keep this confidential as the soldiers are so touchy about any leakage –

BL MS Room, 5th Lord Lansdowne Papers

10
Lord Kitchener to Queen Victoria

[Holograph]   Pretoria
6th June 1900

Your Majesty will have heard by telegraph the details of our recent march here –

The troops are all well and in excellent spirits, they have marched splendidly and whenever we have experienced resistance they have fought very steadily.[56] The cavalry and mounted Infantry have had most of the fighting, and have greatly improved since we started – The Artillery and Transport have also done well, I hope however we shall get some improved guns after this campaign is over –

Lord Roberts is very well and stands the hard work he has to do wonderfully –

We have a very long line of communications and the activity of the Free State Boers is a source of anxiety – There are now no less than three divisions as well as a large force of Yeomanry and Mounted Infantry and 2800 men of General Brabants mounted colonial troops on the Heilbron, Lindley, Senekal, Ficksburg line; but the Boers manage to get through and threaten our railway, they have recently succeeded in surrounding a battalion of Yeomanry[57] and in cutting off one of our convoys of supplies[58] –

I expect to leave here tomorrow for the South to look after matters on the line – If General Buller could get clear of Langs Nek either to the North or into the Free State it would be a great assistance –

It is very difficult to prevent our troops being caught in traps carefully prepared for them by an enemy that does not wear uniform, and can at any moment pose as honest farmers – They are apparently getting heartily sick of the war and it may collapse before long   I hear the burghers are only kept in the field by the greatest persuasion of their commandants and the threats of Mr Kruger and Steyn of imprisonment and confiscation of property for all who hand in their arms –

This is a pretty town consisting mostly of a number of villas in gardens with broad roads. The climate must be very like Cairo as I noticed all the flowers and flowering trees that flourish there do extremely well here – The forts are small but are not badly constructed and their positions have been well selected[59] – There are a few good buildings for public offices and barracks[60] – Mrs Kruger[61] and Mrs L. Botha[62] wife of the Commandant General are both here and being treated with every respect –

It has been a great pleasure to release the prisoners[63] they are looking pale and worn, and I hear some of the officers quite broke down and wept tears when they saw the troops marching through the town with bands playing and knew that their captivity was over –

RA VIC/P10/36[64]

11
Queen Victoria to Lord Kitchener

[Manuscript]   Balmoral Castle.
                                                     June 8, 1900.

The Queen-Empress thanks Lord Kitchener for his very interesting & kind letter of April 26th, received May 19th. She rejoices with him, Lord Roberts & the whole Army in South Africa at the relief of Mafeking,[65] & the capture of Johannesburg & Pretoria.[66] These events, which must have caused much anxiety & difficulty, have been hailed with wild delight & thankfulness in [the][67] whole country.

The Queen was sorry to hear Lord Roberts had not been well,[68] but she hears he is quite recovered, & that Lord Kitchener himself is quite well.

She fears there is still much trouble in store, though she trusts not much more fighting of a serious nature. But you have to contend with a most treacherous foe.

We have got the new Sirdar (Sir R. Wingate)[69] here for two nights. He has been very unwell with influenza, but is getting better. He has had a very anxious winter. He has brougth his Arabian servant with him, who served Lord Kitchener, & we were much interested to see him.

We leave this on the 20th to receive the Khedive[70] on the 22nd.

TNA reference PRO 30/57/16/R6 (original) and R26 (copy)

12
Queen Victoria to Lord Kitchener

[Manuscript]   Windsor Castle
                                                June 29, 1900

The Queen-Empress writes a few lines to Lord Kitchener to tell him of the Khedive's[71] visit here which took place yesterday & lasted till this morning.

Nothing could go off better & he has quite changed & become most friendly towards us of late & used of his own accord the expression of his "fidélité constante"[72] towards the Queen.

He was very ill indeed for a few days on arriving at Queensborough, & fears were at first entertained that he was going to have diphteria. He remained on board from the 21st to the 27th. We thought him very pleasing.

The Queen thanks Lord Kitchener for his last letter of the 14th May, [which][73] she received the day after hers went, on the 9th.

There have been good [?] news from South Africa, but troubles & [?]. The losses of people you know have been sad and the amount of sickness very distressing, still the end seems less distant than it did at one time.

She is glad Lord Roberts is well again, & trusts he will continue so, as also Lord Kitchener.

The present Sirdar,[74] who seems to be doing very well, has been very unwell again with influenza, but seems now much better.

The Queen must add, the beautiful donkey [he] gave her has been in the Queen's garden –, or rather donkey-chair, & was very quiet, & will be very useful.

P.S. – The Queen intended also writing to Lord Roberts, but must put it off till next week. Pray tell him so.

TNA reference PRO 30/57/16/R7a (original) and R27 (copy)

13
Lord Kitchener to Queen Victoria

[Holograph]   Kro[o]nstadt
30th June 1900[75]

The Boers have given us lately considerable trouble on our long line of communications – Having blown up all important bridges and culverts we had to repair the line with wooden baulks, and these are easily destroyed by fire; the enemy have three times succeeded in burning our bridges but their last two attempts failed as our posts along the line were able to drive them off[76] –

I hope in a few days [from] now we shall be in a position to deal with these Freestaters who are still kept in the field by the exertions of Mr. Steyn – General Clements is now moving from Senekal to Lindley where he will join General Pagets force and act against Bethlehem and the Southern position of the country still occupied by the Boers, while General Hunter who has replaced General Ian Hamilton, unfortunately disabled by an accidental fall from his horse, is moving south from Heidelberg and will probably occupy Reitz before long[77] –

The Derbyshire Militia regt were I regret to say captured in one of these raids on the railway though the position they had to hold was naturally a very strong one – The boers surrounded them during the night and at daylight poured a terrible fire into their camp and drove their outposts which were not well placed off the Koppie. Had the regiment been on the Koppies instead of camped underneath on the plain the enemy could not have turned them out.[78]

Pretoria is I am glad to say up to the present much more healthy than Bloemfontein and the troops are doing well there – A large building for the courts of Justice just finished,[79] but not occupied, has been turned into a splendid hospital and when complete will give accommodation to between eight and nine hundred cases. Sir William Thomson has been most active in fitting out and starting this hospital,[80] they are still rather short of nurses but there are a number on the way up only delayed through the breaks on the railway, thirty went on from here to Pretoria today –

Lord Roberts is very well   he has changed his house to a rather more comfortable one in Pretoria.[81] I return there in two days if all is quiet again in this neighbourhood – I think it is very probable that when Mr Steyn and the Free Staters now out on commando have been dealt with that Mr Kruger and the Transvaalers will give in and the war will be over –

RA VIC/P10/127

14
Queen Victoria to Lord Kitchener

[Manuscript]   Osborne.
                                                          Aug. 10, 1900.

The Queen Empress has not yet thanked Lord Kitchener for his two last interesting letters of the 6th and 30th June,[82] but she has so lately received so sad a blow in the loss of her beloved son, which came quite like a thunder-clap,[83] that she could not write.

The Queen follows the War with the greatest interest, which alas! seems to drag on, though it is inevitable. She sees that Lord Kitchener has been going about in many directions,[84] & she is thankful to hear that he has always kept well though his work must be severe.

If only Krüger and the other dreadful people could be caught!

The Queen's best wishes always attend Lord Kitchener.

TNA reference PRO 30/57/16/R10(a) (original) and R22 (copy)

15
Mr Neville Chamberlain[85] to General Ian Hamilton

[Holograph]   Chilwell
                                                                    Notts.
                                                            2nd May 1918

I find it difficult to reply to your question – As Private Secretary
in S. Africa I was kept so busy with all the letters I had to write
that I did not see much of how the actual "military" work was
being carried on – But I should say, from my recollection of what I
did see, that the relations between Lord R. and Lord K. in South
Africa were not exactly those of either a Chief of the Staff, or of a
"Second in Command" – Prior to the war Lord R. had, as you will
remember, always been his own Chief of the Staff, and when "K"
joined him he utilized his services as a sort of understudy of
himself, and delegated to him a very large amount of authority –
For instance, when French got Cronje at bay at Paardeberg Lord
R. sent "K" on to act for him, and the latter practically ran the
first part of the business, though, if I recollect right, Kelly-Kenny
was senior to him[86] –

Almost immediately after Paardeberg there was trouble on our
line of Communications – "K" was sent off at short notice to the
borders of Cape Colony, to put it right, and there again he acted
with the full authority of an "understudy" & commanded to all
intents and purposes on the spot, as if Lord R. himself had been
present, and without referring his plans to the C. in. C[87] – No
doubt a Chief of the Staff would often take on himself such a
responsibility, but I know Lord R. had such an implicit confidence
in "K" that it was a relief to him to give the latter a free hand on
such occasions – as you suggest "I should say . . . he employed
Lord K. in doing special odd jobs . . .".

When "K" had rejoined from such excursions he used to be
busy with the A.G. and QMG. staffs (as we called them in those
days) but I am confident that whenever Lord R. & Lord K. were
together, it was Lord R. who issued practically all important
orders about military operations – No doubt he kept Lord K. fully
posted in what he was doing & consulted him about most matters,

but he kept in his own hands the orders connected with any specially important moves which were in hand – I don't think I can say more & I hope that what I have said will be of use.

Yes – things are busy in France – I have <u>implicit confidence</u> in the British soldier – if only our miserable politicians will give our Generals enough soldiers to carry on the work. But that is the difficulty – Plumer is putting up a grand fight and after the terrible licking he gave the Boches last Monday, it really looks as if he will hold them all right[88] – Good bye old chap. I rejoiced to read that nice Royal message to Bristot in which you were referred to.

LHCMA, Hamilton 13/21

16
Lord Kitchener to Queen Victoria

[Holograph]   Pretoria
25 Augt 1900

I beg to express my humble thanks for the gracious letter Your Majesty was good enough to send me –

When de Wet broke through General Hunter's cordon, Lord Roberts sent me to take charge of the operation against him on the Vaal[89] – The object was to surround the boers on the Southern side and force them either to fight, or to cross the Vaal and thus clear them out of the Orange River Colony –

Lord Methuen was at the same time working from Potche[f]stroom so as to close in de Wet from the north – As I anticipated, when we pressed de Wet from the south he crossed the Vaal,[90] and broke north and though Lord Methuen attacked vigorously the boers managed to pass him – We all started immediately in pursuit but were somewhat delayed in crossing a difficult drift over the Vaal[91] and were only able to come up with the enemy's rear guard which we shelled – The Infantry marched splendidly over bad roads and bad drifts   they made an average for the first ten consecutive days of 18 miles a day –

The boers were so pressed that they had to drop their wagons and blow up a considerable amount of ammunition – Lord

Methuen captured one of their guns;[92] but as they each had two ponies and their transport was in light carts they were able to travel so fast that by making every exertion we could only keep in touch with their rear guard; the prisoners we took said they were very hard pressed – Unfortunately the pass over the magalies Berg range of hills at Olifants Nek was not held by our troops so that de Wet was able to get over and hold the hills against us. It was a great disappointment.[93] I then received a message from Lord Roberts that Lt Col Hore was surrounded by the enemy at Elands river station on the Rustenberg [Rustenburg]-Mafeking road,[94] I therefore marched with all speed to his release –

Col Hore had 480 Australian bushmen with him and had made a most gallant defence in a position much exposed to Artillery fire – The enemy cleared away as we approached leaving only a few hundred men to snipe at us in the hills. The garrison were naturally delighted to see us and cheered heartily as we rode in –

We then marched to Pretoria via the Rustenberg road completing 280 miles march in 15 days –

Lord Roberts is very well   he left yesterday for the East and I follow him in a day or two as soon as I can make arrangements for the march and entraining of the troops going out there – I think that when the enemy are beaten and in full retreat to the hills from their Machadodorp position the war may be practically considered over, they will never stand any where again; but catching them in this vast and broken country is a very difficult problem –

If a proclamation were published annexing the Transvaal and flying columns formed to act as police I think the country would soon settle down. They are all very tired of the war –

Lord Roberts has already approved of five flying columns for the Orange River Colony, and four for the western portion of the Transvaal, each column has a district to work in and I feel sure they will soon clear out all disaffection –

The troops are all well, but are tired after their long marching & we do our best to give them as much rest as possible, but the distances are so great they are obliged to have long marches –

RA VIC/P12/66

17
Lord Kitchener to Queen Victoria

[Holograph]   Pretoria
12th Octr 1900

I feel sure Your Majesty will be pleased to hear that the war is almost over, though there are still several bodies of the enemy in the field they can do very little harm now, and are running short of ammunition –

I have recently returned from Komati Poort where we have now established a garrison – It is a very low feverish place and I fear the troops stationed there will suffer when the rains begin. I have chosen as healthy a site as possible for the camp on the hills near the Portug[u]ese frontier and we are putting up huts so that everything will be done to make the men comfortable, they will be able in case of necessity at any time, to get change of air at sea in Delegoa [Delagoa] Bay –

The local Portug[u]ese authorities were very polite and gave us every assistance in their power but they seem to be much tied by orders from Lisbon, for instance the boers ran some of the Cape Colony, Natal and Orange River railway trucks that they captured into Portug[u]ese territory, besides a very large quantity of the netherlands railway material,[95] these they refuse, under orders from Lisbon, to give up.[96] They acknowledge they have no right to retain the former though there may be some question about the latter, as they seem to be very fond of money I told them they would have to pay £5 a day for each of our trucks they detained, they are now I believe reconsidering the matter. They are of course very anxious to keep the railway from Lorenzo [Lourenço] Marques to Pretoria open, it is a very bad line the grades and curves are terrible, and at one place trains have to be got up five miles of so steep an incline that a rack is necessary, the same as is in use in Switzerland; the result is that only very little can be carried on the line. I expect both Cape Colony, and Natal will do their utmost to shut up the Delegoa [Delagoa] line so as to get the Transvaal trade through their ports and railways in that case Lorenzo Marques would soon cease to be of any importance and the Portug[u]ese might give it up – for a moderate sum –

Mr. Kruger was staying with the Governor at Lorenzo Marques.[97] The Governor's nephew told me he was a most unpleasant guest, they rarely see him except at meal times, he then marches in sits down at the head of the table and after saying a long grace eats his dinner without speaking to anyone, when he has had enough without waiting for anyone else or for the end of dinner he says another long grace in dutch   lights his pipe, and walks out – One evening they had a little music but he sent out word from his room that they were disturbing him while he was reading the Psalms, so the music had to be stopped.

Lord Roberts is very well and will shortly return to England where I am sure he will receive the enthusiastic reception he deserves. Some of the colonial troops will also soon return to their colonies –

RA VIC/P14/27

18
Lord Kitchener to Queen Victoria

[Holograph]   Johannesberg [Johannesburg]
8th Novber 1900

The whole army feel deeply for Your Majesty and Princess Christian[98] in your great sorrow at the sad loss sustained by the death of Prince Christian Victor[99] – There is no doubt had he been spared he would have occupied later a high position in the army, to the great advantage of the service to which he was so thoroughly devoted –

He was always a keen soldier, and never spared himself in the least, always setting the highest and best example of true soldierlike spirit. I do not think there was anyone more loved and respected by all ranks – I greatly fear that his services with the Army in many unhealthy climates, particularly Ashantee, had undermined his naturally strong constitution –

The day before he was taken ill he was playing cricket in Pretoria, and seemed perfectly well and full of life – Everything that was possible was done for him, and he suffered no pain –

Poor Lord Roberts has been extremely anxious about his daughter, she was yesterday most dangerously ill, and the doctors at one time hardly thought she would live through the day. Lord Roberts suffered dreadfully and I was quite nervous about him – I am glad to say that today she is much better and we hope the crisis is over[100] –

I have just received Your Majesty's most gracious letter of the 12th Oct – Some time ago Lord Roberts, I believe recommended me to the Secretary of State for the Indian command, and there is nothing I should like better than to gain experience in that country which seems to me to be one of the most vulnerable portions of Your Majestys vast empire –

When the Ameer of Afghanistan dies,[101] it is not unlikely that there will be some trouble on the north west frontier of India, and I should like very much if possible before anything of the sort happened, to have some experience with the native troops of India –

I feel that with Lord Roberts and his staff at the War Office,[102] the changes necessary for the good of the Army will be in absolutely safe hands – I do not think that in his new work my services would be of much use to him; he has however suggested that I should after returning from South Africa work for a few months with him at the War Office before going to India; during that time any questions in which I could help him would be thoroughly gone into, and as far as possible settled – I have great hopes he will receive the permanent assistance he requires in the War Office from the far more capable hands of Your Majesty's son, the Duke of Connaught, who has such ample experience of the home Army[103] –

The Boers still keep up a hopeless struggle hoping for some form of European intervention through the mediation of Mr Kruger – we have just heard the sad news that Colonel Le Gallais, a very gallant and capable cavalry officer, has been killed   he served with me all through the Sudan campaign and was specially promoted for distinguished conduct in the field – The Boers lost heavily and we captured five guns and three maxims besides one hundred prisoners[104] –

RA VIC/P14/64[105]

19
Queen Victoria to Lord Kitchener

[Manuscript] Windsor Castle.
Nov. 16, 1900.

The Queen-Empress thanks Lord Kitchener for his interesting letter of the ......[106] October, received just before she left Balmoral.

Alas! alas! – the news of the untimely and unexpected loss of her dearly beloved grandson has overwhelmed her with grief, and the Queen knows how fond Lord Kitchener was of our darling Christian Victor, who was much attached to Lord Kitchener. He had gone through the greatest dangers & hardships unscathed, & we thought him safe now. But the malarial & enteric fever together were too much, strong though he was. He was good as he was brave and is a very great loss to the Army & [the][107] country, as well as to his broken-hearted Parents,[108] Sisters, & Brother. The Queen's poor daughter bears up with wonderful courage and resignation, & wishes the Queen to thank Lord Kitchener for all his kindness to him.

The Queen feels much upset and shaken by this event & the loss of a dear grandson who was very useful to her, & at whose birth she had been present.

The War drags on, which is very trying.

TNA reference PRO 30/57/16/R11(a) (original) and R23 (copy)

20
Lord Kitchener to Lieutenant-General Horace Smith-Dorrien

[Holograph] 26th Nov. [1900][109]

Thanks for your letter only received today – As soon as I can get Steinackers[110] men to Komati [Poort] there will be the Komati and Kaapmuiden M.I. available the 3rd and 4th MI and all for your line and have been filled up but it is hard work & long work getting new organisations into order – I hope Alderson will get you a good many Canadians[111] It was necessary to do it through him – I hope before long we may start active work both South & North of your line   Hope you will catch L. Botha if he tries to get through[112] –

Keep your men fit and ready for action

[Postscript]
I am trying to make Rundle disgorge a squadron of 5th Lancers for you but he resists a good deal

IWM, Papers of General Sir Horace Smith-Dorrien, 87/47/6

Part 2
December 1900 to March 1901
From the Escalation of the Guerrilla War to the End of the Middelburg Peace Negotiations
Introduction

By the time Lord Kitchener became Commander-in-Chief of the British forces in South Africa on 29 November 1900, the outcome of the war had for quite some time no longer been in doubt. From the end of February to the end of November 1900, most of the fighting took place on republican soil, but Lord Roberts left a legacy of many complex, unsolved problems to his successor. This can primarily be attributed to Roberts' underestimation of the Boer character, and of the Boers' tenacious Afrikaner nationalism, love of liberty, and resolve to resist the numerically far superior British force. Furthermore, Roberts attached too much importance to the symbolic and practical value of the republican capitals, and he was over-eager to annex the republics, doing so before the complete subjugation of the Boer forces in the field. Roberts also had to take responsibility for many of the administrative blunders, including the problems with the transport system and the red tape of the hospitals. When first the capture of their capitals and later the annexation of their countries did not force the Boer commanders to surrender, Roberts – in desperation – resorted to a scorched earth policy. This was in effect an admission of his failure to find a clear-cut military solution to the problem of continued Boer resistance.[1] Ironically, however, the harsher measures probably prolonged the war, because in due course the guerrilla war escalated – a problem with which Kitchener had to deal soon after he became supreme commander.

Roberts outmanoeuvred the Boers strategically, but was unable to defeat them tactically after the fall of Bloemfontein. Thus, by the time Kitchener took command, the British forces controlled almost all the towns and villages, but in the vast expanses of the South African veldt the Boers to a large extent roamed about freely, threatening the British garrisons and lines of communication. The war had in fact become a war against space [32, 34]. The British underestimated the Boers' ability to continue the military struggle, and in December 1900 – when the Boers once again invaded the Cape Colony – it was as if a totally new war had broken out. As one can imagine, Kitchener was a very frustrated man [27, 28].

When Kitchener took over as Commander-in-Chief, he had approximately 210,000 white soldiers under his command, plus several thousand blacks and coloureds, at that stage still primarily serving the British Army in a non-combatant capacity. Against this large force, there were probably about 30,000 Boers left in their mosquito army[2] in the field; definitely not more than 35,000. Although the British forces seemed to be overwhelming, this was not necessarily true in practice. For example, nearly 100,000 of the white troops were used to guard the vital railway lines, and several thousand others were passively deployed as garrison troops in the many towns and villages dotted all over the war zone [24]. Soon Kitchener realised the need for more – and more effective – mounted troops, organised in smaller mobile units, called columns. There were only 38 of these columns when Kitchener became overall commander in South Africa; in due course this number would double.[3] By May 1901, Kitchener would have a total of some 240,000 white troops under his command (with approximately 100 heavy guns, 420 horse artillery and field artillery guns, and 60 pom-poms)[4] – more than at any other time during the war; and to that number must be added more than 120,000 blacks and coloureds who served in the British Army in South Africa in various combatant and non-combatant capacities. But although he now commanded more troops than ever before in his career, Kitchener must have known that in South Africa there was no possibility of defeating the Boers in the 'Omdurman style'.

The first indication of renewed Boer activities came on 13 December 1900 when Generals C.F. Beyers, J.H. de la Rey and J.C. Smuts, with a force of about 1,700 burghers, attacked the camp of Major-General R.A.P. Clements' force of about 2,000 men (with ten guns) at Nooitgedacht at the foot of the Magalies Mountain in the Western Transvaal, as well as the entrenched British positions on top of the mountain. The initial Boer assault against the camp was beaten off, but after the British positions on top of the mountain were overrun, the British camp came under renewed fire and the British soldiers fled in panic. Boer casualties amounted to 32 killed and 46 wounded, while the British lost 109 killed, 186 wounded and at least 368 taken prisoner[5] [30].

Soon, however, the Cape Colony became Kitchener's main concern. A decision to re-invade the Cape Colony (and Natal) and take the war once again to remote regions was taken at a 'krijgsraad' (council of war) meeting held at Syferfontein in the Western Transvaal on 27 October 1900. Amongst the prominent Boer leaders present were President M.T. Steyn of the OFS and Generals Louis Botha, J.C. Smuts and J.H. de la Rey of the Transvaal. At this meeting it was also decided that an attempt would be made to raise a full-scale rebellion in the Cape Colony.[6]

In November 1900 General Christiaan de Wet's attempt to invade the Cape Colony was frustrated, first by the clash at Doornkraal, near Bothaville (6 November), when De Wet suffered a rare defeat, and then by the fact that the Gariep was in flood, so that he was forced to retreat northwards, pursued by the British in what became known as the second De Wet hunt[7] [25].

De Wet escaped and he and other Boer commanders planned to continue their efforts to break through into the Cape Colony with a view to enlarging the size of the operational area so that the pressure on the Boer commandos in the (former) Boer republics could be relieved, and so that the struggle could be taken into British territory. For this reason a series of incursions took place from the middle of December 1900. On the night of 15–16 December Judge (General) J.B.M. Hertzog crossed the Gariep at Sanddrif, between Norvalspont and Petrusville, with about 1,200 burghers. His force occupied Philipstown on 17 December and Britstown on 22 December. The Boers then moved as far south-west as Vanrhynsdorp (19 January 1901). Some of the burghers went to Lambert's Bay on the Atlantic coast, where they fired at the British light cruiser HMS *Sybille*, which retaliated with a few gunshots. The bulk of Hertzog's force eventually returned to the ORC at the end of February 1901 in the company of De Wet (whose second invasion attempt on 10 February 1901 – see below – was successful). Another invasion force of about 300 men, under Commandant P.H. Kritzinger, also crossed into the Cape Colony on the night of 15–16 December 1900. Kritzinger returned to the ORC in April 1901 (only to launch two further invasions at a later stage), but portions of his force, under the command of Commandant Gideon Scheepers and Commandant W.D. Fouché, reinforced by Cape rebels, continued to operate over a wide area in the

Colony.[8] So, almost as soon as he had taken over as Commander-in-Chief, Kitchener had to contend with an escalating guerrilla conflict.

General De Wet was determined to embark on an incursion into the Cape Colony in spite of his failed attempt in December 1900. On 10 February 1901 he entered the Cape Colony at Sanddrif with at least 2,000 men. From the start, his commando was pursued and attacked by British columns. On 16 February Kitchener himself took command of the operation to capture De Wet [35]. Kitchener arrived at De Aar on 16 February. He organised seventeen mobile columns (about 14,000 soldiers in total) to chase after De Wet. According to Kitchener, De Wet was 'as usual everywhere' [33]. The Boers moved westwards across the De Aar-Kimberley railway line, but on 19 February they came up against the Brak River, approximately 16 km east of Prieska, where they found that the river was in flood. The closest British column was only about 16 km behind them. De Wet realised that there was no other meaningful alternative than to abandon the incursion and to return to the ORC. Under cover of darkness, De Wet and his commando sidestepped the British pursuers and retreated in a north-easterly direction. After Hertzog joined him on 27 February, De Wet led the commandos back across the Gariep into ORC territory. The third, or great De Wet hunt was over. For obvious reasons Kitchener was very disappointed that De Wet had not been killed or captured. Even at this stage of the guerrilla war, Kitchener was convinced that if De Wet could be eliminated, the war would be over [31]. On his return to the ORC, De Wet divided the area into seven military districts, each under the command of an Assistant Chief Commandant. A small portion of De Wet's commando, under Commandant Wynand Malan – cut off from the main force on 12 February – stayed behind in the Cape Colony, mainly operating in the Midland districts of Aberdeen and Graaff-Reinet. Malan sometimes co-operated with the commandos of Scheepers and Fouché, destroyed British communications, caused Kitchener great annoyance, and forced him to send more reinforcements to the Cape Colony[9] [63].

The geographical escalation of the war underscored the need for an elaborate British anti-guerrilla strategy. Earlier, on 21 December 1900, Kitchener had convened a meeting of the Burgher Peace Committee, consisting of handsuppers (i.e. Boers who had surrendered voluntarily). Kitchener supported their idea of sending emissaries to commandos in an effort to convince the Boers who were still in the field, that continued resistance was futile. But this scheme failed, and the Boers retaliated by executing some of the emissaries, for example J.J. Morgendaal [64].

On 28 February 1901 Kitchener and General Louis Botha, Commandant-General of the Transvaal, met for peace negotiations at the Eastern Transvaal town of Middelburg [37, 38]. This meeting was preceded by telegraphic and other correspondence between Kitchener and Roberts regarding the terms that should be offered. Each commander put forward his government's conditions for the cessation of hostilities. Kitchener was in favour of a negotiated peace settlement, but was adamant that republican independence was out of the question and would not be discussed. Using the talks as a basis, Kitchener drafted the proposed terms of settlement. He was even prepared to give amnesty to the Cape rebels. The terms hammered out at Middelburg and accepted by those present, included the following: general amnesty for all republicans, including rebels (although the latter would temporarily lose their voting rights); the speedy return of all republican prisoners of war; self-government as soon as possible to the ORC and the Transvaal Colony; £1,000,000 to be supplied by the British government to pay the republicans' state debts; both Dutch and English to be used in schools; assistance and compensation to farmers for losses; no special war taxes to be levied; certain farmers would be allowed to keep fire-arms, and the question of political rights for black people would be postponed until self-government was granted to the ORC and the Transvaal Colony. These terms were modified by the British High Commissioner in South Africa, Sir Alfred Milner (backed by the Colonial Secretary, Joseph Chamberlain) and by the British government, and subsequently rejected by Botha on 16 March 1901. Kitchener criticised Milner for the refusal to grant an amnesty to the Cape rebels (which he regarded as the main reason for the breakdown of the talks) [45], but it seems that even if that condition had been granted, it is highly unlikely that the Boers would at that stage have opted for a peace settlement.[10]

Kitchener was exasperated by the failure of the Middelburg peace talks. The war continued, and Kitchener had to contend with a British government that needed a speedy conclusion to the hostilities, Milner who gave advice concerning how operations should be conducted [42], and Boer forces who did not play the military game according to any rules known by conventionally-trained European armies. Kitchener said towards the end of March 1901 that the war would drag on for another year [43]. He could not have known for sure at that stage how right he was, albeit that in actual fact the war continued for another year and a little more than two months.

21

Lord Kitchener to Lord Roberts[1]

[Holograph]   4th Decbr. oo.

You will have received all the news about operations by telegram so there is no necessity to repeat – C. Knox is I think doing very well and I hope now that he has got sufficient force that he will have a successful coup –

This place seemed a very sleepy hollow quite as if no war existed   officers riding about with ladies probably of boer extractions as if they had nothing to do

I think until we get the police out into the country we better not appoint more officers to civil work   they have absolutely nothing to do and set a bad example – White Royal Marines D.C. at Ladybrand will have to be dismissed for drunkenness.[2]

I am afraid there has been a good deal of neglect in collection of arms ammunition and horses in the southern portion of O.R.C. with the result that all the farmers are out again and we have to face considerably more opposition than we ought to meet at this stage of the war.

Hunter is not well but he is not ill   he is tired and I think should go home before long but there is no immediate hurry about it[3]   since I have been here I think he is far happier   I have not been able to see Macdonald yet but Hunter agrees with your estimation   he says Mac knows he has made a reputation and he is not going to risk losing it, he is therefore so cautious that he is practically useless – I rather dread losing Hunter as C. Knox is so useful in the field and this place would tie him up with office work How would you view sending out another Major General, Brook is I believe a good man and I think the W.O. offered him for service in South Africa not long ago –

The women question is always cropping up and is most difficult there is no doubt the women are keeping up the war and are far more bitter than the men   I have arranged that Mil[itary]

Gov[ernor] shall look after and feed destitute women of those that have to be removed for inciting the men to continue the war   I really think the only solution that will bring them to their senses is to remove the worst class to Kaapmuiden & form a camp there – I have told Mil Govr to keep the women divided into two classes those that are merely destitute separate from those who have their relations out on commando and are still actively hostile to us –

I hope you had a pleasant trip in Natal and that your arm and leg are now all right again[4] – I shall stop here   until the present rather anxious time is over it is not over   comfortable as Pretyman & his family now occupy Govt House[5] & though he kindly offered to put me up I did not feel equal to it & would not disturb him   There was no other house available   so I started in the train but found that impossible   so have taken up my abode in a disused hospital   the one on the hill next door to Govt House[6] I hope we shall not get enteric – I think however Govt House ought to be available as these makeshifts make our work harder   if a bachelor G.O.C. occupied it there would not be the same difficulty – I am issuing stringent regulations about fortifying positions and getting CREs[7] to build block houses everywhere they are needed[8] –

P.S.[9] I am afraid my chance of India is small but am sure you will do the best you can for me   When you get home I cannot be sufficiently grateful for all you have done for me

NAM. 1971-01-23-33-4

22
Queen Victoria to Lord Kitchener
[Manuscript]   Windsor Castle.
                                                      Dec. 14, 1900.

The Queen thanks Lord Kitchener for his last most kind and sympathetic letter of Nov. 8th.[10] She was sure that he would quite share the general grief for the untimely and very unexpected loss of her beloved soldier grandson.[11] She knows how much Lord

Kitchener appreciated & liked him, which was sincerely reciprocated. He will be much missed in the Army, to which he was so devotedly attached.

Upon the very important question of Lord Kitchener's ultimate employment here or elsewhere the Queen thinks [it] is not possible to decide anything yet. –

The Queen's best wishes accompany Lord Kitchener on his present arduous duties. –

TNA reference PRO 30/57/16/R12(a) (original) and R24 (copy)

23
Mr St John Brodrick to Lord Kitchener

[Copy]   Dec 15. 1900
Strictly confidential

I received your message from Col Sandbach,[12] the substance of which I had already heard from other quarters. I should already have been glad if you had been able to write to me direct on this very important matter, as I can assure you that I have nothing more at heart than the desire to obtain the best possible arrangement of the commands under very difficult conditions.

Will you allow me to write to you perfectly frankly about your proposal?

Your view, as I understand it, is that your position during this year has not been commensurate with your services, that you do not see any advantage in coming to the War Office, and on the other hand would by doing so give up your chance of the Indian Command which you earnestly desire.

Putting the public interest aside, I think there are some considerations which I may lay before you. I have heard a great deal of the course of events in the last year – I imagine your position has been a difficult one – The question of rank[13] struck me early in the year & although I had nothing to do with the War Office, I put it forward – The moment it was in my power I redressed it & have also settled with the Treasury for a more proper adjustment of your pay –

In reference to the conduct of the war, it was of course impossible to interfere from here. But if there has been any divergence of view between yourself & Ld Roberts (of wh. neither he nor you have given us indication) I would remind you that the positon in the War Office is very different from the position in the field – If for instance you have strong views as to reorganizing the Army, you would have in the War Office a direct access to the Secretary of State & the Cabinet (through him) wh. causes the best & strongest view to prevail.

At this moment, the Army can be reformed. Five year[s] hence there will not be the same opening – What is done now may perhaps stand for a generation; it will not be easy to force Parliament or the country into new measures, after the machinery has been readjusted.

That will be done, so far as I can secure it, or I shall cease to be Secretary of State –

Your ambition India – Have you fully considered it? I am not suggesting any question of your talent or ability for any command – But India is peculiar. For 40 years you have had a succession of men who have had long service in India & knowledge of the Indian Army – I think you once told me you had never been in India – Then there is the language difficulty & a body of 240,000 men to deal with of whom 2/3 belong to races, and serve under conditions peculiar to the country, and whose management without previous experience may try the power of any man whatever his military talent and ability. I was in India in 1892 with Ld Roberts & could not help being struck with the degree to wh. his hold on [the] Indian Army was due to knowledge of the language of the troops. Are you sure that the Indian Command is as good an avenue to other high military positions at home or in the field as the War Office ?

It is of course impossible for me to urge upon you service wh. would be distasteful to you – I can only say that not only should I welcome your cooperation, but the public fully count on it, and as I have written you before, I will take care you have the fullest scope & opportunity.

In any case I beg you to write me frankly and on no account to assume that I would do anything willingly to retard your prospects or stand in your way –

I have a very severe task on hand but the Cabinet will back me – I trust you will quietly think over the future before you give your final opinion.

[Postscript]
In any case as you know the Cabinet decides on the Indian C. in C.

TNA reference PRO 30/57/22/Y8

24
Lord Kitchener to Mr St John Brodrick

[Holograph]   Pretoria
20th Dec. 00

I fear from your letter of the 24th Nov.[14] you will have been much disappointed at the recent developments of the war out here.

As I telegraphed to you there has been a very considerable revival of hostilities everywhere and many more boers are now in the field than there were a short time ago[15] –

You may be sure I will do my utmost to reduce expenditure and I have I think recently been able to save between £80 and £90,000 a month by abolishing Weils contract for transport and taking the whole into our own hands[16] – When I get a little more time I will look further into expenditure going on – I think a great number of useless hangers on m[a]y be cleared out – The want of care of the horses supplied the troops has already been frequently strongly pointed out to all concerned, but without much effect – I shall I fear have to make a serious example of some com[man]ding officer to bring it home to all how serious this matter is[17] –

Expenditure in the English Army is not so easy to control as in the Egyptian Army and there does not appear to me to be a proper feeling amongst officers that unnecessary expenditure of Govt. money is culpable & that they are bound to look after the govt interest when dealing with contractors

The transport expenditure shocked me considerably when I looked into it   I think now it will be handled economically – I think that possibly a careful and rigid examination in the W.O. into contracts and current market prices might lead to good results, but I fancy you would have to get someone that has no connection with the service to do it –

There is no doubt that many of the troops out here are stale and tired and any fresh troops to replace them would be an immense advantage –

The difficulties of the present situation out here are that we have to protect very long lines of railway & road and supply garrisons to the many towns & villages that have been occupied all over the country whilst the mobile columns we have in the field are principally taken up in escorting supplies to the various garrisons   We have therefore no striking force of any importance & it is most difficult to find troops in any case of emergency such as the Cape Colony invasion for instance – If we withdraw garrisons it has a bad effect as the boers at once put up their flag and start a sort of government again –

I estimate there are still <u>20,000</u> boers out on commando in the two colonies   Some officers put the numbers considerably higher[18] – These men are not always out on commando but return at intervals to their farms & live as most peaceful inhabitants, probably supplying the nearest British garrisons with forage milk & eggs until they are again called out to take the place of others in the field   Just now they apparently got these all out with the result that they suddenly show in considerable numbers and act with great boldness when they get a chance – Owing to the reactions of the country the boers can roam at pleasure and being excessively mobile they are able to surprise any post not sufficiently on the alert

Every farmer is to them an intelligence agency & a supply depot so that it is almost impossible to surround or catch them   I sincerely hope the people of England will be patient the boers trust to weary us out but of course time tells heavily against them –

To meet some of the difficulties I have determined to bring in the women from the more disturbed districts to laagers near the railway & offer the burghers to join them there.

We shall now be able to work on the feelings of the men to get back to their farms out of which they will be only kept by de Wet and Co – The burghers are now in many cases ….. going out on commando and do not like it at all –

I am afraid I have troubled you with a long letter and am sorry I couldnt give you better news   I will let you know at once when I see hopes of peace in the near future.

TNA reference PRO 30/57/20/Y9

25
Lord Kitchener to Lord Roberts

[Holograph]   Pretoria
                                                    21st Dec 00

Since I last wrote we have been having an anxious time – De Wet was successfully chased north by Knox[19] leaving only a few scattered boers in Zastron district which were being looked after by Grenfell and Herberts column.[20] These boers numbered about 700 passed between Rouxville and Aliwal [North] and to the astonishment of everyone crossed the [Gariep/Orange] river at Rhenoster Hoek[21] and are now being chased in the direction of Steynsberg [Steynsburg]   At the same time Hertzogs commando considerably reinforced   crossed near Sand drift[22] – I had to rapidly get in some of the M[oun]t[ed] troops with Knox and send them down   luckily the boers seem to have moved with great timidity and have given us time to get the troops down – I quite expected they would cut the railway by blowing up some of the important bridges near Colesberg and then get away south with a good start, but now they are apparently making north west which cannot be what they intended as it shows no combination and they could have far easier crossed the Kimberley line at Grasspan and the river further west where it was unguarded had they originally intended to go west – All possible steps are being taken and I am confident if nothing worse happens this attempt will be a complete failure[23] – The colony appears to be behaving well and Milner is not quite as alarmed as I expected –

I had been anxious about Clements   for some days he seemed to have so little go, allowing de la Rey to play about in Hekpoort while he was at Nooitgedacht   no doubt he was over confident and was surprised not in the sense of the men being caught unprepared by the enemy but by the enemy being able to bring up such superior forces and attacking with such boldness – When he had driven off de la Reys attack he and the whole camp thought it was all over and they were absolutely surprised when the attack on the hill above them succeeded and their position became untenable[24] –

I hope this renewed activity will soon cease as there is much organisation to be done –

We are getting on to de Wet really well   his forces were quite demoralised when they crossed the Thabanchu Ladybrand line[25] and Knox had any amount of men. Boyes had got to Senekal,[26] delisle [De Lisle] & Crewe were at Winburg   these would have held the old Winburg Trommel Ficksburg line long before de Wet got up to it but when the Colony invasion occurred I had to bring Boyes to Winburg in case of contingencies & delisle [De Lisle] had to go to the Colony and though Knox still followed de Wet he had only Barker,[27] Pilcher[28] and White[29] with him

I think I shall have to send Broadwood home and put Knox 18th Hussars[30] in his place   Broadwood has never been the same man since Sannahs post[31] & French thinks he ought to go   Poor fellow he is a splendid soldier and I fear it will hurt him very much – how he did not help Clements is a mystery to me – I have brought Lyttelton in here for the moment as I may at any time have to go off South if matters do not go well in the Cape Colony

I think we must bring in all the women from the farms and ….. burghers who voluntarily surrender to live with them – When Beyers came down to attack Clements he rode the last 40 miles hard without any transport, but bread was ready for his whole force in the farms south of Magaliesberg directly after the fight – I hope before I write again things may be surer then   We will all do our best but do impress in British public & press that they must be patient   there is only one ending possible and time tells against our adversaries

Best regards to Lady Roberts & the Misses Roberts

NAM. 1971-01-23-33-7

26
Circular Memorandum No. 29[32]

[Printed document] December 21st, 1900.

The General Commanding-in-Chief is desirous that all possible means shall be taken to stop the present guerilla warfare.

Of the various measures suggested for the accomplishment of this object, one which has been strongly recommended, and has lately been successfully tried on a small scale, is the removal of all men, women and children, and natives from the districts which the enemy's bands persistently occupy. This course has been pointed out by surrendered burghers, who are anxious to finish the war, as the most effective method of limiting the endurance of guerillas, as the men and women left on farms, if disloyal, willingly supply. Burghers, if loyal, dare not refuse to do so. Moreover, seeing the unprotected state of women now living out in the districts, this course is desirable to ensure their not being insulted or molested by natives.

Lord Kitchener desires that General Officers will, according to the means at their disposal, follow this system in the districts which they occupy, or may traverse.

The women and children brought in should be camped near the railway for supply purposes, and should be divided onto two categories, viz.: – 1st, Refugees, and the families of neutrals, non-combatants, and surrendered burghers; 2nd, Those whose husbands, fathers, or sons are on commando. The preference in accommodation, etc., should, of course, be given to the first class. The Ordnance will supply the necessary tents and the District Commissioner will look after the food on the scale now in use.

It should be clearly explained to Burghers in the field, that if they voluntarily surrender, they will be allowed to live with their families in the Camps until it is safe for them to return to their homes.

With regard to natives, it is not intended to clear Kafir [sic] Locations, but only such Kafirs [sic] and their stock as are on Boer farms. Every endeavour should be made to cause as little loss as possible to the natives removed, and to give them protection when brought in. They will be available for any works undertaken, for which they will receive pay at native rates.

South African Field Force. Republication of the Principal Circulars issued during 1900. Army Headquarters, Pretoria, January, 1901, p. 22[33]

27
Lord Kitchener to Mr St John Brodrick

[Holograph]   Commander-in-Chief's Office,
                                                                South Africa.
                                                    Pretoria 4th Jany 1901

Many thanks for your letter of the 8th Decber[34]   I fear it will be some time before we can reopen the mines   the latest development of this guerilla warfare having been a wanton destruction of mine property of considerable value – Ld Roberts will no doubt explain to you the difficulty that exists in protecting all the mine property on the rand[35] – I have seen some of the managers of the mines and will give them every facility in getting up guards from the Uitlanders and making them as efficient as possible   this is the best way to protect the property –

We have been I think unsuccessful in our meat-contract which should give us a saving of £1200 a day about   I have asked Paymasters and heads of spending dep[artmen]ts to bring to my notice any points that occur to them where economies might be made and I will do my best to curtail expenditure

I am sorry the war shows no signs of ending   I have been doing my best to show the people the uselessness of this struggle but I fear they have in many cases become intensely fanatical and quite beyond listening to reason   At the same time all the principal Burghers here say that my remarks to the Peace Committee[36]   a copy of which I have enclosed to Ld Roberts   ought to do a good deal towards bringing the war to a close   I am having it widely circulated throughout the country –

I hope you will be able to send me some Yeomanry drafts as they are a very useful body of men   Ld Chesham has written a memo which I have forwarded with the object of doing away with any cumbrous organisation in England for getting recruits for Yeomanry –

I shall be very glad indeed to have more Colonials   they are splended men and most useful   Canada does not seem to be sending any more – I sincerely hope by the time you get this matters will have so improved out here that there will be no question of sending more men but if such is not the case you might remember Canada.[37]

TNA reference PRO 30/57/22/Y13

28
Lord Kitchener to Lord Roberts

[Holograph]   Commander-in-Chief's Office,
Private   South Africa.
                                        Pretoria 4th Janry 1901.

A most astounding blow came on us last Sunday when we heard that Ben Viljoen's men had surprised and rushed Helvetia at 2.30 am on Saturday and captured the 4.7 [inch] gun without a shot being fired – The sentries must have all been fast asleep and as there have been many cases lately of men sleeping on their posts – I have issued a warning that I will confirm death sentences in such cases – The boers got off with the gun on the Dullstroom road   My brother[38] brought down some men and tried to follow but was too late   Machadodorp also sent out a small column but could not get in touch[39] –

Major Cotton   Manchesters   was in command at Helvetia   he was wounded but from the accounts we have at present he seems to have been quite incompetent and to have ordered the surrender of men who held out   A court of Inquiry is sitting and will probably lead to a Court Martial – I was somewhat disappointed that Lyttelton did not do much but he did not like weakening any point on his lines and expected an attack from the south –

The attack on Vreiheid [Vryheid] was of precisely a similar nature though fortunately it was there driven off;[40] the papers with my remarks on the subject go to you by this mail –

I have reinstated the orders for barbed wire entanglements to be put up everywhere particularly round positions of guns   there seems to be contradictory evidence about wire entanglement at Helvetia, but this will be cleared up[41]

Cape Colony continues to be unsatisfactory   the raiders are few but we cannot apparently get at them   I have sent down Douglas Haig[42] with local rank of Col[on]el to see what can be done and take charge in the field – Though our efforts have not been decidingly successful they have prevented the raiders from doing any harm,   they have been chased everywhere and have not got recruits or support in the colony – Milner has been quite calm and I have had to wake up Chowder [?] with some rather strong telegrams –

Of course having 4000 mounted men in the Colony hampers my action considerably both in Orange river [Colony] and here at the same time   I am acting as vigorously as possible against the enemy everywhere & am trying by working up peace committees & giving good terms to induce burghers to leave the commandos and surrender – If only the Cape Colony disturbances would end I could do more –

I have put Clements under French and Commando Nek under Tucker

Clements moving with a convoy to Rustenberg [Rustenburg] reported very large numbers of the enemy at Buffelspoort   I reinforced from here and Paget moved round in the north but as I expected the boers did not wait and Clements found himself unopposed yesterday –

Clements does not seem to be very satisfactory   I do not know quite what it is   he did not apparently lose his nerve but he sticks terribly   he is I think somewhat stubborn in the way he takes things   if he is told to do anything, that particular action appears always to him to be the worst thing to do,   he and French do not pull well together   I have given him Benson RA as his chief staff officer but it does not appear to have much beneficial result –

Beyers and de la Rey are now some distance west of Oliphants Nek   French is holding Venterdorp – Reitfontein [Rietfontein] 911. line –

C Knox is still after de Wet – now north of Senekal which we have reoccupied – I sent Bethunes M.I. to Lindley to take on the garrison of that place and form a mobile column to work in conjunction with C Knox   I am not sure de Wet himself has not gone west   about 600 boers crossed the line near Roodewal yesterday but as they did no damage   I hardly think de Wet could have been with them[43]

Louis Botha is somewhere near Bethal & report says he talks of peace but I do not put much credit in it   The wanton destruction of mine property at Boksburg shows that they are really bent on Guerilla warfare   The mine managers are getting guards up for all their property on the rand   I have brought in the Jagersfontein and Phillipolis [Philippolis] garrisons to form a column to clear the Zastron district where the boers are still congregated and supporting those in the Colony

I hope you will do something to send us some drafts for the Yeomanry   they are dwindling to nothing and are worth keeping up, Chesham is writing a scheme so as to avoid any large home establishment or committee and to arrange for counties to send men out direct   these men will have to get the new Yeomanry pay 5s[hillings] a day –

I congratulate you most heartily on being an Earl and K.G.[44] and also the Countess and the Ladies Roberts   I wired today on hearing the news   I hope by the time you get this you will have got over the fatigue of your reception in England though I fear you will have more than you care for to go through for some time.[45]

P.S. I see there is some trouble with Colvile[46] so I enclose copies of telegrams which may be of use –

I also enclose a printed copy of some remarks I made to the Burghers Peace Committee which are being widely circulated through the country   my view is that if we could only hit hard, and at the same time leave the door open we might get the boers to give up but I am not sanguine of success –

NAM. 1971-01-23-33-9

29
Queen Victoria to Lord Kitchener[47]

[Manuscript]   Osborne
Dictated.   Jan. 11, 1901.

Though the Queen-Empress has no letter to answer, she is anxious to express her satisfaction to Lord Kitchener at the manner in which he is conducting this very difficult, anxious & troublesome guerilla warfare with the Boers & the entire confidence she reposes in him to bring this to a close.

Though we are fully certain of the ultimate result, it is grievous that there should be so much bloodshed – such unnecessary bloodshed, which is certainly not our fault, but caused by the obstinacy & almost fanatacism [sic] of the Boer leaders, who must know that it can but end in their ultimate defeat.

The Queen trusts the wounded are doing well, & he himself in good health. She hears great praise of Lord Kitchener's Brother.[48]

We have to deplore the loss of many brave officers, young & old, as well as of brave men.

TNA reference PRO 30/57/16/R13(a) (original) and R25 (copy)

30
Lord Kitchener to Queen Victoria
[Holograph]   Commander-in-Chief's Office,
South Africa.
Pretoria 18th Janry 1901[49]

I beg to humbly thank Your Majesty for Your Majesty's most gracious letter of the 14th Decbr.[50]

Since Lord Roberts left the boers have been more active in the hopes of tiring out the troops – They have made some very bold attacks and though they have generally been driven off with considerable loss, they have twice succeeded lately in capturing our positions.[51] I believe the troops have learnt by these experiences a lesson that will I hope prevent any recurrence of such sad events – They were mainly due to over confidence and an underestimation of the enemy's fighting powers –

When Col Lambton[52] visited the position on which he had four companies at Nooitgedacht the day before the attack, all the officers said they only wished the boers would come and attempt to take the place –

The other day a considerable force of the enemy dressed in Khaki made an attack on Kaalfontein and Zuurfontein. I am glad to say they were driven off with loss although the small garrisons of those places were almost entirely comprised of young soldiers only just out here[53] –

The invasion of Cape Colony has been a great disappointment to the enemy as they expected to find large numbers in the colony ready to join them, whereas up to the present only 20 or 30 men have done so[54] –

I am also much disappointed that our troops have not been able long before this, to drive the enemy northwards over the border – No one however who has not been there can realize the difficulty of bringing off a decisive action against so mobile an enemy in such a difficult and vast country, where the inhabitants though not openly hostile to us are still more friendly to the enemy and help them secretly with horses, food, and information

The surrendered burghers here and at Kro[o]nstadt, and other places, have formed peace committees to try and induce the leaders in the field to give up a useless struggle which is ruining their country and to let the boers out in the field know the truth as to how matters stand – I must say there has not been much result up to the present and the boers appear to be more determined than ever to carry on the war – In the Orange River Colony de Wet continually evades our troops – We have been near him several times lately but he manages to escape; I have two columns out chasing him and we hope to catch him between them[55] –

RA VIC/P15/114

31
Lord Kitchener to Lord Roberts

[Holograph]   Commander-in-Chief's Office,
South Africa.
Pretoria Janry 25. 1901.

The death of the Queen seems terribly sudden.[56] We can hardly realise it. She took such an intense interest in all that went on out here that I greatly fear the strain of this war may have shortened her life –

I hope on Sunday to begin an important move eastwards to clear the country between the Eastern and Natal railways   I enclose a copy of my orders which will show you pretty clearly what it is intended to do   A map is being also issued to each commander with his course and that of the other columns marked out so I do not think any mistakes are possible[57] –

Clements evidently required a rest so Cunningham has taken his column and Clements has come in here to replace Tucker gone to Bloemfontein – Clements was in a great state about my remarks on Nooitgedacht. I have told him I could not write anything else particularly as there have been so many cases of carelessness lately I am sending in a memo from him on the subject by this mail – Clements has done some good work and will again I think –

Lyttelton is I fear very disappointing   he sticks in Middleberg [Middelburg, Transvaal] surrounded by forts and a large garrison and never moves a man out   the result is that the boers are really in occupation of the country all around him[58] –

I went out the day before yesterday to explain to him & Smith Dorrien the projected moves east, but when I got to Oliphants River 13 miles from Middleberg I found the hill ahead 5 miles from Middleberg held by the boers   we were just stopped in time and got back to Oliphants River after some time   I got Lyttelton to send out some troops to clear the hill & when after 3 hours that was done we started again but the train ahead of me was blown up by a mine the boers had had time to lay & the line was hopelessly blocked so I returned here – 2 companies on the hill would have made all secure   I hear today the boers are on the same place again & have blown up the line   it has always been a well known place for them –

Lyttelton has the same number of troops as when you left which was supposed to include a mobile column   I cannot make out what it is that makes him cling to the lines without protecting it –

Smith Dorrien moves out tomorrow against the boers at Carolina   I have reinforced him by 4 battalions and the 2nd I.L.H. regt besides an additional number of M.I.   I expect he will have a fight as the boers in Carolina are pretty numerous and as you know a good fighting lot –

I am doing my utmost to catch de Wet   Bruce Hamilton has now joined the chase and I have given them de Wet as their only objective   Of course de Wet is reported to be definitely in 3 different places every day[59] –

I enclose a telegram describing a cold blooded murder by de Wet of a british [sic] subject who went out on a peace mission and was taken to his laager[60] – I am letting Botha know the sort of people he is associated with –

If we could only catch de Wet about the time we got to Ermelo I believe it might finish the war –

Have you thought of sending me Featherstonaugh [Fetherstonhaugh] if he is now fit again, H.C. Dixon[61] of 25th Regt

Dist and Beatson from India – so many leaders are getting tired and used up that they would be very welcome

We are very short of regimental officers   I hope you will let your military Secty[62] hustle some of them out   this is an excellent climate for them –

Methuen has cleared Griqualand [West] and is now back on the line again[63] –

They seem to be telling serious stories in England about killing prisoners & stopping letters   As regards the forces our men are a great deal too weak   over and over again lately boers have apparantly surrendered and then shot our men and galloped off[64]   Nothing is altered since you left in any such matters –

With kind regards to Lady Roberts and your daughters –

NAM. 1971-01-23-33-12

32
Lord Kitchener to Mr St John Brodrick

[Holograph]   Commander-in-Chief's Office,
                                                            South Africa.
                                                              1.2.1901

Many thanks for your letter of the 5th Janry.[65]

I think I could find you a good many men from the Yeomanry and Colonial troops who would make good officers, I am taking a certain number on probation for transport service which is very short of officers and when they have been tried I propose to make them local lieutenants   these would in most cases make good officers – I suppose you will write officially about these and their militia commissions you speak of in your letter –

I am having the cases you enclosed looked into – I know Ld Harris and when he arrives will do all I can for him –

Considering the stale and jaded state of the troops I think it would be a very good thing if I could at once reward any exceptional good service in the field – Immediate recognition would I am sure have wonderful effect, how I can make it ..... but

I can do nothing to make the difference in the case of personal bravery and service that come before me –

The men are getting indifferent   the boers treat them very well as prisoners and I believe they are not always very pleased when they are released   The process of giving an immediate reward, used very sparingly, would I believe have a startling effect as they say it will no doubt be forgotten before the war is over   what is the use of trying – my powers I believe   extend to promoting a corporal to be sergt   a private to be corporal. I am afraid it will be difficult to make any change but I have no doubt if it were done that you would get better service out of the men in the field –

The boers show no signs of any wish for peace without their independence   I cannot say how long it will go on – not counting surrenders we reduce their forces at the rate of about 1000 a month   that was my bag for Decbr and Janry may be a little more – It is a most difficult problem, an enemy that always escapes, a country as vast that there is always room to escape, supplies such as they want abundant almost everywhere.

De Wet & Steyn are now going for the Colony and I fear this time I shall hardly be able to prevent them getting in but I will send 5000 mounted men to keep them moving and preventing their being able to do much harm[66]

Our having kept them out all this time has given us time to do a good deal towards organising the Colonials for resistance & preparing the country, by removing horses forage etc, for invasion – I think more in these ways might [have] been done but a good deal has been already accomplished –

I wish I could give you better news before parliament meets but unless we have a real stroke of luck on the Eastern side where French is operating[67] I fear I shall have nothing good to tell you

TNA reference PRO 30/57/22/Y19

33
Lord Kitchener to Lord Roberts

[Holograph]   Commander-in-Chief's Office,
                                                    South Africa.
                                                8[th] Febry 1901.

French is going on well and I hope will force Botha to clear off the high veldt – De Wet is as usual everywhere   he means to go into the Colony if he can but up to the present has not liked to face it –

Lyttelton and Paget are now at Na[a]uwpoort where the KOE [?] and new M.I. had all concentrating with Plumers brigade   I have now something over 11 000 mounted men in the Colony   we have plenty of horses and I am giving each force a liberal supply of spare horses,   I think this will be a great saving in horse flesh – We are rather hard up for saddles but shall have just enough to pull through until more arrive – As you know we are short of officers so I have not been able to let any go other than those invalided –

I do not think it could be possible for Sir E. Wood to come out under me. I hope my telegrams on the subject were what you would have wished – I do not think it could have worked unless he came over, or independent of me.

I am very glad to see more troops are coming out   you know how they disappear in this enormous country and the wastage is very great –

I am sending home the dewetsdorp Court Martial[68]   it is not pleasant reading but I think should be confirmed as it will have a good effect here –

I hope I respond sufficiently and that you will tell me if I ought to do more   The report that all prisoners are killed has reached Capetown where the Attorney Genl is prosecuting the paper for libel   It is most absurd as they see the reports of our taking prisoners most days and also see the prisoners passing through to Ceylon but people will believe anything – The reports on farm burning asked for by parliament go home this mail[69]   totals Transvaal 256 and Free State 353   this includes every hovel or building of any kind   mills etc. & does not really mean genuine farms in many cases   all the same there may be some unrecorded I think if 50 were added for this it would be a liberal estimate –

I wish I could see any way to bring the war to an end but I fear it can only be done by hard knocks and as you know it is not easy to give those to an enemy that always runs away

With kind regards to the Countess & Ladies Roberts

NAM. 1971-01-23-33-14

34
Lord Kitchener to Lord Milner

[Holograph]   12th Febr 01.
I hope Girouard and Brabant
are working well   I do not think
the East will be attacked[70]

Many thanks for yours of 8th I shall be delighted to see you up here as there are several points I should like to discuss with you –

I have been doing my utmost to keep de Wet out of the Colony but the country is too big and there are so many places to guard it was practically impossible to stop him. However there will be between 11 & 12 thousand mounted men after him so I hope he will have us rest [sic] unless he goes very far west[71] –

Chowder [?] seemed to me to be very slow at waking up to the necessity for preparing the Cape Colony for invasion but since then a great deal has evidently been done –

I have advocated moving all stock   in fact once when I was asked I replied stock in C.C. [Cape Colony] should not be moved – I am rather worn out with the disappointments that a British army bring but hope to worry through somehow. I wish I could see my way to a run like you though you deserve it more than I do – I hope de Wet will not do much harm in the colony   I have done my best to prevent it

Bodleian Library, Milner Papers, Microfilm 175, f.159

35
Lord Kitchener to Mr St John Brodrick

[Holograph]
Commander-in-Chief's Office,
South Africa
D'Aar 16th Febr 1901.

I wish I could make some sort of estimate of the duration of the war but it seems quite impossible to do so –

De Wet has now started in the Colony just as the first two commandos were being succesfully driven out[72] – It all seems endless and I do not know how to answer your telegram asking for even an approximate time when this war would be over – If we had only some native troops who could for one moment forget their stomachs and go for the enemy it would be very different –

We have reduced the expenditure on transport by approximately £200,000 a month and on meat by £250,000 other smaller items some £50000 altogether   I estimate we ought to be costing about half a million less a month but it is difficult to get figures owing to the system of finance in the Army – I hope when Mr [G.D.A. Fleetwood] Wilson arrives I shall be able to know more exactly what is being spent. I fear the Ordnance have been somewhat extravagant but it is impossible to control them   I have sent a staff officer to overhaul their work in Cape Town –

It is of course absolutely premature to foresee the end but I think it would be wise to consider what can be done   If we could make peace with Botha I believe in such a case it would all stop, but if there are to be no terms we might catch Botha & others and still have roving bands for a long time – I have said I will meet Botha should he desire it, but I have no idea what the Gov[ernment] would be prepared to agree to if Botha could absolutely terminate the war – Perhaps it will be time enough to consider this when I do meet Botha and wire you his views – I have to thank you for your kind letter   I am writing in the train[73] so excuse a stupid letter.

TNA reference PRO 30/57/22/Y23

36
Mr St John Brodrick to Lord Kitchener
[Copy]   Feb. 23. 1901.
Private

Your letters of Jan 25 to Lord Roberts and myself[74] gave us the first real inkling we had of your position & prospects and were of the greatest service & interest. If I may say so, the more you take us into your confidence, the better we can help you – Your letters to me are seen by no one but Lord Roberts – occasionally by Ld Salisbury, Mr Balfour & Mr Chamberlain. But as you can imagine finding ourselves engaged in a war for wh. we have to take another £60.000.000 in the coming year, and which entails such great efforts, we are most anxious for any light we can get.

I am very sorry to hear of the staleness of so many of your generals. Especially Lyttelton who had previously done so well – Everyone hopes for great things from Bindon Blood – & I should be glad to feel you had not the whole Cape Colony work to superintend actively as well as the two Boer Colonies

I will get some lawyers on to a reform of Mil[itar]y Law as soon as ever I hear your points & the man who can best represent your views

Any brevets or like honours that you wish bestowed promptly after an engagement shall be dealt with the moment you telegraph & shall be published here –

Strictly Confidential
As regards India, I have done all I can for you in a difficult situation. The Indian authorities say Sir Power Palmer who has acted for nearly a year has done very well[75] & it is difficult to displace him, the more so as you could not hand over command in S. Africa under the most favourable circumstances for some little time to come, and insist then come home –

As the best compromise I have arranged with the Cabinet that Sir Power Palmer should be allowed to complete Sir W. Lockharts term,[76] or to complete 3 years from his own acting app[ointmen]t – This will bring the date to Nov 1902 or March 1903. The exact arrangement depends on a telegram from the Viceroy.[77]

The effect of this would be that the appointment will be open again at latest 2½ years from now, wh. would enable you to complete the war, get some holiday & give us your advice here for a short time. I can make some suitable post for you in Gt Britain subordinate only to Ld Roberts & if necessary of a temporary character so as to secure you proper status & pay.

I trust this arrangement may commend itself to you. I am telegraphing in a day or two about it, and I can think of no other way of combining all the difficult considerations we have to meet.

I do not think you will have cause to regret it, if you are in England while our reorganization is being worked out after the war, & if I may speak of myself, it would be the greatest personal assistance to me. Lord Roberts would welcome this arrangement being as earnest as I am to make the best provision for meeting your wishes.

TNA reference PRO 30/57/22/Y27

37
Lord Kitchener to Lord Roberts

[Holograph]   Middleberg[78]
28th Feby 01

Many thanks for your letter of the 31st Janry[79]   I have written to Brodrick about my meeting with Botha and hope you will see it[80] – If the Govt wish to end the war I do not see any great difficulty in doing so but I think it will go on for some time if the points raised by Botha cannot be answered – Clearing the country and thus rendering the war impossible will be a very long business – They evidently do not like their women being brought in and I think it has made them more anxious for peace – I do not think Botha is likely to be unreasonable   there is a good deal of sentiment about it particularly giving up their independence which they feel very much –

Botha seemed quite reasonable about the conduct of the war   he said we ought at first to have sent every man to Ceylon as they were all bound to serve and we had a right to call them out again after they had taken the oath of neutrality

He asked that greater care might be taken in bringing in the women and I told him I had issued special instructions that where sufficient transport was not available they were to be left on their farms until transport could be provided   he made no complaints about burning farms. He had a narrow escape of being caught by French's columns[81] and said the country was so big that he could always evade us and find a place of safety for his men –

I hope we have knocked de Wet out of the Colony   he has certainly lost heavily and his men are quite disheartened but I shall not feel sure until he is caught or over the Orange River again[82]

The horses are doing much better but we have lost a good many through horse sickness which is bad at Pretoria and in many places – Chowder [?] gives me some trouble but not more so than he used to do   I wish he had a really good staff officer   I fear Verner is not up to much.[83] General health of troops is fairly good. Interic[84] is not on the increase   I am arranging to bring in Vrede garrison where interic has been very bad. We shall soon get some fresh troops into the field now which will be a great thing

I have no doubt the new Yeomanry will soon pick up the work and they will be very useful to fill up the gaps. I am sending home all overseas colonials that have done a year's service replacing them by the contingents now coming out –

With kind regards to Lady Roberts and your daughters.

NAM. 1971-01-23-33-17

38
Lord Kitchener to Mr St John Brodrick

[Holograph]   Middleberg[85]
28th Feby 01

I have had a long day with Louis Botha   he came in at 10 am and left at about 3 pm. He brought 4 staff officers with [him] and they lunched with us – Botha has a nice unassuming manner and seemed desirous of finishing the war but somewhat doubtful of being able to induce his men to accept without independence in some form or other – I told him that independence in any form was impossible and that any modified independence would be extremely dangerous considering the mixed population the effects of the war and previous experience. This he agreed in with evidently some regret. He came prepared with a list of points which he considered should be answered before he could lay the matter of peace before his Govt and the people[86]

I have telegraphed the 10 points to you and will only now add my impressions during the conversation –

He seemed to think that representative Govt might be granted at once on cessation of hostilities but did not press the matter   He spoke very strongly about the feeling of his burghers about Milner's appointment[87] and at one time seemed to think it would entirely prevent any chance of their giving in – I assured him that Milner was a first rate man and that in a short time they would all agree and that I thought there was no chance of a change – Botha's military Secty[88] who was present was also very strongly against Milner

When the Kaffir question was brought up it at once turned on the question of Franchise for Kaffirs to which they are greatly opposed – He stated it would be most dangerous for the burghers on their distant farms   I suggested it should be left open for a representative Govt to decide upon later   this he thought satisfactory[89] – He was anxious that legal debts of the republic should be paid out of revenue   he says that under the law they were allowed to issue notes for a million   these have not all been issued but if they are repudiated it will entail great loss on farmers – In conversation it was suggested that such claims might be equitably considered by a judge but I gave no opinion on the point – He however considered it one of great importance & said he felt personally responsible & hoped that the admission of these debts as valid against the Transvaal would not be refused

The next important point which he spoke strongly about was amnesty to all for bona fide acts in the war   he mentioned Cape and Natal rebels and said they could not desert them to be severely punished   he did not see much objection to their being disfranchized –

The minor points he referred to were Church property to remain untouched – Public trusts and orphans funds ditto – language english & dutch to be equal in schools war tax on farms.

Govt assistance to rebuild and restock farms –

Date of return of Prisoners of War – He had notes on the above points and evidently came prepared – I asked him if he agreed in the settlement of the points raised whether he could be certain that all commandos or bands would submit and lay down their arms

He said he was more or less bound to the Free State but he felt sure he could influence de Wet (if terms were same for the O.R.C.) and in that case he could guarantee complete cessation of hostilities and a general laying down of arms & Briton and Burgher would then be friends again and he & his officers would give the best assistance to the goverment

We talked about the conduct of the war without any bitterness he promised not to take our ambulances again & I agreed to let him have the medicines – He repeated that he and his people felt bitterly losing their independence but he evidently did not think it impossible for them to agree to do so – He said incidentally that he could carry on for some time I pointed out the hopelessness of the struggle on their part and that they had no right to ruin the country further He was very bitter about those that had surrendered & did not like the peace committees but he could not justify de Wets murder of the peace envoy without trial[90] he said he feared it was the result of demoralization caused by the war –

L Botha is a quite capable man and I have no doubt carries considerable weight with the burghers he will be I should think a valuable assistance to the future govt of the country in an official capacity –

It seems a pity that the war should go on for the points raised by Botha which appear to me all capable of adjustment and supposing it cost 2 millions[91] that is to say 1 million for notes issued by Transvaal govt and 1 million for rebuilding and restocking farms which is the most possible it would only represent one months expenditure out here on the war I promised to write to Botha when I received the reply of the govt on the points raised and he will then at once take steps in the matter –

The Brenthurst Library (Johannesburg), Earl Kitchener Papers, MS 182/1⁹²

39

Lord Kitchener to Mr St John Brodrick

[Holograph]   Commander-in-Chief's Office,
                                                        South Africa.
                                                      7 March 1901.

A most extraordinary fatality seems to have attached itself to the telegram about my interview with Botha   The first delay was at Middleberg [Middelburg]   I asked if it had got off as the wires were cut during the night, and by a mistake I was told it had, the clerk referring to my second telegram about Milner – I have always my own telegram clerk with me & as I started the first thing in the morning it was not until I reached Pretoria that I heard that the telegram no 60 had not got through from Middleberg [Middelburg]   it was however at once despatched from Pretoria and I was completely astounded at getting your wire on my way back from Bloemfontein that you had not received it – The delay has been traced to negligence in the Kimberley civil transmitting office and the Post master General is inquiring into the matter & I will see that proper punishment is awarded   The curious thing is that this is the first time I have had to complain of any delay though I have frequently pointed out to the Post Master at Cape Town that it was a great mistake to have the transmitting office at Kimberley when either Na[a]uwpoort or d'Aar [De Aar] would be far better   he has always replied that he could not manage the change and I had sent Colonel Heppesly [?] to Cape town to see him on the subject – I am very sorry for the delay – I thought the best thing to save time would be for me to join Milner as soon as possible   so I came down to Bloemfontein and met him there & he sent after consultation a proposed draft reply to Botha to the Colonial Sec[retar]y – We are waiting for the reply of the cabinet and the letter as amended by Mr Chamberlain is all ready to go[93] – I cannot of course say how Botha will take it but I think it will be all right – I have just heard that he told some boers who wanted to surrender not to do so as he wished all to surrender as a nation   of course this may be only ..... but it is evidently far better to get them all to give up together than to only get Botha and a section of the boers leaving the irreconcilibles still out   I fear Botha will have some difficulty in the Orange River Colony but he seemed pretty confident of his power to bring Milner in if the Transvaal accepted the terms offered –

Your letter of the 8th Febry[94]   I am glad that from your telegram you subsequently received information required but it is rather difficult when writing to you and knowing you will not get the letter for three weeks to foresee what points will be of interest to you   Do not please imagine I am reticent   I write on every point that I think will interest you   As regards horses commandeered and purchased in Cape Colony I cannot get much information out of [Forestier-]Walker (Why not give him Scotland I could replace him by [a] far better officer) I know the numbers of horses but I hear a very large portion of them are not fit for service though they may be useful to the boers   I am sending you by this mail a statement about remounts and are sending Lt Col Bir[k]beck[95] to Cape town to find out the real state of the case about the colonial horses –

I am also sending you a statement about supplies   All in that dept is working satisfactorally [sic]   if it were not I should at once bother you – Ordnance has been a difficulty but I sent down one of my staff and the dept at Capetown has been reorganized   I believe now it is working well and the great strain is over   my staff officer is on his way back but has not rearrived to report details –

I am sending you a despatch about my past operation by this mail[96]   I wished to see something definite about de Wet's manoeuvres to get into the Cape Colony before writing – I was also curious to see Ld Roberts despatches so as to keep up if possible some continuous line, these were some of my reasons for not writing before   I hope you will approve of what I have written –

Staff diaries of operations in South Africa go to the War Office monthly –

I am sending you also by this mail some details about the distribution of our guns as well as statement of the enemy guns and what we have captured this may be of interest to you – I also enclose the last health report which is satisfactory

Komati Poort is of course very unhealthy but with the hospital ship[97] in Delagoa Bay we have done well and mortality has been very slight I have just been speaking to the PMO[98] on this subject and he considers we have done very well and been far healthier than the boers once were in the low country –

The refugee camps for women and surrendered boers are I am sure doing good work it enables a man to surrender and not lose his stock and moveable property which are otherwise confiscated by the boers in the field – The women left on farms give complete intelligence to the boers of all our movements and feed the commandos in their neighbourhood Where they are brought in to the railway they settle down and are quite happy they even may give some intelligence but it is very little –

I have handed over all arrangements about these camps with Milner's approval to the civil authorities[99] and they regulate rations etc. and have their own civil officials looking after the camps –

As regards negotiations with the boers I am sending you a list of all correspondence that has passed between Generals and boer leaders they are mostly of a trivial nature and of very little importance I have told Generals not to correspond on any important points without reference to me and personally my first letter was to say I would meet Botha at Middleberg [Middelburg] in answer to his request for me to do so –

Milner has received the telegram giving the cabinets mission and the letter will go to Botha today[100] –

The peace committees have been an outside independent organization allowed by me, to do their best to induce the boers in the field to see the hopelessness of their struggle for independence & to show them that a considerable local feeling exists against the continuance of the war which must ruin their country –

Harris has taken up duty as A.A.G. under Chesham they will have a good deal to do to arrange for the relief of hard cases in the Yeomanry and organize the new men coming out

With the reinforcements coming I hope to be able to act more vigorously in every direction

Our bag of killed severely wounded and prisoners of war actually known has been over 1100 for each of the last 3 months this does not include voluntary surrenders French has done very well I write every mail to Lord Roberts and tell him about the Generals and troops as a rule I think that very probably you saw my letters to him – If you send me a wire on any Thursday about any point you wish me to write about, Our mail goes on Friday & I will not fail to let you know all I know on the subject –

I am being so constantly interrupted that I hope you will excuse this scrawl – I really wish to give you every information of interest but it is difficult to see what will be of interest three weeks hence when you get this letter – I hope and trust by then we may be in a fair way towards peace if Botha really works for it I have little doubt he can make them all agree to give in – Of course independence is the great difficulty he has to get over – Some of the points insisted on by the Colonial office such as only giving assistance by loans to reconstruct farms and introducing a question about natives which was not asked will I fear make it doubtful Botha will have great difficulties in inducing the majority to agree before however you get this you will know the results by wire –

Do not swear at me for putting in all the enclosures[101] you can throw them away if they do not interest you & I put them in on the chance of hitting off something you want to know I hope you will approve of my despatch it is long but I cannot see how to curtail it more than I have done

TNA reference PRO 30/57/22/Y30

40
Lord Kitchener to Mr St John Brodrick

[Holograph] Commander-in-Chief's Office,
South Africa.
15 March 1901.

Many thanks for the trouble you have taken on my behalf in arranging the Indian command I had almost given up hope of ever going to India and now I feel there is still a chance of doing so if all goes well out here –

No news from or of L. Botha I cannot quite make out where he is or what he is doing we got a receipt for the letter sent out to him so he has got it all right he probably is arranging with Schalk Burger at Roos Senekal but he may have gone further to see De Wet near Senekal – in the O.R.C. I do not think the delay is in anyway serious –

We have had about 12 days of almost continuous rain all over the country rendering all movements of the troops almost impossible. This has quite upset my calculations for French's columns as the country he is in is quite impossible and it has been most difficult to keep him supplied – It is very important to clean up the corner into which he has driven so many boers with their stock and to do this thoroughly he will probably take until the 12th April[102]

Lyttelton is sweeping up the O.R.C. from the Orange river to the Thabanchu line his columns today ought to be at Dewetsdorp Columns moving parallel to each other are found to be most useful and puzzle the enemy

The bands still in Cape Colony are being vigorously pushed and we are now capturing their horses and catching more of them than we used to do I hope before you get this we may have completely cleaned Cape Colony unless de Wet makes another attempt which is not impossible though certainly improbable after his last experience[103]

I have been organizing the new Yeomanry as to have everything ready for them when they arrive We shall have 72 old squadrons refilled with drafts and then form 13 new squadrons out of the uniformed men – The remainder will come out as formed squadrons – I think it will work all right the drafts that have arrived are quite ready to go anywhere and join any existing unit but of course we are sending them as much as possible to their county unit – All hard cases are being relieved and sent home first –

The volunteers are also being sent home as their relief arrives and I am getting them moved down country by degrees so that they may feel they are on their way home I wish I could send them before their reliefs come and will do so when I can get these roving bands out of Cape Colony but while they last a number of small garrisons are necessary to prevent mischief being done –

You wrote to me that a certain number of commissions would be placed at my disposal but though I have twice wired on the subject I have heard nothing official – Reuter also reported that commissions would be given out here – I have a good many young men who would make good officers, I feel sure –

Fleetwood Wilson has arrived at Cape town he is just looking round there and then coming on here to me – I enclose a statement of expenditure in supplies F[leetwood] W[ilson] will have to look into the local expenditure which I have been unable to do – I think economies can be made but I fear we cannot expect anything very large – I am selling and eating as much captured stock as I can I sent you the distribution of supplies last mail –

I enclose some paper about the redistribution of commissions and troops in the O.R.C. These are not yet out but are what I am trying for Gen[eral]s Elliot & Beatson have not yet arrived from India but are expected shortly I also send you our bag for Febr I hope I shall do as well in March everything put down is vouched for and not just the reported numbers put out of action –

I see they are having a lively time in the House of Lords – I hope you have not been much bothered in the Commons; as you have not worried me for replies to parliamentary questions about the war I suppose the opposition have not found much ground for annoyance –

As regards Ordnance it appears to have been very badly managed at Cape town not so much from want of supplies as from want of distribution articles we urgently required were reported as non existent in the country whereas an ample supply really existed, an entire want of ongoing action seems to have prevailed at Cape town resulting in extraordinary demands on War Office – Col Clarke seems to have gone off his head,[104] and Colonel Hobbs[105] is evidently inefficient – I think they should be both sent home   The work is now being done under Col Barrett[106] and the office organized by Major Jackson who is the best Ordnance officer I have seen out here[107] – The details are too long to give you now and I will go into the matter fully with Chowder [?], and send you further information next mail – Fleetwood Wilson will also have to take up the local expenditure on ordnance where I fear money has been wasted – I will try and frame estimates on which peak demands can be made cancelling those rather widely sent in without any knowledge but the whole dept wants thorough overhauling in Cape Town

TNA reference PRO 30/57/22/Y31

41
General Christiaan de Wet to Lord Kitchener

[Typed copy of English translation][108]   In the Field, District
Heilbron,
18th March, 1901.

With this I have the honour to bring to your Lordship's notice the following facts:

In the last times (of late) with your Lordship's troops you are using armed Kaffirs, and coloured persons, against my Burghers, which comprise a great majority of your fighting men – against which and on behalf of my Republic I strongly protest, and request you as Commanding His Majesty's troops to remove all armed natives over the border.

Firstly it can be proved that natives, subjects of the Republics, against their will are fighting, and it is against the Hague Convention signed by your Government, yourself or your Officers, have armed and forced to fight against the Burghers of the Republics. You have also used coloured persons from outside the Republics to fight, which is against all civilized law of civilized nations, which you term yourselves.[109]

Further these natives have illused widows, unprotected women and children and old men in a most shameful manner.

Further it can also be proved in some instances, and this by sworn affidavits, which can be produced before civilized nations, also your troops have expressed their indignation at such acts.

I request your Lordship in a friendly manner, still with earnest hope, that this protest will be forwarded and that you will reply to my request at your earliest date.

[Note added in longhand]
No answer was sent to this letter.

TNA reference PRO WO32/7958

42
Lord Milner to Lord Kitchener

[Typed copy]   Johannesburg,
March 20th, 1901.
Private.

I enclose a wail from Goold-Adams.[110] I have had similar wails before from other persons in the O.R.C.

It does seem to me that something might be done, not indeed to make the policy of "clearing the country" more harmful to the enemy, for I expect the columns already do all that is possible in that direction, but to prevent its hitting our own friends.

I should have thought that there would be no difficulty in settling upon certain areas sufficiently within the protection of our posts and garrisons to justify their being exempted from a general order to sweep up all the livestock of the country.

Surely the G.O.C. and Goold-Adams could between them agree which districts might receive such favoured treatment. Gradually, as the country becomes more settled, an increasing number of areas might be brought within the category of more favoured districts.

The idea of exempting certain districts from the sweeping process, as opposed to that of driving all stock indiscriminately into a few camps, has the following advantages:

1. It will make a distinction, intelligible to everybody, between enemy's country and <u>our</u> country, and a distinction to the advantage of the latter. This must tend to make people desire to settle down:

2. It will encourage the tendency of the Boers under our protection to take up arms, to help to keep the other Boers off. They will fight for their cattle on their own ground as they will for nothing else. This will widen the breach, which it is all our interest to widen.

3. The cattle will live instead of dying. I am getting seriously frightened about the congestion of stock in a few places, where fodder will presently give out. If the cattle starve by thousands, we may have something like a pestilence caused by rotting animals.

4. While alive, they will be less easy to raid (of course I am speaking of districts, within a reasonable distance of our garrisons, not of distant districts virtually in the occupation of the enemy. The more we clear the latter the better). The cattle, herded together in one spot, can be swooped on, as 1700 were lately quite close to Johannesburg. It is much more difficult to collect them from a lot of different farms, with all the owners on the alert to prevent it.

Bodleian Library, Milner Papers, Microfilm 175, ff. 175–6[111]

43
Lord Kitchener to Lady Ilchester

[Holograph]   Pretoria
                                                         22. March [1901]

Very many thanks for your letter   it was most kind of you to remember me –

The war does not look much like ending now and we may be out here for another year   If they would only fight we could soon finish them off but they have quite given up any idea of doing more than cut off any weak party moving alone or blowing up a train by a mine set at night under the rails It seems rather hopeless but I suppose it will have to finish some day –

It seems quite extraordinary that we now have a King and the state ceremonial must have been very interesting I have just got the picture papers with it all in –

I have got some fresh Generals and fresh troops so I hope soon to make Botha somewhat regret that he did not accept terms unfortunately this plague[112] is rather delaying matters

With kind regards to Lady Londonderry –

BL MS Room, Holland House Papers, Add MS 51370

44
Lord Kitchener to Mr St John Brodrick

[Holograph]   Commander-in-Chief's Office,
                                                          South Africa.
                                                    22nd March 1901.

I am enclosing some papers that may be of interest to you – Regarding the ordnance of which I send you a full copy of correspondence that has passed   my view is that when such large financial interests are involved and the efficiency of the Army in the field is at stake all personal feeling as regards officers position and security must be put on one side   we want the best men for the work whoever they may be and I am not in favor [sic] of keeping a senior man merely because he is senior – I think it is very well known that Colonel Hobbs is not a man of very great capacity for Ordnance work though no doubt capable if carrying on ordinary routine and I cannot agree to General [Forestier-] Walker's view of kicking him upstairs in order to get rid of him   I hope you agree with me – I feel sure things will work better now and in a short time all will be straight again   in the mean time I am not short of anything for the present moment & I see no cause for anxiety –

You will find a full report on the Refugee camps in the Transvaal which I hope you will consider satisfactory – The reports for Orange River Colony and Cape Colony will be sent as soon as forwarded but we have really no refugee camps in Cape Colony; only a few women at Port Elizabeth as far as I know[113] – The ORC camps are run on exactly the same lines as the Transvaal and the Inspector has been round and reported; though they are not all quite so good now they will be very shortly – These camps are all under complete civil control. Fleetwood Wilson has arrived & I have plenty of work for him to do   I hope his office will be a success and inaugurate a system by means of which you could decentralize the army to a far greater extent than at present and at the same time complete financial security   only I should like to see the Financial advisors taken from military officers and abolish the present paymasters, any ordinary civilian clerk could carry out their duties at quite low pay if guaranteed for certain sums. Each General would then have his Financial staff who could correspond with the Financial Sectry at the W.O. and advise the General who could then act, if the F[inancial] A[dvisor] and the General disagreed the matter might be referred to W.O. before any action could be taken – over such a system

You would have I believe great economies as the departments of the army would be looked after financially on the spot which is not now I believe the case –

My new Generals from India have arrived   Blood   Elliot and Beatson   I like them all and hope great things from them   troops are also coming in well but this plague at the ports is causing great delay in getting them forward   I hope it will not develop further all possible precautions are being taken

Regarding exchange of troops with India these Indian Generals all say that India could quite well send time expired men from India for exchange at the ports in S.A. which I could manage – India would be about one month (taking the time of a good transport from Bombay to Durban) without the full number of troops and I could get fresh men for those that have had a year in the field   they all say the time expired men in India are very keen to come   I hope this may come off   I wired to the Viceroy[114] to tell him what could be done viz that I could exchange any number of troops at the ports in S.A. but that without relief I could not send to India more than 500 men at a time

The horse sickness[115] is now less and I hope we are getting to the end of it   I propose before long to send an expedition under Plumer to Pietersburg[116] which will cut off Botha's retreat when we push him from Middleberg [Middelburg] and Belfast which I shall do as soon as I can get French's men back – We have had continuous wet weather which has delayed all operations everywhere   it has been practically impossible to move – Lyttelton drew the country from Orange River to the Thabanchu line with a lot of columns but they went so slowly the enemy got through and what I hoped would turn out a good bag was nothing but some stock[117]

In the colony the clearing goes on rigorously   our men go with stripped saddles and keep the boers on the run   a certain number have been killed and horses have been captured   I do not think it can last long in Cape Colony and once clean I hope we shall never let them in again

The difficult problem is to see how to get any finality to this war it is always before me, and I can find no infallible solution other than exhaustion – With new troops we shall no doubt do more but when can we see the end, it may be another year though I hope the winter will try them highly – If we catch Botha and the govt. there will be still a lot of scattered bands and we know from our experience in Cape Colony how difficult they are to deal with   I hope BP. police[118] will help to pacify the country but they have done nothing yet – and will not apparently be ready for some time –

Our best chance was terms with Botha but that is now gone I fear –

I see by the worries you have been having in the house [of Commons] you have been letting me off, many thanks, but do not fail to bother me if it will be any help to you –

I suppose you will send the Ordnance papers to Brackenbury[119] I only send them to you as I know you are interested in the matter – Do you think it would be a good thing to let the press know that the fact of a press message having passed the censor does not in the least vouch for its accuracy – We do not correct messages sent even about military operations – The boers get the mail papers as soon as we do – I was rather sorry to see Bothas refusal of terms wired out from England as the uncertainty of whether the Transvaal was giving in was having a good effect in Orange River & Cape Colony –

TNA reference PRO 30/57/22/Y33

45
Lord Kitchener to Mr St John Brodrick

[Typed copy]   Commander-in-Chief's Office,
South Africa.
22nd March, 1901.

I was afraid Botha could hardly accept the terms offered. The Boers have a good deal of sentiment of honour amongst them, particularly the leaders, and leaving those that had helped them to go to prison for 6 years, as has been done in Natal, would, I felt sure, make it almost impossible for them to accept. I, therefore, insisted on my views being sent home in Milner's telegram to the Colonial Secretary. I hardly expected, however, after Milner's strongly worded objection to my proposition that the Government would decide differently to what they did.

I did all in my power to urge Milner to change his views[120] which seem to me very narrow on this subject. I feel certain and have good grounds for knowing that an amnesty or King's pardon for the 200 or 300 rebels[121] in question (carrying with it disfranchisement which Botha willingly accepted) would be extremely popular amongst the majority of the British and all the Dutch in South Africa, but there no doubt exists a small section in both Colonies who are opposed to any conciliatory measures being taken to end the war and I fear their influence is paramount; they want extermination and I suppose will get it.

My views were that once the Boers gave up their independence and laid down their arms, the main object of the Government was attained, and that the future civil administration would soon heal old sores, and bring the people together again. After the lesson they have had, they are not likely ever to break out again. Milner's views may be strictly just, but they are to my mind vindictive, and

I do not know of a case in history where, under similar circumstances, an amnesty has not been granted.

We are now carrying the war on to be able to put 200 or 300[122] Dutchmen in prison at the end of it. It seems to me absurd and wrong, and I wonder the Chancellor of the Exchequer[123] did not have a fit.

Mrs. Botha has written to ask her husband if the amnesty question is the only one they are now fighting for. If he replies in the affirmative, could anything be done, if Botha was induced to ask for better terms for the rebels, and for a reconsideration of their case? Should this be possible, please wire me.

TNA reference PRO 30/57/22/Y36

46
Lord Kitchener to Mr St John Brodrick

[Holograph]   Commander-in-Chief's Office,
South Africa.
29 March 1901.

Troops are now arriving rapidly and when I get them into the field we shall be in a far better position to deal with the enemy – What I have seen of the Yeomanry drafts I like and I think they will turn out with a little practice very good men in the field – The Colonial contingents from Australia and New Zealand are a very fine lot of men and as keen as possible.[124] It is a great pleasure to see fresh troops –

The reckless loss of horses by mobile columns is causing me a good deal of trouble, I have issued the most stringent orders and personally impressed the great necessity of care in all commanders, but I am afraid with not much result   I shall have to make an example by removing an officer from his command for neglect of orders if it goes on much longer – It is not very easy to find good men to command in the field and in this sort of warfare almost everything depends on the leader –

I am very glad you did not press matters against Clements   he is a fine gallant soldier but made a serious mistake of judgement as regards what a defensible position should be[125] – Many have made similar mistakes in this war – Take Dewetsdorp[126] for instance the positions taken up were occupied for a long time and inspected by several very clever officers, and yet when tested by attack it was evident that the dispositions of the troops were very faulty –

Clements showed great gallantry and soldierlike qualities in getting so well out of the difficulty & he has I believe the entire confidence of his men –

I hope you are going to make some changes in military law so as to give back the power to the confirming officer, who has the advice of an officer of the Judge Advocate Generals department, to deal with miscarriages of justice

A fresh trial can of course be ordered but in the field this is generally impossible, and I believe in peace quarters it is very rarely used so that various cases of injustice are passed over unrectified and though an officer who has been president, or the whole court, may get wigged, the discipline of the army and the confidence of the soldiers that equal justice will be meted out to all ranks is seriously affected   Something ought also I think be done to lay down procedure for Martial Law when declared – My view is that when there are civil institutions for the administration of justice in a country martial law should interfere with such courts and magistrates as little as possible and only when distinct military reasons necessitate such interference – When necessary, assistance may be given to the local administration by lending officers; but when for military reasons a case is taken out of the hands of the civil administration or has in the first instance to be tried under martial law, then, unless the General commanding (who has full power) has reason to change the ordinary procedure of a military court in the particular case, a regular court martial should assemble and try the case under military law –

There is a great tendency amongst the civil authorities to deal with martial law as if it was a power given into their hands to wield, instead of being strictly in the hands of the GO.C. and this is being done in Cape Colony where to my mind very irregular courts are formed under martial law of civilians and officers ..... and in which the regular procedure of court martial is omitted – By means of the courts with the unlimited powers of martial law civil authorities are able to administer possible justice, but certainly not the law of the land – As Milner has arranged this and the Govt of Cape Colony like it, I have not interfered, but it does not seem to me a proper manner to use martial law when it is declared for military reasons in a country – I am arranging with Mr Solomon the Attorney Gen here that civil courts quite independent of military should start here at Johannesburg and at Bloemfontein to try all purely civil cases –

I have asked Fleetwood Wilson to go carefully into the whole question of claims and liabilities when the war is over. As you know practically nothing is being paid out here until hostilities cease though receipts are given for articles taken from farms – These receipts are marked "on commando" when the owner of the goods is out with the enemy, and such receipts will of course be valueless after the war – As I found that receipts and claims were being bought up by Jews for 10 to 25 percent of the face value, a notice was issued in the Govt Gazette and army orders that only those to whom the receipts were given or by whom the claim was made, or their regularly appointed agent, would be dealt with by the authorities when the claims were settled[127] –

A number of claims for damages and loss of stock have been investigated here, but though some valuable information has been recorded nothing final can be done until the war is over – On the cessation of hostilities I think after one notice say a month, a period should be fixed, say another month, in which all claims or receipts must be presented, otherwise they become void – Where there is no doubt payment could then be made at once and all doubtful cases after being carefully stamped and registered as presented during the month could be received for examination and arrangement. Receipts marked "on commando" would be destroyed without payment unless the presenter could prove that he was not fighting against us at the time – By this means we shall know exactly what we have to face and be able to grasp the difficult subject of the disputed claims without having others continually being produced against us – Do you approve of these ideas   they will have of course to be worked out and elaborated by Fleetwood Wilson –

I am much obliged for the presentations I asked for   I am sure it will have a very good effect on the army and I will only use the permission to wire for promotions sparingly and where I am sure it is for the good of the service – I have not yet got Babingtons report so cannot say what I shall recommend. There has been some unpleasantness between Babington and Shekelton and though I intend removing the latter from his command[128] I am not quite sure that Babington has acted quite rightly   however the whole matter is under investigation & at present I can form no opinion   Colonel Grey distinguished himself most I think and deserves a C.B. but you will have no doubt had a wire from me on this subject before you get this letter –

It is always difficult to write about matters that will be of interest to you 3 weeks hence when you will get this letter – Just now the Boers are very subdued and I hope by the time you get this they will be even more so – I am doing all I possibly can to kick them hard and make them regret bitterly that they did not take the terms offered – The weather has put out my calculations as to the time French's movement would take but I hope soon to be at Botha with fresh troops & in the meantime I am preparing to occupy Pietersburg to cut off his retreat to his former sanctuary –

De Wet may attempt the Cape Colony again – It is the only thing he can do   I doubt very much whether he will be able to work up his men to start on another disastrous expedition after their last experiences but it is possible & as I said before he has nothing else to do[129]   I have written you fully in official correspondence sent this mail on the treatment of foreigners, treatment of Germans and some foreign claims – I enclose reports of refugee camps in O.R.C. & Natal & the terms on which the mines have started work again at Johannesburg & a few other papers that may be of interest to you –

I hope this long letter does not bore you –

TNA reference PRO 30/57/22/Y38

Part 3
April to December 1901
Methods of Barbarism?
The Guerrilla War Drags On
Introduction

With the failure of the Middelburg peace negotiations of February–March 1900, hope of a relatively early end to the guerrilla war faded, and Lord Kitchener, urged on by Lord Roberts, had no other choice but to invest a great amount of time and money, as well as many men, in the designing and implementation of an elaborate anti-guerrilla strategy. Kitchener was under enormous pressure to end the war as quickly as possible, but he knew that it would take time [75]. In the final analysis, it became a war against space, with a large number of British troops, backed up by an elaborate blockhouse system, striving desperately to find, corner and destroy mobile die-hard Boer commandos.

In order to defeat the Boers, Kitchener needed more mounted troops. This meant that he also needed more horses – a big problem in the light of the fact that not many horses were available in South Africa. Consequently many horses (and mules) were imported [46, 81], for example horses from the United Kingdom, India, Australia, Canada, the United States of America, South America and Austria-Hungary, and mules from India, Spain, Italy and the United States of America. In the course of the war the British Army in South Africa used a total of 669,575 horses, mules and donkeys. Of these 400,346 were killed or died – in many instances they were not acclimatised and were not fed well [24]. (The Boers also lost some 100,000 horses.)[1]

It angered and frustrated Kitchener that the Boers were not willing to engage the British in battle [49, 61], and he described the elusive Boers as 'sly and cute' [74]. The British were forced to take drastic action in order to ensure victory over the Boer guerrilla units in the field. As a result, many conventionally-organised British units were transformed, in the course of time, into mounted (anti-commando) columns in an attempt to take on the Boers on their own terrain. Furthermore, an extensive blockhouse system was developed which eventually consisted of approximately 8,000 blockhouses, mostly built in lines across a distance of about 6,000 km, which criss-crossed over large parts of the war zone, dividing up the war zone into more manageable cages [55, 62]. The blockhouses varied from sturdy structures built of stone, to mass-produced circular Rice-type blockhouses, named after their designer, Major S.R. Rice, of the Royal Engineers. The blockhouses were manned by a total of about 60,000 white soldiers and 25,000 blacks and coloureds. The cost involved in erecting the blockhouses amounted to some £1,000,000. The aim of this blockhouse network was, among others, to safeguard strategic railway lines, bridges and other key points. Furthermore, the blockhouse lines were intended to limit the Boer commandos' freedom of movement and prevent them from launching more incursions into vast areas such as the Cape Colony. During the various occasions on which hot-pursuit operations were conducted by the mobile columns against the commandos, it was presumed that the commandos would be trapped against the blockhouse lines. The British blockhouse system was an expensive, yet essential emergency measure adopted in order to sway the geographically escalating guerrilla war in favour of the British. Eventually, the system played a significant strategic and tactical role, and although this system did not restrict the Boers entirely, it did nonetheless hamper their freedom of movement to a greater or lesser extent.[2]

Under Kitchener's command, the number of mobile British columns increased, as did the number of drives against the Boer commandos. For obvious reasons, Kitchener was always keen to hear how many burghers had been 'bagged' (i.e. taken prisoner) during a drive [50, 71]. But those who escaped were often the 'best' burghers, and more difficult to deal with [76].

The longer the war lasted, and the more it spread over ever-enlarging parts of the war zone, the greater the manpower demands were on the British Army. But Kitchener was always under political pressure from Britain to reduce the number of troops [68]; i.e. to save money for the tax-payer. As a result, more and more black and coloured inhabitants were employed [41, 96], for example, as blockhouse guards and as guides for the mobile columns. There were also cases where entire columns were made up of, for example, coloured soldiers, in most instances under the command of white officers. In general, Kitchener played down the role played by blacks and coloureds in the British Army in South Africa, and there are not many references in his letters to their crucial contribution [94].

Generally the Boers displayed a ruthless attitude towards blacks and coloureds who were armed, and several of them, once taken prisoner, were executed on the spot[3] – actions that may indeed be regarded as war crimes. It must, of course, be borne in mind that the Boers held strong racial views, and regarded the employment of blacks by the British in a combatant capacity as a very serious matter [41]. By the time hostilities ceased, the war had, in certain areas, degenerated into a civil war between white and black (or coloured). Furthermore, there were also other controversial incidents that jeopardized race relations, for example, the actions that led to Abraham Esau's death,[4] and the events at Leliefontein in Namaqualand.[5]

In addition, the execution of 44 Cape rebels (out of a total of 435 condemned to death) resulted in great bitterness.[6] It is important to note how many death sentences were in fact commuted by Kitchener (391 out of 435), and that he deliberately refrained from acting too harshly with regard to the rebels [65]. After all, he knew that once the war was over, Boer and Briton would have to work together in rebuilding South Africa. The restraint with which he acted is commendable.

The fact that approximately 5,500 burghers and officers, after they had surrendered, had taken up arms (or served in some capacity in the British Army) against their former comrades (i.e. had become joiners), resulted in much division during and after the war. The joiners consisted of approximately 1,500 National Scouts (i.e. those Transvaalers who had joined) and the Orange River Colony Volunteers (i.e. those Free Staters who had joined). The ORC Volunteers were formally established on 3 March 1902, with General Piet de Wet (brother of Christiaan) as commanding officer. This unit never numbered more than 448 men.[7] Kitchener was pleased with the work done by the joiners [89].

As has already been mentioned in the introduction to Part 2, by May 1901 Kitchener commanded more troops than ever before in the course of the war, namely approximately 240,000 soldiers; moreover, there was also an ever-increasing number of black and coloured men who served in his army, either as combatants or non-combatants. Of his white force, some 80,000 were mounted men (including cavalry, mounted infantry, Yeomanry, and local and overseas colonials), and in due course this number would increase further. Kitchener also had at his disposal about 100 heavy guns, 420 other artillery pieces, and 60 pom-poms.

As time passed, the British military strategy affected ever-increasing numbers of ordinary citizens – white as well as black and coloured. For example, to prevent the roving commandos from obtaining shelter, food, medical assistance and information, eventually as many as 30,000 farmhouses and more than 40 towns were partially or entirely destroyed in the ORC and Transvaal. Roberts inaugurated the scorched-earth policy, and formally authorised the establishment of internment camps in September 1900, but Kitchener extended and applied the policy more rigorously, even though he would have preferred to avert the destruction of property [66]. Soon this policy, which started as a military necessity and as part of the overall military strategy, got out of hand. In most cases, the civilian victims of this scorched-earth policy were transported to camps. These camps were not merely refuges (i.e. refugee camps) for Boers who were homeless or who had surrendered voluntarily and had their black or coloured servants with them, but can be regarded as concentration camps where recalcitrant Boer men, but especially women and children who had been removed from their destroyed farms, were housed – as part of an elaborate anti-commando military strategy. However, for the purpose of this study, the less emotional and less controversial term 'internment camp(s)' will be used. Of the at least 160,000 whites and 160,000 blacks who at one time or other were held in camps across the war zone, more than 28,000 whites (i.e. more than 10 per cent of the Afrikaner population of the OFS and Transvaal) and more than 23,000 blacks died (although the latter number is most probably much higher in reality), in many instances as a result of neglect and incompetence. The British simply could not cope with the stream of refugees.[8] The British Army also did not have any experience in administering camps of this nature. But the death of those who were moved to the camps was never intended.

Kitchener set out the purpose of the camps in his Circular 29 of 21 December 1900 [26]. This document can be regarded as Kitchener's master plan for the scorched-earth policy. Earlier, Kitchener had identified the Boer women as the main force behind the continued Boer resistance [21]. He also wanted to ensure that the Boers on commando would no longer receive supplies and other assistance – including information [39] – from the civilians who stayed on on the farms [24].

Mr St John Brodrick, the Secretary of State for War, was very concerned over the conditions in the camps [48]. Kitchener said that all that was possible was being done for the inmates of the 'burgher' (i.e. internment) camps, and according to him they were well looked after. However, he established the camps out of necessity, and he wished he could dispense with the camps [51]. He repeated his wish to be rid of the camps on more than one occasion [65], was worried about the conditions in the camps [65], and even wanted to banish the Boers in order to get rid of the camps [60]. He even thought of letting the civilians out of the camps, and sending them to the Boer commandos, with some food, although he was not prepared to force them to go [82]. The problem, of course, was that the British Army had no experience of looking after thousands of civilians, and many Boer civilians had no experience of living in the veldt in close proximity to many other people. Kitchener had no intention of causing the death of thousands of people – but he neglected to take the necessary precautionary measures. The result was a humanitarian disaster.

It must be kept in mind that the Boers on commando were to a large extent dependent on the civilians on the farms for food, shelter and information; i.e. the farms and the civilians on the farms were part of the expanded Boer guerrilla system. However, those same Boers on commando were not in a position to look after (or even safeguard) their civilians. In a sense the Boer commandos thus sold out their civilians to the British anti-guerrilla strategy, in particular the scorched-earth policy. Kitchener was not committing a crime by taking action against the Boer civilian population – from a military point of view he had no other option, albeit that on a humanitarian level it led to many problems, including the death of thousands of people, as well as much bitterness.

Brodrick attached great value to Kitchener's letters [56] and had certain portions typed, for example Kitchener's letter to him of 26 April 1901 [49], so that he (Brodrick) could use the information contained in the letters to inform the British cabinet [53, 56]. So, through his frank correspondence, Kitchener influenced cabinet decisions, for example to send more troops to South Africa; or at least not to withdraw troops [56].

Kitchener had always set his sights on the post of Commander-in-Chief in India, and often referred to this matter in his correspondence [18, 21, 23, 36, 40]. But first he had to bring the war in South Africa to a successful conclusion. Towards the end of 1901 this still seemed to be a long way off. In September 1901 the British had to cope with a new invasion in the Cape Colony. Former Transvaal State Attorney, Jan Smuts, left the Western Transvaal on 1 August 1901 in what became, in due course, an epic trek through large areas of the war zone. He moved through the ORC, and in the early hours of 4 September 1901 crossed the Gariep in the Herschel district with a commando of about 250 men. He moved southwards, then westwards and eventually northwards, recruiting rebels along the way, finally reaching the Vanrhynsdorp area in November 1901 after several clashes with British columns. In the North-Western Cape Colony he took over command of all the Boer forces in that region and re-organised them.[9] For obvious reasons, Kitchener was very worried about conditions in the Cape Colony [63, 64].

Since Buller had driven the Boers out of Natal in June 1900, there had been no military operations in that colony. In September 1901 this tranquillity was threatened when General Louis Botha left the Eastern Transvaal on 7 September with a commando of about 1,000 men and moved southwards in the direction of the Natal border. At Blood River Poort he defeated a British force of approximately 1,200 soldiers commanded by Lieutenant-Colonel H. de la P. Gough (17 September 1901). At least twenty British soldiers were killed and 241 (including at least 24 of the wounded) were captured. The British also lost three guns that were captured by the Boers. On the Boer side only one burgher was killed and three wounded. Botha then divided his commando into two. One section attacked a British post at Itala (25–26 September), just inside the Natal border, south of Babanango [73], while the other section launched an attack against Fort Prospect (26 September), east of Itala. Both attacks were unsuccessful. Total British casualties during both these clashes amounted to 23 killed and 68 wounded, while the Boers lost at least fifteen killed and 42 wounded. Botha then fell back to the Eastern Transvaal.[10] There, on 30 October 1901, he dealt the column of Lieutenant-Colonel G.E. Benson a shattering blow at Bakenlaagte. Benson's column consisted of some 2,100 soldiers with four guns and two pom-poms, while Botha had approximately 1,200 men with him. The British lost at least 66 killed, 165 wounded (including Benson, who died of his wounds) and 120 taken prisoner. Boer casualites were fewer than 100. The British also lost two of their guns.[11]

In the light of the problems the British Army encountered in South Africa, and their apparent inability to bring the war to a successful conclusion, Kitchener often despaired – and on more than one occasion his frustrations came to the fore in his letters to Roberts and St John Brodrick. He told both Brodrick [76] and Roberts [77] that they should replace him if necessary. Although there was a possibility that Roberts could be sent back to South Africa as Commander-in-Chief [83], this did not happen in practice, and Roberts tried to encourage Kitchener to continue with his important work in South Africa.[12] Brodrick assured Kitchener that both he (as Secretary of State for War) and King Edward VII wanted him to finish the work in South Africa [80]. Kitchener was prepared to stay on as long as his sovereign and his political and military masters had confidence in him [83].

How near Kitchener sometimes was to breaking point, and to losing his nerve, is clear from his letter of 21 June 1901 (written three days before his 51st birthday) to Mr St John Brodrick – probably the most drastic extant letter he ever wrote (albeit that possibly, not too much should be read into it), in which he referred, *inter alia*, to the Boers as 'uncivilized Africander savages with only a thin white veneer' [59]. It must be kept in mind that Kitchener had up to 1899 been a very successful commander, and that it was embarrassing to him not to be able to bring the war against the Boers to a swift end. Furthermore, he was frustrated by the attitude of the British press towards him and his efforts to end the war[13] [78, 81], had to deal with the actions and complaints of Emily Hobhouse[14] [78] – and then there were also the political squabbles in the Cape Colony that Kitchener had to deal with [68, 71, 72].

In July 1901 the British government appointed a six-member all-women committee under the chairmanship of Mrs Millicent Garrett Fawcett (a prominent feminist) to inquire into the conditions prevailing in the internment camps. The so-called Ladies' Committee visited several white, but not black, camps, and their report (submitted in December 1901) contained several important recommendations, for example with regard to the management of the camps, overcrowding, sanitation, and supplying adequate medical facilities, food, water and firewood. The implementation of some of these recommendations led to the improvement of conditions in several camps.[15]

In an effort to bring the war to a successful conclusion, the British government sent more troops to South Africa. By the end of May 1901 more than 30,000 reinforcements had arrived, mostly Yeomanry from Britain, as well as local and other colonial volunteers [86]. But even with ever greater numbers of troops at his disposal, Kitchener was unable to defeat the elusive Boers in the field. He then tried to scare the Boers into submission by issuing several proclamations, for example the one published on 7 August 1901, threatening those Boers who did not lay down their arms by 15 September 1901, that they would be banished permanently[16] – but these proclamations, disparagingly referred to by the Boers as 'Kitchener's paper bombs', did not have the desired results. Interestingly enough, Kitchener himself questioned the value of the proclamations [66]. He admitted that the proclamations would not force the Boers to surrender; rather, a scorched-earth policy would have to make the war zone uninhabitable for the Boers [68].

On the evening of Friday 29 November 1901 Lieutenant-General Ian Hamilton arrived in Pretoria to take up his new post as Lord Kitchener's Chief of Staff, having been appointed as such on 7 November. Hamilton already had an excellent military reputation. He had spent many years in India and in Africa, and was severely wounded and captured at Amajuba on 27 February 1881. Hamilton had previously rendered extensive service during the Anglo-Boer War. He had accompanied General Sir George White as AAG to Natal in September 1899, fought with distinction at Elandslaagte (21 October 1899), Rietfontein (24 November 1899) and Lombardskop (30 October 1899), and was besieged in Ladysmith (he fought bravely at Platrand/Wagon Hill on 6 January 1900). After the relief he went to Cape Town, but Lord Roberts summoned him to Bloemfontein. As GOC of the Mounted Infantry Division he took part in the advance from Bloemfontein to Pretoria, and once again he rendered sterling service, taking part in several clashes in the OFS and Transvaal. On 11 December 1900 he left South Africa in the company of Roberts, to serve as the latter's Military Secretary. When it became clear that Kitchener needed assistance, Roberts (in his capacity as Commander-in-Chief at the War Office) sent Hamilton back to South Africa. Hamilton sincerely hoped that he would be able to lighten the South African Commander-in-Chief's burdens, but Kitchener's temperament made it difficult for him to use Hamilton's services to the full. Consequently Hamilton was never more than a nominal Chief of Staff. Kitchener, who found it very difficult to delegate authority, never used Hamilton to formulate campaign plans, or to transmit orders to subordinates.[17] Nevertheless, Kitchener was very glad to have Hamilton at his side [78, 79], and was pleased with the work done by him [86].

Almost every week Hamilton wrote a fairly long letter to Roberts, and vice versa. Hamilton's letters are of particular importance because they were the most comprehensive letters written to Roberts from the war zone, and gave the Commander-in-Chief at the War Office an excellent idea of what was happening in South Africa during the last crucial six months of the war. These letters also shed light on Kitchener's role as Commander-in-Chief. In a previous volume – on the role played by Roberts during the Anglo-Boer War – several of Hamilton's letters to Roberts were published,[18] and in this present volume on the role played by Kitchener, additional letters written by Hamilton to Brodrick [88],

Winston Churchill [95, 105, 110] and Spenser Wilkinson [107] have been included. These letters shed interesting light on Kitchener's doings, as well as his frustrations and achievements as Commander-in-Chief in South Africa.

President M.T. Steyn and General C.R. de Wet were the most important obstacles in the way of a British military victory in South Africa, and if Kitchener really believed by the end of 1901 that the war was no longer a real war, but only a police operation [84], he was in for a rude shock. Steyn, whose health deteriorated towards the end of the war,[19] usually accompanied De Wet's commando. On Christmas Day 1901, De Wet surprised and defeated a British force in the Eastern ORC [85]. The Boers stormed and overran a British camp on the summit of Groenkop (henceforth also known as 'Krismiskop', i.e. Christmas Hill). The British lost at least 57 killed, 84 wounded and more than 200 (including most of the wounded) taken prisoner. The Boers (who lost fourteen men killed and 30 wounded) also captured a vast amount of arms, ammunition and stores.[20] New plans would have to be implemented if Kitchener wanted to bring the war to a close – and then go to India.

47
Lord Kitchener to Mr St John Brodrick

[Holograph] Commander-in-Chief's Office,
South Africa.
5th April 1901.

I have not got very much for you this mail, at which I daresay you will be pleased after the amount I have sent you in previous mails which I fear must have bored you –

Generally everything is going on all right. Botha and de Wet have met but I do not know what they have settled to do.[1]

The terms of peace were published by the boers at Ermelo with only one mistake. they said Boer farms would be specially taxed for the war. this may have been a slip of my report, but if not it will be corrected

There is evidently a certain amount of divergence of opinion amongst them as to whether the terms should have been accepted or not – Milner is here staying with me and I propose to discuss with him today whether we should not now introduce more confiscation of property etc to bring about the end of the war – Any such action will be telegraphed –

I am arranging for active operations in the neighbourhood of Roos Senekal where the so-called Transvaal Govt now is – I shall I hope put 6 columns into the field with the view of either surrounding or driving the enemy on to Pietersburg where I hope Plumer will meet them – I have a meeting of Generals today on the subject and to make final arrangements[2] –

I think we have advanced the question of how to deal with local Claims against military forces – We now think it advisable to get out a proclamation by Milner to the effect that all claims for compensation for damage done by military or for the repayment of receipts in commandeering notes up to the 31st March inclusive must be presented for registration before the 31st May next at the

General of the districts office or at other central offices and that any claims not so presented will be null and void – This only of course applies to the inhabitants residing at the time in the country. A complete register of claims will thus be made for each district and most of the inquiries on them can be proceeded with at once so that at the end of the war, boards of officers in the district will be able to settle most claims straight off by an offer of each down –

If the war goes on we can later by similar proclamations again bring in and register all claims up to some future date say 6 months hence –

By this means we shall have the great advantage of knowing our liabilities and by dealing with claims under martial law we shall avoid legal complications   I hope by next mail to be able to send you the full detail of the scheme worked out by Fleetwood Wilson –

I fear if we leave the door open until the end of the war many of the boers now in the field may produce claims against us and it would be very difficult to prove they were actually fighting –

Of course we do not intend to pay any claims until the war is over – I only intend to register and stamp the claims and leave the documents (after taking all the information we require for inquiry) in the hands of the applicants   It is of course possible we may bag a few of these men with their claims before the war is over & thus cancel our debt –

My march [March] bag was over the 1000 but it is not yet completely made up   we have also done well in guns pompoms & Mausers[3] –

The mines at Johannesburg are now starting work and we shall soon be turning out a certain amount of gold, I expect this will have a depressing effect on the boers – Since writing the first part of this letter Milner, Solomon, & Self have had a meeting and Solomon is prepared to get out a proposal for confiscation not on the grounds of the boers being rebels but that we exert our right of conquest over the properties of those who remain out after the notice – Of course it will all be fully reported before any steps are taken

TNA reference PRO 30/57/22/Y40

48
Mr St John Brodrick to Lord Kitchener
[Copy] <u>April 12. 1901</u>

Your last two letters have given me infinite pleasure as they have told us so much.[4] I am also greatly indebted for the photo of you and Botha wh. has been a great interest to many – I always exchange letters with Ld Roberts, so it is not safe for you to abuse me to him or vice versa!

We follow all your movements with the utmost keenness. I am very glad you & Milner are agreed as to the temporary High Com[missio]n[er]ship.[5] Personally I was afraid with these immense operations to conduct you would find our additional claim on you a burden – but the fact that you both agree entirely satisfies us & we would far rather it was in your hands than others.

I am a little wondering however, how you will get on for generals considering the number leaving you for home on various grounds. The King spoke to me twice about Oliphant & Ld Roberts. I have telegraphed to you. I see you do not wish for him & there is no more to be said.[6] I put the King off – but Evelyn Wood formed a good opinion of him at manoeuvres & Buller I know thinks well of him. Probably you have about you someone who has a different view, but the feeling here was that Wolseley was hard in preferring Bar Campbell[7] to him last year –

I am glad Lyttelton is to get a rest[8]   I note I have not bothered you too much with questions – but I have ridden the high horse successfully so far in H[ouse] of C[ommons] – One point however we shall have trouble about   I wired to you for a full report on the laagers for refugees – Pretty bad reports have been received here of state of the Bloemfontein laager in Jany – insufficient water, milk, rations, typhoid prevalent – children sick. No soap – no forage for cows – insufficient medical attendance – Norvals Pont better. Aliwal [North] still more so – but little soap. etc.[9]

I think I shall have a hot time over there [sic], probably in most cases inevitable sufferings or privations – War of course is war – & we cannot expect everything, nor have I personally a very strong bias in favour of those who are still fighting being assured of all they care about being in comfort, but we must do the best we can for them. Tell me all that will help the defence

We are bringing out a big Honours list directly. I hope it will put spirits into some of our people. My big scheme for redividing England & working it in Army Corps districts will be keenly debated in H of Commons, but I expect the whole of our reforms & increases to be carried – I only wish you were there to assist in them –

Lord Roberts is in splended form & I think very happy. We are going to readjust some of the W.O duties, but as you are not to be with us, I have made no second post of the character I had proposed.

In getting rid of 5000 prisoners between Bermuda & India[10] I think we have done pretty much our best for you – Australia is set against them –

I do hope the new troops will not prove too raw for use. We are most grateful to you for clearing out the volunteers & dealing with hard cases in the Yeomanry. When you get the whole of the new lot & they are settled down, perhaps you might be able to <u>offer</u> the old yeomen their Conjé.[11]

Post going

TNA reference PRO 30/57/22/Y43

49
Lord Kitchener to Mr St John Brodrick[12]

[Holograph]   Commander-in-Chief's Office,
                               South Africa.
                               26th April 1901

Botha has lost considerably by these abortive peace negiotations there is considerable division amongst his people, a great number think that he ought to have accepted the terms and are somewhat unhappy to find while they were talking we took Pietersburg,[13] and that they will not be able to go to the Bushveldt, hence a considerable number of surrenders which shake their confidence in their cause and in their leaders – In a speech De la Rey said the other day the terms were good but as the rebels had to be punished they must go on fighting   this was not popular at all –

The boer leader is an excellent actor and would take almost anyone in but below the surface he has the mind of an unscrupulous pettifogging attorney and in attempting to overreach anyone he has to deal with, he gets taken in – I have no doubt a good many of the younger leaders thought because I met Botha and seemed anxious for peace that we were tired and would give up; but I am glad to say the troops were never better than they are now – After the first phase of the war when Ld Roberts left they were certainly played out, but now they are quite fit again and full of go – The new troops are also a great help and enable me to carry on the war much more vigorously – We have cleared them out of Roos Senekal and the north is in our hands, now I shall turn on a good many troops to this the only district they have between the Natal & Delagoa [Bay] railways   as we have cleared up all around they will find it difficult to know where to go to – Our bag has increased considerably lately and I hope this month I shall be able to show 2000 taken out of the field. I cannot get reports of two captures at Roos Senekal but I have very little doubt we shall have a good haul[14] –

I see the terms of peace were not very favourably received in England but I daresay if some of those who object to them knew more about affairs out here they would change their opinion – If you had an unconditional surrender tomorrow I think you would have to follow very closely the lines laid down in the above terms of peace in dealing with the boers, that is to say if you really want to live in peace and security with them and be able to give them self government later.

The strain on the Empire will be very great if we are to have our Alsace 6000 miles away instead of next door as Germany has –

The boers are a bigoted people   they will always say they have been overpowered not beaten. The reason for this is of course, that they do not defend their country, but merely carry on hostilities as far as suits them always bolting before risking defeat which the nature and vast area of their country enables them to do with impunity – However they will never recognise this and our own and the foreign press continually assures them of their military power and genius, they are quite sufficiently conceited without these tributes of praise, but if they have the least doubt in their own mind that they are all heroes, it is swept away by European opinion and the parliamentary utterances of the opposition –

I think the only safe way for the future is to put in as many English and overseas colonials as possible and give them self government as soon as possible, they will fight a good deal amongst themselves, there is already a very bitter feeling between those that are fighting and the surrendered burghers or hands uppers as they call them & this feeling will be very useful in the future, if, however, they are not treated as they think fairly they will come together again. Take the Dutch language for instance if you absolutely and openly attempt to suppress it entirely they will start their own schools and keep up the language as a national sentiment.

I am afraid I am going entirely outside my province in writing above but as you say write freely I give it you for what it is worth and hope you will tear it up and not abuse me for boring you –

What is the opinion of the Govt. about the confiscation of property of boers on commando. I gave Milner a project for a proclamation on the subject but of course nothing has been done and I do not think he has yet referred it home – If it is to be done I suggested to Milner that perhaps it would be better if the proclamation came out after he had left – In the mean time we are getting lists of properties of officers and principal men ready, this the boers will hear of and it may have some effect – I enclose a letter on subject written by S. Marks for a paper but not sent – S. Marks is a very wealthy mine and land owner –

Milner has issued a proclamation which I enclose about claims this will greatly facilitate one dealing with all local claims against military funds, and it ought to be an incentive to those boers still on commando who have claims to come in and present them, though of course if it is known they were out on commando they would not get any payment for their claims –

I have been so much interrupted while writing this rather hurried letter that I hope you will excuse its defects – We are all going strong and well and mean to make it lively for the enemy – On the 28th I shall have some more columns in motion which will sway them[15] –

The honours gazette has given great satisfaction   I am much obliged for the GCMG but I like better the reason you gave for its being awarded me than the decoration itself – We are all trying to do our very best –

TNA reference PRO 30/57/22/Y48

50
Lord Kitchener to Schomberg MacDonnell[16]
[Holograph]   Pretoria
9th May 01.

Many thanks for your letter   It was really good of you to take the trouble to write to me. I am full of work so I am not going to give you a proper answer but I do not like you to think that I am not grateful   also if you have the opportunity you might convey to H.M. how highly I appreciate his kind message.

We are all doing our best to bring this beastly war to an end & I think the bags I have wired lately must show you we are steadily reducing the enemy's forces   I am rather afraid of the whole thing degenerating into uncontrolled brigandage which it may take years to suppress   therefore if Botha decided that all should lay down their arms it would be a distinct advantage   this was the main reason for terms and I impressed on Botha that if any resisted he would have to bring them in by force which he was prepared to do – As to the rebels they are all brothers, cousins and close relations of the burghers in the field and if an amnesty is given I cannot for the life of me see a great difference between them – However that is all over and we are still at it

PRONI D/4091/A/3/2/4/2

51
Lord Kitchener to Mr St John Brodrick

[Holograph]   Commander-in-Chief's Office,
                                                         South Africa.
                                                         9th May, 1901.

Last month we took 2000 Boers out of the field   a good many
rifles and over half a million rounds of ammunition – Clearing up
the north has done a great deal of good and as far as I can make
out the enemy have no plans – There is a large and I hope growing
party amongst them who think the terms offered should have been
accepted & that their leaders are betraying the people   possibly
for personal reasons – The number of surrenders have greatly
increased in the Transvaal which does not look as if the burgher
camps were so very bad –

Things are not quite so satisfactory in the O.R.C.   De Wet,
Brand[17] and Hertzog seem to be able to keep up the irreconcilable
feeling and suppress all moderate councils – Steyn's influence
seems to have decreased   I cannot make out what they intend to
do beyond keeping up a hostile attitude and taking advantage of
any slips we may make –

The S.A. Constabulary are now getting out and forming posts,
when we get protected areas we will let the surrendered burghers
go from the camps to their farms and the irreconcilables will see
that ordinary life is going on in spite of all their efforts – I had
hoped that we should have been able to do this on a small scale
earlier but the S.A.C. have been very slow in getting organized
all their work at present is being done in the O.R.C.

I started the mines working at Johannesburg last Saturday and I
hope this will also have a depressing effect on the Boer enthusiasts
– Our being able to do it shows that the country is getting slowly
settled. Attacks on railway lines have greatly decreased owing to
our improved blockhouses and the lines are now gradually forming
barriers through the country which hostile forces cannot cross; this
breaks them up into areas which we will gradually clear –

Having cleared the Roos Senekal district a good many columns
will now be available to clear the country East of Carolina which

has not been touched and is a Boer stronghold. Vigorous operations are also going on against De la Rey in the west[18] and an expedition has started for Louis Trichardt on the north[19] – In the O.R.C. Elliott is sweeping the country along the Vaal [River] moving East until he reaches the Natal frontier.[20] Rundle is in Fouriesberg [Fouriesburg] and operating from there.[21] C Knox will in a day or two move west of the line on Bothaville[22] and Bruce Hamilton[23] is clearing up the southern frontier along the Orange river   In the [Cape] colony the small bands are being cleared everywhere and the colonial defence force is now taking a greater part and is useful

I have written you another despatch up to the 8th May[24] but shall wait for the mail as you may make some remarks on my former despatch 8th March[25] which apparently has not been published

I have had no further communication with Botha – I send you some letters caught on the enemy's despatch riders – You will see the absurd lies spread by the leaders to keep their men in the field – It seems impossible to believe the credulity of the boers – a large party were coming in yesterday to surrender when they were told from Johannesburg that war had broken out between Russia and England, and so they all went back –

We are really doing all we can for the burgher camps and I hope soon to be able to let the surrendered burghers take their cattle to the bush veldt – I do not think people from England would be of any use or help to the families in camps as they already have a number of people looking after them but funds might help them if properly administered – I wish I could get rid of these camps but it is the only way to settle the country and enable the men to leave their commandos and come in to their families without being caught and tried for desertion. Milner has gone and I have taken over his work – I do not think I shall find it excessive[26] –

TNA reference PRO 30/57/22/Y52(b)[27]

52
Lord Kitchener to Lord Roberts

[Holograph]   Pretoria
9th May 01.

I have been wiring you a good many captures lately principally from the columns operating under Blood in the Roos Senekal district. The whole move came off very well as it was planned Plumer cooperating effectively from the north – Now the columns are in and resting before undertaking fresh operations to the East of Carolina – We have had a quiet week as regards our railway lines   they seem to be giving up the attempt to stop our trains which is a great blessing and relief – The Yeomanry are gradually all getting into the field but of course it is a considerable strain getting up sufficient remounts for them –

Wools Sampson is all right   he has taken on with Blood as intelligence officer and is quite happy   so is his regt not to have him –

I am sure the changes you have approved in cavalry commands will be for the advantage of the service, the 5th Lancers and 17th want a lot of looking after and I think the 2nd in command who is not fit to command should also go – If this were done both the 5th and 17th would require fresh men –

I am putting Babington in command of a cavalry brigade forming at Middleberg [Middelburg] working under Blood consisting of the 18th 19th and 5th Lancers   Featherstonhaugh [Fetherstonhaugh] will take over Babingtons present command and will I think improve matters in that direction   Mildmay Willson is not much use and does not seem to improve   he is distinctly the worst of the new Genls that have been sent out – All the others are doing well and Blood and Beatson are quite excellent – I hope soon to let Settle go home relieving him by Colin Mackenzie who under the new organisation is not required in Johannesburg   I should like Settle back if the war goes on –

I hear that in the Indian Staff Corps in special cases quicker promotion is sometimes allowed – Would you recommend Birdwoods case to the India office   he is well deserving of promotion and would then qualify for the reward given him in your gazette[28] –

I have got rid of H.P. Young from being press censor[29]   I have had some very curious cases of how officers do the duty of press censor, but I hope matters are now working better, as far as I know all the correspondents are quite satisfied –

I have taken Appelbe as C.O.O. Hdqts and hope to get the department organized on business lines   it will take a little time to do this as there has been great confusion in the Ordnance – I must say the demands on them for S.A.C. colonial defence, Town Guards[30] have been very great and very irregular so that the Ordnance has hardly had a fair chance –

I am sending you the first batch of my recommendations for commissions   they have been very carefully gone into and I hope the selections will turn out well – I made them sign a certificate of which I enclose a copy   thus caused several applicants to withdraw their requests –

Major Baker R.A.[31] and Major Wintour[32] have been ordered home

We have done our best to get the recommendations for reward and mention, but it is most difficult to get C.O.s. to answer, I have had to threaten the most severe penalties if orders from Hdts are so disregarded   I hope now you have the whole batch except the 7th D[ragoon] G[uard]s and 3rd South Wales Borderers   the C.O.s of these have been asked for their reasons in writing for such a long delay and disregard of numerous written and telegraphed orders and these I will forward to you –

If you think it advisable to send out Oliphant pray do so   I personally know nothing of him. his reputation does not seem to point to his being a great success but I do not put much trust in reputations which have been gained in the street or club and not in the field – I offered Oliphant to Methuen but he respectfully declined and as he was short of senior officers at the time I rather judged that he probably knew more of the value of the officer than I did –

I wish I could tell you when the end of the war would come – We are nearer to it   that is all I can say – I much dread the war degenerating into the uncontrolled brigandage which might take a very long time to suppress and cause incalculable damage to the country and enormous expense, hence my desire for terms with Botha who could control the enemy's forces, however that is probably all over now and how it will end I cannot see – That they are being visibly weakened there is no doubt but the end "Khudu Jauta"[33] –

My best regards to the Countess and Ladies Roberts

[Postscript]
I enclose a translation of a letter purporting to be from a boer to his friend describing Rawlys capture[34] –

NAM. 1971-01-23-33-27

53
Mr St John Brodrick to Lord Kitchener
[Copy]   May 18. 1901.
Private

We had a serious discussion in the Cabinet yesterday on the duration of the war. Thanks to your full private letters, I was able to give more light than I would otherwise have done – Although home coming generals like Lyttelton are sanguine of an early collapse, we cannot help feeling that your efforts to localise the war seem not to have yet succeeded to your full satisfaction. Your last letter[35] referred to Cape Colony & I presume until you can report Cape Colony & O.R.C. clear, you will not be able materially to reduce force – What is in some minds is this; If you were able to drive all but a few marauding Boers north of the Vaal [River], could not the war be pronounced at an end in the 2 Southern Colonies, & Natal and all further opposition be punished in that area as brigandage?

We feel that some point of this kind must be looked to as neither finance nor policy would permit us to maintain 250.000 men in the Colonies indefinitely.

Not improbably before this reaches you some further overtures will be made by Botha as I imagine every week at this time of year adds to his difficulties.

We quite approved your proposed change in the communication to Botha – What struck us was that we might be seeking some co operation from Kruger in bringing pressure to bear on his colleagues, and that it might pay us not to shut the door entirely.

After you receive this anything you can tell us as to the possible localisation of the war, wh. I gather from your correspondence you are considering on the <u>Cordon</u> system will help us extremely in our conclaves with Milner –

I have carried our Scheme for Army Corps districts by a large majority, and we are beginning at once to raise the new troops. We are also reorganizing the Medical Dept and a good many others but if possible I shall leave the question of Transport till you can confer with us here – In this & many other respects I would have given much for your counsel –

TNA reference PRO 30/57/22/Y55

54
Lord Kitchener to Mr St John Brodrick

[Holograph]   Pretoria
18th May 01

Many thanks for your letter. Botha is nibbling again, there is a considerable party amongst the boers who think he has done wrong in not accepting the terms offered and they are very discontented. It is rather amusing to see that he has now discovered a fundamental law which requires reference to Kruger after having told me that he could make peace and would guarantee to bring everyone in if terms were accepted[36] – I believe this move is engineered by old Reitz[37] to gain time and keep the boers out over the winter waiting for a reply – I am glad you accepted the second version of the reply as it will make them show their hand. I have sent off the letter this morning –

I see you have been asked how I let Botha know that I would meet the Old ex president   Pretorius[38] went out on his own request to see Botha about making peace and had an unsuccessful interview   he told me Botha would not listen to anyone who was a burgher but he thought if I met Botha matters could be easily arranged   I said I had no objection to meeting Botha if he asked for an interview and on the distinct understanding that the subject of independence was not to be discussed – Some days afterwards Mrs Botha[39] asked to see me and required permission to go out and see her husband which I allowed, she then asked if she might give Botha a message in the same sense as I had told Pretorius   I said yes laying considerable stress on the latter part viz that the subject of independence was not to be raised. She brought back an official letter from Botha asking for the interview and assured me she had fully explained to Botha that independence was not to be discussed – The rest you know –

News from the north is satisfactory and I do not expect much more trouble from the Waterberg and Zoutpansberg districts   I have now 12 columns operating between the Natal and Delagoa [Bay] railways so Botha will have [to] skip about to escape being taken by one of them   I have given the columns a very free hand and though they work on a system they are not tied down and can follow up any advantage they may gain   their instructions are to follow up and chase any boer commandos met –

Did you ever receive my official despatch of the 8th March. I see it has not been published, and I have never heard of your having received it – I have written another bringing operations up to the 8th May but I do not like sending it off as there may have been something wrong about the 1st despatch which I could correct –

Milners work as left for me is not excessive   I can manage it all right and I think his affairs are going on smoothly   he has a very good legal advice in Solomon – I am of course sending all civil matters to Mr Chamberlain

At Milners request I am sending home (on leave) Girouard to keep him in arranging the future of railway matters – I am very anxious to get better rates on the Natal line which are fearfully high, I have sent Girouard to Natal to explain matters fully to McCallum there – Natal is making such a good thing out of the war that peace is the last thing they pray for – They would then lose the present golden harvest they are reaping but I am trying to induce them to modify their greed and not kill the golden goose as there might be retaliation in the future – I sent F. Wilson down on the same mission but he is so intensely diplomatic that as far as I can gather nothing was done – The question of the rates we are paying for money is also one of great importance

The bank now takes the risk on our lines and I do not wish that altered as one loss of specie would put us very much to the bad, and I feel sure if the bank did not run the risk the movement of specie would be <u>far more</u> likely to get known – Up to the present nothing has been lost, I do not approve of a change of system only a change of rates which are now too high – Fleetwood Wilson is looking into this matter with the Standard Bank at Capetown.

I think I shall get the Ordnance into businesslike working soon. Col Appelbe has taken charge and has gone to Cape town to put things in order[40] – <u>I am afraid the local expenditure there will lead to awkward questions</u>[41] –

I have not bothered you with many enclosures lately but I think you may like to see our last months bag and a state of the transport with expenditure on same may be of interest –

The plague hospital questions at Cape town have all been arranged satisfactorily by Wynne[42] –

[Postscript]
I note your wish about telegraphing to you when I wire to colonial office about any terms –

TNA reference PRO 30/57/22/Y54

55
Lord Kitchener to Lord Roberts

[Holograph]   Pretoria
24th May 01.

Many thanks for your letter – We are working away as hard as we can to enclose and catch the boers, but it is difficult work and they have got remarkably cute lately. I expect everyday to hear that Blood has had a good haul but it does not come off: of course he is working in very difficult country – Botha has asked to send a telegram to Kruger but I have no idea what the result will be[43] – There is no doubt a large number of his men want peace and are going on much against their will, but there are a good many, principally Cape and Natal rebels who think they can still stick it out some time longer – The boer ammunition is running short everywhere – De la Rey seems to be the only one with any supply and now that the north is gone from them they I think realize they cannot go on much longer – I wish the press was more careful in England   it gives the waverers heart to see the comments about the budget and how tired England is of the war – We must now carry this thing through and there is no good crying out – The boers have had good terms offered them and ought not to get anything more

French is still ill, but would not go home in a change as I wanted him to do; when he recovers which will I hope be shortly, I will put him in charge of the operations in Cape Colony and Haig can then go to his regt –

I am sending home by this mail the Helvetia Court Martial;[44] it has only just come in so that I have not had time to read it properly. I think Jones though acquitted might be got rid of as an unsuitable officer, as far as I can judge he evidently acquiesced in the surrender. I hope Cotton will be dealt with at home –

Rawlinson is doing very well in command of a column, & will I feel sure merit his Col[onel]cy when the time comes   I have made him a local Col. I do not think he has any idea of India later –

[Forestier-] Walker issued some 20,000 stand of arms to town guards in Cape Colony without my knowledge, I have been trying to replace them with Martini Henri rifles but Wynne finds great difficulty in doing so, I do not at all like town guards in Cape Colony have our ammunition, and I believe already some has leaked up north from them, but it is terribly difficult to get back on a mistake once made, I shall however stick to it –

We have had a considerable loss of clothing in the Tantallon Castle.[45] I am asking for it to be replaced but I think we can get on all right without the saddles as we have saddles coming from India now –

B[aden] P[owell] and the S.A.C. are still very unsatisfactory he is spending a lot of money and no result; I cannot get them to do anything, & in the mean time a great number of his men are going sick. Organizing is as far as I can see the last thing B.P. can do: some of his officers are getting disgusted and wishing to leave him – As this is one of Milners departments I do not like to interfere but I hate seeing waste of material and money – They have got some posts out from Bloemfontein as far as Petersburg [Petrusburg] which we hold, and that is practically all they do at present –

By fortifying and increasing our posts on the railway lines they form barriers which the Boers cannot cross without being engaged. I am getting blockhouses at every 2500 yards and at night parties from each meet and sleep out between, waiting for any attempt to cross. this has proved very successful – The Eastern and Natal line are complete and the others will soon be so –

I have nearly got all the old Yeomanry away, and shall try and send you more militia than you send me but you know how Lvfl's [?] scream for men – I have enclosed a distribution up to date in Brodricks letters, & some translations of papers found at Roos Senekal showing how important the invasion of Cape Colony might have been had de Wet had any success –

Who is looking after the large expenditure on sea transport? I cannot help thinking a good deal of money might be saved in that Departement – I suppose Stanley is responsible[46] –

NAM. 1971-01-23-33-29

56
Mr St John Brodrick to Lord Kitchener
[Copy]   May 25. 1901
Private

Your letter of April 26th [47] which arrived last mail was so complete a review of the situation and so important that I had portions of it typed for the cabinet.

I was very anxious they should be seized with your view of the position as to the campaign and the negotiations before the meeting with Milner wh. have begun this evening. I have impressed your opinion most carefully both on Balfour & Chamberlain and we realise that the present rate of expenditure & strain cannot go on indefinitely. I shall take care no fresh steps are decided upon here without referring to you, especially as I am hoping for some opinion from you as to the possible localisation of the war.

My colleagues are inclined to ask that troops should be brought home. My reply is that till a substantial portion of your communications are safe from attack, you cannot part with troops.

You often wonder in your letters how what you write will interest us in 3 weeks time. You will I trust realise from the above that your letters are our main guidance & although much may happen in the coming 3 weeks both here & with you, I will ask you when this reaches you to answer me, if you can, the following questions,

1. If and when do you see your way to reducing the theatre of the war?

2. Assuming Cape Colony & O.R.C. to be clear up to the line across O.R.C. which you propose to draw, what troops could you dispense with?

3. Supposing as an extreme ..... you were asked at the end of July to reduce your forces by 100,000 what portion of the country could you hold?

4. Do you still hold that amnesty is the only or main cause of the Boers refusing our terms?

I do not put these questions idly, but you will not I am sure read into them more than I intend. I want to be in a position to argue the case in Cabinet from every standpoint. We do not mind public opinion, but a further heavy demand for money coming on Estimates of £88.000.000 would cause a very 'cold' fit here.

I am glad to see Lyttelton in such good health and spirits. Will you when you have leisure – if such a thing ever is – tell me whether you still think he is the right man to command the 'standing army' after your work is done – give a sort of list of what General Officers you would leave with him? Also I would like to know who of your present Generals you wish us to consider for

Home Commands. The Army Corps Scheme has passed & we shall begin with Aldershot, Ireland & Salisbury Plain on wh. large barracks are beginning to be raised.

I am so glad the honours list gave satisfaction. We hope to have the reg[imen]t[al] list ready in a month. Just now I am pretty busy reorganizing Medical Dept [,] War Office [and] Order in Council as to Headquarters Staff and getting a loan for Barracks etc This with 9 hours a day House of Commons & all the current business brings me too often to 2 & 4 a m as tonight. The main change in the new Order in Council will be the Subordination of A.G. to the C in C – whose ….. he becomes in company with Mil Secy & Mobilization & Intelligence.

The QMG – DGO[48] – IGF[49] remain autonomous. No one man could control them all & the only man we wanted as Chief of the Staff has chosen a warmer post – so there will be none in the new organization. All the above is strictly for yourself alone –

TNA reference PRO 30/57/22/Y57

57
Lord Kitchener to Mr St John Brodrick

[Holograph]   Pretoria
                                                              7th June 01

I am sorry McCallum again raised the Zulu question without any reference to me otherwise I could have told him that for more than a fortnight before his telegram   Bottomley[50] had left and the status quo auth[ante] which has really never been disturbed was left severely alone – This he found out and had to admit when I collared him on subject – The Natal Govt are too absurd about the Zulus   I quite understand that they should be nervous but they so evidently know nothing of what is going on in Zululand that it almost seems to be dangerous to leave the management of the Zulus in their hands   The Zulus are quite quiet, and the whole business which of course increases one's work is the excited creation of Natal – I am now sending a commission to inquire & I hope it will prevent this sort of thing recurring again.

I did not expect McCallum would have allowed himself to be let in without inquiry – I enclose the telegrams that have passed between us on the subject –

I have arranged much better railway rates with Natal and hope to get better terms with Cape Colony shortly   I enclose copies of correspondence which will show you how the matter stands – I am afraid our claims for £129 000 against Natal stated in my letter would not stand very strict examination but it may bluff them into giving me the ..... to the 1st Janry which will mean at least £125,000 –

I see by your telegram you are anxious to reduce the forces here – You may be quite sure I will send home as many men as I possibly can but I really think it would only make the war last longer to reduce now   The very least change is caught hold of by the boer leaders and used effectively to keep the boers in the field – The last thing Botha told them at the meeting a few days ago[51] was that he guaranteed that in two months we should be worn out and give them back their independence – It seems incredible that they can still be taken in by such absurdities – Everything seems to look better and to show that the end is not far off – Our columns are pressing them everywhere and they have no rest and no fight left in them, except when they get a chance like they did at Dixon's column & then they got as good as they gave[52]

The numbers of the boers were exaggerated but under cover of a veldt fire they got close and fiercely attacked Dixons rearguard, almost all the damage was done before the other troops could come up in support when they were easily driven off – As far as I can see our troops behaved well and no blame attaches to anyone –

I am afraid some of the new Yeomanry were somewhat wild but that must be expected at first – These boers are now being chased by three columns and show no signs of wishing to come to close quarters again – I hope we may catch some of them – Delarey was not there as he and de Wet have gone to see Botha[53]   I have warned everyone about their movement & hope for a lucky chance to catch them   they only travel with four men each and go fast & mostly at night – We caught Comdt Malan[54] travelling in this way but it was pure chance our doing so as the country is too vast and open to make any certainty of it –

I think you must be tired of my writing you my bag so I am not sending you many telegrams as it would be impossible to describe the movements of columns, I will begin again in a little while – I enclose our bag for May which was better than I expected: the exhausting process is going on steadily –

I wonder if you had the telegram for Botha to Kruger deciphered I suppose a little money would do it through the F O I should like to know what he said I expect he is asking for money – When the answer comes we shall soon see the result[55] – A great many boers expect then to surrender and if the order comes to go on I anticipate a large number will come in –

I am doing my best to keep down expenditure but it is no easy task and I do not see my way to do much more in any large war – Pay of S.A. irregulars worries me a good deal as it is difficult to get it properly checked and they are all robbers

The moment peace comes we will clear that expenditure off I wired about Yeomanry pay The 5/ rate being only for while in S.A. would I think be an improvement –

Appelbe has been down to Capetown and arranged the ordnance on new lines – I have asked him to write a report which I will enclose if I get it in time for this mail Shortly the system is that of a large firm Retail, Wholesale and manufacturing depts –

You are the manufacturing dept. Our base depots in Cape & Natal are our wholesale dept[s], and our retail shops are the District Ordnance stores under GOCs Appelbe is General Manager and watches the wholesale Dept seeing that proper orders are sent to the manufacturing Dept and proper issues are made to the retail shops I hope no G.O.C. in future will be able to issue all my rifles without my knowledge as they will not be able to touch the Wholesale Dept.

I am afraid there are no dividends to be got out of this firm but I hope in future it will work on business principles –

I hope you will not send [Forestier-] Walker back I should find it very difficult to place him as the Cape is working much better on the new regime and does not now require a Lt. Gen. to command there – I do not want any more Gen[eral]s in fact I could spare you two or three if you require them –

I would send them home but they are not anxious to go and I do not see any advantage in forcing them   Still if you are hard up for Generals there are Hart, Barton, W. Knox[56] & M. Willson quite at your disposal –

The German Consul General from Capetown[57] has been up here and at Bloemfontein lately   I think I have sent him away satisfied that all that is possible is being done for German subjects – Bloemfontein is the only place where trouble exists and I hope matters are settled there now – The German Consul General claims every German whether he has given up his nationality and been a burgher for 13 or 14 years or not even when they have signed a sworn declaration that they have given up all allegiance to their Emperor   Once a German always a German is his contention –

TNA reference PRO 30/57/22/Y60

58
Lord Kitchener to Lord Roberts

[Holograph]

Pretoria
14 June 01.

The war drags on without any definite signs of soon ending – Kemp's commandos that attacked Dixon dispersed as soon as Featherstonhaughs [Fetherstonhaugh's] columns came on the scene[58] –

Featherston [Fetherstonhaugh] tried to drive them north and I sent Dixon to hold Boshoek pass, but as usual they passed through Featherstons [Fetherstonhaugh's] columns and appeared south of him   It is always the same way chasing Quicksilver, still they must feel the steady reduction in their numbers – Bruce Hamilton has done some good work in the South West portion of the O.R.C.[59] and the [S.A.] Constabulary posts are at last becoming of some use –

Elliot has just come in to Kro[o]nstadt after a long trek, but I have not yet heard the result of his operations between Vrede and Lindley[60] –

Plumer has been to Piet Retief for [a] surprise visit and caught Emmett Botha's brother in law[61] –

Bullock, Beatson & Grey, are chasing the government carts everywhere, and Blood will soon move south to join them in the hunt[62] –

All columns are working hard – In the north all the country East of a line running due north through PP Rust[63] may be said to be quite clear and we are going to tackle the West in a few days where Beyers has collected about 100 men – I wish I could see an end to it but this process of exhaustion must in such a country as this be a long one – I do all I can and think all I know I cannot see my way to do more –

I wish the Govt would agree to confiscate the property of the leaders giving them a months notice so that they might have time to come in –

As they do not seem inclined to have peace might not the French Govt be approached with a view of their taking the Prisoners of War as settlers in Madagascar I could send their families and so clear the burgher camps and we should be relieved of a bad and dangerous lot –

Two armed and one unarmed Burgher tried to get out of Pretoria to join De la Rey, they were caught after firing on the police and wounding one man, there is strong presumption that they had been out and in here before and were therefore spies – The court sentenced them all to death and I confirmed the sentence in the case of the two armed men,[64] this has had a very good effect in the town – Maxwell also taking more stringent measures about registration of people in the town and searching for arms[65] –

We have now caught about 30 Cape Colonists who joined Kritzinger and co.[66] I think if some of them were shot[67] these bands would very soon clear out of Cape Colony, they are merely brigands and murderers I have asked whether carrying out a death sentence in such cases would be approved of at home

Krugers answer to Botha will be delivered shortly   I hope it may have some effect. Have you any idea what the nature of these communications were? I know nothing here –

Chesham is going home   the distribution of Yeomanry is complete   they are doing well but are still green and therefore liable to more casualties than they should have. Another month will I expect make them all right –

All departments are working all right and the army is in good spirits and full of hope that it cannot last long now –

With kind regards to Lady Roberts and your family

NAM. 1971-01-23-33-32

59
Lord Kitchener to Mr St John Brodrick

[Holograph]   Pretoria
<u>Very Secret</u>   21st June 01.

I very much wish we were anyway near the position of affairs out here indicated by your questions in your letter of May 25th [68] – I have answered the questions by telegraph and I do not think I can say anything more – I do not see how you can reduce the forces here until something definite is settled as it would certainly put off the end of the war indefinitely – I enclose an actual statement of the number of troops in the field, the remainder are either time expired, on their way home, or sick in hospital –

You say you like to have my views on the future – A good deal may happen in the next few days as Botha is being pressed, and has not yet I think received Kruger's message – I cannot make out what the message contains; but I fancy it will either result in a surrender, or give the boers fresh impetus for carrying on the war, which will take them over the winter –

The boers have practically no guns & are very short of ammunition – Still doing all we possibly can we find it very difficult to catch even a few of them – The process of exhaustion will take a very long time –

The South African white (Cape or Natal colonists or Transvaal uitlanders) is very inferior to the boers, both in knowledge of the country, capability of standing hardship, and hard work, and in guts and determination – You have only to compare Kritzingers invasion of the Cape Colony with 500 men passing unhind[ered] through all the Cape Colony defence forces, and mounted troops, backed up by a large force of Imperial troops;[69] and the Jameson raid[70] to realize the situation –

The boers naturally see these points very prominently, and possibly exaggerate their prowess, and the longer the war goes on the more it is brought home to them that they can, with small forces and short of ammunition, still stand up and do a great deal of damage, and some of them probably consider that were it not for the large forces of Imperial troops, they could still make short work of the local whites, and carry out their original scheme of a united South Africa under the Dutch[71] –

I know that this is not the view of the loyal colonist, but when have they ever told us one single thing that turned out true –

There seems to me to be only two safe courses to pursue – Settle on some island or country where we can safely establish the boers, Fiji for instance, or get some foreign provider to take them such as France to populate Madagascar – Send all the prisoners of war there and let their families join them, have no more voluntary surrenders and ship all as they are caught to the new settlement – We should then only have the surrendered burghers left, and the country would be safe and available for white colonists –

The alternative was what was in my mind when the terms of peace were proposed, i.e. get them to agree to give up their independence, and let them settle down to quarrel amongst themselves, there are already two parties amongst them ready to fly at each others throats viz the surrenders or "handsuppers" as they call them and those that have unjustifiably carried on the war to the ruin of their country –

The howls with which the terms were received in England and by the Cape Colonists have to my mind put off the termination of the war for a very long time, and made it almost impossible for Boer and Briton to settle down peaceably, so this course having failed we are as far as I can see forced into the more objectionable first course proposed –

I have no doubt you will say both courses are too extreme; we must find some intermediate course for the future of the country   I wish I could see a safe one but I own I entirely fail to do so – These boers are uncivilized Africander savages with only a thin white veneer. The people who have lived all their lives with them have only seen the veneer, hence they have no idea what bringing up in this wild country has produced, savages – The boer woman in the refugee camp who slaps her protruding belly at you, and shouts "when all our men are gone these little Khakies will fight you" is a type of the savage produced by generations of wild lonely life – Back in their farms and their life on the veldt they will be just as uncivilized as ever, and a constant danger – Change their country and they may become civilized people fit to live with –

The leaders and towns people are sufficiently educated and civilized, I only refer to the bulk of the population who live in distant farms and trek into the Bush veldt with their cattle every winter – This explains the anomalies of the conduct of the war by the boers, the leaders enjoin civilized treatment but occasionally the uncivilized boer is met and shows all his native savagery –

I fear it will be many generations before they forget or forgive this war and that they will bide their time and when we are least prepared for it try the issue again – Will the English people after their experience care for another boer war possibly coming when they are busy elsewhere, and if they hesitate the whole of S.A. may go –

We have now got more than half the boer population either as prisoners of war or in our refugee camps[72] – I would advise that they should not be allowed to return – I think we should start a large scheme for settling them elsewhere and S.A. will then be safe and there will be room for British to colonize the country – If the scheme is costly it will pay in the long run by the security it ensures and the value of the vacant farms here would go against the cost of establishing the boers elsewhere –

I fear the so-called loyalists will never live at peace with the boers though we may force the latter into a cessation of hostilities, we shall I fear never bring them down to consider themselves thoroughly defeated, and to be ready to crouch and lick the feet of the local white settler whom they despise – In South Africa it may be said with more or less truth that "the tail wags the dog" – I have therefore very little hope in a permanent settlement by any intermediate course between the extreme ones above mentioned –

By the time you get this it will be clear whether Krugers messages allow a surrender or not – If peace is near, as I pray it may be please tear this up but should we still be pegging away I think the subject may be with [worth?] your consideration – It gives you the reasons for my telegram of yesterday to W Chamberlain[73] –

It was very like a present[i]ment of evil when in my last letter to you I said we had to be careful, next day I heard of the Australians under Beatson being surprised[74] – I fear it was a gross case of want of ordinary precautions   I have told Blood to hold an inquiry and have placed Beatson under his orders, he was acting independently before – [The following two paragraphs have been scratched out in the consulted manuscript]

I can only say 'mea culpa'[75] about Lukin's D.S.O.[76] I had no idea that Ld Roberts had included him in his list but there is no doubt I should have known, and I will square it with Lukin at the end of the campaign.

I am sending you by this mail a long report by Fleetwood Wilson on the local expenditure mismanagement in the Ordnance Dept, as Fleetwood Wilson leaves at the end of the month   I daresay you will see him before further inquiry in England is instituted

I hope I have not bored you by this long letter but it seems to me as well that you should know what is passing through one's mind out here, though possibly I have touched on subjects that are not in my province –

TNA reference PRO 30/57/22/Y62

60
Lord Kitchener to Mr St John Brodrick
[Holograph]   Pretoria
28th June 01

Our intelligence is very conflicting and I cannot make out very definitely what decision has been come to by the boers – The day before yesterday we heard from two sources that a meeting had been held, and that it was decided to continue the struggle; Since then we have heard that no decision was come to and that the meeting is to be on the 30th – I feel sure Krugers telegram has not been published to the Burghers as we have a good many spies who would certainly let us know, and surrendered Boers know nothing of the contents – I also feel pretty sure that when it is decided to go on we shall have a good many surrenders from amongst a certain number of boers who are only waiting to possibly come in with the others – There is a good deal of movement going on amongst the leaders which is difficult to follow – I think the solution is that the leaders held a meeting and have gone to consult their commandos and will there [then?] probably meet again to come to a final decision[77] –

With regard to the proposals in my last letter and telegrams about establishing irreconcilable boers in some other country, would not the Dutch Colonies of Java etc. accept them as settlers – I think if they were approached they might do so but of course steps would have to be taken to prevent them return[ing] to S.A. – We could then get rid of these refugee camps to a very great extent – I wonder why you do not hand over the questions about these camps to the Colonial Secty – They are entirely worked by the civil administration of the Transvaal and O.R.C. and returns are regularly sent to the Colonial Office, everything that is possible is being done for them and I have allowed Mrs Rendal [sic] Harris who has been sent out by some relief committee to come up and go round all the camps[78] –

One or two other ladies have asked for permission, but as I have received letters from home that they belong to the proboer party[79] and are merely going for political motives I have refused –

I wish we could get rid of these camps, but I do not see how to do so if the war goes on, unless you make some arrangement for removing them –

Fleetwood Wilson goes home by this mail, and will no doubt be able to give you any information that you may want, which I have not supplied – He has shown tact, skill and energy in carrying out this work and has been of great assistance to me – Most of the important financial questions that were worrying my mind, but which I had not time to go into myself, have now been cleared up – I think the office of F[inancial] A[dvisor] should go on as it is a check on expenditure, and is able to stop anything going wrong at once before the evil is done – you will no doubt consult with Fleetwood Wilson about a successor, I should have liked an officer, but the right man is most difficult to find – There is a Major Armstrong here who has shown considerable ability and who might do, I may perhaps try him as a temporary measure –

Baden Powell is going home on sick leave – I have been getting more lately out of the S.A.C. and they have at least completed the line across the O.R.C. but I fear it is not impervious to boers moving through at night – I cannot however say that I am satisfied with the result obtained from 8000 men that B[aden] P[owell] now has – I shall keep on trying to get more out of them –

I enclose some papers about the boer trial of Meyers de Kock and a legal opinion[80] –

Has it ever occurred to you that when Mr Cardwell carried out his great reform[81] amongst officers of the army by the abolition of purchase thus taking away their personal ..... regimental rights, that reform only went half way and left the personal regimental rights of officers, called the regimental system, still existing – I cannot help thinking that the immense improvement in the training of officers caused by Mr Cardwells reform points to the corollary that a change or abolition of the regimental system would give you far more efficient officers in the higher ranks, by teaching them throughout their career that the Army is their profession, not the narrow groove of any regiment which seems to contract their minds, dwarf their intellects and from the bright young man who joins the regiments turns out the present unsatisfactory senior officer –

I know you do not mind my giving you, for what they may be worth, my opinions such as the above –

I had greatly hoped that my despatch of the 8th July[82] which I must now set to work at would have been a final one, and it is a sore disappointment to realize that it is only one of a series –

TNA reference PRO 30/57/22/Y66

61
Lord Kitchener to Lord Milner

[Holograph]   Pretoria
                                                                  4th July 01

Many thanks for your letter of the 7th June.[83] We are pegging away as hard as we can but the boers will not stand at all   I was first starting a new system of Kraaling the boers up into areas by lines of our patent blockhouses when I got the telegram from the W.O. which you no doubt saw – I have cleared out those boers N.W. of Johannesburg and now hold a line north of Krugersdorp

It evidently does not much matter what terms we give the boers as de Wet and De la Rey & their following can outvote Botha & those who have had enough of it   after the recent decision to carry on the war I do not expect there will be any serious attempt at peace again before Sept unless of course the Govt would take some serious steps that would upset their calculations   then of course there is no saying but we might have peace. I suppose you have done all you can about confiscation in any form but there seems no hope of getting the Govt to agree [I enclose Perry's programme for what it is worth][84] everyone out here considers confiscation the only chance of bringing these people to their senses –

Talking of changes I only hope my head may grace that lordly dish   I am not too enamoured of the Army after 6 years continual war & would give a good deal to sink into oblivion and peace

I wonder when the winter is over whether we could not again finish the war and let a very tired person say his nunc dimittis[85]

All your children[86] are working well and smoothly and are giving me no trouble – Solomon produces a good many proclamations but except those referred and app[rove]d of by you or C.O. they are not of much importance –

I hope you will be out to meet the Cornwalls as I have not much time for such trips[87] – I am starting a few more stumps which will give joy to your heart

Bodleian Library, Milner Papers, Microfilm 175, ff. 75–6

62
Lord Kitchener to Mr St John Brodrick
[Holograph]   Pretoria
5th July 01.

Considering the enormous expenditure going on, Ld Roberts' telegram on the subject of reduction of the forces in South Africa was not a surprise – I have been for some time fortifying the railway lines with blockhouses so as to reduce the numbers employed in defending the lines, which duty takes up by far the greater number of the troops in S.A., and I am glad to say these works are now so far forward that to my mind (though in this some of my generals do not willingly agree) a substantial reduction of the forces can be safely carried out

I do not propose to send you the full scheme worked out by this mail, and am writing to Ld Roberts in some details, but by next mail I hope you will have complete detail of the proposed new distribution of the troops – One thing is of great importance and that is that the battalions left here should be kept up to strength by drafts – From one cause and another some battalions out here are very weak in efficient strength, and for the protection of lines I hope you will remember every man counts –

Out of the 140,000 men proposed by Ld Roberts I think I may calculate on having 100,000 infantry and mounted troops, leaving 40,000 for Artillery   Engineers Departmental Corps and sick –

The 100,000 infantry and mounted troops would be divided into approximately 70,000 infantry and 30,000 mounted troops; but I do not wish to go more into the details of the scheme until I can see it thoroughly worked out –

The only source of danger in this project is the possibility of a rapid concentration of the enemy at any point making it necessary to undertake operations of a larger nature than the troops of the district could safely contend within; but under present circumstances this is not a very likely contingency and there will be sufficient troops in reserve to act when necessary –

I do not estimate the boer forces now to be much over 13,000[88] – There have been a great many more killed and severely wounded in the last few months than those reported, as to present exaggeration I have been very strict in obtaining only known numbers

There is no doubt these flying columns, on extended operations in Transvaal country, only in great measure beat the air, as the mobile boers clear off the moment they hear of [a] column being sometimes 20 miles away – My project had been with the numbers of troops economical off the lines, to divide the country up into paddocks by lines of blockhouses and to restrict the area in which boers could operate.

The reduction will of course stop this plan being carried out very extensively

Cape Colony is exploiting the British tax payer to a vast extent – it is most difficult to control as G.O.C. L[ines] of C[ommunication][89] has from time to time approved of very large financial matters – I have made him now refer for approval when any large expenditure is involved, but a great deal of harm has been done, and under the head of colonial defence the Cape colonists have got their fingers into the imperial pocket and it is very difficult to get them out again – I will do the best I can – I am very glad to see in Ld Roberts telegram that you consider they should defend their own lines of railway, they have even refused to allow a reduced rate for imperial troops moving along their lines for the defence of such railways –

General [Forestier-] Walker allowed guards in Cape Colony to have Lee Metford rifles, since then they have lost a number of them to the boers with a considerable amount of ammunition, and from various sources I have heard of ammunition passing up to the O.R.C. and Transvaal from these town guards. so many boers have now got our rifles that it is of the utmost importance to safeguard all Lee Metford ammunition – I told Wynne that he must arrange for the town guards to be armed with Martini Henri rifles & I have asked for some from home for the purpose – Now I have received a protest from the Cape Ministry forwarded by the Governor[90] against changing the arms carried by town guards – I asked French what he thought and he entirely agrees with my view of the necessity of the change – I will write to the Governor and point this out

I hope you will look into the expenditure on oversea transport it seems to me enormous, but is outside my jurisdiction – I am however dealing with certain very high landing charges at the ports –

I am very grieved that we have not been able to absolutely end the war or rather the resistance to our rule which is more what is going on now than actual warfare, but I hope by the end of August we shall have rendered the resistance so that with certain safeguards it may be ignored and the industries of the country may be again safely undertaken and developed

I am again allowing a small increase of mining industry & if we can only go on gradually we shall before long have all the mines working again

The reduction of the troops will enable the railways to cope with larger civil requirements as at present we are only just able to keep the troops and existing population supplied –

I will send you a despatch next mail dated the 8th July[91] which will explain the operations that have been undertaken   I hear that the press are rather discontented at my not sending more telegrams   I always send you anything of real importance but the numerous small engagements are better I think recorded in the weekly bag of boers knocked out of action – Of course in killing and capturing boers we must have some casualties and where so many columns are engaged and so many skirmishes occur all over this vast country it would be unending if I wired you about each and give an undue importance to the operations – One thing I think I can safely claim is that the boers have had no rest for the last few months and so it will be in the future – If only I could get the Cape Colony clear I should be happy for this I rely on French –

TNA reference PRO 30/57/22/Y69

63
Lord Kitchener to Lord Roberts
[Holograph]   Commanding-in-Chief's Office.
Pretoria, 12th July 1901

I hope by this mail to send you the complete scheme of the distribution of 140,000 men – It has been rather hard work as every line of communication has had to be carefully gone through, and as far as possible reduced – I have also been trying to trace the difference in numbers shown in states as the strength of units – I feel sure there is a great leakage, owing to men being taken on extra regimental employment. We have already had orders on the subject, but they are much disregarded in the army – I am now issuing the enclosed order and intend to send a staff officer (Gaisford)[92] round to all stations to actually investigate on the spot the cases of all employed men – I am also having a complete census taken of all troops in South Africa – The AGs returns must I think be very misleading, as units very often do not know for months of men being officially struck off strength, and I suppose he does not take account of men at sea on their way home –

As regards the distribution I have calculated on holding all the country we now hold, and for having columns to strike out from the lines at any assembly of boers and keep them on the move –

For instance the Eastern line has its L[ines] of C[ommunication] troops, and depots held and in addition has three mobile columns on the line, and one at Lydenberg [Lydenburg], with 3 battalions of infantry for these columns, or for reserve troops where required – Each command thus has a certain reserve ready for action in the district or it may be used as a temporary measure outside the district, wherever boers concentrate or threaten

Cape Colony is my one sore   I am sending more troops to French and hope to swamp them out; but I hear of fresh ideas of sending more raiders down from de la Reys[93] men, I hope they will not go, but if they do I will give them a hot time of it, and follow them up the whole way –

Blood is starting one column of picked troops, to follow up the Transvaal Govt, and I have arranged that Rimington starts another from Heilbron on the 21st after de Wet –

I mean to send the Johannesburg Mounted Rifles, Kitcheners Fighting Scouts, and the 2nd ILH each separate with a free hand after de Wet, but these latter corps are just now in one of their usual transition states, when old men are going, and new have not joined, so it will be a little time before they can start –

My former tries of this nature after de Wet did not come to much, as he managed to entirely disappear taking another name – he has now however had a quiet time and has gained confidence so we may have a chance at him –

We shall never get our men British or colonial to work like the boers can in their own country, we may catch de Wet, but it will be by good information, or chance – Rimington selects his own men & runs his own intelligence –

What the boers can do in Cape Colony is amazing, constantly hassled, and followed, they seem to move about just where they like, the only thing is they do very little harm, and I believe the dutch are getting very tired of feeding them

I am trying to hold the railway line Stormberg-Rosmead, Rosmead-Na[a]uwpoort, Na[a]uwpoort-D'aar [De Aar] & make it impervious for boers, but I fear small bands will always succeed in getting through our lines at night – I have great doubts about the S.A.C. posts west of Bloemfontein stopping boers that mean to get through –

We have taken a large number of wagons, and carts, lately which interferes with their arrangements for supply –

I hope something may be done before long to bring it home to the boers, that they cannot carry on the present system of warfare with impunity – I feel sure that strong measures would soon end the war –

NAM. 1971-01-23-33-37

64
Lord Kitchener to Mr St John Brodrick

[Holograph]   Secret

Pretoria 19th July 01.

I fear you are rather
optimistic at home I
have had so many disappointments
I do not think it wise to count
on an early finish[94]

I am anxious about the state of affairs in Cape Colony. French is doing all he can, but does not make much progress – The enemy know that it is our vulnerable point where they can do us most harm and keep the sore festering and now intend to make it again the theatre of operations – The country is frightfully difficult for our troops and the assistance given everywhere to the rebels creates a very unpleasant situation – I enclose a copy of a letter I have received from the Governor on the subject, and some correspondence by telegraph that has passed between us –

I went down to see Gen. French at Middleberg [Middelburg, Cape Colony] to consult with him as to steps to be taken, and to judge of the result of the death sentences that have been confirmed – I saw a Mr de Vaal, a bond leader, and one of the principal dutch inhabitants of Middleberg[95] – he is a clever man and talks a great deal – he however said the bond had always been against rebellion, but practically admitted that now that rifles had come into the question the bond had lost all power over the people – He said if leniency was shown to those rebels that came in willingly and laid down their arms, he thought a good many would do so, and that he would do all in his power to influence them in that respect if an order was published to that effect; after consulting with French I gave him the order which I have telegraphed to you today – Amongst other things Mr de Vaal seemed to think the bond ought to have been approached about the war. I said such an idea was absurd but that I had heard criticisms in the bond for not having done their utmost to avert the present state of affairs – Both Gen. French & I gathered that the bond have now no power with the people, they have started heated feelings which have now got entirely beyond their control – I have not yet received Mr Chamberlain's telegram to which you refer, but I hope it may not be to cancel the order I thought advisable to give Gen. French, as I fear doing so would have a bad effect –

The letters found in Steyn's baggage and the correspondence with Kruger shows very clearly the state of affairs[96] – The Free Staters are evidently those that now keep the war going and I will do my best to make them regret it – At the same time I do not think we shall get an end of the war a long time yet unless we use some more pressure. I have wired you on the subject today – I hope I may be allowed to do as I suggest, it would I believe bring these people to their senses –

With reference to a previous letter to you on the subject of the danger of letting these people return, I enclose copy of a letter from Smuts to Steyn, stating if they give up now it will be with the intention of fighting again when England may be in difficulties[97] –

If Cape Colony goes on in its present state the reduction of troops as proposed will be impossible – I am sending Ld Roberts a state of effective troops now in Cape Colony and I may shortly have to send further reinforcements there as there is no doubt the boers' intention to keep on sending small parties down to swell the rebels in Cape Colony –

I fear I shall have a very bad week as many columns have come in to refit & restart out again –

I asked Steyn's Secretary[98] about de Wet's murder of Morgenda[a]l; it took place practically as reported, they look on it as a case of manslaughter, which it will probably turn out to be as there was a good deal of excitement at the time due to the approach of one of our columns and there does not appear to have been a deliberate intention of murdering Morgenda[a]l[99] –

TNA reference PRO 30/57/22/Y74

65
Lord Kitchener to Mr St John Brodrick

[Holograph]
Pretoria
26[th] July 01.

I send you by this mail a report on my action regarding my proposed notice that Cape Colony rebels who surrendered willingly would not be awarded more than one years imprisonment if tried under Martial Law, and all telegrams that have passed on the subject –

In dealing with this matter I have been guided by Solomon's advice and it has been a rather severe blow to us to be thrown over particularly as the Cape Colony sentences for Treason in their own courts are much less severe than what we proposed to give – However as Mr Chamberlain evidently considers the matter political, though for the life of me I cannot see why – I thought it better to drop the matter – It comes to this, I commute sentences in martial law cases that come before me under certain circumstances to a years imprisonment on Solomons advice; if however I let this be known with a view of helping to end the war, it becomes a political question –

Of course all cases tried under martial law will come before the Cape Legislature to be confirmed or revised when the war is over, When however that happens we shall have achieved our main object, and from a military point of view it is quite immaterial if cases condemned under martial law are maintained or not –

We tried to the best of our endeavours to use the powers given us under martial law to bring about the early end of the war, and it seems to me a grave responsibility to stay the hands of the military authorities on the spot for some political reason –

I am not at all sure that some Cape Colony officials are very anxious to stop the war; they have got their hands well into the Imperial money bags and while present operations are going on it is very difficult to get them out – Notwithstanding this I was certainly much surprised, considering that the sentences given by the civil courts in Cape Colony for Treason have been far more lenient than a years imprisonment, though the rebel had to be caught, at their now recorded opinion, that only in cases of surrender, the extreme penalty should be commuted; if carried out this would mean that we ought to hang wholesale batches of 30 or 40 as we catch them – I am sure anything of that sort would never do and I do not feel prepared to carry out such drastic measures –

If my confirming powers in cases brought before me are not properly used, I should be glad if you would let me know – Solomon, St. Clair,[100] Kelly[101] & myself read the cases, and then meet when after discussion if necessary confirmation is finally decided on and recorded –

I must say I feel rather hurt at the manner in which this matter has been dealt with, but I do not wish to trouble you with my personal feelings – I certainly thought it was within my power to publish, if I thought it advisable, what I intended to do as confirming officer – As you know the same course is frequently followed as a warning or otherwise; now I have had to correct my order on the subject and this naturally weakens my position out here –

I hope you will give the matter your consideration as hampered in this way I do not know what I can, or cannot do to bring the present state of hostilities in Cape Colony to a rapid end and until that is achieved the wishes of the Govt for the reduction of troops and consequent expenditure must I fear remain in abeyance[102] – I presume you will communicate my report to Mr [Joseph] Chamberlain –

I am glad to say surrenders are again on the increase and there is every sign of exhaustion amongst the enemy, but it is weary work, and as they get less it becomes more difficult to find and catch them – I am glad to get a telegram from Milner which looks as if something would be done, if we could bluff them a little the end would come –

I am sending you by this mail a number of reports on refugee camps – Dr Kendal Franks' report[103] should be of value – We are doing all we possibly can for the inmates but it is impossible to fight against the criminal neglect of the mothers – I do not like the idea of using force which Dr Franks recommends but I am considering whether some of the worst cases could not be tried for manslaughter – How I wish I could get rid of them and I daresay you do also –

I hope sufficient information is being sent you on the subject of these camps   we do our best to meet all requirements   I hear the request for information about the numbers of children born caused rather a flutter as some ladies had been an inconvenient time separated from their husbands –

The governor of Natal[104] has sent me as H[igh] C[ommisioner][105] a long document from his ministers about some severe measures that they would like to see adopted: no doubt the idea must have come from here – It is very difficult to keep anything secret but I do not think much gets out from Hd Qts

P.S. I am doing my utmost as regards Cape Colony   also special mounted corps with a definite objective – I fear there may be some trouble about the executions in Cape Colony. I left the carrying out of the sentences to the discretion of Gen. French Com[man]ding in Cape Colony. On hearing however that there was some feeling on the subject I at once issued instructions that the sentences should be carried out as quietly as possible   officials only being present – When two prisoners were quietly executed here in gaol the dutch people refused absolutely to believe they had been executed and insisted they had been quietly removed.

TNA reference PRO 30/57/22/Y77

66
Lord Kitchener to Lord Roberts

[Holograph]   Pretoria
9th Aug[us]t [1901]

The articles in the Daily Mail will do a great deal of harm out here, as anything of the sort the boers can get hold of, they use with great effect in keeping their dissatisfied men in the field

I have little doubt those articles will prolong the war by I should say three weeks or a month – It is very sad to see that England has so little patience – The people stood the dark days out here with great credit; but they seem now unable to realize the immense amount of work that has to be done to finish the business – It is not now a case of stirring warfare, but steady hard work catching every man and thoroughly clearing the country –

These ebulliences of impatience and keen attempts to exaggerate atrocities only play into the hands of our enemies, and prolong the war, which we all want so much to end quickly –

If only the english [sic] press would treat us as a matter of small moment, and not use so many highflown adjectives, and make so much of every little skirmish, we should be able to end the war much sooner out here – I wish you could let them know this   These conceited boers are delighted to have so much fuss made about them and consider themselves quite hero[e]s when they see their deeds exaggerated and made much of in our press –

You must remember they get the English papers almost as soon as I do –

The new proclamation is out[106]   I fear it is not strong enough The boers will not believe in banishment as they feel sure a change of Govt would bring them all back again – Confiscation is the only thing that will touch them – I quite understand that confiscation is repugnant to British lawyers, but in this war we had to do much that is repugnant to us all, and where the loss of many valuable lives and destruction of property can be avoided, I should [have] thought the Govt would have taken the only really effective course to stop the war –

It looks very much as if old Kruger was spending a good deal of money on the English press, & I should not be surprised if he was following Rhodes' plan of subscribing to the Irish cause to get what he wants out of the English people –

All this agitation and lies about the refugee camps seems to me to come from ..... from Holland –

When Lyttelton arrives he will be able to replace Hildyard in Natal as the latter will want leave and may accept the Australian office[107] – Rundle will also require a change, and I am trying to get some of his battalions away so as to gradually get troops into the new distribution – I think he better go home and I shall not require him out again[108]

The King telegraphed to me about Paget coming out again[109] so I presume he will be starting at once & if you send me Oliphant I will return Bar Campbell or Inigo Jones into store[110] – I have given Tullibardine local rank of Lt Col his name has been very useful[111] –

I am going down to Natal in a day or two to meet H.R.H. and have arranged for him to present some VCs and DSOs.[112]

I shall not trouble Mr Brodrick with a letter in this mail   I have nothing of importance to tell him and he must still be suffering a great deal[113] –

P.S.[114] I have had two good days: yesterday 103 today up to 4 pm 104 killed and prisoner[115]   If I could only keep this up it would soon be over

NAM. 1971-01-23-33-41

67
Lord Kitchener to King Edward VII

[Manuscript]   Pretoria
16th Aug[u]st 1901

Lord Kitchener presents his humble duty to Your Majesty, and begs to inform Your Majesty that he had the honour to meet their Royal Highnesses the Duke and Duchess of Cornwall and York at

Pietermaritzburg – Although His Royal Highness looked rather thin both Their Royal Highnesses appeared to be in excellent health and not over fatigued by the hard work they have had to perform during their extended tour – The visit of Their Royal Highnesses to Natal has been a great success, and will have an excellent effect on the loyal inhabitants of that colony; they were everywhere received with the utmost enthusiasm[116] –

His Royal Highness decorated nine officers and N.C.O.s with the V.C.[117] and 51 officers received the D.S.O. from the hands of His Royal Highness on a parade of the 2nd battalion Scots Guards, a detachment of the Cameron Highlanders, and a large force of Natal Volunteers and cadets.

The services of the recipients of the V.C. were read out on parade – Subsequently the Zulu chiefs and natives of Natal presented an address to which His Royal Highness replied –

Your Majesty's Army in South Africa is in excellent health and spirits and Lord Kitchener cannot speak too highly of the splendid manner in which both Officers and men carry out the difficult task now before them in order to bring the war to an end –

The enemy are in scattered parties of from 30 to 200 over an immense area, and sometimes in most difficult country, with which they are naturally thoroughly acquainted these have to be captured by Your Majestys troops – They have excellent scouts and information and generally move away rapidly before our columns can get within 20 miles of them – At the same time if they get a chance at a weak party unsupported, or by any carelessness on our part, they take immmediate advantage of it – Long railway lines have also to be thoroughly protected by the troops, and this is done by a system of blockhouses 1600 yds apart, with men lying out at night between each blockhouse – There are now over 1500 blockhouses in the Transvaal and Orange River Colony for the protection of railways besides 61 mobile columns scouring the country in every direction, some of these columns are specially fitted out to travel light and fast and have the boer leaders as their objective –

The recent proclamation has been issued but the effect is not yet known,[118] the general opinion appears to be that without confiscation of property the proclamation will hardly end the war, as the boers do not believe in their banishment being permanent should there be a change in Your Majestys Government –

From all accounts it does not seem possible that the boers can resist much longer, their food, ammunition, transport, and horses, are almost exhausted

The monument on the grave of His Highness Prince Christian Victor has been erected here in the cemetery and is being well cared for.[119]

All arrangements have been made at Cape Town for their Royal Highnesses' reception and a detachment of the 2nd Battalion Royal Fusiliers will form the guard of honour there –

Lord Kitchener hopes that Your Majesty and Her Majesty the Queen[120] are in perfect health, and begs to humbly assure Your Majesties of the deep sympathy felt by everyone here in your recent loss[121] –

RA W60/130

68
Lord Kitchener to Lord Roberts

[Holograph] Pretoria
23[rd] Aug[u]st 01

I am very puzzled about the Generals and staff – As long as the War lasts though the troops may be reduced to 140,000 from the present 189000 out here I do not see how I can spare many valuable generals or staff officers – I shall lose Blood   Elliot and Beatson, and presume I may get Lyttelton, Paget, Little[122] and perhaps Oliphant –

Hildyard will evidently have to go home for a rest, he is quite worn out. I was quite shocked to see him lately at Pietermaritzburg looking so ill and weak –

I could also send home Barton, Hart, M Willson, Cooper[123] from Heidelberg, B Campbell, Babington and Brigs Gens Barker & Cunningham – I do not see how I can send any other Generals as we shall want to still push the war on vigorously and the number of columns in the field will not be very greatly altered except in Cape Colony – I am very glad you gave your opinion that the reduction should not take place until Cape Colony is clear. I have always based my calculations on that contingency; and, as almost all the militia that would have to go home are in Cape Colony, if I had to replace them by troops from other places I should be very pressed to hold the railway lines in the O.R.C. and Transvaal – A certain amount of Artillery could be spared without waiting for Cape Colony to be clear as I have already informed you –

If you mean at the end of the war what Generals and staff officers will be available, then no doubt there will be a large number – One of the advantages of fighting this struggle out to the bitter end, as the boers seem determined to do, is that we shall require fewer troops to garrison the country when the war is over – I am sending you enclosed a list of the Generals that would be then required but even this may be reduced when we see how things go at the end of the war –

As regards staff officers so many required change and have already dropped out from various causes that we have found some difficulty in meeting our requirements out here – so that until the war is over I do not see how we can spare many – Of course when the war is over a considerable number will be available to fill staff billets at home

India has been now for nearly two years without five British cavalry regts   Would it not be as well to permanently reduce the normal garrison of India by two British cavalry regts and allow them to at once increase their native cavalry by four regiments which would probably be equivalent in the nature of cost – We should then only have to send three cavalry regts from here to India – I believe there would be no difficulty in India finding men and raising these requirements in a very short time –

Our extra mobile corps (I prefer that title to the Corps d'Elite as it creates less jealousy) have been long marched and covered a lot of ground but have not yet hit on their objective. As far as I can see Rimington is the best of them – Spens is a great improvement on Bullock and I am glad I made the change –

I am concentrating the 1st & 2nd I.L.H. together at Bethlehem under Dartnell[124] as another extra mobile column to search for de Wet & Steyn. I hope they will have some success as Rimington & Spens are pretty sure to drive the quarry south of the Lindley Reitz district[125] –

I wish the Cape Colony Government would do a little more to help. They might do a great deal and I cannot understand why it is they take up a line of more obstruction than help. I sent down Solomon to see them but he wires me he has had no success. I hope when Milner arrives he will have more influence with the Cape Colony Govt – Hely Hutchinson has done his best[126] but is evidently not equal to dealing with them – It is not the loyal Cape Colonists but the Govt under Sir G. Sprigg that seem to be the obstructionists[127] –

I am afraid there is not much chance of the boers giving in on the last proclamation. They are quite impossible people to deal with and the only way will be to wear them out by continually catching their men and rendering the country uninhabitable – It is weary work but patience will eventually end the war; I do not see how anything else will do it – I look more to the numbers we kill or capture than to anything else –

I am reducing the size of columns and doing my utmost to increase their mobility   long marches are necessary now to catch boers –

Methuen has just come here to stay the night with me   his column is at Klerksdorp   he is looking very well and tells me his Yeomanry have greatly improved   I am arranging with him further moves at De la Rey

I fear we shall not have much of a bag this week   so many columns are watching the Cape frontier that they are not available for catching boers –

With kind regards to Lady Roberts and your daughters –

NAM. 1971-01-23-33-43

69
Lord Kitchener to Mr St John Brodrick

[Holograph] Pretoria 30th August 01

I am sending you the first monthly despatch by this mail,[128] I am sorry it was not got off sooner but your request to send more frequent despatches only reached me the last mail, and I could not get the despatch written in time. Next despatch will be more up to date, as I am already at work at it – I am in great hopes of getting a more satisfactory financial arrangement with the Cape Colony regarding colonial defence expenditure   The negotiations have been most difficult with the Cape Government, but the Governor has been very helpful and I hope before long we may have a proper financial basis to work on –

I have done all I can to render all columns more mobile, and I think the distances they travel (50 or 60 miles is quite an ordinary trek, hard as they can go, to catch 20 boers) proves that considerable improvement in that respect has been made – I have also tried to get picked men for extra mobile columns with a definite objective and a free hand to follow up leads anywhere – It is found that definite corps or regiments are better for this work than mixed forces and the term Corps d'Elite is not liked as it creates jealousy – All are doing their best, some to the flyers, others to feed and play up to the flyers – In some parts it is rather nervous work sending out these men without equipment for long treks, as the boers are very quick at concentration, and getting back is not always easy. 200 boers on a strong position are very difficult sometimes to get out – From the boers own account we are giving them a bad time of it, and they have to keep on the move all night – I have just heard of de Wet and Steyn again, as we had lost them for some time. If the intelligence is correct Elliot is beautifully placed, but of course you will have heard of this by telegram if anything happens. I hope and trust we may have a coup[129] –

My weekly bag will not be as large this week as I have had to throw out a number of columns from the task of catching boers to prevent Kritzinger and Smuts, with some Transvaalers getting back into Cape Colony – Up to the present they have not been able to penetrate our line, but it is a long one to guard & I am always afraid of their making a dash through[130] –

French is having hard work in Cape Colony, he has got plenty of men but the difficulty of catching these small scattered roving bands is very great in a country where everyone outside the towns actively assists the enemy –

I am sending you the correspondence with the boer leaders,[131] and a memo from Blood on his conversation with B Viljoen about which I wired you.

I have not seen Milner yet, as he is delaying in Cape town. I am anxious to meet him and hear what he has got to say about the impressions on the war at home – I intend to propose to him that the civil administration should take over the entire management of recovery of funds expended on refugee camps by public sale of farms, under the proclamation; I hope he will agree to this –

I am letting up some more people to Johannesburg owing to increased safety of railway lines, and am opening more mines there.

After the 15th Sept[132] we shall be able to get rid of some very unpleasant and dangerous people still out on commando When we catch them – It will be a great help to Milner in future administration

TNA reference PRO 30/57/22/Y82(a)

70
Lieutenant-General Bindon Blood to Lord Kitchener
[Holograph]   M' Burg [Middelburg, Transvaal]
11.9.1901.

Walter[133] started on the evening of the 8th but I fear missed his way and got bogged. I have had no satisfactory news from him yet (11 a.m.). Campbell[134] started with this convoy of his own and Walter's columns on the morning of the 9th, and is moving along the Wonderfontein-Ermelo road – probably today at Smutsoog 143. Benson started last night with Sampson and all available mounted men to round up Pullenshope 213 and De Groot Rietpan 231, where bags are hoped for.[135] No news yet. His convoy started this morning. Lieut Malan Staats Artillery[136] and P.S. W Viljoen came here yesterday. I took him to the Boer Refugee Camp[137] this morning and he saw the whole of the arrangements, and talked to a number of women. Afterwards he told us all that the women said they were all right – but that the meat given them was poor. But we are all complaining of that. Malan told us openly that there were no complaints, and that the women seemed quite contented. Montagu[e] Bell,[138] who takes this to you was present when Malan rode round with me, and can tell you all about it. It strikes me that this may be useful as a counterblast to the pro-Boers. Malan tells me that Viljoen has written to Botha about peace and expects to meet him in a few days – which does not look as if Botha were south. I send you a letter herewith from Viljoen. Malan goes in about an hour, and if anything further of interest transpires, I will write again –

NAM. 1971-01-23-33-47

71

Lord Kitchener to Mr St John Broderick

[Holograph]   Pretoria. 13th Sept 1901.
Private

There is not much change in the situation out here – We are constantly reducing the enemy forces, and they are becoming more and more discontented with their leaders; but I fear the war will go on until we reduce their numbers to a very small residue – I am glad to say our <u>bag</u>!!! [sic] has not fallen off as rather expected it would – Considerable areas are being entirely cleared and kept clear of boers & this makes them thicker in the positions they still occupy so that our columns get at them almost better than they did before as boers are forced out of their own country and hiding places – This process is naturally a very long one, and takes up a large number of troops, but satisfactory progress has been made and the results are rather better than I anticipated –

153

We are still doing all we can to catch Steyn and de Wet and some more columns will shortly be available to fill up gaps and work the country he is in thoroughly

Botha has been lately threatening to invade Natal   he might possibly get 1000 men together for a raid, but I do not think now it will come off, all precautions have been taken and Lyttelton will soon take action against the concentration in the Piet Retief district[139] –

We are also doing all we can to prevent boers slipping through into Cape Colony, with such a large extent of wild country this is not easy – You will see from enclosed morning report what the blockhouse lines do in this respect –

I have no doubt you must be very anxious about the reduction of forces and of expenditure – I am doing all I can to send home as many men as possible particularly the 5/- a day men. Another battalion of militia is leaving very shortly for England, and as I have before informed you there is some artillery ready to go but sending you regular troops will not cause such a reduction of expenditure as getting rid of irregulars altogether and this I am doing as much as I can – A great difficulty in carrying out these reductions is the impossible ministry now at Cape town – They will do nothing and obstruct in every possible way – Milner and Hely Hutchinson are equally powerless to deal with them or even to influence them to more sensible courses – Can nothing be done from home to coerce them as they are costing the Imperial Govt vast sums, and greatly assisting our enemies – While the present state of things lasts in Cape Colony I do not see how I can carry out any more reductions of troops –

If only the Prime minister in Cape Colony[140] were changed something might be done, but everyone agrees that under the present regime no arguments, no imploring, nothing is of the least use – A weak conceited individual upsets all necessary action – It is very hard on His Majestys troops that this state of things should be allowed to continue and it causes a great deal of feeling throughout the Army particularly amongst the S.A. Colonial forces

I have had a talk with Milner on the subject and we decided the best way was to wire and ask Sir G. Sprigg to come up and see us;

but we have very little hope that the result will be satisfactory – In the mean time the enemy are obtaining ammunition and recruits from Cape Colony to carry on the war –

I enclose correspondence about Martial Law in Cape Ports which shows the attitude taken up by the Cape Government – It is nothing less than one of actual hostility to HMs forces & the same is going on throughout the Colony –

I have asked Milner to take over under the civil administration all sales of property under the proclamation and this he will do and is getting out a proclamation on the subject I fear Mr Chamberlain's interpretation of the selling clauses will take away greatly from the strength of the proclamation and be considered a great sign of weakness in carrying it out as it has not been so understood here – Leaders will I fear now escape with all their property –

A Revnd Mr Murray from Cape Colony has been out to see Steyn and de Wet at his own request[141] the latter treated him rather badly but Steyn appears to have discussed matters freely they were both quite irreconcilable and said they meant to carry on the war as they felt sure from the information they had that England could not long stand the financial strain of the war and would have to make terms They intended to continue to send raiding parties into Cape Colony so as to divide our forces and if the Africanders of the O.R.C. were ruined and had to give in they hoped the Africanders of Cape Colony would also share the same fate – Mr Murray was much disgusted with them –

I am sending you a despatch[142] by this mail I very much wish we could do more but I feel sure you will give us credit for doing all we possibly can – The troops are wonderfully fit and well & are never better than when out on the trek – A King's Medal would put fresh life into them and they really well deserve it – Day after day they are at it and I never hear a grumble I cannot speak too highly of the tone of the Army all through –

I enclose a letter[143] caught on a despatch rider from Gen Liebenberg[144] to Gen De la Rey which shows the trash by means of which the burghers are kept in the field –

TNA reference PRO 30/57/22/Y85

72
Lord Kitchener to Mr St John Brodrick

[Holograph] Pretoria 20[th] Sept 01.

I very much regret three unpleasant occur[r]ences coming one after the other – Gough's affair might happen to anyone he fell into a carefully prepared trap in very difficult ground – The bait was 200 men of enemy off saddled and the whole force of enemy were carefully concealed[145] –

The squadron 17[th] Lancers in Cape Colony severely mauled by Smuts' commando fought well – the boers were surrounded and determined at all cost to get through, which they did with severe loss – The only mistake was that the boers being dressed in khaki were allowed to get to close quarters before they were fired on[146] –

The loss of 2 guns and a company of M.I. south of the Waterworks near Bloemfontein is quite the worst thing I know of and is now under investigation. The force was sent out without Gen. Tucker's knowledge and of course should never have gone – It was as good as giving the time and place away[147] –

We shall do all we can to retrieve these unpleasant affairs and I hope you will consider that we have been a long time clear of anything of the sort – Three coming so close one after another is somewhat trying –

I enclose copies of telegrams that have passed between Governor and myself about martial law. I only addressed one telegram to the Admiral of which also a copy is enclosed. My ADC however sent a wire to General Wynne's A.D.C. asking him to arrange for my mails to be brought up from Durban should the mail steamer be sent there – This was after my telegram to the Govr no. 7407 asking ministers to decide in time for me to take action regarding the mail – From the A.D.C's telegram the idea was started in Cape Town that I had interfered with mail steamers which I had not in any way attempted to do –

I enclose a letter from Wynne on the difficulties that are being experienced with the Attorney General. Until the arrival of Rose Innes there was peace between the civil and military in Cape Colony[148] – He immediately began a campaign – Luckily I had

Solomon here, late Attorney General, to whom I handed over the case and they have been hammering away at each other until Solomon became exhausted and tells me he thinks Innes is off his head – Milner will I understand get Innes out of Cape Town as soon as possible on the pretext of making rules for the High Court here – We shall then I hope have peace again, but the damage done will I fear be far reaching in Cape Colony – Martial law is always a difficulty but it is rendered ten times more so if every unfounded complaint is taken up by an irresponsible official. I wonder how Innes would like us to criticize his legal proceedings   I fear they would not come out very well –

It is a great pity that the Cape Govt have taken up the present line: of course they feel that after the war is over they will score in votes, and that whatever their personal feelings may be they cannot afford to lose votes by acting in such a way as might bring the war to a more rapid conclusion – Natal certainly sets them an example; martial law is exactly the same there but it is rather popular, as was shown in a recent debate in their House.

I leave all questions of martial law in Cape Colony to Gen Wynne who I think acts with discretion and tact in a very difficult position; he has to face a violent attack with a very weak Governor to back him –

I suppose the present state of affairs will be all over before this reaches you but I feel sure you can understand how worrying & unpleasant it is to be mixed up with such political affairs when I have 64 mobile columns to attend to –

I wish very much we could do better towards bringing the war to an end, but I fear we shall have to go on until we so reduce the enemy in numbers that they cannot show anywhere – This of course must take time and patience but it is apparently the only solution –

TNA reference PRO 30/57/22/Y88

73
Lord Kitchener to Mr St John Brodrick

[Holograph]   Pretoria 27th Sept. 01.

Having failed to get into Natal across the Buffalo River, Botha is apparently making a dash for Zululand at Melmoth – Itala post has been attacked, but held out though I fear they have had a good many casualties, of which I have no details yet[149] – A column is following the boers and the drifts on the Tugela are held – I hope they will not be able to get into Natal – These raiding parties are very bold and it is difficult to block every place they can get through – Lyttelton is directing operations and he has 20,000 men so there ought not to be much anxiety, unfortunately my experience of the number of times what ought to be, does not come off, makes me feel somewhat uncertain as to the result. Luckily I had brought Elliott's division to Harrismith so they will be available to train down to Natal in case of necessity

All this rather upsets my arrangements for catching boers and I fear the bag will suffer and consequently the time necessary to end the war; nothing else seems to have a certain result on the resistance of the enemy, but the weekly drain must tell, and already some commando's are either reduced to impotence or wiped out altogether and a large tract of country is entirely in our hands and clear of boers –

A court of inquiry is sitting   Major Fraser[150] who sent out the party from the waterworks – It is rather hard when one is trying all one can to give the enemy as little chance as possible, to be given away in this way – I fear Lovat's Scouts sat down too long in one place without making it sufficiently strong; the boers knew exactly how and where to attack and brought off a night attack[151] very much the same as we give them almost every night somewhere in the country[152] – As a rule boers do not dare to do this unless they have had plenty of time to thoroughly reconnoitre our position & know its strength accurately –

I am afraid such affairs are inevitable   do what one can to avoid it, and extremely unpleasant as they are, they do not in any important degree change the situation –

I have done nothing more regarding the Cape Govt – I hear that the Prime Minister and Attorney General are coming up to Johannesburg where I shall see them, in the meantime all sorts of assistance to the enemy is pouring in through Cape ports, and the state of affairs in Cape Colony is if anything growing worse – French and Wynne both do their utmost, but with a country in active sympathy with the marauders, the 28,000 troops in Cape Colony find it most difficult to keep the rebellion under – Kritzinger has not yet got back, but I am in daily fear he will evade us somehow and succeed in doing so[153] –

I am sending you by this mail some boer correspondence; I should like you to look at my reply to Schalk Burgher as you might possibly think it a good thing to publish it in England – Schalk Burgher's letter would want a good deal of cutting down if it were published. I am having my reply and the list of banished leaders scattered about the country and have sent copies to the principal leaders –

Milner & I have a special telephone wire between our houses on which we converse on all subjects –

I wish I could reduce expenditure more, but it is no easy task and the biggest reduction which I have in view, by an arrangement with Cape Colony, to take over local defence forces, is always being postponed by the unpracticability of getting the Cape ministers to agree to anything, however I hope now they are coming up that we shall at last get it settled

TNA reference PRO 30/57/22/Y90

74
Lord Kitchener to Lady Ilchester

[Holograph]   Pretoria
                                                               4th Oct 01

I am so glad to be able to congratulate you on your engagement   I wish you every joy and though rather filled with envy of the lucky one I hope when I get back I may have the pleasure of seeing you again.

I cannot get these boers to give in   their resistance is quite hopeless & their efforts are absolutely useless but still they stick out hoping for something to turn up   principally a change of Government in England which they hope would give them back their independence –

Plenty of hard work as we have to catch everyone of them & it is no easy business as they are very sly and cute –

I am so glad you are quite happy

BL MS Room, Holland House Papers, Add MS 51370

75
Lord Kitchener to Mr St John Brodrick

[Holograph]   11th Oct. 01.

Martial law has been proclaimed in Cape ports[154] so I hope we shall prevent the enemy getting further assistance from that source – The very fact of there being martial law will make shippers very careful about what they bring out and even if we catch nothing I expect the importation will cease as soon as they hear of martial law.

I am sorry the word "bag" slipped into a telegram, it seems to have caused some excitement amongst the proboer press –

Botha has got into some trouble by his intended raid on Natal and is still in a difficult position but I fear he will escape as there is still a way out – You will have had the result by telegraph before you get this[155] –

Our bags have fallen off considerably I am sorry to say; but the move of so many troops to Natal, and a large number being taken up in preventing Kritzinger getting back into Cape Colony, rendered this result inevitable – I have not taken any credit for boer losses at Itala[156] and Prospect,[157] which were undoubtedly severe, but have not been definitely proved –

I enclose a tracing which if you put on a Jeppe map[158] will show you the country in which there are now no boers, owing to our lines of blockhouses – I find this is the only way of making the country actually ours, for even if the boers break through our lines in small parties, they are so chased and find no food or help that they have to surrender –

I am anxious to send away such women as Mrs Smuts,[159] Mrs Steyn[160] and others whose husbands will be banished when caught, they do a lot of harm here, and I think Kruger should keep them as he promised the burghers he would do – I think these women should be merely deported from South Africa, to go where they like – Mrs Smuts from Natal certainly gave Botha information, and I think if they were removed the Boers would begin to believe that we intended to carry out the proclamation which they do not at present –

Milner has been staying with me for the last few days, we are getting on with more mines and more refugees returning to Johannesburg, and I think he is satisfied that everything possible is being done. It could be very rash to go too fast & have to send people away again & close mines –

We are having very wet weather which retards all moves, and the rinderpest amongst the cattle is a serious matter,[161] we are inoculating everywhere, and I hope shall not lose many; but it throws the oxen out of work for a time –

I wish I could give you a date when we could finish the war, but though steady progress has been made, I cannot say when it will end – Fighting to a finish in this country and with these people, means extermination and is a long and very trying business. We are all doing our best, & the troops are fit and well; but there is no doubt it must take time, and I cannot see how to hasten the end with the troops I have – I fear you must be anxious about money I am doing all I can to cut down expenditure out here – Could not something more be done at home in this respect –

TNA reference PRO 30/57/22/Y94

76
Lord Kitchener to Mr St John Brodrick

[Holograph]   Pretoria
18th Oct 01.

Botha has escaped from Natal by passing through Swaziland. I am sorry we were not able to stop him but I think he has lost considerably both in prestige as a leader, and materially in the numbers of wounded and loss of transport – Lyttelton did all he could I think, but bad weather made the movement of troops very slow, and enabled the boers to get away by abandoning their transport –

There is no doubt the boers are depressed by the result of the Natal enterprise and the failure of the attack on Kekewich's camp;[162] but they seem as fanatically disposed to continue the war as ever, and I fear it can only end by our catching all or almost all of them – It is hard work for our men and horses, and must take a considerable time. I think you ought to be prepared for this –

If you think that someone else could do better out here, I hope you will not hesitate for a moment in replacing me. I try all I can but it is not like the Soudan and disappointments are frequent – You must remember that as we go on catching boers, we weed them out, and the residue left in the field are generally their best men and therefore more difficult to deal with –

The state of affairs in Cape Colony has improved, and French has got a good grip of the commandos still moving about – I do not attach any great importance to the Western move South, they will soon be driven back again and the country round Calvinia cannot support any large bodies of the enemy[163] – The colonial local forces have I am sorry to say again distinguished themselves by disgracefully giving in without fighting, and thus enabling the boers to refit themselves with horses and ammunition[164] –

It is most annoying when local troops behave in this way – I hope martial law in the Cape ports will do a lot of good, everything is apparantly working smoothly at Cape town & I do not anticipate any trouble there – I hope soon to get the definite arrangement about payment of local forces settled, but any work with people like the Cape ministry takes an enormous amount of time and labour to bring about any definite result. Armstrong who is acting as my financial adviser has gone to Cape town to see about it, and I have also seen Colonel Crewe who will I expect replace Gen Brabant at Cape town, the latter is quite incompetent and has muddled the colonial forces terribly, but I hope they will now be placed on a practical footing –

P.S. I am sending you a monthly despatch[165] by this mail

TNA reference PRO 30/57/22/Y95

77
Lord Kitchener to Lord Roberts

[Holograph]   Pretoria 1st Nov[em]b[e]r 01.

I am very much upset at this most sad affair of Benson's column, I have just heard that he has died of his wounds; but I can hardly believe it as last night he was reported wounded but not severely – The casualty list is very heavy   9 officers and 54 men killed – The enemy got close up to the rearguard in heavy mist and fog and were at first taken for their own people – I have no details of the fighting yet but you will have had all the details before you get this by wire[166] –

What can one do to prevent these sort of occur[r]ences, Benson was one of the best commanders, knew the country, and had an excellent intelligence, his column was extremely efficient and they were not more than 20 miles outside our line of posts – There was bad luck in the matter, When Botha escaped through Swazi land to Amsterdam, I sent Rawlinson and Rimington combined at him between Ermelo and Amsterdam – They very nearly got him and captured his papers[167] –

My instructions were after clearing Botha to move west through Ermelo, and drive any boers between Ermelo and Bethal on to Benson who would be at Trichardts fontein – Unfortunately they found amongst Botha's papers an order to Opperman[168] who was south of them in the Elandsberg and Randberg to at once attack the new blockhouse line between Wakkerstroom and Piet Retief, they therefore decided on going for Opperman and asked Plumer to cooperate. Botha must have at once collected all his men and gone for Benson with the sad result you know –

The boers have become so aggressive that [it] is evident I shall have to strengthen columns and work them more together and the greatest care must be taken.

If I had not sent so many men to Natal, where I thought we were bound to catch Botha's concentrated force, I would have had more working with Benson in that area but still he might have been quite safe as it was –

I see the papers say I am not much good as a strategist – I try to do the best I can, I enclose my project for the North Eastern portion of the O.R.C.[169] – By moving columns in a zigzag way boers are much puzzled and lose sight of our objective – I planned out the different moves after consultation with boer prisoners taken in the neighbourhoods, inside the circle is the rendezvous and principal source of supply of the boers of the whole neighbourhood –

Can you get anyone to do it better, if so please do not hesitate – A new man at the head might evolve some new ideas for finishing the war – I try my best I am afraid it is not much – Would a considerable increase to the troops finish it? It would I think hasten the end but not finish it for some time – Since Benson's affair I am inclined to ask for more troops – You are sending me two cavalry regts; but if I send two on from here to India I am only in the same state as before – I do not think I should say I will do this until the time comes, and the state of affairs at that time is known, It may be improved if so, I should be glad to help –

I have just seen my brother[170] he absolutely declines to go on leave until the war is over – I cannot help thinking it would be better for him to go as he has been at it from the first, but as he seems fairly well I do not see that I should insist on his going, so please cancel what I said on the subject last mail –

164

[Postscript]

This policy of the boers is greatly due to the row in the English press about Vlakfontein,[171] they think by attacking columns violently under cover of some advantage they will tire the British public of the war and gain their ends – Delarey [De la Rey] stated this idea and I suppose has communicated it to Botha above from prisoners

NAM. 1971-01-23-33-55

78
Lord Kitchener to Mr St John Brodrick

[Holograph]   8th Nov[em]ber 1901

I am very pleased at the prospect of getting Hamilton as Chief of the staff.[172] I often thought of appointing one out here and I tried Lyttelton for a short time – Hamilton will I am sure do the work extremely well and relieve me of a good deal of worry, besides I shall be able to get away much more and see column commanders personally

The article in the Spectator of which kind friends sent me 13 copies as well as the comments in the papers on the war naturally led to the conclusion that I would shortly be removed from this command – I do not think anyone was to blame that the report was widely spread through the army –

The papers do a great deal towards keeping the war going – Steyn and Botha get all the papers almost as soon as I do, and they extract choice articles for the boers – If the press really wished the war to end they might I think stop the present system of urging the disheartened boers to still stick it out by pointing out how tired we are of the war and what sacrifices it is costing us –

Our weekly captures show how we are bringing them down, but the most advantage we ought to obtain by so constantly defeating them is robbed from us by our own press –

We might possibly make more of our constant successful skirmishes resulting in captures, but I do not think it is a good thing for the army to glorify engagements that do not result in a definite step towards the end of the war – At the same time if the reverses the boers suffer continually were ours instead of theirs what a row the press would make about them[173] –

There is no doubt the boers are becoming desperate and we must expect severe fighting; when you have to kill a wild cat in a room there is generally a good deal of damage done –

I hope by vigilance to take full advantage of the present tendency of the boers and I hope that when they see how useless their struggles are, the depression that will follow may lead to good results, if only you can keep the English press from giving them heart again, and thus enabling their leaders to keep them together –

I wish I could find out some way of finishing the war; but it is really most difficult – We do all we can to capture the leaders but they are too well guarded to get them by surprise, and concentration of columns find no one – It is really most disheartening, but by steady perseverance we must get them in time – I wish those that say the war ought to be over would come out and show us how to do it –

I enclose some more of the Botha correspondence taken by Rimington – Milner asked me about Miss Hobhouse[174] being allowed to land at Cape Town and we agreed that considering the attitude she had taken up and the untruths she had published, that it would not be desirable in the present state of the colony to allow her to do so. I enclose copies of the letters on the subject to Milner and myself – I daresay if they were published in the press it might give the public a clearer insight into the sort of lady? [sic] she is[175] –

Our captures this week are not good – The columns have been refitting after the Natal operations and are only just at work again now. Oh for a little luck but I never get any –

I was much obliged for your kind telegram saying the government still had confidence in me, I must say I should not have been surprised if my failure to bring the war to an end had induced the Govt to come to a decision that a change was advisable – We have all done our best and mean to stick to it and see this war through & I sincerely hope it will not be long before we see the end, no effort shall be spared to bring that about as soon as possible

TNA reference PRO 30/57/22/Y101

79
Lord Kitchener to Lord Roberts

[Holograph]   8th Nov. 01

It is very good of you to let me have Johnnie Hamilton, nothing could suit me better. he is just the man I want – The war has been going on so long that I sometimes have qualms as to whether I am doing all that possibly could be done with the means at my disposal – I shall be able to discuss it with Hamilton and he will either suggest something or I shall be reassured –

I am kept pretty hard at it for 14 hours every day and it is beginning to tell, Hamilton will relieve me of a lot of work – I do not mean to suggest that my present staff do not do every thing possible to relieve me of work or worry, I cannot really say enough for them, I do not think any GOC has ever had a better and more devoted staff, but as you know there are so many things a chief of staff can do which others cannot without hurting peoples feelings – Altogether I am absolutely delighted   it gives me quite a fresh heart –

I have given Colin Mackenzie Bensons column, I have no doubt he will do well though it will be difficult for him to keep up Benson's record –

I fear the Buffs did not behave well with Bensons column, I have asked Featherstonehaugh [Fetherstonhaugh] to inquire into the truth of some stories that are flying about, in the mean time I have changed the regiment and sent them back to L[ines] of C[ommunication] – Had the infantry been in position, as I fancy they should have been, instead of dealing us a blow, the boers would have received a really hard knock – Bad luck was it not, I had only just changed the A[rgyll] & S[utherland] Highlanders who had been treking with Benson for a very long time for the Buffs.

The reinforcements you are sending will enable me to do a good deal more. I am quite ready to send troops to India as soon as they come – I should like to see some changes of the more tired cavalry and Infantry regiments for fresh troops from India   I will keep the 9th Lancers and 5th D[ragoon] G[uard]s ready so that they may be got out without trouble or notice –

It is evidently getting daily more difficult to catch boers, we have got down to the best of them and they are really wonders at getting out of a tight place – They are getting hard up for horses I am glad to say – and when the horse sickness[176] begins we will press them well into it – In Cape Colony French has been able to clear the Midland districts and has now only to deal with the East and West   the latter is such a barren country that I do not think much harm will be done by leaving the enemy a good deal alone, as long as they are prevented from getting south of Clanwilliam –

When I capture another 2000 or 3000 the war will be practically of no great serious imput [sic] –

The railway lines have not now been touched for some time, and I am about to double the 100 refugees a week that are now allowed to return to Johannesburg – Extension to the mines is arranged at 50 stamps per 400 refugees returning –

Column commanders are now much more pleased with the Yeomanry & the weeding that has been given has resulted in greatly increased efficiency – Chesham has been round inspecting & is very satisfied with what he has seen –

Wynne has recently been here to see me to arrange matters so that the Cape Govt may entirely take over the Colonial defence forces – I hope now all will work smoothly   I had to take Brabant away at Sprigg's request so as to leave them a free hand for reorganisation – I am rather afraid the Cape Govt is making a mess of it, but we are giving them a free hand & only ask them to pay for what they do –

I was also able to arrange certain questions of martial law administration with Wynne &c as to bring in the civil magistrates and check a tendency of martial law being used to deal with matters not really affecting the army, & thus greatly reduce the numbers of officers dealing with martial law questions –

NAM. 1971-01-23-33-57

80
Mr St John Brodrick to Lord Kitchener

[Copy]   Nov. 16. 1901
Private

I did not write last week because Ian Hamilton was starting and I thought he would carry my messages & tell you all the latest from that 'den of iniquity' the War Office. I trust he will be able to relieve you a little. One cannot help feeling from the nature of the case & reading through the lines in your letters that you are suffering from the strain a little – and I want you to feel quite at ease as to the future. We all want you to keep on as long as possible. The cabinet feel it keenly and the King has written me strongly in the same sense – But we will take care you get a good rest before India. If necessary you must not go there till the autumn. My hope is you may be able to stay till it becomes possible, either to send home troops or to divide up the command – At a pinch Lord Roberts is perfectly willing to go out again, but this could only be on the ground of your health, as we have no reason whatever for asking you to come away.

It is a long pull for all of us. You will have heard by telegram the measures of relief we propose – In all you will get 6 fresh battalions for the loss of 2 tired battalions; 4 Cavalry Regts at once for the surrender of 2 tired regts (in March next); about 2000 more mounted troops & the Militia reliefs. In addition Canada has offered a fresh contingent of 600 men[177] wh. we shall accept & some Yeomanry recruiting is going on. Your last telegram asks for 1000 Yeomanry per month from Jan[uar]y. This of course opens a new vista, but I will carefully consider what can be done –

The strong measures which you are taking about rebels and Kaffir murderers, made me take rather a truculent line in a speech wh. I delivered two days ago. It has been well received and I do not think in the latter case you can be too severe – The accounts of these atrocities help us to make head against the feeling naturally aroused by the loss of life in the camps –

I have had to publish a Blue Book on the latter as all sorts of reports had been promised at different times. I fancy Dr. Kendal

Franks' contributions will make the pro Boers sit up a bit, and establish the difficulties under wh. you have been labouring with these people[178] – the account of the progress of your blockhouse system has given great encouragement. If only it can be made effective, it will be most telling.

I fear the removal of the wives of leaders is troubling you – It is not a question of sentiment with us but this is exactly one of the points which touches people most. If we can make out a military case for it, well & good – You have no doubt considered that these people, if their stage management is good may give a good deal of trouble on the continent –

All our friends abroad urge us to bring the war to a rapid conclusion. This is not possible at present, but we do not want to triply arm our opponents as it is not good business nationally

TNA reference PRO 30/57/22/Y104

81
Lord Kitchener to Mr St John Brodrick
[Holograph]   Army Headquarters,
South Africa.
29th Nov 01.

I fear our progress is much slower than you expect – The advance made in a week or fortnight in such a vast country is very small, but I believe it to be real. I hope my telegrams lately have improved, but it is not easy without giving undue importance to events to make very much of a weeks or fortnights work towards the end of the war –

There have been constant reports from secret agents that the great majority of the boers do not intend to go on much beyond the end of the year, owing to want of food and ammunition – We have heard such reports before so I only mention them for what they are worth which may be very little – From one of de Wets letters we know Botha wants to arrange to meet de Wet, probably to discuss the future as Bothas men are very discontented with the way things are going and at being led by the O.F.S. – Ben Viljoen is doing all he can to bring about peace, and his men are anxiously waiting to give up – De Wet's own men are much more discontented and insubordinate than they used to be – At a meeting the other day de Wet had to shambok[179] one of his men for openly saying they were being deceived and asking how long they were to be kept on at this hopeless struggle[180] – There have been several quarrels amongst the Free Staters lately – No one now cares to go down to the Colony, and de Wet has to exert all his influence to get men to attempt it – Kritzinger after refusing for a long time has at last been induced to make another attempt, but he has only started with 60 men though he may gather some more en route[181] –

De la Rey's men seem to have more heart for going on than any others and he has also the intention of going to the Colony, though I much doubt that he will really start after having the reports from there[182] – The people we really want to catch are Steyn, De Wet, and De la Rey, the first two are always being followed by light mobile columns who know what a good reward they will get, & Methuen has got a fitted out column for the same purpose as regards De la Rey, but he has not yet been able to let it go. I hope he will soon   I am constantly urging him to do so. Of course there must be a very great element of chance in catching these men, for by the time the quickest intelligences can come in of their movements, they have started again in some other direction, and we have been near them so often that they are very much on the alert –

There is a certain Dr. J.A. Kay living here as a civilian doctor, I believe he came up with Bullers troops, he was in the siege of Ladysmith and his brother (a very good man) was Lambton's[183] paymaster there – He is a regular firebrand apparently rather mad in the wild imperialist style of the editor of the Empire – He is not an authorized correspondent but [the] press censor has found him trying to send very untruthful accounts to Pall Mall – He might have been deported, but I thought he was safer here under control – Last mail he posted the enclosed two letters which [the] press censor took, but did not open – The man is entirely unreliable –

I have just seen Capt Crowe the Consul General at Lorenzo [Lourenço] Marques[184] he has apparently got the chance of getting possession of certain munitions of war intended for the boers, I have agreed to purchase these as the prices are far below what the articles could be produced for. I hope the negotiations will go on satisfactoraly as we may be able to draw considerably on the Boer European resources by this means, and if the boer agents can be led to suppose they are supplying their forces in the field by this channel they will not try in other ways –

The loss in horses, both in columns in the field and in the veterinary hospitals, has always been very serious especially during the winter months when grazing is not procurable – We have done our best to rest horses after their sea voyage, only the fittest landed are issued after an average rest of three weeks or a month, whilst poor horses who have stood the journey badly are kept a considerably longer time at remount depots before issue – Glanders[185] has been bad especially with horses from New Orleans – We have had to destroy 7500 from this cause alone since Feby – Horse sickness is another evil we have to contend against and accounts for 5000 since Feby   We have increased our Vet[erinar]y Field Hospitals from 15 to 32 and I have issued a number of orders and regulations on the subject of care of horses (copies enclosed) besides special telegrams to those column commanders who show want of care of horses – The mounted troops we employ are some of them very bad in the care of horses – Colonials are terrible, Yeomanry and Mounted Infantry are bad, and column commanders and officers have the greatest trouble in getting moderate care taken of the animals – I tried fitting out columns with extra horses as the boers have but the loss through want of care was so terrible I had to give up the plan – Where boer poneys thrive, our horses simply die – A number of our men are now mounted on rough boer poneys, but what will carry a boer who has two or three spare poneys well, fails in most cases to carry the colonial or cavalry soldier – The work our mounted troops have to do in finding the boers is also so much greater than that of the boers who remain in hiding, that we lose a much larger portion though the boers have lost very considerably;[186] the number of horses that there were in the O.R.C. and Transvaal was something prodigeous, there are still a large number remaining so wild in the O.R.C. that neither we nor the boers can catch them –

I have sent Col Long Ra [Royal Artillery] an excellent horse master to inspect closely all Veterinary Hospitals and farms, half our casualties occur in them, and I do not think we are quite on right lines about the farms – I have frequently inspected the Veterinary Hospitals & there is now a marked improvement both in care and accommodation for the horses –

I have changed column commanders for want of care of horses, but what can one do when officers like Elliott, Spens, French and Plumer have the worst results the last named is the worst –

It is only in the most exceptional cases of military necessity that horses do not get a good rest after a trek – The result is I know unsatisfactory, particularly in a campaign that has been going on for so long, but it is difficult to see what more can be done if we have to catch the boers – General Hamilton will be here tomorrow and I will get him to take up the whole subject specially and will send you a full report on the whole matter – I am restricting the issue of horses to columns without full investigation of the cases, and establishing as far as possible reserves in certain depots so that tired and unfit horses may be more easily exchanged before a column goes out –

As regards the six boer ladies I think it is better to let the matter drop. I fear we shall not catch their correspondence though there is no doubt communication does go on –

I have to thank you very sincerely for your letters and hope you will have a happy Xmas

[Postscript]
I enclose translations of a manuscript sort of paper circulated amongst the boer commanders in O.R.C.[187]

TNA reference PRO 30/57/22/Y108

82
Lord Kitchener to Mr St John Brodrick

[Holograph]   6[th] Dec[em]b[e]r 01.
Private

We have had some better captures lately and the boers in the Eastern portion of the Transvaal under Louis Botha are more demoralized and broken up than they have been for a long time – De Wet about Reitz is concentrating his men, to attack our columns or blockhouse lines, but I do not think he will be able to do much. Elliotts [Elliot's] division from the Kro[o]nstadt Lindley blockhouse line and Rimington from Frankfort will operate against this concentration in a few days. I am anxious to be certain how many men de Wet can get together. The action of the ..... mobile columns chasing de Wet is the cause of this concentration and he hopes to catch one of them either at night or in the day time, after they have had a long march –

Sir W. Harcourts[188] letter "Guerilla War" seems to us all out here a most pernicious publication – I have little doubt it will have the effect of making the war go on for three months longer than it otherwise would have done – It looks as if Sir W Harcourt cared little for the loss of life he thus causes and is responsible for –

It is curious to see how the English papers affect the boer leaders   I can almost tell exactly when they get the papers of a certain date, as they immediately follow up, out here, any agitation started in the press at home – A little while ago it was the employment of natives by us in offensive operations,[189] when they found that they could prove nothing they gave it up – now it is the concentration camps, about which I am sending you a despatch, covering a protest sent to Lord Salisbury – I consulted Milner and we agreed on the attached reply being sent which I expect will make them drop the subject and beg us to continue keeping their women and children from them – if they can take them I shall be glad to send them out with a certain amount of food and every facility for those that wish to go, of course we could not force women out – I do not however expect they will take them

I think I have hit on the right man in Col Long to go into the force management question – I was much pleased at his first inspection which pointed out defects that had escaped notice – I will do all I possibly can to improve and I feel more hopeful of being able to do a good deal, than when I last wrote –

As regards Cape Colony, I think what we want most is to prevent reinvasion – French can perfectly well deal with the rebel forces and boers now in Cape Colony; but fresh bands breaking in should be prevented and this can best be done as far north as possible, so that by a dash they cannot get through the lines and disappear in the hills as they are so fond of doing – When we have a good cleared area and get at them far enough away from the frontier we can break them up and prevent their getting through. Kritzinger has been trying unsuccessfully for more than two months[190] –

I am very glad to have Hamilton   he greatly helps and lightens my task in every way –

I wish the press and particularly the Times would be a little more careful what they put in, a letter from a civilian which was published in the Times and quoted in other papers is absurdly wrong and for ignorance might have been written by a private soldier – It makes the army feel disgusted that the press at home should show delight in running down their work, and criticising from a comfortable armchair or railway carriage what is being done. Though there are and must be mistakes and slackness, on the whole you may take my word for it the army is doing work that no continental army would do without a grumble.

TNA reference PRO 30/57/22/Y109

83
Lord Kitchener to Lord Roberts

[Holograph]   Pretoria
                                                13. Dec. 01.

Many thanks for your letter and what you say about the Indian appointment – Please remember as long as you have confidence in me and I am required out here I desire to remain and see this through – It is very good for you to think of coming out; but I cannot see what the Army would do if you left the helm in Pall Mall, much as I should like to show you personally what has been done during the year I have been in command – Hamilton is I believe writing to you fully his impressions which will be more valuable as he is fresh from home and has not seen the whole thing creeping on slowly[191] I wish we could move quicker with results, but it is a great comfort to have the candid opinion of a newcomer that everything that can be done is being done –

I think about April we shall have pretty well exhausted the boers, and so enclosed them in areas that they will find it very hard to keep up much form of resistance – Of course for some time there may and probably will be a few bands of irreconcilables in difficult country, but these will be easily confined to districts –

The blockhouse system is telling very well, but takes up a large number of infantry – I am using every means I can lay my hands on and reducing all garrisons to a minimum, I was rather shocked to get a wire from AG[192] asking which battalion I could send to Antigua   I shall have none to spare if I carry out my projects, so I hope you will find a militia battalion to go to Antigua when we have filled up Bermuda –

Our recent captures have been good, they consist of some of the finest boers I have seen all first rate young men – Surrenders are coming again more freely and all round I hear the boers are much depressed and inclined to give up only the leaders urge them on as they have always done with false promises of European intervention and that we are tired and will soon go –

Before I left for Harrismith I wired you about Rundle, however when I got there I found things better than I expected, & I do not think a change necessary unless of course you want Rundle – I had intended putting Bar Campbell at Harrismith and giving Oliphant Bar Campbell's present work in the Brandwater basin – It is not very easy to find work for a new hand like Oliphant, but we shall manage it all right, I propose to attach him to either Methuen or Elliot to learn a bit first – The boys have arrived and are getting their horses fit at Stellenbosch, I have not settled yet where they better go to as there is plenty of time, if the horses get a month I think it will be sufficient as they will start with light work –

French especially asked for the Guards M.I. & I said he might have them as I thought the Guards probably would like to serve near their own battalions in Cape Colony, if I find they would prefer Rawlinson I can make a change later –

I have acted on your suggestion about R.A. Mounted Infantry and hope in a short time to have 700 men started under Dunlop[193] who will make a good C.O. – I wonder how this never occurred to us out here –

I enclose the last distribution list of the effective troops & by next mail I hope to send some maps of the distribution of troops in S.A.

With best wishes for the New Year

NAM. 1971-01-23-33-63

84
Lord Kitchener to Mr St John Brodrick
[Holograph]   Pretoria
                                                 13 Dec. 01.

The boers are at present more depressed than they have been for some time – Unfortunately they are so broken up and divided that they do not know exactly what is going on in different parts of the country, so that their leaders are still able to deceive them by supposed successes in distant parts of the country – European intervention is also being freely promised by leaders if the men will only stick it out a little longer –

I feel sure you will like to have for parliament the latest possible information of the position of troops out here – I am therefore preparing maps, or tracings of maps that can be fitted on at home, giving the exact position of the troops and enemy's commandos, with numbers as nearly as we can ascertain them in each case – I will send you three by next mail and three by a telegram on the

13th or 14th Janry, I will correct positions, and you will I hope be able to put up maps in parliament giving the fullest and latest information of where everyone is –

I have been away again driving the week, and have inspected at Standerton and Harrismith besides seeing Lyttelton at Newcastle – I am sure it is a good thing for me as well as for the troops that I should personally see them as often as possible and now that I have Ian Hamilton I can get away without trouble or stopping the continuity of work –

The blockhouse line now going out from Standerton to Ermelo, is very strong, a boer prisoner coming in along the line was asked what he thought of it, he said "well if the wind blew my hat over the line I can quite see I should have to go round by Ermelo to pick it up" I rode out about 10 miles along the line and was much pleased with the work done, no escorts are required and the country around is now entirely left by the boers –

At Harrismith I rode out on the Blockhouse line to Bethlehem, though good it is not nearly as strong as the Standerton-Ermelo line; but when the line is complete it is intended to strengthen it by interpolating additional blockhouses[194]

A few men have got through our lines into our enclosed areas and wander aimlessly about, I expect they will starve or surrender in the mean time I have offered a reward of £5 to any one who brings in a boer caught in our enclosures – I hope this will keep these areas absolutely clear of boers –

I am much obliged to you for your letter of the 16th [195] just received. I think I shall want a rest before going to India, unless you will change the law that the C. in C. in India cannot leave the country. I think we can fairly count on the boers not keeping me here much after April so that I could get out to India in the autumn without any difficulty – If however this estimate of time is not realized, as long as the Government have confidence in me, I should like to stick to South Africa and see this struggle through –

It is no longer real war out here but police operations of considerable magnitude to catch various bands of men who resist and do all they can to avoid arrest – Like wild animals they have to be got into enclosures before they can be captured. The boers cordially dislike the blockhouse lines –

P.S. I see by a telegram from you that you consider the daily intelligence map giving the enemy's position as accurate, it is only a summary of the news that I have made so that I can see at a glance where boers are reported, I see on yesterdays map 100 boers marked that have since turned out to have been only a herd of blesbok & a great deal of the information shown on the map is subsequently corrected, but it is useful to me as it is, for directing operations

TNA reference PRO 30/57/22/Y111

85
Lord Kitchener to Mr St John Brodrick

[Holograph]   Johannesburg
27th Dec[em]b[e]r. 01.

I am very sorry to have to report another loss – Firmans column[196] covering the blockhouse extension from Harrismith to Bethlehem has been rushed at night by de Wet. The boers were evidently in the camp before the men could get into their positions with the usual result   great confusion and loss of life

The boers captured a gun and a pompom and a considerable amount of ammunition – I fear this result is due to some carelessness in the posting of picquets on the top of a precipitous incline instead of both at the top and bottom – The column had been warned that de Wet was moving in their direction; there is no excuse for any want of attention in looking after the security of a camp at this period of the campaign

I cannot say for certain that my supposition as regards neglect is well grounded though the result seems to point to it – I am having careful inquiry made[197] –

De Wet & his men are certainly rendered somewhat desperate by the lines of blockhouses gradually being drawn round him, and we must and did expect these violent attacks – I only wish he had not picked out Yeomanry to go for –

It is very sad and depressing that the boers are able to strike us such blows, but I fear until all is over we shall always be liable to something of the sort from an unchecked rush of desperate men at night –

The new troops from India are just arriving, and I have the two regiments that have to go there to replace them quite ready to embark – The ship requires a few days for coaling etc before she is ready to return but there will be no delay as regards the troops –

I am trying to arrange regulations under which black boys can be got up from Portuguese territory to work in the mines – Milner considers it essential though I much fear it will open the door for introduction of letters & perhaps ammunition from Delagoa Bay We will take all the precautions we can, but with 10,000 natives passing up the railway every month I am afraid things will get through notwithstanding all we can do –

I cannot help thinking we could do quite well for the mine labor [sic] by importing mine labor [sic] from our own territory in the north where there are any quantity of natives; I have during last month sent 10,000 boys to Johannesburg from Pietersburg and they will naturally take back their wages and eventually enable us to get taxes from native extensive territories in the north –

The mine managers naturally like Portugese [sic] boys best, as they are trained by previous work in the mines when the boers did not allow the boys from the northern Transvaal to be recruited for fear of the European influences they would come under if they worked in the mines

However I fear there is not much use in trying to prevent this danger to the army and to the prolongation of the war as the mine managers are determined to get the Portugese [sic] boys, and Milner thinks they should be allowed to do so notwithstanding the risk incurred – I would have liked to see a rule made that until every available boy was recruited from our own territories and we were therefore unable to supply the mines with the labor [sic] they required, no boys should be brought in from Portugese [sic] territories

I am sorry you thought I delayed to act on your telegram re sending prisoners to Bermuda, Your telegram only reached me on the day the ship sailed and though I wired Cape town the ship was gone – Further accommodation for prisoners will be shortly required as before you get this I hope I shall have caught the 1000 that St Helena can take but I should think St Helena could take many more[198] –

P.S. I enclose an extract from our papers that had been circulated in boer camps[199]

TNA reference PRO 30/57/22/Y116(b)

Part 4
January to April 1902
The New Model Drives
Introduction

From 27 January to 17 February 1902 a drive took place from near the Johannesburg-Pretoria railway line to the mountains on the border between the Transvaal and Natal.[1] But the greatest danger was elsewhere. By the beginning of 1902 Lord Kitchener had at long last learnt to respect the Boers [92, 94], in particular the role played by President M.T. Steyn and General Christiaan de Wet, and he went all-out to defeat them [71, 91]. In a desperate effort to eliminate De Wet and his commandos as a factor in the war, Kitchener launched a series of so-called New Model Drives, primarily in the North-Eastern ORC, utilising the blockhouse lines as an integral part of his tactics to drive on, corner and destroy the elusive Boer commandos.

The first New Model Drive was launched in the North-Eastern ORC on Wednesday 5 February 1902 in an effort to defeat De Wet. Approximately 9,000 British soldiers formed a line of some 90 km stretching from Frankfort to Kafferkop (thus comprising an average of one soldier every 10 m). They were to 'drive' the Boers against the Kroonstad-Wolwehoek-Heilbron blockhouse lines. These lines (comprising a total of some 300 blockhouses) were also reinforced with some 8,000 additional soldiers, while four armoured trains were sent out to patrol the Kroonstad-Wolwehoek railway line, and three armoured trains to patrol the Wolwehoek-Heilbron railway line. On 7 February De Wet and about 700 men moved south and broke through the Kroonstad-Lindley line, west of Doornkloof. Also on 7 February, another Boer commando, under Commandant D.H. van Coller, some 300 strong, broke through the Heilbron-Frankfort blockhouse line. When the first New Model Drive ended on 8 February, the British claimed 286 Boers killed, wounded or captured, but the latter apparently included young boys forcibly removed from their homes.[2]

The second New Model Drive was also aimed at eliminating De Wet and his forces. It was launched in the North-Eastern ORC on 13 February 1902. During the first phase of the drive, some 30,000 British soldiers swept the area between the main Natal railway line, the Natalspruit-Brandfort blockhouse line, and the Harrismith-Winburg blockhouse line. Six large mobile columns lined up from Doornberg to Kroonstad, and moved towards the Lindley-Bethlehem blockhouse line [92]. These six columns reached the last-mentioned blockhouse line on 15 February, but in the course of the two days' drive, only about ten Boers were captured. The next day (16 February), the second phase of the drive started with a sweep between the Natal railway line and the Wolwehoek-Heilbron-Frankfort blockhouse line. Most of the Boer commandos broke through the British blockhouse lines or sweeping cordons. By the time the second New Model Drive ended on 27 February, the Boers had lost about 50 killed, plus 778 captured. Although De Wet, Steyn, and most of the Boers escaped, this was the biggest haul of captured Boers since Chief Commandant Marthinus Prinsloo had surrendered with more than 4,000 men in the Brandwater Basin in July–August 1900 (see the Introduction to Part 1 for more information). The Boers also lost some 25,000 head of cattle, 2,000 horses and 200 wagons and carts in the second New Model Drive.[3]

The third New Model Drive started on 4 March 1902. It ended on 11 March, on the Kroonstad-Wolwehoek-Lindley blockhouse line, having led to the capture of only about 100 Boers.[4] The fourth New Model Drive started on 20 March 1902. This time the area to be swept stretched from the Heilbron-Frankfort-Botha's Pass blockhouse line (northern flank) to the Lindley-Bethlehem-Harrismith blockhouse line (southern flank). Five large columns, consisting of a total of some 14,000 British soldiers, took part in the drive. Heavy rain and impassable rivers hampered this drive, and by the time the drive ended on 5 April, only ten Boers had been killed and 76 captured. Three Krupp field-guns, 178 wagons and carts, and some 4,800 head of cattle and horses were also captured.[5]

The fifth and final New Model Drive in the North-Eastern ORC commenced on Thursday 1 May 1902. It consisted of a number of movements, for example, on 6 May a total of 121 Boers were captured in a sweep from the Heilbron blockhouse line to the Kroonstad-Lindley blockhouse line. A return sweep on 8 May produced only 22 Boers captured. The drive ended on 10 May, without anything else having been achieved.[6]

During these last months of the war, blacks in British service played an ever-increasingly important role in the struggle against the Boers. The blacks knew the terrain, knew where water could be found for men and horses, and were skilful guides at night. Questions were asked in Britain about the employment of 'non-whites' in a so-called white man's war, and Mr St John Brodrick had to obtain information from Kitchener, though it is clear that Brodrick did not always know what to believe, or what to make of the information Kitchener supplied him with in this regard [96]. Kitchener admitted that he was not fully in control of the employment of black people by the British Army in South Africa [99].

The war in the Cape Colony continued over large areas, albeit at a low level of intensity. On the night of 15–16 December 1901, Commandant P.H. Kritzinger invaded the colony for a third time. On 16 December 1901 he was seriously wounded and taken prisoner. After spending several weeks in hospital at Naauwpoort, Kritzinger was taken to Graaff-Reinet. In March 1902, he was tried by a military tribunal on charges of murder and train-wrecking, but was acquitted[7] [93]. In the meantime, in the furthest north-western region of the Cape Colony, General Jan Smuts – after reorganising the commandos – led an expedition southwards, but after suffering a defeat on the farm Windhoek (25 February 1902), he besieged and captured the mining towns Nababeep, Springbok and Concordia. However, the British garrison in another mining town, Okiep, could not be forced into surrendering. At the end of April 1902 Smuts departed from this operational area to take part in the peace negotiations at Vereeniging and Pretoria[8] (see Part 5 for more on these negotiations).

In the meantime, in the Western Transvaal, General Koos de la Rey (assisted by Generals J.C.G. Kemp and P.J. Liebenberg) inflicted severe losses on British columns. Between Yzerspruit and Jagdspruit, on Tuesday 25 February 1902, a convoy escorted by Lieutenant-Colonel W.C. Anderson was attacked by about 1,000 Boers. Anderson had about 700 soldiers under his command. When the attack commenced at about 05.00, thick morning mist limited visibility. Two Boer charges were repulsed, but a third broke British resistance and the convoy was captured. The British lost at least 33 killed, 129 wounded (most of them taken prisoner), and about 240 unwounded soldiers captured, plus two field-guns, a pom-pom, and a large amount of ammunition. The Boers lost at least twelve killed and 31 wounded, of whom three died later[9] [94].

At about 05.00 on Friday 7 March 1902, General Koos de la Rey (assisted by Generals J.C.G. Kemp and J.G. Celliers), and about 750 men, attacked a column led by Lord Methuen (about 1,300 strong) near De Klipdrift in the Western Transvaal [94]. Methuen was trekking from Tweebosch in the direction of Lichtenburg, co-operating with Colonel R.G. Kekewich and Lieutenant-Colonel H.M. Grenfell in an effort to corner De la Rey. British losses amounted to at least 68 killed, 121 wounded, and more than 800 prisoners of war, as well as four field-guns, two pom-poms, and about 100 wagons and carts captured. The Boers lost at least eight killed and 26 wounded. Methuen was among those wounded and taken prisoner. Amid calls of protest from several Boers, De la Rey magnanimously decided to set Methuen free as soon as the latter's wound had been attended to. Accompanied by a doctor and a few others, Methuen was sent to Klerksdorp. Soon after his departure, pressure was exercised on De la Rey to reverse his decision. Messengers overtook Methuen's company, and they were taken to Gestoptefontein. At a meeting held on 9 March De la Rey more or less convinced the burghers that it would be in the interest of the Boer cause to set Methuen free. Methuen finally reached Klerksdorp on 13 March and fully recovered.[10] Alarmed by these reverses, Kitchener was in favour of stricter action against officers whose negligence led to losses [98, 102]. Kitchener was so upset when he heard of Methuen's capture that he collapsed and stayed in bed for more than a day, without eating[11] [94].

On 31 March 1902, two British columns were camped at Boschbult – a total of about 1,800 soldiers with four guns, commanded by Lieutenant-Colonel G.A. Cookson and Lieutenant-Colonel J.L. Keir. At approximately 13.20 they were attacked by some 2,000 Boers under the command of De la Rey and Kemp. The British succeeded in beating off the attack. British losses amounted to 27 killed, about 70 wounded, and approximately 100 taken prisoner. On the Boer side, six were killed and some fifteen wounded.[12]

On 5 April 1902 Kitchener put Ian Hamilton in overall command of all British forces in the Western Transvaal. This meant that Hamilton had sixteen columns (a total of some 17,000 soldiers) under his command. Hamilton travelled by train from Pretoria to Klerksdorp, and then across the veldt to Kekewich's headquarters at Middelbult. Hamilton took charge and organized an elaborate drive against the Boer forces that were still at large in this area. At about 07.15 on 11 April some 800 Boers under the command of Ferdinandus Jacobus Potgieter, Commandant of the Wolmaransstad commando, charged the columns of Lieutenant-Colonel S.B. von Donop and Lieutenant-Colonel H.M. Grenfell (across open veldt) at Rooiwal. The British forces totalled about

3,000 men with six guns. The attack was beaten back, with the Boers losing at least 43 killed (including Potgieter), more than 50 wounded (of whom 40 were taken prisoner), while 36 unwounded prisoners were taken. The British lost about twelve killed and 75 wounded. When Hamilton arrived on the scene of the attack he ordered a general pursuit. Later, Lieutenant-Colonel H.S. Rawlinson's columns also joined in the pursuit, but the Boers eluded them. The British recaptured two of their own field-guns and a pom-pom they had lost at Tweebosch-De Klipdrift.[13]

By the time the action at Rooiwal took place, members of the Transvaal and OFS governments had already gathered at Klerksdorp (9–11 April) to discuss the possibility of entering into peace negotiations with the British authorities. Although Kitchener did not realise it at this stage, the war was nearing its logical end, and soon he would – at long last – be on his way to India.

86
Lord Kitchener to Mr St John Brodrick

[Holograph]   Johannesburg
                                                     3rd Janry 02.

We are now keeping de Wet hustled so he has done no more
damage – I have sent Chesham to hold an inquiry into the Firman
incident[1] – I fear there must have been slackness and that
Christmas[2] was in some way responsible; the position in which the
troops were is I understand excellent for defence in every way[3] – I
am enclosing some notes of what I said in the Burgher camps on
my recent inspection with a view to the boers outside hearing
about it – As I anticipated the contents has become widely known
amongst the boers with the result that we have had a good many
surrenders lately and the feeling against their leaders has become
intensified and may lead to further developments   The press have
heard nothing about these speeches and I think that possibly you
may find something useful for debate in the house [of Commons]
in them –

I feel we are now getting a much closer grip on the boers in the
Eastern Transvaal and the O.R.C.   the blockhouses are doing well
though of course the boers can and do occasionally force their way
through them at night with loss   even then they are a great help
by pointing out where the boers are – We do not claim that these
lines are impervious barriers   in fact I rather like the boers to get
through sometimes as they thus get separated and out of touch
with each other – the proof of their utility is the cordial manner in
which they are detested by the boers –

I have sent you a financial telegram today   I hope it is what you
want and that you will not think that I have gone beyond my
province in referring to all military expenditure and not only what
we are spending out here – With a budget of 80 millions I fancy
we could run the war as long as it lasts out of the General army
budget – The war would then take the place of manoeuvres, and

no special grants and unpleasant debates would be necessary – Perhaps this is Utopiac but I cannot help thinking with strict economy everywhere it might be managed – The Chancellor of the Exchequer would have to relax Treasury rules regarding transfer of funds from different headings of the army budget – I suppose he will get a fairly large unexpended balance on the present army Budget at the end of the financial year –

I am anxious about our meat contract and as you doubtless know have sent home Col Morgan to arrange matters I hope he may be allowed a free hand as he is quite reliable and knows the subject and my views thoroughly

I hope we may be able to make a considerable saving though it will not be so large as the reduced figures might make one think as there will be no more cattle here to capture and we shall have to pay for all meat rations instead of only some. Still we shall make a large profit by supplying civil inhabitants and I have little doubt at the end of a year's work we shall be able to float a company and get a million pounds fully paid up shares for it – I expect the S.A. Cold storage will rather scream but they have had their time and done us badly and are arrant rebels and proboers of course if they like to tender at a dead loss we will accept and get a bit back of that reserve we enabled them to put up – It would pay them well to supply us at a loss so as to get the army contract, and proboers money is just as good as any other, though Milner and Natal will not much like the S A C[old] S[torage] getting the contract which will ensure their monopoly in S.A.

Many thanks for your kind words we are doing all we can and Hamilton is a great help to me and just gives me that reassurance that I want sometimes that all that is possible is being done not only to end the war but also to prevent as far as possible unpleasant incidents I enclose a correspondence about opening Cape parliament[4] I have as you will see taken Milner's advice I had intended to ask Hely Hutchinson as well, but Milner thinks it would place him in an awkward position as he is supposed to act on the advice of his ministers and his opinion against the proposed elections is pretty well known –

TNA reference PRO 30/57/22/Y117(b)

87
Lord Kitchener to Mr St John Brodrick

[Holograph]   Johannesburg
                                                 10th Janry 02.

I have been kept very busy with de Wet during the past week, but I am sorry to say without much result except that his horses are getting done up – He has been continually on the move in his now rather restricted area, & it has been most difficult to follow him – I fancy he means to burst out and go for the colony again if his men will follow him but that is doubtful – He made an attempt to go to join De la Rey but that was prevented by our columns being too close on his heels[5] – Boers will not risk attacking Blockhouse lines if our columns are pretty close behind them – I am always hopeful of getting him into some corner, but up to the present he has evaded any such mishap by very quick turns, however I am getting more troops around him and we will give him no rest –

I have been rather exercised to know what is the reason for your desire to do away with the military farms which produce vegetables for the hospital convalescent camps and troops and green stuff for our sick horses – It is the greatest boon to the troops to have fresh vegetables, which they cannot get on trek, and as we have some scurvy in the Army it is essential to have a good liberal supply of fresh vegetables – You seem to think that the civil administration could take up the production of the vegetables for the Army, but why should they – They have no means for doing so, and they do not want to – If they did take up the work they would not produce what we want as the Army Service Corps do, and I feel convinced all they could produce would be absorbed at enormous prices by Johannesburg so that the Army would suffer – The civil administration naturally refuse to take up a contract for the supply of the Army where they could get prices elsewhere, and where the risk of considerable loss, and almost innumerable lawsuits would hang over their heads for occupying and cultivating land which did not belong to them –

When I first got your telegram I thought Milner was at the bottom of this proposed change, but I am glad to say after seeing him on the subject he is almost as strongly averse to any change as I am – Milner feared that some remarks he had made to Mr Chamberlain on a misapprehension of what was being done without reference to me, had influenced you in this matter; but we have since found out that his letter could not have reached the Colonial Office so it is difficult to follow what the reasons were, they are not financial as we are doing well in that respect and it is not as if the civil administration have not larger areas along the railways they could cultivate if they liked, and make a considerable profit by supplying Johannesburg if they wished to take up that line, and could arrange with the owners which is a difficulty for them but not for us –

I sincerely hope that you will allow us to go on – I am quite convinced there is under present circumstances no other means of supplying these necessities to the Army – I am anxious about the matter as it is exceptional for the Army to have to do this work, but while the war lasts I am sure it is necessary for us to do it as no one else can – Directly the war is over of course the farms will have to cease as the owners will again come in and be able to cultivate them. Some of these farms are good land –

I am sending you by this mail the despatch on executions under martial law, I hope it is what you want – Ian Hamilton is a help in getting such matters forward and I hope there is not much outstanding work – There is a little delay in answering questions in my AGs dept as it is not always easy to trace people in South Africa, but with this exception I fancy we answer fairly promptly I should like to know if you find this to be the case –

[Postscript]
Please excuse a bad letter   I have been going through constant interruptions –

TNA reference PRO 30/57/22/Y118(b)

88
Lieutenant-General Ian Hamilton to Mr St John Brodrick

Army Head Quarters,
[Typescript copy with additions in longhand[6]]   South Africa.
January 16th 1902.

Rough Draft of letter which Lord R. held back & it
was never delivered –
Ian H
27.1.04[7]

I am impelled to write to you by the accident to poor Miss Sybil,[8] who, I most sincerely trust, is quite herself again now.

I have long meant to send you a letter, but as a rule[9] I should have only been duplicating my lengthy communications to Lord Roberts, so I have hitherto left it alone.

Things military are, I really believe, going well, and our plans are well advanced for making a serious impression on the enemy in the Northern Orange River Colony, who have hitherto suffered comparatively little at our hands.[10]

But the political situation does not seem to me nearly as plain sailing a matter as the military one. When I dined at your house two days before sailing for South Africa, Mr Joseph Chamberlain remarked to me that it was indeed *a* most singular *and to him inexplicable fact* that in talking *face to face* with Lord Kitchener, General Lyttelton, or myself, he found that we were in entire accord with his views, whereas when we came out here and talked with him over the wires, differences of opinion began slowly to accumulate, until finally they reached such a pitch, that one *correspondent* could hardly understand what on earth the other was driving at. I have since thought that one reason for such a gradual drifting apart of opinion might be that Englishmen in South Africa keep coming more & more into practical touch with the situation, whereas Mr Chamberlain remained all the time influenced by the press-created public opinion of our dear old foggy native land. There are dozens of minor instances which I could make use of in illustration of my theory, but the important one of all is with regard to the best method of concluding this war. I wrote to Lord Roberts some time ago, endeavouring to make clear to him that if we do not have peace by settlement, and with terms regularly subscribed to by both parties, we may have war again within the next few years. Further, that in such case we should have to go on until we catch the last commando.

Steyn and De Wet, our two most irreconcilable enemies, are just as anxious as Mr Chamberlain and Lord Milner, that we should offer no terms, and that we should insist on unconditional surrender. For they know *as Lord K & I know* the extraordinary law-abiding nature of the Dutch, and that if they once agree to terms they would keep them, whereas if there are no terms they will consider themselves perfectly free to rise again.

Lord Milner speaking to me on this matter the other day declared his strong opinion that if they were crushed and beaten down to the bitter end, they would never rise again, but it seems to me that, as soon as Johannesburg is fairly engrossed in gold-making, and as soon as each Burgher has smuggled in a rifle, they might easily collect a few thousand men and, with the extraordinary celerity and precision which characterizes them, blow up one or two railway bridges, and then --- [sic] would the English people agree to start a big war over again? *If not, then Johannesburg would make terms and a Dutch South Africa would be a fait accompli.*

On the other hand, it is my firm belief that if we did come to terms with them, we might rely upon them *so absolutely to observe those terms honorably* [sic] *that* we could withdraw practically all our troops, within a reasonable period, leaving only the S.A.C. with the National Scouts[11] (the latter to steady the Johannesburgers) to run the show quite comfortably.

With regard to Johannesburg, when I read of Ministers at home discussing when, or in what measure, they will grant representative government, or to what extent the mines are to pay towards the cost of the war, I rub my eyes and wonder if such things can really be. I trust you will believe me when I assure you that these Johannesburgers mean to run the show now, and no mistake about it. *I trust you will believe me also when I assure you*

that running the show does not include money subscriptions! They
have let us smash the Boers for them, just as the Boers let us
smash the Zulus for them,[12] in the old days, and unless we guard
against it the result will be the same. The moment the fear of the
Boers is withdrawn from them, they mean to have representative
government, and if they don't get it there will be trouble between
the Rand Rifles and the Johannesburg garrison, but the threat will
probably be enough, and we shall climb down.

Loyalists from conviction are, in this country, few and far
between. There is a sprinkling throughout South Africa but,
comparatively, they are precious scarce. Loyalty here is too often
cast off like a garment for the most trifling reasons of personal
inconvenience, or personal advantage. Not only is it thrown off
like a garment, but when thrown off it is liberally stamped upon.
There is in fact, I regret to say, far less true loyalty here than you
people at home are inclined to think, except in so far as loyalty is
the South African political expression meaning anti-Dutch. Need
I add that there is absolutely no trace of gratitude for anything
done by the English nation or the Army. Therefore on all and
every ground I say make terms with the Dutch, and do not reduce
them too low. *Lord Milner can see no good of any sort in description
in any Dutchman – He regards them as a low lot   not to be trusted
further than they can be seen. This was a very excellent attitude as
long as no question of peace was allowed to intrude itself, but in a peace
maker the attitude is devilish bad. If you want peace* you have only to
give Lord Kitchener a free hand, and peace will very shortly
follow. I say very shortly, because he could not take the initiative in
discussing such a theme, but some opportunity would soon arise,
and within a month of its arising peace would be made. This is
where the War Office should come in, and not the Colonial Office.

In my humble opinion, the Boers will never make peace with
Lord Milner, whom they regard as a Johannesburger, and their
enemy. This is hard for anyone to realize who knows the gentle
and charming nature of the High Commissioner, but it is a fact
nevertheless. Whereas, in their eyes, Lord Kitchener is connected
with no political party, and is merely regarded as an Englishman,
whom they certainly do not hate, although they may dislike him,

Milner *on the other hand* is irretrievably identified with the *hated anti dutch* South African political party.

Political hatred is at the bottom of the continuance of this struggle, and not military hatred. There is intense political hatred; there is practically no such thing as military hatred, but rather mutual respect, and in many instances a strange sort of mutual liking.

Therefore when you come to make peace it should be engineered through the military, and not through the political channel.

I feel that if I could only succeed in persuading you of this, you might perhaps see your way to make the War Office influence more felt than it has been in this part of the business.

The War Office and Lord Kitchener can make peace. I do not think that anyone else can.

I have opened my mind very freely to you, otherwise I think it would be worse than useless for me to take up your valuable time. I need hardly say that I alone am responsible for the ideas I set forth.

P.S. My impression, mind you it is only an impression, is that Lord Milner himself is not quite so bitterly opposed as he was a short time [ago] to any moderation of absolute unconditional surrender, but no doubt he fears we have gone too far with the principle to draw back now.

P.S. (2). I am writing to Lord Roberts today to beg him to make sure that *a troop of Boer* National Scouts, wearing S. African medals, form part of the coronation procession.[13] We will send you some real wild six-footers from Zoutpansberg. They will make the blood of the little Piccadilly loungers run icy cold with fear.

[Note in longhand at end of manuscript]
Similar letter only stronger and freer sent to George Wyndham[14] and Winston Churchill[15] – IH

LHCMA, Hamilton 2/3/12

89
Lord Kitchener to Mr St John Brodrick

[Holograph]   17. Janry 02.

Your campaign has now started again and I hope you will have every success. Let me recommend the blockhouse system; I have no doubt it would have an excellent effect in parliament; you pin your adversary down to certain areas and stop anything like diffuseners [sic], but I fear I am writing about that of which I know nothing –

I have been paying a considerable amount of attention to the horse question and it appears to me from some of the horses I have inspected that a good deal more attention should be paid to the purchases and selection of these horses. Of course I am aware with such large purchases there is no doubt considerable difficulty in finding suitable animals; but you will see from my reports that a great number of totally unsuitable animals have been shipped out here which is no doubt due to some of the officers purchasing for the War Office not having sufficient knowledge or taking sufficient care in selection

We have of course to issue the good and bad to columns as soon as they are physically fit, and there is no doubt that the latter owing to their unsuitability almost at once drop out of the ranks and increase our persentage of losses enormously[16]

The Australian shipments have at times arrived in the most wretched condition, so much so that some of the horses are never able to be got into condition to take the field while others though every care is taken of them   would require 12 months to recover from the effect of the voyage –

I have been talking to Milner about the wish of some boer prisoners in Ceylon and elsewhere to come back and join the Burgher corps.[17] I think it would be a good thing for the future if carefully managed as once these boers have taken the field they can never be trusted by or join the irreconciled element again, and we shall therefore have a party amongst the boers themselves depending entirely on British continuity of rule out here

I think if the colonies where these prisoners are would let us know the names of the applicants to join, either by telegraph to save time or letter, I could then find out from the boer officers with the National scouts[18] which could be trusted and would be useful to us – I think the sooner this is done the better as the effect will doubtless be considerable on the boers in the field when they hear that the prisoners are coming back to fight against them –

The National Scouts have done very good work and are improving; there has been no case of a boer serving us ever having let us in in any way and many of them have behaved extremely well – As a rule they are not very keen for severe fighting & carry out boer tactics of only going when they are convinced of being much the stronger and have the best positions; then they show dash and are very good at following up scattered and flying boers –

I enclose a translation of a letter sent to Steyn from a Mr Vilonel who is about to raise a Burgher Corps in the O.R.C. He is a man of considerable local influence and if he takes the field will have a good effect[19] –

I am very glad the farm question is settled. I am still rather puzzled how it got started. It was either Fleetwood Wilson or Morgan trying to become a highly paid civil employee out here – The new meat contract is I think good as regards prices and will save us a lot of trouble and some risk though we might have done it a penny cheaper ourselves; on the other hand we might not have succeeded as well as we hoped to do

TNA reference PRO 30/57/22/Y12(b)

90
Lord Kitchener to Mr St John Brodrick
[Holograph]   24th Janry 1902

I suppose Reuters telegram must have given a wrong impression of what Mr [Joseph] Chamberlain said in the house [of Commons] about amnesty to rebels   There is very little doubt that this is the crux of the situation at present, particularly in the Transvaal where the boers are thoroughly sick of the war and are only kept in the field by their leaders, to whom it is a point of honour not to desert the rebels with them – For instance De la Rey had a meeting a few days ago and spoke of peace, but the Cape rebels with him abused the boers for thinking of leaving them to their fate, so nothing came of the meeting –

I have interviewed General Erasmus[20] and enclose a statement he sent me, he says they all want peace. I particularly asked him about De la Rey, whose sentiments I am not sure about, Erasmus assured me De la Rey was more for peace than Botha – He also told me if we caught Schalk Burger that Botha would declare himself president – The Boers are being continually told that if they keep the war going a little longer, England will be financially ruined and have to stop – I enclose a translation of some Boer accounts of expenditure on the war which are interesting – I am sending you separately some financial papers, Armstrong has done a good deal and is I think well worth his pay – Next week I will send you a further report on the work of his office – I have been trying to settle up outstanding railway charges with the Cape Govt, but they are most difficult to deal with and do not at all like the idea that the milch cow is objecting to being milked freely – I have first heard from Girouard, who I sent down to try and arrange certain matters, that the Cape Govt refuse even to go to arbitration, which they are bound to do by their agreement in case of dispute with the Imperial Govt. I shall have to bring a little pressure to bear by stopping payments and I daresay in time we shall get them to run straight as we have on previous occasions, but all this makes it difficult not to have accounts – You may be sure we are doing our best to clear up everything outstanding –

I was astonished to hear of the arrival of Ardagh at Cape Town[21] as I had heard nothing from the War Office about his coming out and what he is coming for – He wires me that he has come out to deal with foreign claims, but I cannot understand how he can do so – I have sent down Gordon,[22] my staff officer for that work, to explain what we are doing re claims –

As we are not paying any claims until the war is over I do not see how we can go into disputes about them – We are registering and examining all claims and shall be prepared at end of war to say what is allowed – If the foreigner then refuses to accept the money offered him, the disputed claim could be gone into by Ardagh and foreign representatives, but until we know what to offer and do offer, no dispute can arise – I expect a large majority will accept the ready money offered rather than him wait for a disputed claim to be settled and we shall only have a few cases to go into by a special commission with foreign representatives on it – I hope you approve of this way of dealing with local claims by foreigners

I suppose you are having a hard time with parliament, though the opposition do not seem able to do much – I am writing to Ld Roberts about military operations so will not take up more of your valuable time –

TNA reference PRO 30/57/22/Y121

91
Lord Kitchener to Mr St John Brodrick
[Holograph]   7th Febry 02.

I have had recently an interesting conversation with Gen Viljoen[23] who speaks quite openly   I think he tells the truth. He says they are all anxious for peace, that Schalk Burger is very weary and much under the influence of Steyn and de Wet who are still irreconcilable – Schalk Burger is shortly going to see them in the O.R.C. and try to make some proposals for a conference – Viljoen says if Schalk Burger proposed to the Transvaal unconditional surrender, the people would surrender, but before doing so they would kill Schalk Burger and the Govt. for having led them to such a result after so much loss – Botha according to B. Viljoen is more for peace than I previously thought – There is a strong and growing feeling amongst the burghers that de Wet and Steyn are so implicated in Morgenda[a]l's murder[24] and other similar illegalities that they dare not place themselves in the hands of the law and therefore continue the useless struggle –

Communications certainly pass with Europe through German [South-] West Africa and B Viljoen gave me the name of the boer agent from whom he had seen letters urging the boers to continue

198

in the field and stating our financial resources would soon be exhausted – I have kept on good terms with Herr von Lindequist German Consul General at Cape Town and when Colonel von Estoff[25] was passing through Cape Town to take up the command in German [South-] West Africa, I had him up here and did him well sending him out with a column to see the boers, so I have been able to privately communicate with these two about the agent and they have replied that they will do their best to get him removed – B Viljoen says they shortly expect ammunition from German [South-] West Africa   that they are very badly off and if it fails cannot last much longer – He says they have no communications with Portugese [sic] territory –

On the whole I think things are looking promising though it may take longer than we anticipate to bring about the complete end of the war – The burghers are very determined that next time a conference starts that it shall not be broken off without some result on the differences being submitted to them as was not done at the Middleberg [Middelburg] conference[26]

Steyn and de Wet, B Viljoen puts them in that order, are the main obstacles to a settlement   I am doing my best to hustle them both and I do not think they feel very comfortable at the present moment[27]

The work required from our horses continues very severe   All recent captures have been made after long night marches of from 20 to 50 miles followed by gallops of from 8 to 12 miles in pursuit We have at present in our depots the following horses which will be ready for issue in a month   Cape Colony 800 art[illery], 9.000 riding horses O.R.C. 150 art[illery] 1.600 riding horses Transvaal 100 art[illery], 1200 riding horses & Natal 100 Art[illery], 3,000 riding horses[28] –

Lord Downe is apparently unfavourably impressed with the class of horse landed – It may be that the rough coats make them look common as they come off ships, but it is a continual complaint that there is want of quality – My own observation of the horses in the remount depots leads me to think that many of the horses sent are what is known in the trade as light "van horses"   not riding horses at all and this class of animal cannot do our work – Recent shipments have landed generally in good condition but of the English horses many are unsound concerning which full reports have been sent to General Ternen specifying the Army number of the horses complained of – Many are too big and heavy   not at all of the right stamp – This has been constantly pointed out   for example the horses landed from the Kent are reported to include 50 per cent of unsuitable animals and Lord Downe classes 200 riding horses as artillery [horses] –

I do not think sufficient care has been made for the preparation of the horses for shipment – Conducting officers report much strangles on board shortly after sailing which looks as if the horses had gone straight from yards to the ship and this was specially noteable in the case of the Fifeshire and Idaho –

The majority of the Russian shipments[29] are considered suitable but once bigger horses have been included notably in the ship America which were like artillery horses of bad stamp – The Australian C.J.F. shipments[30] are improving in condition but the stamp is generally unsuitable   they are mostly unshaped weeds with quality and nothing else – The American horses[31] generally are good and in good condition but among them are some badly selected animals notably in the Mount Royal shipment and 5 percent of the horses shipped in the Montreal were ..... Lord Downe considers the Canadian horses[32] too big and underbred – I hope I have not bored you by the above but see you are anxious on the subject

TNA reference PRO 30/57/22/Y125

92
Lord Kitchener to Lord Roberts

[Holograph]   Pretoria
                                                            14 Feby 02

The drive came off as I intended and though the results were considerable they were disappointing[33] – De Wets escape was most unfortunate due I fear to the carelessness of the 4th R.B.'s[34] on the Lindley B. H. [blockhouse] line – The boers were however much scarred and all their plans broken up, we got a good lot of their riding horses, not the wild animals in the veldt we generally bring in, but real saddle horses quite done up by being over ridden by the boers in their attempt to escape, they will most of them turn out useful animals after a rest –

I am now driving the outside coverts as you will see by the schemes enclosed and there I hope to give them a repetition of the original drive   only this time I shall hold the Valsch [River] South of the Lindley B H [blockhouse] line as well as the B H line itself[35] –

I have been away the whole week as after seeing the arrival of the troops from the drive and giving them fresh instructions   I went down to Na[a]uwpoort and saw French – He was quite changed and happy about the progress made, though it appears to me slow, we agreed that Munro[36] was not much use and should go home, and some other changes, also at last he has written that Sprot[37] is not in his opinion fit to command a Cavalry Regt, this you will get officially next mail – French told me Col Morris[38] at East London was quite useless and I have noticed this myself, through Morris' carelessness the boers got through a blockhouse line without damage against which French had driven them –

I arranged with French and Jones that the 1200 guards drafts should take the place of the men of the brigade that marched into Pretoria with you, so that if you want them they might be got out without upsetting existing places. This is being done quite quietly nobody knows   I suppose we must get all the old Militia relieved first and I am doing all I can in this respect –

I am sending Brooke [Brook] to take Rundle's place and Tucker wants leave so C Knox will be able to go there for a time – I shall send Cunningham home as Oliphant from Johannesburg can include all his work in his command – Willcocks[39] has I hear arrived at Capetown but also orders for him to go on at once to India if he accepted a brigade there, he said he would like the brigade but also to stop in S.A. I said in reply you had told me not to keep him so he better go on, but if he liked I would refer the matter home   I have had no answer yet – I hoped to see Downe tomorrow & hear his opinion about the remount establishments he has seen them all now –

I wish I could see an end to the war, but the leaders still keep the boers out in some quite unaccountable way – The reports that they were preparing to make peace have rather died away again now – I do not see how they can stand another winter unless the whole ..... go down to Cape Colony or attempt to do so –

The new troops are giving me the usual anxiety and learning their lessons of how to deal with boers in the usual manner by getting into trouble – the 7th Hussars have lost some men picked up by boers and the new M I from Malta have come to grief at their first meeting with boers[40] – It looks as if they had bolted disgracefully before a very inferior number – Confound them –

What are left of the boers are really very fine fellows and when they do fight they do it well –

I shall be off to Middleberg [Middelburg, Transvaal] tomorrow to get a little more done against old Schalk Burgers [Burger] on the north of the line   I cannot get much done there – They have elected Ben Viljoens brother[41] to replace him   I am glad of this as Muller would have been a more awkward customer[42]

NAM. 1971-01-23-33-75

93
Lord Kitchener to Mr St John Brodrick
[Holograph]   23rd Febry 02
Confidential

Schalk Burger and the Transvaal Govt are moving West through the bushveldt on salted horses to visit De la Rey and try to make their way to meet Steyn in the O.R.C. – This is in accordance with what Ben Viljoen told me they intended to do, if they could not cross the railway lines to the South – The object of the journey according to B. Viljoen was to arrange some proposals for peace, but I think de Wet and the irreconcilables in the O.R.C. will prevent anything coming out of this meeting if it ever takes place –

De Wets opinion is, if they cannot hold the Republics, that they should all go to Cape Colony – I am doubtful whether he will be able to carry out this policy, but there is no doubt he will do his utmost to do so[43] –

I have wired you about procedure of Court Martial on boer leaders in Cape Colony – I think it is a good thing that boer leaders should feel that if with a very small force they evade our frontier guards and enter Cape Colony to obtain recruits from British subjects, and create disturbance in an otherwise peaceful district, that they are straining their position as belligerents to the utmost, and if caught will be liable to be treated with the utmost severity for offences and crimes committed under the cloak of war, but contrary to the rules of warfare, which if they had remained in their own country might have been condoned –

I fancy from your telegram you do not wish Kritzinger tried or certainly not condemned <u>to death</u>[44] – I have therefore postponed the court and ordered all the evidence to be sent here to be examined by my legal advisers – There is certainly some feeling for Kritzinger but as far as I know I understand he was equally guilty with Scheepers,[45] and his proclamation or notice that natives would be shot which he issued as chief commandant in the Cape Colony must tell against him if he is tried[46] – I hope you will let me know definitely what line I should take in these cases –

Some 300 boers broke through our lines and got back into one of my enclosed areas a short time ago   I was rather glad to see what they would do and after a bit I suddenly disturbed them at their eating time   they bolted off leaving everything and they had nothing but fruit to live on, excellent peaches and apples, but not a single mealie or sign of bread stuff – it is rather hard to deal with such people but fruit cannot last very long – The great question is can they get through the next winter, with any ordinary people I should say it was quite impossible, but with boers I am doubtful; as they get starved they become bolder robbers, and the extension of civil life and cultivation which Milner is always pressing on me, gives them many opportunities of getting what they want to carry on –

You remember how carefully I cleared the area of the Thabanchu line and East of the railway to make de Wet pass through a desert if he attempted that way again down to the

Colony – Nothing living was left in the country and I kept columns there though I wanted them elsewhere till there was no doubt nothing was hidden – Now 5 boers come and drive off 500 cattle from the village of Bethulie that have been kept by the civil administration there. Each of those cattle will cost far more than £100 for me to catch them again – You can understand how worrying these things are & how hopeless it makes me feel about forcing a rapid conclusion to the war –

I don't often grumble so please excuse me this time   We will do all we can and hope for the best – Even should ..... lock me up in carnival house it would be better than this –

TNA reference PRO 30/57/22/Y129

94
Lord Kitchener to Mr St John Brodrick

[Holograph]   Pretoria
                                                      9th March 02

I am sorry to say things have not improved since I last wrote – De la Rey has succeeded in giving me two blows which, however much they ought not to have happened must undoubtedly have a considerable effect on the boers[47] – Our successes against them are of course minimized by the report of our superior numbers whereas any stray boer success is exaggerated into a glorious victory – I have always tried to be as careful as warfare would permit, but I do not think anyone could have foreseen and guarded against either of these two mishaps – I must say I was a little anxious about the second, i.e. the move of Methuen from Vryburg to Lichtenburg; but he was so confident and the numbers seemed so safe that I said nothing against it – It is just the boer way to remain quiet after receiving a blow, and apparently disappear by scattering their forces, and then when our troops are somewhat off their guard to reassemble and strike some blow. I cannot say how grieved I am at these occurrences – I will send down troops and hustle De la Rey again, but I am afraid the damage has been done in giving the boers heart to continue the war –

You may be quite sure that strict inquiry will take place, but it always takes some time to get at the truth of what actually happened in an action – I was at Klerksdorp on the sixth, and as far I could gather the disaster to the convoy occurred through the commander being in too great hurry to get into Klerksdorp – He held a good position, and had beaten off two attacks, the third, on his rear, would also in all probability have been beaten off, in which case the enemy would certainly have retreated before the advance of the mounted troops from Klerksdorp, hesitating and slow as that may have been, but the OC convoy thought he would make a push for it and consequently the wagons and two thirds of the force marched away leaving the rearguard so hotly engaged that it could not shift its position – Into the gap there left the enemy pressed, thereby surrounding the rearguard and stampeding the mules in all directions causing the utmost confusion which the enemy took advantage of – This is not an authentic account but what I gathered it may be changed by Oliphants court of inquiry –

It looks as if both these disasters came from Col Anderson's[48] order for the convoy to advance where it ought to have remained parked – Had the boers not succeeded in the first they would never have dared to rush Methuen's column[49] –

You have asked me rather a difficult question about black men who are stated to be actually garrisoning blockhouses etc –

In Cape Colony Cape boys and Bastards[50] are separated by Act of parliament from natives, of the latter we have none in blockhouses though we have some as watchmen between blockhouses[51] – of the former, Cape boys, I believe French has recently allowed some of them to occupy intermediate blockhouses out west – Of the Bastards there has always been a corps at Uppington [Upington] on the German frontier to guard roads and water holes, they may be said to be police. No one else could do the work –

In native states such as Herschell[52] of Cape Colony, Basutoland, Swaziland, natives are employed by the states to protect their frontier from boer incursions – I do not know how many are employed but they all keep well within their frontier, and do not work under my orders – The only natives I pay of all these is a guard on the frontier of Herschell, and the ORC, and a guard of Basutos on the Witzie hoek [Witzieshoek] passes into Basutoland along the Natal frontier, neither of these guards can be employed outside Herschell or Basutoland, and I only pay them to make sure that the native states keep them up, as both points are of strategic importance to me –

In ORC & Transvaal & Natal no natives are used otherwise than as watchmen cattle guards scouts drivers and labourers   I will try and get accurate numbers but it means a vast amount of telegraphing[53]

I enclose a copy of my orders on the subject of employment of natives[54]

The Cape boys and Bastards are only employed as police to guard their country & people from boers who murder them as was done in the case of Esau[55]   they are all west of the railway to Cape Town and are all immediately under control of regular soldiers.

I have wired your question on to Settle at Cape Town, but I fear it will take a little time to get numbers required

With regard to Courts of Inquiry and Courts Martial I must say I much prefer the naval system of trying officers; but the present regulations and Royal warrants prevent such trials – I find the greatest difficulty with A G and Judge Advocate General to get any officer tried – I hardly think that taking evidence on oath and the Court of Inquiry giving an opinion will much improve matters – The only whitewashing that I think should be allowed is acquittal by G[eneral] C[ourt] M[arshal] – after confirmation

I have wired you about selling captured stock to the new meat contractors – If I did not do so they could not possibly take up their contract, and we should be in a hole – I have already had a row with them about the price which I have insisted on being market value, which they did not like as they lose on the subsequent dead weight which they sell to us. I said "take it or leave it", and they then after some grumbling took it – We ought to get half a million for our stock which is all I can set off against what the late contractors made out of us –

The new contractors tried to bounce me out of some conclusion on political grounds; but I said I would have no dealings other than on strict business principles, I think now the air is cleared they will work all right – Rhodes is very ill[56] otherwise I expect he would have been at me about the price of stock they have to pay, as it no doubt makes the contractors work at a loss for some time; but they have plenty of capital to go on –

I am very sorry I missed last mail while I was travelling, my inspection at Harrismith took rather longer than I anticipated and trains ran badly back to Pretoria so I was late – I hope you will forgive this very bad letter – I am rather upset about this Methuen business[57] and am being a good deal worried – I am afraid the answer I sent you the other day on an absurd question in Parliament, that "I do not keep useless men in South Africa", was untrue – I evidently have kept more than I thought It is an unpleasant fact, but must be faced some of these 5/ men are not nearly equal to the boers –

TNA reference PRO 30/57/22/Y31(a)

95
Lieutenant-General Ian Hamilton to Mr Winston Churchill
[Typed and signed letter]   Army Head Quarters, South Africa,
Pretoria. 15th March, 1902.

Private

The present is rather a critical moment in several ways. I will not say much about the tactical position at present, as, after all, you get that pretty well from the telegrams and despatches. The Orange River Colony is getting played out. The women, poor things, have at last become humbled, and during the past fortnight have, for the first time during this War, given willing information to the Columns and have confessed they wish the thing well over. Many of them are reduced to dressing themselves in the forage sacks picked up at our Camping grounds, and enteric is bad amongst them. The Eastern Transvaal does not look dangerous, although a biggish concentration has just been reported East of the Wilge

[River]. The North is full of surrenders and talk of surrendering: The Western Transvaal has now got to be tackled, – a difficult business owing to the vastness of the country and the fact that we cannot well blockhouse it owing to want of water. Methuen has worked it on much more kindly principles than other parts of the country, and it is still full of crops and stuff. This, however, will probably soon now be altered. So much for the military situation. But what I want to write you about is Schalk Burger coming in to talk over terms with De Wet, for which purposes we have granted him a free pass. A special train is waiting for him at Belfast, and he will come in here en route and see Lord Kitchener. Lord K. can talk any of these fellows over if he is left half an hour with them. What he will try and do now is to persuade Schalk Burger to agree definitely to have a Conference before he comes under the pernicious influence of De Wet.[58] Once we have a Conference I think there is some chance of arriving at a conclusion, anyway this is the last chance. If we do not come to some agreement with the leaders within the next two months or so these leaders will lose the last remnant of their authority with their men: there will be no treating possible, and we shall have to catch the lot. In the purely military and political sense this may possibly be advantageous, seeing that the bitter men will continue to be killed off and the children in the Camps to become anglicised, but is it worth the blood and millions of say another year's fighting? Personally, I don't think so. If the Conference were to come off and Lord K. with full powers met the Boer leaders, say Schalk Burger, Steyn, Botha, De la Rey, and some sensible civilian who knows and is understood by the Boers, we should probably have peace if our Government did not get too exultant and rub it in too much to these fellows that they were absolutely humbled and crushed. If however the High Commissioner steps on to the scene I despair. A rough Dutch farmer and the finest product of Oxford are instinctively antagonistic, especially when the latter hails from Johannesburg, wears a frock coat and eyeglass, and has a quietly sarcastic manner.

Now you have all my news. I have an anxious time here, but don't you make any mistake. Lord K. is a big genius, even if he does occasionally display the manners of a spoilt child. He must prevail in the long run over anything, or if he does not then I have never yet met the man who will.

Churchill Archives Centre (Cambridge), Churchill Papers, CHAR 1/34/20-23

96
Mr St John Brodrick to Lord Kitchener
[Copy]   March 22nd-1902
<u>Private</u>

Our mails do not cross today - or rather I do not receive yours before writing – We have been busy getting our estimates through and defending ourselves against suggestions of improper contracts. Campbell Bannerman got a heavy fall over his vote of censure – We carried the war into his camp and beat him by 155 – But we cannot stop their saying things wh. do harm – Incidentally I have been for 9 hours running on the Govt. bench for 9 of the last 12 Parliamentary days, which is very severe with all the work here.

I see you are 'shedding' Generals very fast – Rundle – Tucker – B[ar] Campbell & to our satisfaction B. Hamilton.

If you have a berth for men like Paget or Pole Carew – both are available – but I imagine you only want Column Commanders.

We quite realise how useless you find new troops at first – and I hope the new Yeomanry will have had a good racket before they go to you. Your letters & Ian Hamiltons have made them put Infantry drafts in front of them – We shall have draft ships leaving from next week.

One thing I am troubled about viz. employment of Kaffirs <u>as soldiers</u> I do not want to bother you & your telegrams are explicit – but somehow I can't help having a suspicion that on some lines of country, the C.O's are so reduced in men that Kaffirs are possibly doing soldiers work – I do not want – for your credit as well as my own – to have to go back on anything I may say in H[ouse] of C[ommons] & though I have taken a pretty high line, the letters wh. come through hardly seem to square with our official assertions. I am sure you understand it is only that I want to make sure we are not being let down.[59]

I am repeating your telegram on Australian Horses landed with Commonwealth Rgt to Downe – and if more are to be got of same stamp they shall be shipped at once –

[Postscript]
Thanks for letting me know result of Oliphant's angling into Von Donop disaster[60]

TNA reference PRO 30/57/22/Y134

Part 5
April and May 1902
The Peace Negotiations
Introduction

On Wednesday 9 April 1902 delegations from the ZAR (Acting State President Schalk Burger, State Secretary F.W. Reitz, Commandant-General Louis Botha, General Koos de la Rey, General Lukas Meyer, plus five others) and the OFS (President M.T. Steyn, Acting State Secretary W.J.C. Brebner, General Christiaan de Wet, General C.H. Olivier and Judge (General) J.B.M. Hertzog, plus two others) met in the Western Transvaal town of Klerksdorp to discuss the question of whether the Boers would enter into peace talks with the British government. This meeting was made possible by the mediation of the Minister-President of the Netherlands, Dr Abraham Kuyper, who contacted Lord Lansdowne, the British Secretary of State for Foreign Affairs, who in turn contacted Lord Kitchener, who then gave the Boer governments safe conduct to enable them to hold the meeting [97]. Those present at the meeting gave a review of the circumstances under which the commandos were fighting and of whether it was possible to continue with the struggle. It was decided to negotiate for peace under the following conditions: some retention of republican independence; the Uitlander franchise question had to be settled; the Boers would be prepared to demolish their forts; future disputes were to be settled by arbitration; Dutch and English were to receive equal status in schools, and there had to be bilateral amnesty. These proposals were presented on 12 April to Kitchener in Pretoria [99], who declined to negotiate on the basis of the republics retaining their independence. Lansdowne also rejected the proposals, but authorised Kitchener and Lord Milner to request new proposals from the Boers. The Boer leaders rejected Lord Roberts' annexation proclamations of 1900 as invalid, regarded themselves as the legitimate governments of the republics, and argued that they did not have the constitutional right to negotiate for peace on the basis of losing their independence without having consulted the republican electorate.[1] At this stage Kitchener became more optimistic about the possibilities of a negotiated peace settlement [101].

It was impractical to test the republican voters on the above-mentioned matters, and consequently it was decided that the commandos would elect 30 delegates each for the Transvaal and the OFS, who would then meet at Vereeniging on 15 May 1902 to discuss the basis of the peace negotiations. Although by May 1902 approximately 20 per cent of all Afrikaners in the field were fighting on the side of the British Army, these joiners were not represented at any of the peace talks. The more than 120,000 black and coloured people who served the British Army also had nowhere to air their views. After two days of discussions by the delegates, a Boer commission of five members (Generals J.C. Smuts, Louis Botha, J.H. de la Rey, C.R. de Wet and J.B.M. Hertzog) left for Pretoria on 17 May, where from 19 to 28 May the 'acts of peace' were hammered out in tough negotiations with Milner and Kitchener [104, 106]. Kitchener was in a very difficult position. As a military man he knew the horrors and suffering of war, and he wanted to end the senseless conflict as soon as possible. But he also had to keep his political masters in London happy, as well as local politicians (in particular Milner). At Pretoria, a rapport developed between Kitchener and Smuts which in due course may well have been of decisive importance. Kitchener spoke privately to Smuts and said that there was a possibility that in a year or two the Liberal Party (which had been sympathetic to the plight of the Boers) could come to power, and then grant self-government to the Transvaal and ORC. In practice Henry Campbell-Bannerman's Liberal Party swept to power in 1905, kept their promise, and granted responsible self-government to the Transvaal (1906) and then to the ORC (1907).

From 29 May 1902 the Boer commission was back at Vereeniging where the conditions of surrender were presented to the other delegates, and discussed in heated debates. Die-hards such as Steyn and De Wet resisted the idea of a peace settlement without the retention of independence, but Botha, Smuts, and even De la Rey were in due course successful in convincing the greater majority of delegates that it was in the interest of the Afrikaner nation to accept the British peace terms. Of crucial importance were arguments with regard to the dwindling number of Boers in the field; their lack of horses, arms, and ammunition; the overwhelming British military manpower resources; the fact that

European powers were definitely not going to intervene on behalf of the Boers; the increasing number of blacks and coloureds who were taking part on the side of the British in a combatant capacity; the plight of the Boer women and children in the internment camps, and the fact that it was in the interest of the Boers to accept reasonably advantageous proposals while they were still in a position to do so and while the British were still prepared to make certain concessions, even though the Boer republics would lose their independence.[2]

What the Boers did not know was that the number of deaths in the white internment camps – which had risen sharply since July 1901 and peaked at over 3,000 for the month of October 1901 – had begun to decrease after October 1901, and had fallen sharply in February 1902; and that fewer than 200 died in the camps in May 1902.[3] But that is not to say that the Boers could – or would – have continued their hopeless struggle.

An incident of which the Boers did take note, and which must have had a profound influence on them, was the clash between a Zulu impi and a Boer commando at Ntatshana (Holkrans), about 20 km north of Vryheid, in the early hours of Tuesday 6 May 1902. The Boers, under Field-Cornet Jan Potgieter (totalling 72 men), were all asleep when they were attacked by a few hundred members of the abaQulusi tribe (led by Sikhobobo). The Boers suffered a humiliating defeat, losing 56 killed and three captured. The Zulus lost 52 killed and 48 wounded.[4] Only at Magersfontein (11 December 1899), Platrand/Wagon Hill (6 January 1900) and Spioenkop (24 January 1900) had the Boers lost more men killed in a battle, albeit that they were victorious at Magersfontein and Spioenkop.

Kitchener's role during the negotiations was crucial. Those in the know had always said that in negotiations with the Boers, Kitchener would be a better diplomat than Alfred Milner [88, 95]. Kitchener and Milner did not always get along very well [112, 113]. Milner wanted unconditional surrender, while Kitchener – who had learnt to respect his military opponents – was in favour of a negotiated settlement that would not alienate the Boers and jeopardise reconstruction after the war. In practice, Kitchener was in fact very conciliatory towards the Boers during the peace negotiations [100], and Ian Hamilton noted that Kitchener conducted the negotiations in an excellent way [105]. Kitchener regarded Milner as a negative influence during the negotiations [106]. Although Kitchener would not budge on basic issues, for example the question of the restoration of republican independence to the Boers, he went out of his way to treat the Boer leaders with respect, tried to see their point of view, and valued their dignity. While Milner wanted subjugation, Kitchener was not vindictive and worked in the interest of terms that the Boers could accept with some honour; and Kitchener always kept post-war reconstruction and reconciliation in mind.

Lord Kitchener to Mr St John Brodrick

[Holograph]   Pretoria

30th March 02[1]

The boer Govt have been waiting patiently at Kro[o]nstadt while their messengers have been out looking for Steyn – I have just heard they found Steyn with De la Rey, and the messengers are returning to Kro[o]nstadt – I therefore expect the Govt will leave Kro[o]nstadt shortly to meet Steyn and De la Rey – While staying at Kro[o]nstadt I have had two officers with them and from what I can gather it seems probable that Schalk Burgher [Burger] intends to ask for a conference to settle peace[2] – The point they appear to lay most stress on is that some period should be fixed after which, if all goes well, self Govt would be given to the new colonies – I believe if 2 or 3 years could be fixed, on the understanding that the boers behave thoroughly well, that it could help greatly – I should like very much to know what H.M. Govt think of this point –

They seem to realize that this is about their only chance of getting peace, and if negotiations fail now that their people will be out of hand, and the state of the country and war will be a repetition of what happened in Poland[3] – They think de Wet wishes to pose as a polish patriot and martyr but they seem quite convinced that the Transvaal has had enough of it – Of course they have not seen De la Rey whose attitude after his recent success[4] would not be conducive to peace – I am doing all in my power to hit him hard as soon as possible, and hope soon to succeed My first attempt hustled them severely; but was unfortunately not decisive[5] –

I do not place much reliance on the negotiations coming to anything more than my meeting with Botha did – I think there is a great number who really want peace and see how hopeless this struggle is, but one can never be sure that they will not be talked over by the more bellicose minority and even if not completely brought round to change their views, will be so influenced as to take up an attitude which would make any negotiations impossible – If they come to us and say "we are beaten, be generous", then I think we should treat them with consideration   None of them like the idea of being handed down to posterity as traitors who gave their country away –

I think the above gives you fairly how the matter as it now stands strikes me, and we must leave the result "on the knees of the Gods" –

Of course the main questions will be 1. Amnesty 2. Rebuilding of farms and restocking country and 3. How long, if they behave loyally and well, the period of probation before they get self govt will last – Of these as far as I can gather the last is far the most important as if 2 or 3 years were fixed they could go to their people with something definite & so cover their face with them – They talk a good deal of Polands struggles and polish patriots –

I send you a translation from the Orange Free State Gazette (which is still occasionally published by the boers) which shows what harm Campbell Bannermans speeches do[6] –

I also enclose a statement of the intelligence that was given to Lord Methuen the day before the attack – I do not think the intelligence could do more, the way this news was obtained was an intelligence scout went to a boer woman in a farm, and said he was sick of us, and fed up, and wished to join the boers; but felt he could only get away if there was fighting   the lady replied "then you won't have long to wait as delarey [De la Rey] means to attack tomorrow"   I will let you know when we have losses, but I am glad to say it is not often of course   I do not refer to a cart being caught or a few cattle driven off by robbers –

TNA reference PRO 30/57/22/Y136

98
Lord Kitchener to Mr St John Brodrick

[Holograph]   Pretoria
6th April 02

I am much obliged for your letter of the 15th March[7] – I quite agree with you as regards the strict punishment of those officers and men who by their carelessness or through other causes do so much harm, and I consider that this is most necessary for the good of the army as a whole –

One of the great faults in British officers is that they do not look upon their work sufficiently seriously at all times – They are in many cases spasmodic and do not realize the serious nature of their responsibilities, and if they do so at one time, they easily forget them.

Though this is due in some extent to training, it seems to be a national defect based a good deal on over confidence –

In my opinion strict punishment is very necessary to impress on officers their very serious duties, but at the same time it does no good to act without fullest inquiry and strictly on legal lines –

A hasty judgement creates a martyr, and unless military law is strictly followed a sense of injustice having been done is the result –

Military law requires in my opinion considerable attention to be effective, and to meet cases that have occurred during this war – The slight changes in the court of inquiry procedure are not in my opinion sufficient –

It is always very difficult to elucidate by evidence exactly what has taken place in a fight. I have however tried my best, in every unpleasant case of mishap, to deal with the case on the above lines; but when after exhaustive inquiry and trial the fault is brought home, and an officer is condemned and cashiered it seems to me that the subsequent cancelling of the sentence on a legal quibble is a set back – I refer to the case of Milne-Home[8] – As far as I know the sentence was quashed because an officer sat on the court who, though previously qualified to sit on C[ourt] M[artial] by service in the army, had become disqualified through leaving the service, and joining the yeomanry in which he had not sufficient service –

When C Ms have to take place with military officers, colonial officers, etc as members it strikes one that the objection in this case was a mere quibble, and I think the impression created did some harm with regard to the remarks we so often see in the papers, the Army, I think rightly, feel that examples should be made, but when such an example has to be and is carried out, it should be published to the world as little as possible on the principle of washing our dirty linen at home –

Examples are solely for the good of the Army, throughout which they are thoroughly known and appreciated, and though the public may wish to "turn their thumbs down", it is felt that considering the honour of the Army at home and abroad, they should as far as possible be made to restrain their efforts for our good –

I am having one officer tried for the loss of the convoy, and six officers tried for Methuens disaster,[9] these trials probably will result in other trials, as we get at the truth – You may be quite sure I will not let the matter drop if I have anything to go on upon

Botha is coming in to join the others, and I am sending them all down to Klerksdorp to await Steyn and Delarey there[10] – I have nothing new to report, some think peace is likely to result, personally I am not very sanguine, as they are such difficult people to deal with, full of suspicion – Anyway it can do no harm, and I shall relax nothing until the arms are actually laid down – If they ask for a conference I propose it should take place here in Pretoria –

I enclose some translations of captured correspondence[11] there is not much in the letters, but they may interest you –

I have had the audacity to send you a wire this morning about a King's medal, if it comes to anything I should restrict the issue carefully to only those actually fighting at the end of the war, and who have been for 6 months previously in the field – The only exception would be those that had to leave during the 6 months previous to the end of the war through wounds or very serious illness. If this were announced you would have no difficulty in finding reinforcements & I should have no difficulty in keeping men I want; but whose time was up   the general impression has always been that the war would be over in 6 months –

TNA reference PRO 30/57/22/Y138

99
Lord Kitchener to Mr St John Brodrick

[Holograph]
Pretoria
13th April 02

I send you the notes taken by Hamilton of our first meeting; there were some other conversational remarks but nothing of importance. I did not get your telegram informing me that I should not express an opinion until after the meeting. I do not think what I said did any harm: on the contrary it brought out before them all the absurdity of the position they took up and how little the wire pullers had to say in favor [sic] of it.[12] As far as I can gather the question they will certainly ask is how long a period will elapse if they behave absolutely loyally before they obtain self government.[13]

Milner does not like this I gather, but it will make them very suspicious if no term can be even hinted at – On the whole I am personally rather in favor [sic] of giving them an indication, properly safeguarded, of the time – I cannot help thinking before long we shall have some trouble with the natives all round the Transvaal – They have seen for the last 2½ years white men chased by other white men and have suffered considerably & have got out of hand – The boers have sold them rifles for food and are now much afraid of them –

If the future self govt is tied up by financial arrangements suggested in my last letter I think in 2 or 3 years we should be quite safe with a properly arranged franchise to give self govt and it might relieve us of a good deal of trouble to do so –

Milner comes over tonight and will be at the meeting tomorrow when the telegram just received will be communicated to them   I think the telegram 692 is perfect   it avoids giving them any possible chance of misrepresenting matters to their Burghers which the war party are anxious to obtain.

One of their party tells us most of what passes

There is no doubt Steyn rules the whole   he is well educated[14] and a man of ability but bitterly hostile   he has nice manners   in fact they all are very polite. He is ill and has bad eyes. I have supplied him with a doctor that he asked for & he reports him very bad and that he must shortly go to the coast and have complete rest[15]

The Free staters are a very common classed lot compared with the Transvaalers. De Wet has said very little   he is a low classed man, but from the little he did say I did not gather that he was as irreconcilable as I suspected; he evidently wants if they have to carry on to make out a good case for their burghers: so far he has been disappointed –

As regards the question of amnesty to Cape rebels they may ask that those that they commandeered i.e. forced to join them, who I believe number two or three hundred may benefit with them in the general amnesty leaving all who joined willingly to our care.

The Transvaalers are for peace and will not stick out much for terms – If it all fails I think I may make some arrangement with them for our benefit hereafter –

Baird[16] who talks Dutch though they do not know this, Mackee my adc [ADC],[17] and Leggett,[18] are in constant attendance, the young boers of whom there are a considerable number as secretaries, ADC's etc talk rather openly; they say that if no terms are made and they are forced to unconditional surrender that they will hold themselves absolutely free to begin again when they can get a chance and see England in any difficulties. On the contrary if terms are arranged and independence is officially given up they will be unable to do so and will join us loyally and make the best of it – They were asked how they would start war again without arms and they said it would be difficult and take time but could be managed –

I am on very good terms with them and our people with them say they are rather frightened of me   I give it them pretty straight some times for instance I told them the letter they sent me after my Middleberg [Middelburg] interview[19] was disgraceful, but not so bad as their lying motive, they had officially told the burghers, was at the bottom of my reply to Botha's questions – They had not a word to say – I have also given it their generals pretty hot in their treatment of natives and selling them arms, they are much afraid of a native rising and I have told them they are entirely responsible if such an event occurs and that I cannot detach troops to protect them from the result of their own conduct which has caused the natives in many parts to get beyond my control – They retaliated somewhat feebly by saying our troops incite natives against them I said we only incited natives by example   they (the natives) are an imitative people and when they see us chasing boers over hills, they want to do the same in order to take revenge for the bad treatment of the natives by the boers – They did not much like this and Botha was a good deal impressed and said it was a most serious question – I shall probably discuss it again with them – Of course these remarks were said in conversation   not at the table during the meeting –

I do not think there is much more of interest to you   I am not more hopeful than I was last week but these people will want a lot of talking or they will start some impossible line –

You can understand with all this going on I am having rather a hard time and will excuse this letter if it is not full enough –

Might I suggest that when you take up a line in parliament that I should conform to here that your Secty should write me privately exactly what the point is   For instance the employment of natives to which you refer in your letter of 22nd [20]   have looked through two papers and cannot find your statement on the subject – I sent you the exact numbers employed and by not hearing from you I thought all was well but it is a subject on which I am always nervous as I find I have to be continually checking officers for going beyond or wishing to go beyond instructions on the subject the temptation on the spot to relieve our men of hard work is no doubt great but I am very strict on subject

[Postscript]
Since writing I fear Steyns influence has succeeded in changing the majority   we shall see but I am not more hopeful than I was –

TNA reference PRO 30/57/22/Y140

100
Lord Kitchener to Mr St John Brodrick
[Holograph]   Pretoria
20th April 02

I enclose the notes taken at the meetings from which you will be able to see at once exactly what happened.[21] They all went off in good spirits and I think with the exception of Steyn and Hertzog they are all anxious to put an end to the war.

Besides the official meetings I arranged each day to have meetings with the Generals, nominally to discuss various points such as treatment of natives, wearing Khaki etc   When I got them together I did not restrict our conversations to the points that their Govts thought we were discussing – I think these meetings did good, they are a curious people and if they are taken the right way seem to be very easy to manage, but it all depends on the way it is done – However we can only gauge by results. I was very sorry they took such a long time to get their people together, I worked out for them a different way to do it by which a few days would have been saved, but they preferred their own and I could not insist –

I hope you will agree that I was right to resist armistice   at the same time to give them the facilities for meetings they require, I shall keep a close watch on these meetings and any that are hostile shall have it sharp. A little rest for our men and horses will be a great advantage to us, and give us a really good fresh start if we have to go at it again, I do not mean that I am giving up operations, only going a bit slow and not annoying those that vote solid for peace –

They took all my decisions very well, when Steyn asked for Fisher[22] I suggested the Transvaal might fairly ask for Leyds. Which made them laugh as Leyds is one of the most unpopular men amongst them as they all think his intrigues were a great cause of the war[23] –

I only fear that Steyn in his ponderous way will make a patriotic speech at the meeting, and turn them round, he (Steyn) is head & shoulders above the others, and has great influence owing to his better education and ability – Botha tells me if Smuts from the colony gets up in time for the meeting he will face Steyn, and be able to stop any attempt to ….. the voters – On the whole I think things look well, there is very little doubt that the Transvaal will vote solid for peace – De la Rey was the only doubtful one, and before he went away he said he would go with the majority of the Transvaalers – The Free staters are doubtful, but they cannot go on alone, and we have so chaffed the Transvaal that they are being led by the nose by the smaller state that I really think they will stick out this time

Steyn's eyes are bad, and he is generally ill, he asked to see a dutch doctor friend in whom he had confidence – As the doctor was very anxious for his own purposes, to get the war over, I allowed this, and after examining Steyn he told him that unless he immediately took complete rest at the coast he would die in three weeks, Steyn said "I know it but I must give my life for the people" The doctor said if he would not do as he told him he refused to treat him, so they parted and the doctor went away after telling all the members of Steyns Govt that Steyn was no longer in his present state responsible for what he did   Another doctor was called in, and he gave a similar opinion, but Steyn insisted on going out again,[24] though I think in a somewhat subdued state of mind – I hope this will have a good effect upon him on the 15th at the meeting,[25] he is not likely to get much medical advice on the veldt –

Before the boers left they handed me a statement they had drawn out for the burghers which they are sending round, I enclose a translation   I think it is a fair statement of the case –

They will want to get de Wet off his liability of being hanged for murder, and I suppose we could hardly hang him after he has signed peace – I think it will be better in every way to let bygones be bygones, and try to start on a friendly footing –

The great difficulty is to know what line de Wet is taking in the matter, this is not at all clear yet, but I hope to get information when he begins talking to the boers on the veldt, we are watching him closely –

I am distressed at some Yeomanry in Ternans column again behaving badly – I have told Gen C Knox to try them by C[ourt] M[artial] if possible –

The correspondents here have been rather pestering for news of the negotiations, I wish you could let me know what is allowed out at home, so that I could do the same here, I have given them nothing and they have behaved well –

TNA reference PRO 30/57/22/Y143

101
Lord Kitchener to Mr St John Brodrick

[Holograph]   Pretoria
27th April 02.

I have received and understand all your instructions about dealing with the terms of peace. I have impressed on Botha and others that if they decide to give in they will get far more generous terms by simply owning that they are beaten, and not haggling about terms which would look like selling their country – I expect we shall have some points raised, but I do not foresee any great difficulty if the delegates return from the meeting with a mandate to make peace –

Up to the present the news of the attitude of the boers is distinctly favourable to peace – De Wet who was a doubtful factor seems to be working for peace, I heard that some of the irreconcilables in the Free State are saying that de Wet had been bought in Pretoria

I do not like telegraphing to you yet on the subject as one is so often deceived by false intelligence of what the boers really think; but if I can let you know with any certainty what is likely to happen at the meeting I will do so –

Milner has gone to Capetown where there is a certain amount of agitation about abolition of the Constitution in order to rearrange the electorate – Those that advocate the abolition would have been wiser I think if they had objected to be governed by the present ministers, and given that as a reason rather than show their hand as regards the intended manipulation of the registration of votes. I have been asked to decide what the Cape papers may publish on the subject as there might be a good deal of agitation in the colony on the subject   I replied to GOC Capetown that "Press censors should not allow anything to appear that may in your opinion or that of the Governor lead to agitation in the country especially by the use of inflammatory language. With this restriction I do not consider it possible for me to deal with specific subjects and must leave the decision on such points to the Governor and you to determine" –

I am sending you by this mail a despatch,[26] and a list of officers for honours and rewards at the coronation which I hope you will approve of – I have only chosen a few of those who received previous rewards who have done particularly well, and who I think it is for the good of the service that they should be pushed forward – If the war ends there may be a few other cases that I should like to bring forward –

I think the increase of pay to the soldiers is an excellent thing, I did not write about it as I thought you would like to know the impressions amongst the men particularly as regards reengagement, and this I gave to one of my adcs [ADCs] to find out, but it takes a long time with troops scattered as they are out here to get any really valuable opinion – We are all so busy with the war that no one has much time to think of anything else, but I will let you know the impression created amongst the men as soon as I get something reliable to go on.

I feel some hope that the end is not far off –

TNA reference PRO 30/57/22/Y145

102
Lord Kitchener to Mr St John Brodrick
[Holograph]   Pretoria
                                              3rd May 02.

I have told Settle to post to you by this mail a copy of the martial law regulations in force in Cape Colony – They have been seen and approved of by the Cape Attorney General & Sir R Solomon here, and perhaps you would like to communicate them to Parliament – I do not think there is anything in them that would raise much criticism, and considering the cock & bull stories that are being circulated at home regarding martial law in Cape Colony, it might have a good effect to publish facts –

I am rather disappointed at not having been able to telegraph before this some news regarding the attitude of the boers in the field towards the terms of peace – I get a great deal of contradictory intelligence, but there is nothing definite to go on, and as far as I can judge the boers are about even for war or peace –

There is very little doubt de Wet has been working for peace, but the boers in the field show great opposition to a settlement which they might have had a year ago, and which they were then told would ruin them by the same leaders who now advocate their acceptance of the terms – In some parts of the country they show more inclination to go on with the war than I had expected – I think if they decide to continue we shall have a large number of surrenders –

Capt. Massey [?],[27] who was tried at Klerksdorp for failing to assist the convoy, has been honourably acquitted – The present state of military law is to my mind unsuited to the Army and is not based on the principles of administration of justice which govern all other courts of law –

A court martial is now what an ordinary court of law would be without a judge – The foreman of the jury decides the case and gives judgement, if this were attempted in civil law it would soon break down –

All justice seems to me to be based on the prosecution, the defence, the jury (i.e. the officer of the court martial), and the judge (i.e. the convening officer who acts under warrant) – In military law the judge is left out, and entirely ignored, he cannot bring before the jury the legal aspects of the case, or the value that should be placed on evidence that may have been given to the court – The code of punishment is so vague and elastic that you see almost ridiculous awards given by courts martial, which have afterwards in some cases to be set right, and this shake[s] all confidence in the administration of Army justice – I believe a court martial might be made into one of the best courts of law; as it stands however, it is to my mind in the majority of cases very much what a civil court would be without a judge –

In the case of Capt. Massey [?] I am calling attention of the members of the court to the term "honourably" in the acquittal – I expect the other officers will get off just the same –

I am very glad the Govt have decided to give a Kings medal, it will be most popular amongst the men who have really done hard word [sic] – I hope the issue will be so restricted as to keep up the value of the medal, it makes all the difference in the world how soldiers look at a medal if the distribution is carefully considered and strictly adhered to –

TNA reference PRO 30/57/22/Y146

103
Lord Kitchener to Mr St John Brodrick

[Holograph]   Pretoria
11th May 02

Long before you get this you will have known the result of the meeting to be held on the 15th at Vereeniging,[28] so there is no use in my trying to give a forecast from the very contradictory reports I receive –

If we have to go on it will no doubt take some time to catch the last man, and I could suggest for your consideration whether it would not be wise to husband our resources rather more so as to continue the campaign steadily; but without so much strain on home supplies of men horses etc – The same would apply to the colonies, instead of rushing out men that may be available, they should I think now prepare to relieve the contingents out here before their time is up – It always takes a month at least before a colonial contingent after arrival in this country is ready to take the field, and the hiatus between the contingent leaving and the new contingent taking their place in the field, is always difficult to arrange for satisfactoraly –

I am a good deal worried about operations in Cape Colony, if we have to go on I shall go down and see French, and go thoroughly into the matter   he is always sanguine, but the result is not satisfactory – I know how hard it is in the immense area of the Colony to catch the small parties still wandering about – I think I must make a change again in the colonial troops, they are practically useless as at present organised under the Prime Minister[29] and though we save money by the present arrangements, I think we should do better by not allowing these D[istrict] M[ounted] T[roops] who are merely ordnance depots for the rebels to draw upon –

If only the Prime Minister would do as I advised him at first, and put his money into really efficient police, and leave Army matters alone, it would be much better and finish matters in Cape Colony far sooner; but unfortunately he suffers severely from overpowering conceit and the position of commanding two colonial forces in the colony is so dear a personal satisfaction to him that unless he has that he will do nothing – He has now I fear almost squandered all his money so he will be useless in the future – He might have done a good deal had he taken advice –

I expect if the ..... soon that we shall have a large number of surrenders, I should like if possible to try and protect certain areas with blockhouses and National Scouts, and get the women and children back to their farms – It may not be possible, but if it were the boers still out would see that the country was settling down in spite of all they could do – I think the country East of this would be almost in a condition to allow of my trying this experiment and if it succeeded it would soon spread –

I promised to let you know what the men thought of the new pay – It is very difficult to get any opinion of value – The scheme is generally looked on favorably [sic], but it is thought that it unduly benefits the young soldier   It is thought that men who earn at present good conduct pay should be allowed to keep it, and receive the service pay in addition – I am afraid I cannot give you much now of any value on the subject at present

TNA reference PRO 30/57/22/Y149

104
Mr St John Brodrick to Lord Kitchener

[Copy]
Private

May 24. 1902.

I am glad your telegrams prove you in such good spirits as to the negotiations. As you will have seen from our replies – we are ready to go nearly the whole way with you – but it is absolutely necessary to say not to land ourselves in further trouble. Probably your arrangement as to Arms will cover the points on wh. we are anxious here. We were bound to ascertain what it is proposed to do with rebels, though I know how ticklish a point this is.

The worst trouble is the £3.000.000 for expenses of war – The money does not matter – but the Loyalists will have seeds of bitterness for ever if they are not treated more handsomely <u>in proportion</u> A farmer – loyalist Cape Colony – whose business has been ruined will not be satisfied without some very excessive sum if besides assistance to the Burghers to reoccupy their farms, all the notes given them are to be redeemed, and they find themselves possibly better off than before –

Then we are set ag[ain]st paying Foreign creditors. But I have no doubt a way will be found out of all this & as the telegraph will dispose of much of it in the next few days, I will not write further.

If peace should ensue, I hope you will get things well in train before you leave. No one could take up the command, or deal with the Boers with half your authority & probably what is done in the first few weeks will go far to make for the success of the settlement.

But this ought to be consistent with your getting a good holiday here before you go East[30] –

Do not think I am not supporting you about the £3.000.000 – but we must find a way if possible to put it which will be less crude & offensive to loyalist sentiment both here & in S.Africa than that originally sketched out

I imagine also that the proposals, having been arranged under such great pressure, are open to some modification or close scrutiny.

Thank you much for your full telegrams & most interesting letters.

TNA reference PRO 30/57/22/Y151

105
Lieutenant-General Ian Hamilton to Mr Winston Churchill

[Typed and signed letter]   Army Head Quarters, South Africa,
Pretoria. 24th May, 1902.

I have just arrived here from Klerksdorp, having come up in rather a hurry on a coal truck in order to be at Lord K's. elbow during this crisis.

Thank you so very much for yours of the 15th April. I stupidly have not kept a copy of mine to you, and can only suspect therefore that certain passages therein may not have served to raise me in the opinion of one of the eminent statesmen to whom you showed it. Although far removed from the scene of your struggles and debates, it is not difficult even for an outsider like myself to apprehend that Mr. Chamberlain possesses 'les defauts de ses qualities',[31] and that he is so accustomed to making men do what he wants them to do that he is rather inclined to imagine that Nations as well as individuals should feel as he wants them to feel. If not, 'tant pis'[32] for them. Still, I am entirely and unreservedly glad he saw my letter, because my conscience tells me that, whatever its precise terms may have been, its intention was purely impersonal and in what I believed to be the interests of the Empire and its fortunes. This being so, I am naturally inclined to hope that it is more likely to have done good than harm to the negotiations, which is a point far more vital to me just now than any thought of what impression I may myself have produced.

Things are very exciting here this morning, and as far as our Government, Lord Kitchener, and the Boers are concerned, all looks very hopeful. The only danger is the one I have always anticipated. Lord K. has had an extraordinarily difficult task. Milner says himself he is no diplomatist, and certainly it is always difficult to diplomatise in double harness. I must not discuss this further, but if ever the Minutes are published[33] I think you will say I have not misled you in my previous letters on the subject. It is curious to me to look back now on the Bloemfontein Conference[34] and to realise that, under the circumstances, this bloody War was bound to be the result. So far I believe that this result was little short of providential from an Imperial point of view, but the time has now come when we want quite another sort of wind up to the palaver.

I told General De la Rey this morning that General Tucker had just got married. He said, 'Why he must be 60!'. I replied, 'Yes, but the lady also is no chicken',[35] on which he rejoined 'I hope then the Clergyman may preach to them from the text "<u>Father forgive them: they know not what they do</u>"'.

The Western Transvaal has always been pronounced impracticable for driving purposes. The territory was, it was said, too vast: there were no blockhouses on which to rest the flanks of the line, which must therefore rest 'en l'air'[36] and be open to the circumvention's of the enemy. There was no water except small pools at intervals of from 15 to 20 miles, and it was therefore considered impossible to line out at night.

Well, we managed it. We spread false reports; we filled gaps of 20 miles at night with veld fires and a few National and Native Scouts, until we got close enough to one another to make a continuous line. We did without water, and we dug and worked night and day for all we were worth. It was very hard on the troops, as for four successive nights they were digging and shooting all the time after 20 mile marches during the day, but success made them forget all their past hardships, and the enthusiasm when they found they had got 367 prisoners, mostly irreconcilables and rebels, was something to be proud of.[37]

Good bye for the present, and may your star continue in the ascendant,

P.S. 25<u>th</u>.

I dined with General De la Rey last night, the occasion was the birthday of Smuts.[38] I sat between Botha and De la Rey. On Botha's right was De Wet: on De la Rey's left sat Smuts. I had the most enchanting evening, and never wish to eat my dinner in better company. They told me a great many stories about the War which would give me much joy to repeat to you now only, alas, I have no time. De la Rey and De Wet both told me exciting stories of their escapes from myself and others. It would specially interest you to know, on Botha's authority, that on the evening of the second day's fighting,[39] a messenger from De la Rey carrying a letter saying he had got French in the hollow of his hand and only awaited orders to smash him up, actually crossed a messenger from Tobias Smuts[40] (on Botha's left) saying that De Lisle had carried his part of the position and that the whole line of retreat was threatened. It was this which forced Botha to retire in such a hurry, otherwise he thought he had had a great success on hand. I do not myself think this, but we should certainly have had lively times next morning: as soon as De la Rey had overwhelmed French he was, with 800 men, to gallop for the big guns which were, I think, with the Scots Guards in front of Pole Carew, and Botha was to support this by a vigorous advance all along his line. As you remember, French was almost absurdly weak, and I am inclined to think they would have got him, but the other part of the plan I told them would not have come off.

You would also like to know that the Boer losses at Colenso were 5 killed, 1 drowned, 23 wounded:[41] At Wagon Hill 77 killed, 30 missing, 250 wounded:[42] at Magersfontein, which I had thought their most severe engagement but which turns out to have been only the second worst, they had 72 killed and a proportionate number of wounded.[43]

Churchill Archives Centre (Cambridge), Churchill Papers, CHAR 1/34/58-62

106
Lord Kitchener to Mr St John Brodrick
[Holograph]   Pretoria
                                                            25 May 02

I had hoped these negotiations would have been over by this time but as you know we are still at them and the result is still doubtful – I hope I may never again have to carry on negotiations in double harness, it adds enormously to the difficulties which in this case have not been small –

I do not for a moment believe that Milner would like to see the war go on when peace could be secured without giving the boers any point that would not be conceded if they laid down their arms without terms, but he is very suspicious and rather inclined to haggle about money – His openly shown suspicion makes the boers doubly suspicious that he means some deep plot to ruin them later, and so we go on making sometimes mountains out of molehills and all the time increasing the danger of handing over the peace party amongst the boers to the irreconcilables –

Doubtless before you get this the whole matter will be settled one way or the other – There is no doubt the boers admit they are thoroughly beaten, but in guerilla warfare it is far easier to start it than it is to bring it to an end and this the boer leaders are now feeling –

If peace comes no doubt the future arrangements will be made by telegrams from you, so that it is hardly worth while starting the subject in this letter which will probably only reach you after everything of importance is settled –

I am sending you by this mail the record of the last meetings   I hope you will approve of the attitude I took up.

All the troops have benefited considerably by the rest and we shall all be ready to go on cheerfully when the trumpet sounds, I fear if we have to wait much longer we shall be changing our bits to be at them again –

TNA reference PRO 30/57/22/Y152

Epilogue
31 May 1902 and Beyond
Peace and Aftermath
Introduction

The 60 Boer delegates at Vereeniging had to accept the British peace proposals no later than midnight on 31 May 1902. The 'acts of peace', or rather the conditions under which the Boers were to surrender, contained ten clauses, including the following: all burghers had to lay down their arms and recognise the British monarch as their legitimate sovereign; all Boer prisoners of war could return on condition that they became British subjects (i.e. they had to sign a declaration that they accepted the terms of surrender); the burghers and repatriates would, as British subjects, retain their personal freedom and property; Dutch would be taught in Transvaal and ORC schools, and would if necessary be used in courts of law; licensed arms could be retained if necessary for protection; military administration would be replaced by civil administration, and representative government (followed by self-government) would be granted as soon as circumstances permitted; the question of whether black people should be given political rights would not be discussed before the introduction of representative government (i.e. the interests of black people were sacrificed in the interest of Briton-Boer reconciliation after the war), and the British government would make available £3,000,000 for the reconstruction and development of the two former republics. The surrender conditions were, if all aspects are taken into account, very generous towards the Boers. Had Lord Milner and his followers had their way, the conditions would not have been so lenient.[1] But, ironically, Lord Kitchener would not be remembered by Afrikaners for these relatively liberal terms, but rather for what happened in the internment camps, or 'murder camps' as many Afrikaners referred to them.

On the afternoon of Saturday 31 May the peace proposals were accepted by the Boer delegates [107, 108] by 54 votes to six. (The previous day, President M.T. Steyn had stepped down as President of the OFS, and General Christiaan de Wet became Acting State President. At the bitter end, De Wet decided to vote in favour of the 'acts of peace'.) Members of both republican governments then travelled by train to Pretoria where, at 23.05 in the dining-hall of Melrose House, Kitchener's headquarters, the conditions of surrender were signed by all parties. Lord Kitchener and Lord Milner signed on behalf of the British government; Acting State President (General) Schalk Burger, Commandant-General Louis Botha, General Koos de la Rey, General Lukas Meyer, State Secretary F.W. Reitz and Executive Council member J.C. Krogh signed for the Transvaal, and Acting State President (General) Christiaan de Wet, Judge (General) J.B.M. Hertzog, General C.H. Olivier and State Secretary W.J.C. Brebner signed for the OFS.[2]

While the Boers struggled to come to terms with the humiliation of defeat and the loss of their independence, the British could afford the luxury of congratulating themselves on the successful conclusion of hostilities [109]. Kitchener could, at long last, sigh with relief that all was over, and that he had accomplished what had been expected of him [111]. In the long run, he had been ruthlessly efficient in South Africa.

The Anglo-Boer War was over and it was time to count the cost. A total of 448,435 white soldiers had fought on the side of the British. According to official figures, at least 7,792 of these soldiers had been killed or had succumbed owing to wounds sustained in battle, while 14,658 had died of disease or in accidents. Furthermore, 75,430 soldiers had been sent home either ill or wounded.[3] It is not known for certain how many black and coloured people, who had served on the British side, either as combatants or non-combatants, were killed or wounded. Not more than 78,000 Boers took part in the conflict. At the cessation of hostilities, some 21,000 were still in the field (11,000 Transvaalers, 6,000 Free Staters and 4,000 Cape rebels); i.e. more than double the number estimated by the British. And then there were also the approximately 5,500 joiners who served on the side of the British. At least 3,997 Boers were killed on the battlefield or died of wounds, some 150 died in accidents, while those who had died owing to disease numbered about 1,000. A total of 33,059 Boers were captured: 12,954 Transvaalers, 12,358 Free Staters, 7,587 Cape and Natal rebels, and 160 foreign volunteers. A further 22,098 Boers surrendered voluntarily (handsuppers): 13,780 Transvaalers and 8,318 Free Staters. Since no record was kept during the guerrilla phase of how many Boers were wounded, this number remains unknown.[4]

Apart from white and black civilians who died in the internment camps (i.e. at least 28,000 whites and at least 23,000 – but probably many more – blacks), an unknown number of black and coloured people died in the services of the Boer commandos. The war cost the British taxpayers more than £200 million[5] – about £6,000,000,000 in terms of the value of money a hundred years later (2002). (The seventeen major wars in which Britain had been involved from the end of the Crimean War (which cost Britain £68 million) in 1856, up to the eve of the outbreak of the Anglo-Boer War in 1899, had cost them a total amount of £98.5 million.)[6] The cost of the Anglo-Boer War was in fact enormous, keeping in mind that it is impossible to determine the high cost of the war to the ruined Boer republics.

On Sunday 8 June 1902 approximately 9,500 British soldiers formed up on Church Square in Pretoria for a medal parade, followed by a thanksgiving service [110]. The interdenominational service was led by the Archbishop of Cape Town. At the medal parade, Kitchener awarded nine Victoria Crosses to soldiers, and other awards to several nurses. Kitchener and his staff left Pretoria on 21 June 1902.[7] In the meantime, and for several weeks to come, at various places across the war zone, the Boers continued to surrender and hand in their weapons [114].

On 23 June 1902 Kitchener handed over the overall command of the British forces in South Africa to Lieutenant-General N.G. Lyttelton. That same day (i.e. a day before his 52nd birthday) Kitchener departed from Cape Town on board the SS *Orotava*, accompanied by Lieutenant-General Ian Hamilton, Lieutenant-General J.D.P. French, Colonel H.S. Rawlinson, Colonel W.R. Birdwood, and other members of his personal staff. The SS *Orotava* arrived back in England on Saturday 12 July 1902. The ship berthed at Ocean Quay, Southampton, at 09.00. Kitchener then travelled by train to London, arriving at Paddington Station at 13.50 where he was met by the Prince of Wales, the Duke of Connaught and Lord Roberts. Troops lined the streets all along the route which Kitchener travelled from the station to St James' Palace, where a luncheon was held in his honour. From there he went to Buckingham Palace for an audience with King Edward VII (who was recovering from appendicitis). The king bestowed upon him the Order of Merit. He was also made a Viscount, and was henceforth known as Viscount Kitchener of Khartoum, and of the Vaal in the Colony of the Transvaal, and of Aspall in the County of Suffolk. Parliament voted him a grant of £50,000 (worth about £1,400,000 a hundred years later), and as from 1 June 1902 he had already been promoted to full General.[8] In the weeks following his return to England, Kitchener was invited to several functions held in his honour, and received several additional honours and awards [115].

On 9 September 1902 the British government appointed a Royal Commission, under the chairmanship of Lord Elgin, to inquire into the military preparations and other matters connected with the war in South Africa. The inquiry did not include the conduct of military operations in the field. On Tuesday 14 October 1902 – the second day on which the Commission sat to hear evidence – Lord Kitchener gave his evidence to the Commission, in the process answering no fewer than 105 questions. Amongst the many matters that Kitchener referred to was the need for a more professional army, and better training. He also commented on the medical services during the war, the transport situation, and problems with regard to horses.[9]

On 17 October 1902 Kitchener left Britain's shores and sailed to India where, from 28 November 1902 to 9 September 1909, he served as Commander-in-Chief. His tenure as Commander-in-Chief was overshadowed by clashes with the Viceroy, Lord Curzon. On leaving India, Kitchener was promoted to Field Marshal. En route back to Britain (via the United States of America) he toured the battlefields of the Russo-Japanese War of 1904–5, and visited Australia and New Zealand to advise the dominion governments on defence matters. Back in Britain he served on the Committee of Imperial Defence. From 29 September 1911 Kitchener was Agent and Consul-General in Egypt, as well as Minister Plenipotentiary. In June 1914 he received an Earldom, and was henceforth known as Earl Kitchener of Khartoum, and of Broome in the County of Kent (Broome being the name of his country estate). On 6 August 1914, shortly after the outbreak of the First World War, Kitchener – who had been on holiday in England and was about to return to his post in Egypt – was appointed as Britain's Secretary of State for War. His tenure as Secretary of State was not a happy one, and extremely controversial. Kitchener was like a fish out of water. He foresaw a protracted war and was successful in mobilising the huge new British citizen armies and sending them to France and Belgium – where hundreds of thousands of men died. But Kitchener had no experience of the Cabinet government or of the methods and machinery of the War Office, which led to strained relations with other members of the Cabinet. However, he probably laid the foundation for the Allied victory attained by November 1918. With regard to World War I, Kitchener will always be remembered as the face (and the pointed finger) on the famous

1914 recruiting poster (designed by Alfred Leete) proclaiming 'Your Country needs YOU'.[10]

At about 17.00 on the afternoon of Monday 5 June 1916 (exactly sixteen years after he and Lord Roberts captured Pretoria), Kitchener sailed from the Royal Navy's base at Scapa Flow in the Orkney Islands on board the 10,850-ton 'County' class armoured (heavy) cruiser HMS *Hampshire* to visit Russia, where he was to advise the Russian government on matters pertaining to the war, hopefully instill in the Russians a greater enthusiasm to continue their war effort with more vigour, and establish some co-operation between the Allied forces fighting on the Western and Eastern fronts. In extremely bad weather, near Marwick Head, and some 2.5 km off the west coast of the Orkney Islands, the *Hampshire* struck a mine at approximately 19.40 (5 June). The mine was one of several laid by the German submarine *U-75* on the night of 28–29 May 1916. Almost immediately the ship lost power, could not be steered, and wireless communication was lost. The *Hampshire* sank within fifteen minutes. Of the 655 men on board the cruiser, only twelve survived, and Lord Kitchener of Khartoum was not one of them. His body was never recovered.[11]

107
Lieutenant-General Ian Hamilton to Mr Spenser Wilkinson[1]

[Photocopy of holograph]   31-5-1902
                                                              3-p.m.-

Best thanks for yours of April 14th – Just half an hour ago we heard
the delegates accepted peace[2] – I had run up from the Western
Transvaal to be at the Chief's elbow during the crisis – I can hardly
realise the new situation – but I feel that a mountain has rolled off
my head – Personally of course I wished for nothing better than to
go on, but from the Imperial standpoint I feel it is everything to
have got a solid peace generously granted, willingly accepted –
Even from the selfish point of view too I could hardly hope to
better my good fortune in having begun at Elandslaagte[3] and having
ended, with the end, by commanding at the last general action
(when Potgieter was killed)[4] and at the very last big drive,
particulars of which I attach[5] – I am very anxious for you to read, &
even study, these. Lord K. never gives much detail in his despatches
& I do not remember ever having seen anything giving a really clear
idea of the thought, labour etc involved in carrying one of these out
to a successful issue – There is nothing private about the facts
although the actual wording had better not be used in any way as it
is always just possible that in view to this being the very last drive,
& very opportune in its effect on de la Rey & Kemp, Lord K. might
think fit to publish it – I have shown it to no one else here –

<u>Private</u>
I am perhaps going home via Japan to look at the troops of our ally
– Goodbye my dear Wilkinson – Don't overwork yourself –

<u>P.S.</u> 1 1.6.02
Japan is off!! Am coming home with K.

239

P.S.2 <u>1.6.02.</u>

I have just ascertained that Lord K. has actually freely cribbed from my despatch in writing his final one[6] which H. Hamilton[7] takes home tomorrow – It is just as well you should know this as it makes it clear you should not show before his appears that you have seen an identical document!

LHCMA, Hamilton 2/2/2

108
Lord Kitchener to Lord Roberts
[Telegram copy]   31 May 4.20 p.m.
S 1039 cipher

Secret. Peace terms accepted. I know how glad you will be to hear this. Will you tell Ralli 17 Belgrave Square[8] who is ill.

NAM. 1971-01-23-33-79

109
Lord Roberts to Lord Kitchener
[Manuscript copy]   47 Portland Place, London. W
1st June 1902

Warmest and heartiest congratulations from Lady Roberts, the girls, and myself. Ralli will be informed.

NAM. 1971-01-23-122-4-286

110
Lieutenant-General Ian Hamilton to Mr Winston Churchill
[Typed and signed letter]   Pretoria. 8th June, 1902.

This is probably the last letter I shall write you from South Africa. Thank God, all has gone well, and by going well I do not only mean that the victory is complete, but also that I think history will say Lord K. has done all that he could do, even during that first flush of success which turns some people's heads, to lay the foundations for a permanent friendship and peace between the Dutch and English sections which may, D.V., end in complete amalgamation. Someday, in safe England, I will tell you, perhaps, something of the vicissitudes and struggles through which this has been accomplished. It is wonderful to think how smooth and easy it must all seem to some of the outside world when one has an intimate knowledge of the ups and downs of the struggle.

I think there is no harm in my saying one thing, viz., that Mr. Brodrick (for whom I know you do not profess a very profound admiration) has, nevertheless, played up most splendidly throughout this business. His telegrams, indeed, have been just about perfect, and helped us round many a nasty corner.

There is only one troublesome matter now left on my mind, and I do not think I can give a better notion of it than by the following extract from a letter which I have just written to Lord Roberts.

"Lord K. showed me your remarks regarding the inadvisability of at present bringing some of the more prominent Boer Leaders to England. I wish, Sir, you could take some opportunity of reassuring Mr. Chamberlain as to his fear that there is any section of loyalists who would resent honour being done to the Boers. I am thankful to say that not even the most bitter of the Johannesburghers are quite as bitter as that. Of course some people carry the idea of patting our late enemies on the back to an extent which can only be described as hysterical and ridiculous. Thus I see people talking about giving a Sword of Honour to Christian [Christiaan] de Wet, &c., &c., but to allow the Boers to England and let people pay them what attention their own feelings may prompt them to show is quite another matter, and is one which should be very seriously considered indeed from a practical standpoint before it is rejected. The Pan-Germanic League[9] have asked Botha and De la Rey to go on a tour through Germany to make speeches, and have baited their hook with the promise that they will be able thereby to raise a very large sum of money for the Widows and children of those who have fallen. This idea has caught on, and Botha certainly (with his Secretary de Wet),[10] and probably also De la Rey, are going. After all, they are British subjects, and being so, cannot well be prevented from travelling where they like.[11]

Now, I think Sir, you will credit me with knowing the Boers pretty well by this time; not only do I know the Boers generally, but I know Smuts, Botha and De la Rey personally. The first two are true Boers as regards their impressionability to their immediate surroundings. Their feelings towards us at present are all that any Britisher could desire. Start them, however, on a tour of speechifying in Germany, and the local anti-British atmosphere would turn their heads as they saw time after time how any reference to ill-treatment or farm burning was received with applause. It is hardly in human nature, certainly not in Boer nature, to resist going further and further on the denunciatory tack. There might be no great political harm in this on the Continent – of that I am no judge – but as regards this country the effect would be damnable.

Now, there is a perfectly easy way of preventing all this mischief and trouble, or rather there are two ways. The first I hardly venture to press. It is that Commissions, at any rate honorary, should be given to Botha and De la Rey, which would stamp them definitely as British and render any anti-British remarks uttered in their presence insulting to them, but I feel that in expressing this wish I am going a bit ahead of your views and those generally held in England.

The second method is far simpler, and, if well worked, would, I believe, be equally effective. You have simply to let Botha come home in the ship with Lord K., and appear a few times to enthusiastic meetings in London. He would then publicly give himself away to such an extent by declaring his real feelings as regards our treatment of prisoners and general conduct, that he would cease to be worth a cent to the blighters of the Pan-Germanic League.

I fear I have inflicted an interminable screed upon you today, Sir, but the extreme importance of the subject must be my excuse.

Do not altogether lose your mind to the possibility of my doing a lightning voyage to Japan this autumn. The idea has become so firmly fixed in my head, and also in Victor Brooke's,[12] that to root it out entirely would be too painful. He has already learnt to say in Japanese "What a pretty gal you are", and I can make some simple enquiries about Hospitals and Field Artillery".

In making this extract from my letter to Lord Roberts, the last two paragraphs are outside the subject I meant to refer to you.[13] However, that doesn't matter. I hope you will agree with me in what I say about these Boer Leaders.

I enclose you a Poem[14] which is intrinsically rather amusing, but is really of value in as much as it is a genuine voice from the ranks, having been composed by a Private in the Cameron Highlanders. I think you may take it that the views expressed are pretty generally held in the Army.

We have just had our Thanksgiving Service.[15] K. surpassed himself. He was Archbishop, Choir and Congregation in one. I could not deny him the tribute of my warmest admiration.

Good-bye, my dear boy. More power to your elbow

Churchill Archives Centre (Cambridge), Churchill Papers, CHAR 1/34/67-72

III
Lord Kitchener to Mr St John Brodrick
[Holograph]   Pretoria
8th June 02

Everything is going on well as I have told you by wire and I hope the disarmament will be complete on the 17th   I expect we shall find there were more boers in the field than we anticipated   it was of course very difficult to judge numbers seen – I would swear that they were more than that   we had apparently over estimated our enemy[16] –

I am very grateful for all the rewards that have been showered upon me,[17] but really what one feels is the sense of relief and security that no more regretable [sic] incidents will occur – It was the fear of what might happen any minute that made life so unendurable – Thank God that it is all over now and the end I am glad to say is equally well received on both sides   Hoping to see you before long

TNA reference PRO 30/57/22/Y155

112
Lord Kitchener to Lord Roberts

[Holograph]   June 8th 02.

I am sending
you some photos in
another envelope[18]

We have just held a successful service of thanksgiving in the square[19] – I think it went off well, but what with giving a big luncheon party afterwards my time for writing letters has been cut short –

The surrender is going on excellently   no hitch anywhere up to the present and <u>all</u> the arms are I fully believe coming in. Botha de Wet and delarey [De la Rey] playing up well in this respect – The permits which I was rather afraid of are being very sparingly given so all is well – It is rather difficult to determine whether the peace is more popular amongst the boers or the South African loyalists,   both are pleased –

I am very grateful for all the honours and rewards that have been given me – I think I like my promotion[20] best as it completes the series of my ranks from Capt on having all been obtained by brevet for active service –

I hope to be able to get away about the 21st, the surrender will then be complete, and Lyttelton will know everything   he is now coming here to work with me till I go[21] – Milner will be glad to get me away and really there will be no object in my staying to arrange for the troops going home – I shall not be sorry to get a little rest

Many thanks for your kind messages as also those from Lady Roberts and your daughters[22]

Hoping to see you all again soon

NAM. 1971-01-23-33-80[23]

113
Lord Kitchener to Lord Roberts

[Holograph]   Pretoria
                                                                   15 June 02

So much is done by wire that it is not necessary for me to write to you about the military details that have been arranged

Lyttelton is quite ready to take over[24] and I think shall be …..

I am now fairly ready to hand over everything in good order and settled

I am sending home my brother[25] by this mail so he can get away to India   he has done the surrender in the west well and with great tact   4800 men came in in that district where I only thought there were 2000   In fact our enemy were just about double what we calculated they were[26]   I am glad we did not over estimate them as the civil element kept on stating we were doing, they are now more astonished than I am.

It is curious that all the men who knew the boers well like Wools Sampson Sammy Marks and others should have been so much out in their calculation but I think it is a good thing for us that we were not engaged against such small numbers as they supposed –

I feel I have squared up most things and Milner will be glad to see me away and have Lyttelton to deal with so I hope very shortly after you get this to see you again   I hope to get away about 23 or 24th from Cape town[27] but you have given me no hint yet when you would like me to come.

NAM. 1971-01-23-33-81

114
Lord Kitchener to Mr St John Brodrick

[Holograph]   Pretoria
                                                            15 June 02

Everything is settling up well and I hope it may not be long after you get this before I see you – I have arranged the commands as you wish   Lyttelton taking the Transvaal and ORC   I know that from the Governors of Cape Colony and Natal point of view there is something to be said for this division but I do not think it is from the purely military point of view the best arrangement

I have also at last settled up with Milner what he wants and have just wired you the final result –

The only outstanding account of importance is the Cape Railways account   I shall have another try to settle this when I pass through Cape Town but am doubtful of success as they are quite impossible people to deal with –

The troops and commands are all arranged as also is the sending home of the men as far as transport are available –

The surrender has gone off remarkably well and will be complete on the 17th   I feel sure with good government there may be no fear for the future in this country   nothing could be better than the manner in which the boers have come in   They are now more loyalist than the loyalists

Lyttelton has been working with me lately and know[s] everything now so that when I look round I do not see much to keep me here and as I daresay you can imagine I feel I want a rest away from it all   so I hope before long I may get a wire from you to say come on which I shall not delay long –

TNA reference PRO 30/57/22/Y156

115
Speech by Lord Kitchener[28]
Sword of
Honour
(Capetown)

Lord K.'s Speech: Original – (Autograph Corrections)[29]

[Typed speech with amendments in longhand[30]]   [31 July 1902]

My Lord Mayor,[31] My Lords and Gentleman [sic]. I wish I could adequately express to you my gratitude for the cordiality [deleted] *kindness* with which you have emphasised the far too flattering terms in which this toast has been proposed.

I have already thanked the Mayor and People of Capetown[32] in anticipation, for this beautiful sword, but there are many friends [deleted] *here* representing South Africa to whom I again tender my best thanks together with the expression of a sincere [deleted] *confident* hope that in South Africa at any rate the sword may never again be drawn from *its* scabbard.

I feel sure *that* upon an occasion such as the present one when so many *who* take a deep interest in the future of South Africa are met together all our thoughts must turn to the man who has been left at the helm in that country.

We all have confidence in Lord Milner, we all realise the difficult work he has before him, and wish him, with confidence as well as sympathy, every success in the anxious task which he is now accomplishing in South Africa.

For nearly 3 years I have worked in close communion with the High Commissioner, and I may say that our *old* friendship which existed prior to my going to South Africa has only been strengthened during [deleted] *and increased* by the time of stress which we have passed together.

Although previous [deleted] events *immediately leading up to the War*, may have to some degree influenced the full appreciation of Lord Milner by a certain class *of our New fellow Subjects* in South Africa, still I am convinced that the better he is known the more his high qualities and great ability will be appreciated by all sections of those who have come under his rule.

Nothing will assist Lord Milner more in his great work of reconciliation, and *the* creation of a [deleted] prosperous [deleted] country [deleted] *prosperity* than the rapid development of South [deleted] Africa [deleted] *the country* which is, as you doubtless know, a land full of natural resources, and every description of potential wealth.

Gold iron and coal, are good assets, and if to them you add the development of Agriculture, and the introduction, by assisted immigration, of fresh blood into the Country then Gentleman [sic] you have the makings of nothing less than a new America in the Southern Hemisphere.

The question who will supply the energy brains and money required for this great development is one far more for you Gentlemen than for me but where as in South Africa patriotism is joined to self interest I am not in the least afraid[33] that you will sow the seed and reap the harvest for which we have I hope prepared the soil.

I thank you once more My Lord Mayor and Gentlemen for your kindness which will neverbe [sic] forgotton [sic] by me.

TNA reference PRO 30/57/17/S29-30

Notes

Publication details of all works mentioned in the Notes are given in the Bibliography.

Introduction

1 His first name, Horatio, was originally given to his father (born 1805), in honour of Lord Nelson (who died in 1805). H. de Watteville, *Lord Kitchener*, p. 9; G.H. Cassar, *Kitchener: Architect of Victory*, p. 17.

2 G. Arthur, *Life of Lord Kitchener*, I, p. 3; information supplied by Emma Kitchener-Fellowes.

3 *Dictionary of National Biography* (henceforth referred to as *DNB*) *1912–1921*, pp. 306–7; *Dictionary of South African Biography* (henceforth referred to as *DSAB*), II, p. 365; Cassar, op cit, p. 17; Arthur, op cit, I, pp. 1–3.

4 *DNB 1912–1921*, p. 307; *DSAB*, II, p. 364; Arthur, op cit, I, pp. 4–40.

5 Arthur, op cit, I, pp. 41–139; *DNB 1912–1921*, pp. 307–8.

6 *DNB 1912–1921*, p. 308; Arthur, op cit, I, pp. 140–65; A. Hodges, *Lord Kitchener*, pp. 85–94.

7 Arthur, op cit, I, pp. 165–83; *DNB 1912–1921*, p. 308.

8 *DNB 1912–1921*, pp. 308–9; J. Pollock, *Kitchener. The Road to Omdurman*, pp. 91–143; Arthur, op cit, I, pp. 184–245; P. Magnus, *Kitchener. Portrait of an Imperialist*, pp. 99–134. See also B. Burleigh, *Sirdar and Khalifa or the Re-conquest of the Soudan 1898*, B. Burleigh, *Khartoum Campaign 1898 or the Re-conquest of the Soudan* and P. Ziegler, *Omdurman*.

9 Pollock, op cit, pp. 144–51; *DNB 1912–1921*, p. 309; Arthur, op cit, I, pp. 246–55.

10 *DNB 1912–1921*, p. 309, Arthur, op cit, I, pp. 256–63.

11 See the Introduction to the Prologue, infra, for more information about the appointment of Roberts and Kitchener for war service in South Africa.

12 Pollock, op cit, p. 187.

13 Ibid, p. 219.

14 Ibid, pp. 191, 219.

15 R. Esher, *The Tragedy of Lord Kitchener*, p. 215. For more on Kitchener's character see also, for example, E.S. Grew *et al.*, *Field-Marshal Lord Kitchener. His Life and Work for the Empire*, pp. 1–15.

16 F.M. Richardson, *Mars without Venus. A Study of Some Homosexual Generals*, pp. 117–26.

17 Pollock, op cit, pp. 225–7.
18 *DNB 1912–1921*, p. 307.
19 Esher, op cit, pp. 215–16.
20 Pollock, p. 228. For a list of Masonic appointments held by Kitchener, see ibid, pp. 228–9.
21 Esher, p. 217.
22 See the caption to photo number 11 in D. Judd and K. Surridge, *The Boer War*, between pp. 176 and 177.
23 Richardson, op cit, p. 118.
24 Cassar, op cit, p. 485; J. Adye, *Soldiers and Others I have known*, pp. 189, 191.
25 P. Trew, *The Boer War Generals*, p. 88.

Sources and Editorial Method

1 P. Magnus, *Kitchener. Portrait of an Imperialist*, p. 11.
2 G. Arthur, *Life of Lord Kitchener*, II, p. 114.
3 Transvaal Archives Depot (TAD, now part of the National Archives, Pretoria), inventory of microfilms kept by the TAD, p. 147; TAD inventory of War Office Records (copies) kept by the TAD, pp. 2–5.
4 F.A. Steytler, 'Bronnenavorsing in Groot-Brittanje, 1951–1954', *S.A. Argiefblad* 8, 1966, p. 31.

Prologue
11 October 1899 to 10 January 1900
Introduction

1 *Report of His Majesty's Commissioners Appointed to Inquire into the Military Preparations and Other Matters Connected with the War in South Africa* (Cd. 1789), pp. 21, 34; J.F. Maurice (ed.), *History of the War in South Africa 1899–1902*, I, p. 2.
2 A. Wessels, *Die Anglo-Boereoorlog 1899–1902. 'n Oorsig van die Militêre Verloop van die Stryd*, pp. 4–5.
3 A. Wessels, 'Die Britse Militêre Strategie tydens die Anglo-Boereoorlog tot en met die Buller-fase', pp. 367–9; *Royal Commission on the War in South Africa. Appendices to the Minutes of Evidence taken before the Royal Commission on the War in South Africa* (Cd. 1792), pp. 103–5.
4 Wessels, 'Die Britse Militêre Strategie . . .', pp. 204–16, 288–315; I.F.W. Beckett, 'Buller and the Politics of Command' in J. Gooch (ed.), *The Boer War. Direction, Experience and Image*, pp. 46, 53.
5 J.H. Breytenbach, *Die Geskiedenis van die Tweede Vryheidsoorlog in Suid-Afrika, 1899–1902*, I, pp. 147–51, 153, 156–62.
6 For more on the four main phases of the war, see A. Wessels, *The Phases of the Anglo-Boer War*.

7 For more on the Boers' strategy on the eve of the war, see A. Wessels, 'Die Boere se Strategie aan die Begin van die Anglo-Boereoorlog', *Tydskrif vir Geesteswetenskappe* 39 (3&4), September & December 1999, pp. 227–42.

8 For more on the 217-day siege of Mafeking see, for example, J.P. Botha, 'Die Beleg van Mafeking tydens die Anglo-Boereoorlog', passim; A.P. Smit and L. Maré (eds), *Die Beleg van Mafeking. Dagboek van Abraham Stafleu*, passim; L.S. Amery (ed.), *The Times History of the War in South Africa 1899–1902*, IV, pp. 568–97; B. Gardner, *Mafeking. A Victorian Legend*, passim; I.R. Smith (ed.), *The Siege of Mafeking*, passim.

9 For more on the four-month siege of Kimberley see, for example, H.G. Terblanche, 'Die Beleg van Kimberley', passim; Amery (ed.), op cit, IV, pp. 533–67; B. Gardner, *The Lion's Cage*, passim. Cecil John Rhodes (mining magnate and former Prime Minister of the Cape Colony) – see also Biographical Notes – was in Kimberley during the siege.

10 Wessels, 'Die Britse Militêre Strategie . . .', pp. 380–1.

11 For more on the battle at Talana see, for example, Amery (ed.), op cit, II, pp. 141–74; Maurice (ed.), I, pp. 123–41; Breytenbach, op cit, I, pp. 214–36; G.S. Preller, *Talana. Die Driegeneraalslag by Dundee met Lewensskets van genl. Daniel Erasmus*, pp. 192–221.

12 For more on the battle at Elandslaagte see, for example, Amery (ed.), op cit, II, pp. 175–95; Maurice (ed.), op cit, I, pp. 157–71; Breytenbach, op cit, I, pp. 237–63.

13 For more on the events of 'Mournful Monday' see, for example, Amery (ed.), op cit, II, pp. 212–60; Maurice (ed.), op cit, I, pp. 303–41; Breytenbach, op cit, I, pp. 172–95.

14 For more on the 119-day siege of Ladysmith see, for example, Amery (ed.), op cit, III, pp. 145–205; Maurice (ed.), op cit, II, pp. 531–85.

15 Amery (ed.), op cit, II, pp. 303–17; Breytenbach, op cit, I, pp. 364–85; W.S. Churchill, *London to Ladysmith via Pretoria*, pp. 76–97.

16 *South Africa. Further Correspondence relating to Affairs in South Africa* (Cd. 43), p. 135: Steyn-Schreiner, 11 Otober 1899 (telegram).

17 Amery (ed.), op cit, II, pp. 292–4; Maurice (ed.), op cit, I, p. 275; Breytenbach, op cit, I, pp. 447–55; C.J.S. Strydom, *Kaapland en die Tweede Vryheidsoorlog*, pp. 42–3; Wessels, 'Die Britse Militêre Strategie . . .', pp. 426–8. As far as the role of and dilemma faced by the 'Dutch' (Afrikaners) in the Cape Colony are concerned, see J.H. Snyman, 'Die Afrikaner in Kaapland 1899–1902'.

18 Wessels, 'Die Britse Militêre Strategie . . .', pp. 459–77.

19 For more on the battle at Stormberg see, for example, Amery (ed.), op cit, II, pp. 362–82; Maurice (ed.), op cit, I, pp. 291–303; Breytenbach, op cit, II, pp. 196–225; J. Meintjes, *Stormberg. A Lost Opportunity*, pp. 81–103.

20 For more on Methuen's advance and the battles fought by his army, 21 November–12 December 1899 see, for example, Amery (ed.), op cit, II, pp. 325–61, 383–420; Maurice (ed.), op cit I, pp. 218–60, 304–31;

Breytenbach, op cit, II, pp. 22–183; W.B. Pemberton, *Battles of the Boer War*, pp. 43–54, 59–118; G.R. Duxbury, *The Battle of Magersfontein 11th December 1899*, passim.

21 For more on the battle at Colenso see, for example, Amery (ed.), op cit, II, pp. 421–67; Maurice (ed.), op cit, I, pp. 351–75; Breytenbach, op cit, II, pp. 226–332; H.A. Mocke, 'Die Slag van Colenso, 15 December 1899', passim; C.J. Barnard, *Generaal Louis Botha op die Natalse Front, 1899–1900*, pp. 46–71; National Archives of South Africa (Pretoria), LA, 77A: P.A. Nierstrasz, *Der süd-afrikanische Krieg, 1899–1902* (typed manuscript), pp. 677–86.

22 *Confidential Telegrams*, p. 490, No 26: Buller–White, 16 December 1899 (No 88). See also the note following the published telegram that refers to Buller's telegram to White of 17 December 1899, in which he asked certain 'corrections' to be made to the telegram of 16 December.

23 Breytenbach, op cit, II, p. 340; D. James, *Lord Roberts*, p. 265; D. de Watteville, *Lord Roberts*, p. 126.

24 BL MS Room, Lansdowne Papers, L(5)47: Roberts–Lansdowne, 8 December 1899; published in A. Wessels (ed.), *Lord Roberts and the War in South Africa 1899–1902*, pp. 14–16.

25 Breytenbach, op cit, II, pp. 340–1; James, op cit, pp. 262–3, 265–6; T. Pakenham, *The Boer War*, pp. 245–6; Churchill Archives Centre (Cambridge), Esher Papers, ESHR 2/10: journal entry for 18 December 1899. As far as the strategic management of the war is concerned, in particular with regard to civil-military relations, see the excellent book by K.T. Surridge, *Managing the South African War. Politicians v. Generals*.

26 Maurice (ed.), op cit, I, p. 381; *DSAB*, II, p. 599; Pakenham, op cit, pp. 242–5; G. Arthur, *Life of Lord Kitchener*, I, pp. 265–6. See also Part 1, Introduction, including Note 6.

27 A. Hodges, *Lord Kitchener*, pp. 124–5; Arthur, op cit, I, p. 266; J. Pollock, *Kitchener. The Road to Omdurman*, p. 174; C.R. Ballard, *Kitchener*, p. 110.

11 October 1899 to 10 January 1900

1 Efforts to track down and kill or capture Khalifa Abdullahi after the battle at Omdurman (2 September 1898) failed, until his whereabouts were betrayed to Kitchener by spies. On 24 November 1899 the Khalifa and about 5,000 of his followers were run down by a British force at Um Debreikat, some 300 km south of Khartoum. The Khalifa, his principal emirs and at least 600 other Dervishes were killed. P. Magnus, *Kitchener. Portrait of an Imperialist*, pp. 153–4; G. Arthur, *Life of Lord Kitchener*, I, pp. 262–3; E.S. Grew et al., *Field-Marshal Lord Kitchener. His Life and Work for the Empire*, II, pp. 262–3.

2 Sahlé Miriam (Mariam) was the original name of Menelik II (1844–1913), King of Shewa (Shoa), 1865–89; Emperor of Ethiopia, 1889–1913. In 1896 he repelled the Italian invasion of Ethiopia.

3 Kitchener decided to build the Gordon Memorial College in Khartoum in honour of Major-General Charles Gordon, who was killed, together with his force, in Khartoum in 1885 when their base was besieged and then overrun by the Dervishes. Kitchener laid the cornerstone of the college on 4 January 1899, and opened it on 8 November 1902 (en route from England to India). Magnus, op cit, pp. 144–9, 193; Arthur, op cit, I, pp. 253–5 and II, p. 113; Grew *et al.*, op cit, II, pp. 22–6.

4 See G.E. Buckle (ed.), *The Letters of Queen Victoria*, 3rd Series, III, pp. 450–1 for a published version of this letter. The published version in Buckle's book differs from the original manuscript in the RA in the case of punctuation, paragraphing and spelling.

5 Mary Eleanor Anne (died 1935), daughter of the 1st Earl of Dartrey, and later the wife of the 5th Earl of Ilchester.

6 Kitchener was in Khartoum when, on 18 December 1899, he received the news that he was to accompany Lord Roberts to South Africa. He left immediately on that same day, boarded the cruiser HMS *Isis* at Alexandria on 21 December, sailed to Malta, where he changed to the cruiser HMS *Dido*, and reached Gibraltar on 27 December, where he went on board the Royal Mail Ship *Dunottar Castle*, met Lord Roberts, and sailed for South Africa. Magnus, op cit, p. 159; A. Hodges, *Lord Kitchener*, pp. 124–5.

7 Lady Cranborne?

8 Theresa Susy (or Susey) Helen ('Nellie') Chetwynd-Talbot (1857–1919), eldest daughter of the 19th Earl of Shrewsbury, who married Charles Stewart Vane-Tempest-Stewart (later the 6th Marquis of Londonderry) in 1875. They had one son and one daughter.

Part 1
11 January to 28 November 1900
Introduction

1 BL MS Room, Balfour Papers, Add 49727: Lansdowne–Balfour, 17.12.1899 (letter); P. Trew, *The Boer War Generals*, p. 98.

2 *DSAB*, II, p. 599; J. Pollock, *Kitchener. The Road to Omdurman*, p. 174; A. Wessels (ed.), *Lord Roberts and the War in South Africa 1899–1902*, pp. 126–7.

3 *DSAB*, II, p. 599; H. de Watteville, *Lord Roberts*, pp. 131–3; Pollock, op cit, p. 176; G. Arthur, *Life of Lord Kitchener*, I, p. 274.

4 For more on Buller's Upper Thukela campaign see, for example, J. Symons, *Buller's Campaign*, pp. 194–5, 212–40, 247–58; E.B. Knox, *Buller's Campaign with the Natal Field Force 1900*, pp. 55–132; C.J. Barnard,

Generaal Louis Botha op die Natalse Front, 1899–1900, pp. 107–18; J.H. Breytenbach, *Die Geskiedenis van die Tweede Vryheidsoorlog in Suid-Afrika, 1899–1902*, III, pp. 62–236, 288–330; L.S. Amery (ed.), *The Times History of the War in South Africa 1899–1902*, III, pp. 225–330; J.F. Maurice (ed.), *History of the War in South Africa 1899–1902*, II, pp. 366–422; W.S. Churchill, *From London to Ladysmith via Pretoria*, pp. 293–313, 345–66; O. Ransford, *The Battle of Spion Kop*, pp. 34, 42–3, 59–118; J.H. Cilliers, 'Die Slag van Spioenkop (24 Januarie 1900)', *Archives Year Book for South African History* 23(2), 1960, pp. 1–71.

5 Breytenbach, op cit, IV, pp. 204–31; Amery (ed.), op cit, III, pp. 392–6; J.G. Maydon, *French's Cavalry Campaign*, pp. 140–8.

6 A.J. Smithers, *The Fighting Nation. Lord Kitchener and his Armies*, p. 25, pointed to the fact that until 1900 Kitchener was referred to in the *Army Lists* as being only a Major-General, but then from 1901 onwards he was all of a sudden indicated as being a Lieutenant-General since 23 December 1899. See also *Hart's Annual Army List, Militia List, and Imperial Yeomanry List, for 1906*, p. 4. To complicate matters, Pollock, op cit, p. 188 says that Kitchener was promoted to Lieutenant-General on 29 November 1900 (i.e. when he became C-in-C, South Africa), with temporary rank of General. See in this regard also G.E. Buckle (ed.), *The Letters of Queen Victoria*, 3rd Series: *A Selection from Her Majesty's Correspondence and Journal between the Years 1886 and 1901*, III: *1896–1902*, p. 622: Mr St John Brodrick–Queen Victoria, 21.11.1900 (letter). For Kitchener's confidence as to his seniority, see Arthur, op cit, I, p. 288. If, however, Kitchener was in fact only a Major-General at Paardeberg, the command situation was still complicated, because Kelly-Kenny only had the local rank of Lieutenant-General, and Kitchener had been promoted Major-General *before* Kelly-Kenny, who was ten years his senior. Pollock, op cit, pp. 177, 254 (Note 2).

7 Breytenbach, op cit, IV, pp. 286–323; Amery (ed.), op cit, III, pp. 422–53; P. Magnus, *Kitchener. Portrait of an Imperialist*, pp. 164–9; Pollock, op cit, pp. 178–9; G.H. Cassar, *Kitchener: Architect of Victory*, pp. 118–21; Arthur, op cit, I, pp. 282–91; E.S. Grew *et al.*, *Field-Marshal Lord Kitchener. His Life and Work for the Empire*, II, pp. 90–6.

8 Breytenbach, op cit, IV, pp. 324–430; Amery (ed.), op cit, III, pp. 453–8, 473–87.

9 Trew, op cit, p. 108; De Watteville, op cit, pp. 69–70.

10 C.M. Bakkes, *Die Britse Deurbraak aan die Benede-Tugela op Majubadag 1900*, passim; Breytenbach, op cit, III, pp. 343, 398, 401–43, 476–567; Amery (ed.), op cit, III, pp. 500–6, 513–46; *History of the War in South Africa 1899–1902*, III, pp. 438–55, 463–530; Churchill, op cit, pp. 398–466.

11 For more on Roberts' march from Paardeberg to Bloemfontein see, for example, Breytenbach, op cit, V, 27–115; Amery (ed.), op cit, III, 553–91; Maurice (ed.), op cit, II, pp. 180–238.

12 Trew, op cit, pp. 108–9; Amery (ed.), op cit, III, pp. 479, 492–4, 570, 594 and IV, pp. 2–6; Arthur, op cit, I, pp. 299–301.

13 C.R. de Wet, *Three Years War (October 1899–June 1902)*, pp. 79–80; Breytenbach, op cit, V, pp. 159–67.

14 For more on the battle at Sannaspos see, for example, J.E. Rabie, *Generaal C.R. de Wet se Krygsleiding by Sannaspos en Groenkop*, pp. 5–30; Breytenbach, op cit, V, pp. 196–225; Amery (ed.), op cit, IV, pp. 29–50; Maurice (ed.), op cit, II, pp. 274–99.

15 For more on De Wet's role at Mostertshoek and Jammerbergdrif see, for example, W.L. von R. Scholtz, 'Generaal Christiaan de Wet as Veldheer', pp. 120–7; Breytenbach, op cit, V, pp. 240–58, 269–81; Amery (ed.), op cit, III, pp. 56–75; Maurice (ed.), op cit, II, pp. 314–33; A. Wessels (ed.), *Anglo-Boer War Diary of Herbert Gwynne Howell*, pp. 37–46.

16 For more on Roberts' advance from Bloemfontein to the Vaal River see, for example, Breytenbach, op cit, V, pp. 413–524; Amery (ed.), op cit, IV, pp. 77–141; *History of the War in South Africa 1899–1902*, III, pp. 40–77; D. James, *Lord Roberts*, pp. 315–23; T. Pakenham, *The Boer War*, pp. 419–24.

17 Amery (ed.), op cit, IV, pp. 165–84; *History of the War in South Africa 1899–1902*, III, pp. 259–69.

18 Amery (ed.), op cit, IV, pp. 591–7; B. Gardner, *Mafeking. A Victorian Legend*, p. 191 et seq.; A.P. Smit and L. Maré (eds), *Die Beleg van Mafeking. Dagboek van Abraham Stafleu*, pp. 219–71.

19 Breytenbach, op cit, V, pp. 524–49; Amery (ed.), op cit, IV, pp. 141–64; *History of the War in South Africa 1899–1902*, III, pp. 75–101; D. Judd and K. Surridge, *The Boer War*, p. 183.

20 BL MS Room, Lansdowne Papers, L(5)48: Roberts–Lansdowne, 7 June 1900 (letter); published in A. Wessels (ed.), *Lord Roberts and the War in South Africa 1899–1902*, pp. 97–100.

21 For more on the battle at Diamond Hill (Donkerhoek) see, for example, Amery (ed.), op cit, IV, pp. 269–96; *History of the War in South Africa 1899–1902*, III, pp. 204–25; Breytenbach, op cit, VI, pp. 174–207; A.E. Breytenbach, 'Die Slag by Donkerhoek, 11–12 Junie 1900', passim; H.F. Nel, 'Die Slag van Donkerhoek 11–12 Junie 1900', *Militaria* 15(1), 1985, pp. 52–8 and 15(2), 1985, pp. 17–30.

22 The name of the station/siding Heilbronweg (i.e. Heilbron Road, about half-way between Kroonstad and Vereeniging on the main railway line from Cape Town to Pretoria) changed to Vredefortweg (i.e. Vredefort Road) in 1899, and to Greenlands in 1910 – as it is known to this day.

23 Pollock, op cit, pp. 183–4; D.A. Mackenzie, *Lord Kitchener. The Story of his Life and Work*, p. 124; C.R. Ballard, *Kitchener*, pp. 116, 143; Arthur, op cit, I, p. 311; De Wet, op cit, pp. 146–8. There is some disagreement with regard to the exact date. According to De Wet, the incident took place on the night of 13–14 June.

24 Amery (ed.), op cit, IV, pp. 349–54; *History of the War in South Africa 1899–1902*, III, pp. 236–48.

25 *Army. Proclamations Issued by Field-Marshal Lord Roberts in South Africa* (Cd. 426), pp. 10–11.

26 As far as the events in the Brandwater Basin and the first drive against De Wet are concerned see, for example, Amery (ed.), op cit, IV, pp. 298–343, 414–33; F. Pretorius, *The Great Escape of the Boer Pimpernel. Christiaan de Wet. The Making of a Legend*, pp. 23–209.

27 Trew, op cit, p. 110; L. Wulfsohn, 'Elands River. A Siege which possibly Changed the Course of History in South Africa', *Military History Journal* 6(3), June 1984, pp. 106–8; Amery (ed.), op cit, IV, pp. 357–61, 428–9.

28 Breytenbach, op cit, VI, pp. 317–46; Amery (ed.), op cit, IV, pp. 380–413, 443–56; *History of the War in South Africa 1899–1902*, III, pp. 396–403; B.G. Schultz, 'Die Slag van Bergendal (Dalmanutha)', passim.

29 Amery (ed.), op cit, IV, pp. 474–83.

30 Ibid, pp. 481, 483 and V, p. 27.

31 His appointment was officially announced on 18 October 1900. See, for example, G. Forrest, *The Life of Lord Roberts, K.G., V.C.*, pp. 320–1.

32 Magnus, op cit, pp. 171–2.

33 See the comments and sources referred to in Note 6 above.

11 January to 28 November 1900

1 Major-General Edward Thomas Henry Hutton (1848–1923) took part in Lord Roberts' advance to Pretoria, 1900; and in the advance to Komatipoort, 1900. Previous service in Anglo-Zulu War, 1879; Transvaal War of Independence, 1880–1; Egypt, 1882; Sudan, 1884–5. Returned to the UK, October 1900. GOC, Australian forces, 1901–4; GOC, 21st Division of the 3rd Army, 1914–18.

2 At the end of 1899, after the British 'Black Week' defeats, two more contingents were mobilised in Canada for service in SA, the first of these consisting of 1,200 MI, and a regiment of field artillery. This, the 2nd Canadian contingent, arrived in SA 31 January–21 March 1900. C. Miller, *Painting the Map Red. Canada and the South African War, 1899–1902*, pp. 152–70. For the 3rd Canadian contingent to be sent to SA, see Note 8 below.

3 Lieutenant-Colonel Charles William Drury (1856–1913) can be regarded as the father of the Canadian Artillery. Previous service in the suppression of the North-West Rebellion, Canada, 1885. In South Africa he commanded three batteries of Royal Canadian Field Artillery, 1899–1900. Colonel, 1900; Major-General, 1912.

4 Henri-Alexandre Panet (1869–1951) had no previous war service. In South Africa he first served as a Lieutenant in the Royal Canadian Regiment,

1899–1900, and then as a Captain (later Brevet Major) in the Royal Canadian Artillery, 1900. Back in Canada he was AAG, 1905–7; DAG, 1907–9. Served in World War I, 1914–18 (wounded). Retired as a Major-General, 1930.

5 A total of 7,368 Canadians served as volunteers in South Africa (plus five postal clerks, eighteen nurses, 23 artificers and a hospital unit of 64 men who served with the British forces, as well as about 300 who joined irregular units). At least 270 Canadians died during the war, over half of them from disease. The 2nd Battalion Canadian Mounted Rifles (CMR, known as the 1st Battalion CMR from August 1900) was composed of men recruited in Western Canada. See, for example, Miller, op cit, passim.

6 NWMP – (Canadian) North West Mounted Police.

7 Donald Alexander Smith, 1st Baron Strathcona and Mount Royal (1820–1914) raised at own expense a regiment of Canadian rough-riders (Strathcona's Horse) for service in South Africa – see Note 8 below. Smith was a financier, conservative member of the Canadian federal parliament, 1871–9; played a significant role in the completion of the Great Northern Railway in Canada, 1879, and Canadian Pacific Railway, 1885; Conservative MP for Montreal, 1887–96; Governor of Hudson's Bay Company since 1889; Canada's High Commissioner to the UK, 1896–1914. Baron, 1897.

8 The 3rd Canadian contingent to be sent to SA was Strathcona's Horse, 500 men strong. They began their service in SA in Natal in June 1900, as scouts for General Buller's Natal Field Force. Miller, op cit, p. 289 et seq.

9 Baden-Powell relied heavily on black armed support: to defend the defence perimeter, and to sortie out, harass the Boers, and bring in cattle for food. See, for example, B. Willan, 'The Siege of Mafeking' in P. Warwick (ed.), *The South African War. The Anglo-Boer War, 1899–1902*, pp. 150–6.

10 When the war broke out, there were about 1,500 white and 7,000 black (mostly Barolong) inhabitants in Mafikeng. The Barolong had a long tradition of support for the British against the Boers, and consequently approximately 500 of them were immediately armed to help defend their township as well as the south-western section of the town's defences. One of their military leaders, Mathakgong, led several sorties behind the Boer lines and brought back large numbers of cattle. Baden-Powell did not give the Barolong the credit they deserved for helping to save the town. Willan, op cit, in Warwick (ed.), op cit, pp. 141, 150–2, 160.

11 I.e. members of a local coloured community in Mafikeng, some of whom were armed by the British to help defend the town. Willan, op cit, in Warwick (ed.), op cit, pp. 151–2.

12 I.e. members of the Mfengu community in Mafikeng, some of whom were armed by the British to help defend the town. Willan, op cit, in Warwick (ed.), op cit, pp. 151–2.

13 Kgama III (*c.*1830/8–1923), chief of the baMangwato (1872, 1875–1923), asked (1876) and received (from 1885 onwards) British protection against the Boers. A portion of his land became British Bechuanaland.

14 Lentswe (c.1854/5–1924), chief of the baKgatla, was ordered by the British to assist them in attacking a Boer outpost at Derdepoort (25.11.1899), and henceforth Lentswe participated on the side of the British. During the attack on Derdepoort, Colonel G.L. Holdsworth (see next note) was in overall command, albeit that he sent Lentswe's men, under the latter's half-brother, Segale (Lentswe not being present himself) across the border to attack while he waited on the Bechuanaland side. See, for example, H.J. Botha, 'Die Moord op Derdepoort, 25 November 1899. Nie-blankes in Oorlogsdiens', *Militaria* 1(2), 1969, pp. 3–98.

15 Lieutenant-Colonel George Lewis Holdsworth (born 1862) served in South Africa, 1899–1901. From the consulted sources it is not clear to what attack Baden-Powell is referring, unless the attack on Derdepoort (see previous note) is meant.

16 Approximately 300 members of the Rapulana tribe were armed by the Boers at Mafikeng. They were used to raid British cattle, guard Boer cattle, and manned Boer trenches and other fortifications around the besieged town. Other Rapulana were used by the Boers as labourers, messengers and scouts. The Rapulana used the siege to settle old scores with the Tshidi Barolong, who had sided with the British. P. Warwick, *Black People and the South African War 1899–1902*, p. 33.

17 Chief Saane was captured by the Rapulana people at Modimola and held as a prisoner at Lotlhakane. He was only rescued by the Tshidi Barolong after the siege of Mafikeng was lifted, and he was brought back to the town. Warwick, op cit, pp. 33–4, 38.

18 Bathoën I (c.1836–1910), chief of the baNgwaketse in Bechuanaland.

19 General Jacobus Philippus (Kootjie) Snyman (1838–1925), CO of the Boer siege force at Mafikeng.

20 Lord Roberts' HQ, on a farm approximately 3 km south of the Modder River and 5 km south-east from where General P.A. Cronjé had his laager (see Note 22 below).

21 See TNA reference PRO 30/57/16/R8(a).

22 On 17 February 1900 General P.A. Cronjé (see Biographical Notes) and his force of more than 4,000 men, plus a number of women and children, as well as all his wagons, were surrounded in the vicinity of Vendusiedrif, near Paardeberg. Lord Kitchener's unimaginative frontal attacks against the entrenched Boers failed (18 February), but Lord Roberts (who arrived on the scene on 19 February) bombarded the Boer laager incessantly with artillery fire, and on 27 February 1900 (Amajuba Day) Cronjé and his entire force surrendered. L.S. Amery (ed.), *The Times History of the War in South Africa 1899–1902*, III, pp. 401–58, 473–87; J.H. Breytenbach, *Die Geskiedenis van die Tweede Vryheidsoorlog in Suid-Afrika, 1899–1902*, IV, pp. 232–430; J.F. Maurice (ed.), *History of the War in South Africa 1899–1902*, II, pp. 73–179; J.L. Basson, 'Die Slag van Paardeberg', passim.

23 After failing to break through to Ladysmith at Colenso (15 December 1899) and on the Upper Thukela (three attempts, 20 January–7 February 1900), General Sir Redvers Buller succeeded in breaking through on the Lower Thukela at Pietershoogte on 27 February 1900 (after a series of heavy battles that started on 17 February). Ladysmith was relieved on 28 February 1900. For Buller's campaign in Natal up to 28 February see, for example, Amery (ed.), op cit, II, pp. 421–59 and III, pp. 206–330; Breytenbach, op cit, II, pp. 226–332 and III, passim; C.M. Bakkes, *Die Britse Deurbraak aan die Benede-Tugela op Majubadag*, passim.

24 While Roberts and his main force pursued Cronjé's force in the direction of Paardeberg (see Note 22 above), Major-General J.D.P. French and his cavalry rode into Kimberley on 15 February 1900, exactly four months after the siege began. See C.S. Goldmann, *With General French and the Cavalry in South Africa*, pp. 80–97; J.G. Maydon, *French's Cavalry Campaign*, pp. 140–9. As far as the siege in general is concerned see, for example, H.J. Terblanche, 'Die Beleg van Kimberley'; B. Gardner, *The Lion's Cage*.

25 Colonel B.T. Mahon (see Biographical Notes) advanced from Barkly West on 4 May 1900 in a northerly direction with approximately 1,150 mounted troops, four field-guns and two machine-guns. On 15 May this force combined with the southward moving force of approximately 700 men and eight field-guns of Colonel H.C.O. Plumer (see Biographical Notes) at Jan Massibi's kraal on the Molopo River, about 30 km west of Mafikeng. Meanwhile, an attempt to take the town by storm on 12 May, failed after a battle that lasted for the entire day. After a number of men from the relief force had arrived in the town on the evening of 16 May, Mahon officially lifted the 217-day siege of the town the next day. A.P. Smit and L. Maré (eds), *Die Beleg van Mafeking. Dagboek van Abraham Stafleu*, pp. 219–71; Amery (ed.), op cit, IV, pp. 220, 591–7; B. Gardner, *Mafeking. A Victorian Legend*, p. 191 et seq.

26 Roberts visited Kimberley on Thursday 1 March 1900 (arriving in the course of the day) to discuss matters with Lord Methuen, who had moved northwards from the British base at the confluence of the Modder and Riet River. Roberts returned to his HQ at Osfontein on 2 March. Maurice (ed.), op cit, II, pp. 182–3.

27 Cronjé turned 63 on 4 October 1899.

28 Hester Susanna Visser (1840–1903) married Piet Cronjé in 1857. They had nine children: five sons and four daughters. She accompanied her husband to a POW camp on the island of St Helena.

29 See TNA reference PRO 30/57/16/R9(a).

30 Major-General H.A. MacDonald (see Biographical Notes) was wounded in the foot during the frontal attacks against Cronjé's laager at Paardeberg on 18 February 1900.

31 The third Presidency was completed in 1886 and used as such by President J.H. Brand (1886–8), President F.W. Reitz (1889–95) and President

M.T. Steyn (1896–1900). After the British occupation of Bloemfontein (13 March 1900), it became known as Government House. Roberts resided there, and then Major-General G.T. Pretyman (Military Governor and Administrator, ORC, 1900–1) and H.J. Goold-Adams (Lieutenant-Governor, ORC, 1901–7, and Governor, OFS, 1907–10). It was later used as a school, hostel, offices, library and theatre venue, and has been a museum since 1985. S.M. Botes, 'Van Residensie tot Presidensie: 'n Kultuurhistoriese Studie van Ampswonings in Bloemfontein 1846–1900'.

32 Although only about 10,000 out of a total white population in the OFS of 81,000 were English speaking in 1899, the majority of Bloemfontein's inhabitants were English; as a matter of fact, Bloemfontein was English orientated until at least the 1920s.

33 When more than 8,000 British soldiers went down with typhoid (then called enteric fever) in Bloemfontein, several public and other buildings were transformed into temporary hospitals, including the Fourth Raadzaal (Parliament building), Grey College School (now part of the Motheo FET College), the Ramblers Club and St Andrews School (now the Elizabeth le Roux Hostel of Oranje Girls' School).

34 From Paardeberg Roberts marched eastwards in the direction of Bloemfontein. At Modderrivierspoort, near Poplar Grove Drift, General C.R. de Wet (see Biographical Notes), with about 5,000 men and seven field-guns, took up positions over a wide front. The British forces attacked the Boers on 7 March 1900. When French's cavalry started to outflank the Boer positions, the Boers fled. The British lost eight soldiers killed and 49 wounded, while on the Boer side at least one was killed and one wounded. Both President S.J.P. Kruger of Transvaal and President M.T. Steyn of the OFS were present at the battle, but were unable to stop the burghers from leaving their positions. Amery (ed.), op cit, III, pp. 560–9; Breytenbach, op cit, V, pp. 27–63; Maurice (ed.), op cit, II, pp. 180–207.

35 Lieutenant-Colonel Walter Adye (1858–1915), Royal Irish Rifles. Previous service in Afghanistan, 1879–80; Transvaal War of Independence, 1880–1. DAAG, Army in Natal, 1899–1900. DAAG, Army, 1900–4. The unsuccessful encounter with rebels in the Prieska district refers to the clash on 6 March 1900 between Adye's force (approximately 600 men with six guns) and a Boer and rebel commando (approximately 190 men with two guns) under the command of General P.J. Liebenberg at Houwater, some 30 km north-west of Britstown, on the road to Prieska. The British force was driven back and fell back to Britstown. British losses amounted to at least three killed, fourteen wounded and six captured, while on the Boer side two died and three were wounded. Amery (ed.), op cit, III, pp. 570–1 and IV, pp. 3–4; Breytenbach, op cit, V, pp. 323–6.

36 The philanthropist Edward Cecil Guinness, 1st Earl of Iveagh (1847–1927), was co-owner of the famous Guinness Brewery, Dublin. Baron, 1891;

Viscount, 1905; Earl, 1919. During the Anglo-Boer War he equipped and maintained an Irish field hospital. It was a stationary hospital with 100 beds, but had special transport of its own. A portion of the transport section arrived in South Africa in March 1900 and it was sent to Naauwpoort and then accompanied Kitchener on his expedition to Prieska. In April 1900 the hospital as a whole was opened in Bloemfontein. A portion of the hospital accompanied Roberts to Pretoria, where the whole hospital in due course developed into a large hospital in the Palace of Justice (see also Note 79 below). Amery (ed.), op cit, VI, p. 533.

37 Possibly Dr George Stoker.

38 On 8 March 1900 Roberts sent Kitchener to De Aar to take charge of the operation to quell the rebellion in the North-West Cape Colony. Maurice (ed.), op cit, II, p. 212.

39 General P.J. Liebenberg and approximately 190 men, with one field-gun and a pom-pom, left the Boer positions at Magersfontein at the beginning of February 1900, invaded the sparsely-populated North-Western Cape Colony, and occupied Prieska on 16 February, without encountering any resistance. The area was proclaimed OFS territory. Breytenbach, op cit, V, pp. 319–21; Amery (ed.), op cit, III, p. 493.

40 Lieutenant Edward John Morewood Harvey (born 1875), 2nd Battalion Royal Warwickshire Regiment, had no previous war service. He served in South Africa, 1899–1900.

41 I.e. Bloemfontein, on 13 March 1900. Kroonstad was captured on 12 May 1900.

42 At Karree, some 30 km north of Bloemfontein and about half-way to Brandfort, a Boer force of about 2,600 men under command of General Tobias Smuts (see Part 5 Note 40), General Philip Botha, General W.J. Kolbe and Lieutenant-Colonel S.P.E. Trichardt, on 29 March 1900 clashed with a British force under Major-General J.D.P. French and Major-General C. Tucker. Only after heavy fighting and several charges, were the British able to dislodge the Boers from their positions. The British lost at least nineteen soldiers killed, 180 wounded, and three missing. Three Boers were killed and eighteen wounded. Breytenbach, op cit, V, pp. 186–91; Amery (ed.), op cit, IV, pp. 20–2.

43 I.e. Cape Town.

44 Roberts was joined by his wife (Nora) and daughters (Aileen and Ada) – see Biographical Notes – in the third week of April 1900. D. James, *Lord Roberts*, pp. 314–15.

45 'Francs-tireurs', i.e. fighters who are not part of an organised army and/or persons who operate on their own. The assistance supplied by Professor Naòmi Morgan, Department of French, University of the Free State, in explaining the French words used in the documents, is gratefully acknowledged.

46 See Note 25 above.

261

47 With Kimberley as his base, Lord Methuen in March 1900 aimed at clearing the Boers out of the area between Boshof and Fourteen Streams, in an effort to extend British control north-eastwards along the Vaal River towards Hoopstad. On 12 March he entered Boshof unopposed and, leaving behind a small garrison, seized Barkly West on 26 March. In the first week of April 1900, Methuen was back in the Boshof district where, on 5 April, he defeated a Boer force commanded by the French volunteer Georges Henri Ann-Marie Victor, the 20th Comte de Villebois-Mareuil (see also Note 51 below). The French Count and six of his men were killed, eleven wounded and 51 unwounded men taken prisoner. The British only lost at least two men killed and six wounded. S.M. Miller, *Lord Methuen and the British Army. Failure and Redemption in South Africa*, pp. 184–6; Breytenbach, op cit, V, pp. 355–78; Amery (ed.), op cit, IV, pp. 209–14.

48 Although it is true that the largest percentage of soldiers who contracted typhoid (enteric fever) recovered, Kitchener kept quiet about the fact that by the end of April 1900 a few hundred soldiers had already died in Bloemfontein, and many more would follow.

49 Captain Reginald Arthur Haworth Peel (born 1863), 2nd Battalion Life Guards, had no previous war service. He died from enteric fever in Bloemfontein on 16 April 1900.

50 In practice the British occupied Kroonstad on 12 May 1900 without any Boer resistance.

51 At least 2,615 foreigners fought as volunteers on the side of the Boers, including men from Germany, the Netherlands, Belgium, France, Italy, Switzerland, Ireland, Finland, Norway, Sweden, Denmark, Austria-Hungary, Russia and the United States of America. Some of them were already residing in the Transvaal when the war broke out; most of them came to South Africa after the start of hostilities. The most well-known foreign units were the Hollander Corps, First and Second Irish Brigades, the German Corps, and the Scandinavian Corps. Amongst the more prominent foreign officers were the Frenchman Count Georges de Villebois-Mareuil (see also note 47 above), the German Count Harra Zeppelin, and the Irishman Sean (John) MacBride (executed in 1916 for his role in the Easter Rising, Dublin). Initially the Boers were somewhat wary to use the services of the foreigners, but in practice they played an important role on the side of the Boers until June 1900. They fought bravely at, for example, the battles at Elandslaagte (21 October 1899) and Magersfontein (11 December 1899), but suffered severe losses because they wanted to engage the British in close combat. They were not suited for guerrilla warfare. See, for example, E. Wessels, *They Fought on Foreign Soil*.

52 On 3 May 1900 Roberts and more than 20,000 soldiers with 80 pieces of artillery and 49 machine-guns, resumed their advance from Bloemfontein, all along the main railway line in the direction of the Transvaal. Initially the Boers were only able to deploy approximately 1,700 men along the main

railway line, although this force grew in size as time passed. At Brandfort (3 May), the Vet River (5 May) and the Sand River (7 and 10 May), the Boers tried in vain to stop the British advance. Breytenbach, op cit, V, pp. 413–75; Amery (ed.), op cit, IV, pp. 102–18.

53 Several cases were reported where Boers – either on purpose, or because as civilians with no military training, they did not fully understand the use and implications of a white flag – misused the white flag in battle conditions. According to G. Jooste and A. Oosthuizen, *So het hulle Gesterf. Gedenkboek van Teregstellings van Kaapse Rebelle en Republikeinse Burgers tydens die Anglo-Boereoorlog 1899–1902*, pp. 198–207, five Boers were executed (all of them in the Transvaal) for allegedly misusing the white flag. However, there were also other such incidents; for example, according to Miller, op cit, p. 185, Methuen had a Boer executed for misusing the white flag at Boshof on 5 April 1900 – see also note 47 above.

54 Lieutenant-Colonel E.P.C. Girouard, Roberts' Director of Military Railways (see Biographical Notes), and his Royal Engineers were responsible for repairing the railway lines, which they did admirably under great pressure.

55 Henry Charles Keith Petty-Fitzmaurice, 5th Marquis of Lansdowne (1845–1927). Under-Secretary of State for War, 1872–4, and of India Office, 1880; Governor-General of Canada, 1883–8; Viceroy of India, 1888–94; Secretary of State for War, 1895–1900, and for Foreign Affairs, 1900–5; Minister Without Portfolio, 1915–16.

56 Roberts resumed his advance from Kroonstad on 22 May 1900. Almost no Boer opposition was encountered en route northwards and he crossed the Vaal River unopposed on 27 May. The next day he annexed the OFS (henceforth to be known as the Orange River Colony, ORC), backdating the date to 24 May to coincide with Queen Victoria's 81st birthday. At Klipriviersberg (28–29 May) the Boers gave some opposition, but the British occupied Johannesburg unopposed on 31 May. The Boer forces were not immediately pursued. At Sesmylspruit, just south of Pretoria, the Boers attempted to resist the British advance (4 June), but the next day the Transvaal capital was occupied without any resistance. Once again the Boers were allowed to escape. Breytenbach, op cit, V, pp. 504–47; Amery (ed.), op cit, IV, pp. 135–64.

57 On 27 May 1900 Colonel B. E. Spragge and his 13th Yeomanry Battalion were surrounded by a Boer force about 3 km north-west of Lindley in the North-Eastern ORC. As more Boers and artillery arrived the British force's position deteriorated, and on 31 May they surrendered: 443 officers and men, including 55 wounded (25 were killed). Boer casualties were apparently more or less 70. Amery (ed.), op cit, IV, pp. 252–9; *History of the War in South Africa 1899–1902*, III, pp. 115–20; B.N. Reckitt, *The Lindley Affair. A Diary of the Boer War*, p. 9 et seq.

58 On 4 June 1900 General C.R. de Wet intercepted a supply convoy (consisting of 56 wagons, escorted by 160 infantrymen) at Swawelkrans,

22 km west from Heilbron, the convoy's destination. De Wet bluffed the CO, Captain James Corballis, into surrendering without giving any resistance, by exaggerating the number of Boers and guns that he had at his disposal. W.L. von R. Scholtz, 'General Christiaan de Wet as Veldheer', p. 173.

59 After the Jameson Raid (see Part 3, Note 70) the Transvaal government had four forts built on hills on the outskirts of Pretoria (1896–8): Fort Schanskop, Fort Daspoortrand, Fort Wonderboompoort and Fort Klapperkop. See J. Ploeger, *Die Fortifikasie van Pretoria. Fort Klapperkop – Gister en Vandag*. The ruins of the ones on Daspoortrand and at Wonderboompoort can still be seen today, and the ones on Schanskop and Klapperkop have been restored and are museums.

60 See, for example, the Raadzaal (Parliament building, completed in 1891) and the Palace of Justice (1900) on Church Square, and the buildings of the Transvaal State Artillery (1896–8). These buildings are still in use to this day. For the Palace of Justice, see also Note 79 below.

61 Gezina Susanna Frederika Wilhelmina du Plessis (1831–1901) was the second wife of President Paul Kruger (see Biographical Notes). They married in 1847 and had sixteen children: nine sons and seven daughters, some of whom died young. When Kruger left Pretoria a week before the British occupation (and later left for Europe), Gezina stayed behind in the (former) Presidency in Pretoria, where she died. She was buried in the Old Cemetery in Pretoria – see also Note 99 below.

62 Annie Frances Bland Emmett (1864–1937), an English-speaking woman of Irish descent, married Louis Botha in 1886. They had five children: three sons and two daughters. She stayed behind in Pretoria when the Boer commandos retreated eastwards. In February 1901 she helped in effecting communication between her husband and Kitchener, which led to the Middelburg peace talks (see Part 2, Note 80). Towards the middle of 1901 she was allowed to travel to Europe, where she stayed until the end of the war. See also Part 3, Note 39.

63 When it became clear that the British were about to occupy Pretoria, the Boers carried off eastwards with them about 1,000 British POWs, but left over 3,000 behind at Waterval, just north of Pretoria. The Waterval POWs were released on 6 June 1900, after a force under the command of Colonel T.C. Porter put the Boers to flight. The other POWs were taken to Nooitgedacht in the Eastern Transvaal, where they were in due course joined by about 1,000 other POWs, and only released on 30 August 1900, when the Boers retreated further eastwards. Amery (ed.), op cit, IV, pp. 269–70, 457.

64 With the exception of the largest portion of the second-last paragraph, this letter is published in G.E. Buckle (ed.), *The Letters of Queen Victoria*, 3rd Series, III, pp. 558–9. The published version in Buckle's book differs from the original manuscript in the RA in punctuation, paragraphing and spelling.

65 See Note 25 above.

66 See Note 56 above.

67 [the] inserted in the copy of the letter by an unidentified person.

68 By the time he reached Pretoria, Roberts was a very tired man. After four months in command of a huge army in the field, the strain of overwork and old age was beginning to take its toll. James, op cit, p. 354.

69 Francis Reginald Wingate (1861–1953) served in the Sudan, 1884–5 and 1889–91; took part in the Dongola Expedition, 1896; Nile Expedition, 1897–9. Colonel, 1899; Major-General, 1903; Lieutenant-General, 1908; General, 1913. When Lord Kitchener left for South Africa, Wingate succeeded him as Sirdar (i.e. C-in-C) of the Egyptian Army and Governor-General of the Sudan, 1899–1916. High Commissioner for Egypt, 1917–19. Baronet, 1920. Author of several books.

70 Abbas Hilmi II, 'governed' 1892–1914.

71 See Note 70 above.

72 I.e. constant fidelity/loyalty.

73 Word in square brackets inserted in the copy of the letter by an unidentified person. See also the [?] inserted on two occasions further down in the letter. The original letters are barely legible.

74 I.e. Sir Reginald Wingate – see Note 69 above.

75 Roberts sent Kitchener south along the railway line and into the ORC in an effort to strengthen the lines of communication.

76 Kitchener is referring to the following incidents:

(1)   7 June 1900 – General De Wet launched simultaneous attacks on the British lines of communication north of Kroonstad. At Vredefort Road Station Commandant Steenekamp surprised and captured 38 soldiers without a shot being fired. A troop train that approached from the north turned back after a short exchange of fire. At Renoster River bridge Assistant Chief Commandant C.C. Froneman attacked the 4th Derbyshire Regiment – 36 British officers and men were killed and 486 surrendered (including 104 wounded). At Rooiwal Station De Wet attacked and captured a British ammunition and supply train, as well as more than 100 British soldiers (including 24 wounded) – eight soldiers were killed. After removing between 500 and 600 crates of ammunition, De Wet burnt the train and other ammunition and supplies, with a total estimated value of between £100,000 and £750,000. In all three engagements the Boers lost a total of only one burgher killed and four wounded.

(2)   14 June 1900 – An attack by General P.H. Roux on a British post at Sand River bridge is repulsed.

(3)   22 June 1900 – De Wet launched another three-pronged attack on the railway line north of Kroonstad. At Sterkfontein Siding De Wet cut the railway line, and at America Siding Froneman did likewise, but General J.H. Olivier's attacks on Heuningspruit Siding and the nearby post at Katbos, were repulsed. Total British casualties amounted to four dead and

eighteen wounded, while the Boers lost three killed and twelve wounded. P.G. Cloete, *The Anglo-Boer War. A Chronology*, pp. 156, 161, 163; *History of the War in South Africa 1899–1902*, III, pp. 136–7; Amery (ed.), op cit, IV, p. 268; Scholtz, op cit, pp. 186–7.

77 When Lieutenant-General I.S.M. Hamilton (see Biographical Notes) fell from his horse on 23 June 1900 and broke his collar-bone, Lieutenant-General A. Hunter (see Biographical Notes) was appointed in his place as CO of the British forces in the North-Eastern ORC. Hunter occupied the town of Reitz on 7 July 1900. He then moved his forces southwards, cornering a large Boer force in the Brandwater Basin, and forcing them to surrender (30 July and following days). Amery (ed.), op cit, pp. 300–43.

78 See the events at Renoster River bridge, 7 June 1900, referred to in Note 76(1) above.

79 The Palace of Justice on Pretoria's Church Square was only completed in 1900. After being used as a military hospital during the Anglo-Boer War (see also Note 36 above), the Transvaal Provincial Division of the Supreme Court of South Africa sat in the building. Many noteworthy trials have taken place in the building, including the Rivonia Trial, which led to Nelson Mandela and other senior members of the African National Congress being sentenced to life imprisonment in 1964.

80 Sir William Thomson (1843–1909) was in charge of Lord Iveagh's Irish Hospital (see Note 36 above). Thomson qualified as a medical doctor at Queen's University, Dublin, and lectured at the Carmichael (Medical) School, Dublin. He was surgeon in ordinary to Queen Victoria in Ireland, later honorary surgeon to King Edward VII, and the author of several medical books. In December 1899 he was invited by Lord Iveagh to organise a field hospital for service in South Africa. Thomson obliged and accompanied Lord Roberts on his advance to Pretoria, where he established a 600-bed hospital in the Palace of Justice building. Mainly thanks to Thomson and his colleagues, Pretoria was not as hard hit by typhoid as was the case with so many other places in the war zone. Thomson returned to Ireland in November 1900.

81 On the evening of 5 June 1900 Roberts went to stay in the British Residency on the corner of Rissik Street and Mears Street (where the Boers handed over their ultimatum on 9 October 1899). About a month later Roberts moved to Melrose House in Jacob Maré Street, which became his home and HQ, and later that of Kitchener (and after the war of Lieutenant-General N.G. Lyttelton, who succeeded Kitchener as C-in-C). Today Melrose House is a museum. When Roberts moved to Melrose House, the Residency became the home of Major-General J.G. Maxwell (see Part 3, Note 65), the Military Governor of Pretoria. (The house was demolished in 1945.) P.J. Greyling, *Pretoria en die Anglo-Boereoorlog. 'n Gids tot Geboue, Terreine, Grafte en Monumente / Pretoria and the Anglo-Boer War. A Guide of Buildings, Terrains, Graves and Monuments*, pp. 58–9, 76–8.

82 Printed in this publication as documents [10] and [13].

83 Alfred Ernest Albert, Duke of Edinburgh, and of Saxe-Coburg and Gotha, 2nd son (born 1844) of Queen Victoria and Prince Albert, died suddenly at Rosenau, near Coburg, Germany, 30 July 1900. He followed a naval career: Rear-Admiral, 1878; Vice-Admiral, 1882; Admiral, 1887. C-in-C, Mediterranean, 1886–9; C-in-C, Devonport, 1890–3; Admiral of the Fleet, 1893.

84 Since the British occupation of Pretoria on 5 June 1900, Kitchener was mostly away from the headquarters, superintending urgent details, for example organising the strengthening of the lines of communication. Roberts sent him to the ORC to eliminate Gen. C.R. de Wet's force, but at Vredefort Road (today Greenlands) it was De Wet who captured at least 50 British soldiers, and had Kitchener not been able to rush off on horseback, he would probably have been the Boers' biggest catch of the war. Amery (ed.), op cit, IV, p. 411; G. Arthur, *Life of Lord Kitchener*, I, pp. 310–14.

85 Colonel Neville Francis Fitzgerald Chamberlain (1856–1944) was Private Secretary to Roberts, 1899–1900, and then IG, Royal Irish Constabulary, 1900–16. Previously he served in Afghanistan, 1878–80 (wounded) and Burma, 1886–7.

86 While Roberts stayed behind at Jacobsdal because of a severe cold, Lieutenant-General T. Kelly-Kenny (see Biographical Notes), as (apparently) the most senior officer, was technically in command of the British force at Paardeberg, but in practice Kitchener (who was apparently only a Major-General) had the final say; for example as far as the ill-fated British attack of 18 February was concerned. However, there is a possibility that Kitchener had already been promoted to Lieutenant-General on 23 December 1899. (See the general Introduction and that introduction's Note 6.) Roberts arrived at Paardeberg on 19 February. Amery (ed.), op cit, III, pp. 418–19, 453.

87 On 22 February 1900, while the siege of Cronjé's force continued, Roberts sent Kitchener to Naauwpoort, to inspect the repairing of the railway line and bridges over the Gariep. From Naauwpoort Kitchener travelled to Arundel, and then to Kimberley. Amery (ed.), op cit, IV, pp. 479, 488, 492–3.

88 At the end of April 1918, General H.C.O. Plumer's 2nd Army withstood the German onslaught in the Ypres Salient. A.J.P. Taylor (editor-in-chief) and S.L. Mayer (compiler), *History of World War I*, pp. 255–6.

89 As Hunter's noose closed around the Boer commandos in the Brandwater Basin (see Note 77 above), De Wet, accompanied by President M.T. Steyn, other members of the OFS government and approximately 2,000 men, five guns and more than 400 wagons and carts, escaped across Slabbertsnek during the night of 15–16 July 1900. What followed became known as the first De Wet hunt. In an effort to stop De Wet from entering the Transvaal, and to try and corner and catch him before he even reached the Vaal River,

Roberts sent Kitchener south on 2 August to co-ordinate the operation. F. Pretorius, *The Great Escape of the Boer Pimpernel. Christiaan de Wet. The Making of a Legend*, pp. 111–20.

90 De Wet and his force, with their artillery and most of their wagons and carts, crossed the Vaal River on 6 August at Schoemansdrif.

91 Kitchener and his force crossed the Vaal River on 10 August at Lindequesdrif.

92 On Sunday 12 August De Wet's rearguard fought a running battle with his pursuers (under Methuen) north-west of Frederikstad. Several wagons were left behind, 80 British POWs, as well as a 15-pounder field-gun (ex 77th Battery RFA, captured by the Boers at Stormberg on 10 December 1899). Pretorius, op cit, pp. 163–9.

93 De Wet, Steyn and most of the commando that escaped with him from the Brandwater Basin on 15–16 July, trekked unmolested through the Magaliesberg via Olifantsnek on 14 August 1900. Ian Hamilton, who could (and should) have occupied Olifantsnek, had neglected to do so. Safely north of the Magaliesberg, De Wet rested and reorganised his force, and in due course returned to the ORC to continue his guerrilla activities. The way in which De Wet succeeded in evading several superior British columns under the overall command of Kitchener, cemented De Wet's reputation as an excellent guerrilla leader. Pretorius, op cit, pp. 173–209.

94 Lieutenant-Colonel Charles Owen Hore (1860–1916) took up position at Brakfontein, on the Elands River, in an effort to keep up the connection between Mafikeng and Zeerust. He had just more than 500 men, a muzzle-loading 7-pounder gun and two machine-guns with him. From 4–16 August 1900 this force was besieged by General J.H. de la Rey (see Biographical Notes) with at least 500 men, at least four field-guns, one pom-pom and two machine-guns. Several British columns were sent out to relieve Hore, but it was Kitchener who eventually succeeded in doing so. During the siege the defenders lost at least twelve killed and 36 wounded. Amery (ed.), op cit, IV, pp. 357–61, 428–9; L. Wulfsohn, 'Elands River. A Siege which possibly Changed the Course of History in South Africa', *Military History Journal* 6(3), June 1984, pp. 106–8.

95 The Nederlandsche Zuid-Afrikaansche Spoorweg-Maatschappij (NZASM; i.e. Dutch-South African Railway Company) was established on 21 June 1887, and built and owned most of the railway lines in the Transvaal. As war clouds gathered, the Transvaal government took over the NZASM's railways and workshops on 29 September 1899. On 12 September 1900 the British authorities confiscated all NZASM properties. The NZASM was eventually dissolved on 13 October 1908. *Standard Encyclopaedia of Southern Africa* (henceforth referred to as *SESA*), VIII, pp. 156–8.

96 The Anglo-Boer War placed Portugal in a very difficult position. For centuries the country had friendly ties (and treaties) with Britain, but that was also true of its relationship with the Transvaal, its neighbour in Africa.

The vast majority of Portuguese were sympathetic towards the Boers and were in favour of reinforcements, arms and ammunition being sent via Delagoa Bay to the Transvaal, but the Portuguese government, fearful of the safety of its colonies in Africa, knew that they could not openly allow that to happen. In practice some contraband did get through to the Transvaal, but ships of the Royal Navy patrolled the Portuguese coast in an effort to stop the flow of support to the Boers. In September 1900 some 2,500 Boers crossed the border into Portuguese East Africa (Mozambique), from where they were sent to internment camps in Portugal. O.J.O. Ferreira, *Viva os Boers! Boeregeïnterneerdes in Portugal tydens die Anglo-Boereoorlog, 1899–1902.*

97 From 12 September to 19 October 1900 (when he departed for Europe), President Kruger stayed as guest in the house of the Governor of the Lourenço Marques District, António José de Souza Machado, where he was treated as a visiting foreign head of state. Ferreira, op cit, pp. 36–8.

98 Helena Augusta Victoria (1846–1923) was the 5th child (and 3rd daughter) of Queen Victoria. She became Princess Christian of Schleswig-Holstein (Denmark) when she married Prince Frederick Christian Charles Augustus of Schleswig-Holstein-Sonderburg-Augustenburg in 1866. She founded the Army Nursing Service Reserve (officially recognised in 1897). During the Anglo-Boer War a 100-bed private hospital at Pinetown, as well as a hospital train, were named after Princess Christian.

99 Prince Christian Victor (see Biographical Notes), who served on Roberts' staff, died of typhoid in Pretoria on 28 October 1900, and was buried with full military honours in the Old Cemetery in Pretoria, just west of the city centre, where his grave, with its imposing tombstone, can be seen to this day. In the same cemetery are also the graves of more than 1,000 other British soldiers who died during the war, several Boer commanders and burghers, President and Mrs Kruger, Hans Cordua (executed for plotting to kidnap Roberts), as well as South African Prime Ministers J.G. Strijdom and H.F. Verwoerd. As far as the Prince's role in the war and his death is concerned see, for example, H. Warren, *Christian Victor. The Story of a Young Soldier*, pp. 300–97, as well as Roberts' letter of 1 November 1900 to Queen Victoria, published in A. Wessels (ed.), *Lord Roberts and the War in South Africa 1899–1902*, pp. 140–2.

100 Roberts' eldest daughter, Aileen (see Biographical Notes) nearly died of typhoid.

101 The amir of Afghanistan was Abdorrahman Khan. He died in October 1901 and was succeeded by his eldest son, Habibollah Khan.

102 In the last week of September 1900 Roberts was offered, and accepted, the post of C-in-C of the British Army in succession to Lord Wolseley at the War Office in London.

103 Arthur William Patrick Albert, Duke of Connaught (1850–1942), 3rd son of Queen Victoria and Prince Albert. He saw active service in Egypt, 1882.

Lieutenant-General, 1889; General, 1893; Field Marshal, 1902. GOC, Aldershot, 1893–8; Ireland, 1900–8; Mediterranean, 1907–9. Opened first parliament of the Union of South Africa, 1910. Governor-General, Canada, 1911–16.

104 Lieutenant-Colonel Philip Walter Jules le Gallais (1861–1900) took part in Roberts' advance to Bloemfontein, and to Pretoria. He then commanded a column in the Western Transvaal and ORC. On 6 November 1900 he surprised De Wet's commando at Doornkraal, near Bothaville, in the North-Western ORC. De Wet was en route through the ORC to invade the Cape Colony. De Wet succeeded in escaping, but at least nine burghers were killed and more than 100 (including several wounded) were captured, as well as six pieces of artillery. On the British side at least thirteen soldiers were killed and 33 wounded. The mortally wounded Le Gallais died at 20.30 that evening. Amery (ed.), op cit, V, pp. 13–21; Scholtz, op cit, pp. 276–81.

105 The second half of this letter (minus the last portion of the last paragraph) is published in Buckle (ed.), op cit, 3rd Series, III, pp. 617–18. The published version in Buckle's book differs from the original manuscript in the RA in punctuation and the use of capital letters.

106 There is a blank space in the manuscript. Kitchener's letter dated 12 October 1900 probably refers. See document [17] printed in this publication.

107 [the] inserted in the copy of the letter by an unidentified person.

108 Prince Christian Victor was the son of Princess Helena Augusta Victoria, Queen Victoria's 3rd daughter, and Prince Frederick Christian Charles Augustus of Schleswig-Holstein-Sonderburg-Augustenburg. See also Notes 98 and 99 above.

109 [1900] added in pencil by an unidentified person.

110 Major (later Lieutenant-Colonel) Francis Christian Ludwig, Baron von Steinaecker (1854–1914) served in the German Army, early 1870s to 1879, and then served in Bulgaria during the revolution. He led an expedition into the interior of German South-West Africa (today Namibia), 1888; settled in Natal, 1890, and became a British subject. He served in the Anglo-Boer War from 1900–2: first in the Colonial Scouts, 1899–1900; then raised a unit of irregular horsemen, known as Steinaecker's Horse.

111 Colonel Edwin Alfred Hervey Alderson (1859–1927). Previous service in Transvaal War of Independence, 1880–1; Egypt, 1882 and 1884–5; Matabeleland, 1896. Saw action in North-West Cape Colony, 1899–1900; took part in Lord Roberts' advance to Bloemfontein, and to Pretoria, 1900; anti-guerrilla operations, Transvaal, 1900–1. GOC, Mounted Infantry, 1901–2; IG of Mounted Infantry, South Africa, 1900–2. Major-General, 1907; Lieutenant-General, 1914. GOC, Canadian Army Corps, France, 1915–16; IG, Canadian Forces, 1916–18.

112 Major-General H.L. Smith-Dorrien (see Biographical Notes) was in charge of garrisons that protected a stretch of the Delagoa Bay railway line from Pan Station to the town of Belfast. From time to time Smith-Dorrien

launched attacks against Boer guerrilla groups in the area, and on 7 January 1901 he was attacked by General Louis Botha (see Biographical Notes) at Belfast. The attack was repulsed, but Botha escaped to fight another day. Amery (ed.), op cit, V, pp. 50–2, 122–5.

Part 2
December 1900 to March 1901
Introduction

1 *DSAB*, II, p. 601; T. Pakenham, *The Boer War*, pp. 318–19, 384.

2 A term used by A.J. Smithers, *The Fighting Nation. Lord Kitchener and His Armies*, p. 35. The number of Boers still left in the field were definitely not as high as 60,000 as stated by L.S. Amery (ed.), *The Times History of the War in South Africa 1899–1902*, V, p. 67.

3 See, for example, Amery (ed.), op cit, V, pp. 67–8.

4 Ibid, p. 248; *Army. Return of Military Forces in South Africa 1899–1902* (Cd. 578), p. 1.

5 Amery (ed.), op cit, V, pp. 99–108; M.H. Grant, *History of the War in South Africa 1899–1902*, IV, pp. 11–21.

6 L. Scholtz, *Waarom die Boere die Oorlog Verloor het*, pp. 126–30.

7 W.L. von R. Scholtz, 'Generaal C.R. de Wet as Veldheer', pp. 261–319; Amery (ed.), op cit, V, pp. 1–43; *History of the War in South Africa 1899–1902*, III, pp. 469–96.

8 As far as the Boer incursions into the Cape Colony are concerned see, for example, A. de Wet *et al.*, *Die Buren in der Kapkolonie im Kriege mit England*, pp. 87–95; R.D. McDonald, *In die Skaduwee van die Dood*, p. 22 et seq.; N. Gomm, 'Commandant P.H. Kritzinger in the Cape, December 1900–December 1901', *Military History Journal* 1(7), December 1970, pp. 30–2, 34; J. Meinjes, *Sword in the Sand. The Life and Death of Gideon Scheepers*, p. 101 et seq.; G.S. Preller, *Scheepers se Dagboek en die Stryd in Kaapland (1 Okt. 1901 – 18 Jan. 1902)*, pp. 71–112; P.J. du Plessis, *Oomblikke van Spanning*, passim.

9 W.L. von R. Scholtz, op cit, pp. 321–70; Amery (ed.), op cit, V, pp. 131–57; H.C.J. Pieterse, *Oorlogsavonture van genl. Wynand Malan*, p. 125 et seq.

10 S.J. du Preez, 'Vredespogings gedurende die Anglo-Boereoorlog tot Maart 1901', passim; Amery (ed.), op cit., V, pp. 183–93.

December 1900 to March 1901

1 As far as could be ascertained, this is the first letter written by Lord Kitchener to Lord Roberts after he (Kitchener) became C-in-C in South Africa. Roberts only left South Africa on 11 December 1900, and it is not clear whether Kitchener sent this letter to him in Cape Town, or to England.

2 Lieutenant-Colonel Frederick White (1861–1924), Royal Marines, who previously took part in the Egyption Expedition, 1882–4. He was not dismissed from service, but served in South Africa, 1900–2, for example as District Commander under the Military Governor, ORC. Brevet of Colonel, 1906.

3 Lieutenant-General Archibald Hunter (see also Biographical Notes) was sent home on sick-leave in January 1901.

4 The serious illness of Roberts' daughter Aileen (see Part 1, Note 100) and his fall from a horse, delayed his departure from South Africa until 11 December 1900.

5 Major-General George Tindal Pretyman (1845–1917) served in Afghanistan (1878–80) and was Roberts' Military Secretary in Madras (1881–4). DAG, Bengal (1887–9) and DC, Bengal (1889–94). Came to South Africa in 1899 and served on HQ Staff. Military Governor of Bloemfontein from 13 March 1900, and Military Governor and Administrator of the OFS (later ORC) from 20 April 1900, until transferred to Kimberley in February 1901 as GOC. GOC, Secunderabad District, India, 1902–3; Commander of forces in Madras, 1904; Burma Division, 1906–7. In Bloemfontein Pretyman (joined by his wife, Winefred, née Locke) stayed in Government House, the former OFS Presidency. See also Part 1, Note 31.

6 Probably a reference to either the Green Hill Convent, or Eunice School's Upper House.

7 Major-General Elliott Wood (1855–1931) was Commander of the Royal Engineers in SA, 1899–1902. Previously he served in Egypt (1882) and in the Sudan (1884–5), and he was OC, RE, Malta, 1894–9.

8 The first blockhouses were erected at the beginning of 1901 in an effort to safeguard the railway lines and the bridges. In due course approximately 8,000 blockhouses and other fortifications were erected across the length and breadth of South Africa, mostly in lines, dividing up the war zone in more manageable 'cages' in which drives would take place in an effort to corner Boer commandos. J. Hattingh and A. Wessels, *Britse Fortifikasies in die Anglo-Boereoorlog (1899–1902)*, p. 21 et seq.; Amery (ed.), op cit, V, pp. 396–412 (including a fold-out map opposite p. 412 on which all the blockhouse lines, including dates of completion, are indicated).

9 Written in the left-hand top corner on p. 1 of the manuscript.

10 See document [18] in this publication.

11 Prince Christian Victor. See Biographical Notes and Part 1, Note 99.

12 Colonel Arthur Edmund Sandbach (1859–1928) previously served in Egypt, 1882; Sudan, 1885; took part in Burmese Expedition, 1886–7; Sikkim Expedition, 1888; Hazara Expedition, 1897; Nile Expedition, 1898. Military Secretary to Viceroy, India, 1898–9. In South Africa he served in Natal, 1899–1900 (including Ladysmith relief operations, and march from Ladysmith to Transvaal) and Eastern Transvaal, 1900. Returned to England, 1901. Commandant, 1st Sappers and Miners, Indian Army, 1904–7; CRE,

Aldershot, 1908–10. Brigadier-General, 1910. Chief Engineer, Ireland, 1910–14. Major-General, 1914. Served in World War I, 1914–15 and 1917.

13 When Kitchener was sent to South Africa in December 1899 he was, according to most sources, a Major-General, i.e. junior in rank to a number of other officers serving in South Africa. However, there is a possibility that he had already been promoted to Lieutenant-General on 23 December 1899. See the general Introduction and that introduction's Note 6.

14 See TNA reference PRO 30/57/22/Y4.

15 There were not necessarily more Boers in the field in December 1900, but the second week of December saw a dramatic increase in guerrilla activities. On 13 December a British force was defeated at Nooitgedacht in the Western Transvaal (see Note 24 below), and on the night of 15–16 December the commandos of General J.B.M. Hertzog and Commandant P.H. Kritzinger crossed the Gariep (i.e. Orange River) into the Cape Colony, while General C.R. de Wet's attempt to cross into the Colony was thwarted by a Gariep that was at that stage in flood. (See also Note 19 below.)

16 Samuel Weil (1862–1944) was a businessman who played a significant role in the development of commerce and industry in Southern Africa. He came from England to the Cape Colony in 1876, and joined the firm of his elder brother, Julius, who was a government contractor, general merchant, and landing, shipping and forwarding agent. Samuel organised transport and food supplies for the Imperial forces during the suppression of the Matabele Rebellion (in present-day Zimbabwe), 1896. During the Anglo-Boer War he helped in organising the British transport system. As a Major in Colonel B.T. Mahon's force, he took part in the relief of Mafikeng (see Part 1, Note 25). After the war he became director of several mining and other companies.

17 According to official sources, the British Army used a total of 518,794 horses and 150,781 mules and donkeys during the war in South Africa. Of these 347,007 horses and 53,339 mules and donkeys died during the war. D. Hall, *The Hall Handbook of the Anglo-Boer War 1899–1902*, p. 237.

18 According to Amery (ed.), op cit, p. 67 Kitchener had approximately 210,000 soldiers under his command when he took over from Roberts, and at that stage there were still some 60,000 Boers in the field. The latter figure is a gross exaggeration, because the greatest number of Boers ever to be on commando at any one stage was approximately 47,000 (including Cape rebels as well as foreign volunteers), and that was in the period December 1899 to February 1900 (see A. Wessels, *Die Anglo-Boereoorlog. 'n Oorsig van die Militêre Verloop van die Stryd*, p. 5). At the end of November 1900 there were probably approximately 30,000 burghers in the field; definitely not more than 35,000.

19 De Wet planned to cross the Gariep into the Cape Colony at or near Odendaalstroom, between Bethulie and Aliwal North, but the river was in flood, and on 6 December 1900 De Wet decided to abort his invasion

attempt. He fell back northwards, pursued by Major-General C.E. Knox in what became known as the second De Wet hunt. De Wet escaped, and entered the Cape Colony in February 1901. C.R. de Wet, *Three Years War (October 1899–June 1902)*, pp. 249–276; L.S. Amery (ed.), *The Times History of the War in South Africa 1899–1902*, V, pp. 28–42.

20 Lieutenant-Colonel Harold Maxwell Grenfell (1870–1929; previous service in the Sudan, 1898) commanded the 2nd Regiment Brabant's Horse, also known as Grenfell's Horse, in the ORC, 1900–1, and in the Cape Colony, 1901. Lieutenant-Colonel Edward Bleiddian Herbert (born 1858; previous service in the Anglo-Zulu War, 1879) saw action in Natal, 1899–1900, and took part in anti-guerrilla operations in the ORC and Cape Colony, 1900–1.

21 The farm Rhenoster Hoek lies on the southern side of the Gariep, between Bethulie and Aliwal North. At 02.00 in the early hours of 16 December 1900, Commandant P.H. Kritzinger and approximately 300 men crossed the river at this farm. R.D. McDonald, *In the Skaduwee van die Dood*, pp. 5, 67.

22 Judge (General) J.B.M. Hertzog and his commando of approximately 1,200 men crossed the Gariep at Sanddrif, between Norvalspont and Petrusville, during the night of 15–16 December 1900, and trekked south-westwards in the direction of Philipstown. (See also the next note.)

23 Hertzog's commando occupied Philipstown on 17 December 1900, and Britstown on 22 December. On 26 December the Boers clashed with a British force at Houwater, and Vosburg was occupied the next day. Hertzog's advance guard reached Calvinia on 7 January 1901, and Vanrhynsdorp was occupied on 19 January. Some of Hertzog's burghers went as far south-west as Lambert's Bay on the Atlantic coast, where they fired on the cruiser HMS *Sybille* – which retaliated with a few gunshots. At the end of February 1901 the bulk of Hertzog's force returned to the ORC in the company of De Wet (whose second invasion attempt on 10 February was successful). The Boers failed in their attempt to stir up an uncontrollable rebellion in the Cape Colony, but their invasion led to a second (albeit limited) rebellion and until the cessation of hostilities the Cape Colony would remain a very active operational zone. A. de Wet *et al.*, *Die Buren in der Kapkolonie im Kriege mit England*, pp. 87–95.

24 Kitchener is referring to the battle at Nooitgedacht, north-west of Pretoria, 13 December 1900, when Generals C.F. Beyers, J.H. de la Rey and J.C. Smuts (with about 1,700 burghers) attacked the camp of Major-General R.A.P. Clements' force (about 2,000 soldiers with ten artillery pieces) at the foot of the Magaliesberg, as well as the entrenched positions on top of the mountain. The initial Boer assault against the camp was beaten off, but after the British positions on top of the mountain were overrun, the camp once again came under fire and the British fled. The Boers lost 32 killed and 46 wounded; the British 109 killed, 186 wounded and at least 368 POWs. M.H. Grant, *History of the War in South Africa 1899–1902*, IV, pp. 11–21; Amery (ed.), op cit, V, pp. 99–108.

25 On 14 December 1900 De Wet and his commando (accompanied by President Steyn) broke through the Thaba 'Nchu-Ladybrand blockhouse line at Sprinkaansnek, apparently losing eight men killed, 17 wounded and 33 captured in the process. They regrouped and in due course moved south again and succeeded in crossing the Gariep into the Cape Colony on 10 February 1900. W.L. von R. Scholtz, 'Generaal Christiaan de Wet as Veldheer', pp. 308–10.

26 John Edward Boyes (1843–1915) previously served in Egypt, 1882–4, and in the Sudan, 1884–5. Major-General, 1898. In South Africa he served as OC, 17th Brigade, 1900–1.

27 Colonel John Stewart Scott Barker (1853–1918) had no previous war service. He served in South Africa, 1899–1902: took part in advance to Bloemfontein; operated in the ORC, 1900 and 1901–2, and in the Cape Colony, 1900–1. Retired as a Major-General.

28 Colonel Thomas David Pilcher (1858–1928). Previous service in West Africa, 1897–8. Saw action on Kimberley front under Lord Methuen, 1899–1900; took part in Lord Roberts' advance to Bloemfontein, and to Pretoria, 1900; anti-guerrilla operations, Transvaal, ORC and Cape Colony, 1900–2. Major-General, 1907. GOC, 17th Division, BEF, England and France, 1915–16 (wounded).

29 Lieutenant-Colonel William Lewis White (1856–1931) previously served in the Sudan, 1885. Military Attaché, Madrid, 1898–9. He served throughout the Anglo-Boer War, in the Cape Colony, OFS/ORC, and Transvaal; OC of a mobile column, 1900–2. DAQMG, Portsmouth, 1902; DAAG, War Office, 1903. Colonel, 1905. Commander, School of Gunnery, Shoeburyness, 1909; IG, Royal Garrison Artillery, 1910–12; DAG and QMG, IVth Corps, BEF, 1914–16.

30 Major-General C.E. Knox – see Biographical Notes.

31 Brigadier-General Robert George Broadwood (1862–1917) in practice fought until the cessation of hostilities. Before the Anglo-Boer War he saw active service in the Dongola Expedition (1896) and in the Sudan (1897–8). As GOC, 2nd Cavalry Brigade, he fought on the Kimberley front, 1900. The first guerrilla clash of the war took place on 31 March 1900 when De Wet with about 1,500 men ambushed and defeated Broadwood's force of about 1,800 men at Sannaspos, some 30 km east of Bloemfontein. The British lost at least eighteen killed, 134 wounded and 426 taken POW, as well as seven artillery pieces and over 100 wagons and carts captured. On the Boer side at least three were killed and five wounded. (J.E. Rabie, *Generaal Christiaan de Wet se Krygsleiding by Sannaspos en Groenkop*, pp. 5–30.) After the war Broadwood was C-in-C, Natal, 1903–4; ORC, 1904–6; China, 1906. Major-General, 1906. He was killed in action in France.

32 Issued by Major-General W.F. Kelly, AG (see Part 3, Note 101), on behalf of Lord Kitchener.

33 Also published in Amery (ed.), op cit, V, pp. 86–7.

34 See TNA reference PRO 30/57/33/Y6.

35 Witwatersrand, i.e. Johannesburg and surrounding areas.

36 On 21 December 1900 Kitchener met with the Burgher Peace Committee, consisting of surrendered Boers who wanted to co-operate with the British in an effort to end the war. Kitchener supported their proposal to send emissaries to the Boer commandos to try and convince them to lay down their arms. A.M. Grundlingh, *Die "Hendsoppers" en "Joiners". Die Rasionaal en Verskynsel van Verraad*, pp. 82–91.

37 By June 1900 three Canadian contingents had arrived in SA (see Part 1, Notes 2, 5 and 8). It was only in March 1902 that the next Canadian contingent arrived in SA (see Part 3, Note 177), and in April 1902 an additional 2,036 Canadians were recruited for service in SA, but they arrived too late to participate in operations. C. Miller, *Painting the Map Red. Canada and the South African War, 1899–1902*, p. 414.

38 Major-General Frederick Walter Kitchener (1858–1912). Previous service in Afghanistan, 1878–80; Dongola, 1896; Sudan, 1898. Fought in Natal, 1899–1900; Transvaal, 1900–2. Lieutenant-General, 1906. C-in-C and Governor, Bermuda, 1908–9.

39 The British military post at Helvetia, about 10 km north of Machadodorp, formed part of a line of fortified posts that stretched from the latter town all the way to Lydenburg. The OC at Helvetia, Major S.L. Cotton (see Biographical Notes) had about 350 men under his command, with one 4.7-inch naval gun, the 'Lady Roberts'. At approximately 03.00 on 29 December 1900, about 580 Boers under the command of General B.J. Viljoen (see Biographical Notes) and General Chris Muller attacked and overran the British positions. The British lost eleven soldiers killed, 29 wounded and 235 taken POW, while the naval gun was also captured. (The Boers later blew up the gun to ensure that it was not recaptured by the British.) Boer casualties were apparently few in number. Amery (ed.), op cit, V, pp. 121–2; Grant, op cit, IV, pp. 25–7.

40 At 02.15 on 12 December 1900 approximately 1,000 Boers under the command of General Chris Botha attacked the British garrison at Vryheid in the South-Eastern Transvaal (in 1903 to become part of Natal). After an intense battle, the Boers fell back by 07.00, having lost an unspecified number of dead and wounded. British losses amounted to at least six killed, twenty wounded and 29 missing (presumed POWs). Amery (ed.), op cit, V, pp. 117–18; Grant, op cit, IV, pp. 30–1.

41 There were in fact several wire entanglements at Helvetia. See, for example, Amery (ed.), op cit, V, p. 121 and fold-out map opposite p. 126.

42 Major-General Douglas Haig (1861–1928) previously fought in Egypt (1897) and in the Sudan (1898). During the Anglo–Boer War he saw action in Natal and on the Colesberg front, 1899; took part in Roberts' advance, 1900, and in anti-guerrilla operations in the Cape Colony, 1901–2. Major-General, 1904; Lieutenant-General, 1910; General, 1914. GOC, Aldershot,

1912–14; GOC, 1st Army, 1914–15; C-in-C, BEF, 1915–19. Field Marshal, 1917; Earl of Bemersyde, 1919.

43 On the evening of 1 January 1901 De Wet was near Roodewal Station on the main line between Bloemfontein and Johannesburg. The next evening De Wet was in the vicinity of the bridge over the Renoster River, where the Boers dug up ammunition they had buried there earlier. The night of 4–5 January De Wet and his commando crossed the main railway line near Vredefort Road (previously known as Heilbron Road, and since 1910 as Greenlands), unnoticed by the British. De Wet, op cit, pp. 243–4.

44 On arrival in England on Wednesday 2 January 1901, Roberts was awarded an earldom (he was henceforth known as Earl Roberts of Kandahar, Pretoria and Waterford), and created a Knight of the Garter (KG). Parliament voted to give him a grant of £100,000 in recognition of his services in South Africa. D. James, *Lord Roberts*, pp. 369–71; G. Forrest, *The Life of Lord Roberts*, K.G., V.C., pp. 324–6.

45 Roberts arrived back in England on board HM Hospital Ship *Canada* on 2 January 1901, landed at Cowes on the Isle of Wight where he received a rousing welcome, was presented with an address, and delivered the first of many speeches. He immediately went to Osborne to be received in special audience by Queen Victoria. The next day Roberts received a hero's welcome on arrival in London and was driven through the city, where 14,000 troops lined the streets and spectators stood six or more deep along the route. Many official receptions followed in the next weeks. James, op cit, pp. 369–71; Forrest, op cit, pp. 324–6.

46 Major-General Henry Edward Colvile (1852–1907) previously fought in the Sudan (1884–5), and was Acting Commissioner in Uganda (1893–5). Served on the Kimberley front (1899–1900), commanding the 1st (Guards) Brigade of the 1st Division. GOC, 9th Division (1900) – as part of Roberts' force. Incurred the disfavour of Roberts and Kitchener because he did not go to the assistance of the British forces that were defeated at Sannaspos (see Note 31 above) and Lindley (see Part 1, Note 57). He was ordered back to England in November 1900, and when on arrival he gave his version of events to the press, was compelled to take his discharge from the Army in January 1901.

47 In the left-hand margin of the copy it says that the original letter is in the handwriting of Princess Helena (i.e. Queen Victoria's 3rd daughter – see Part 1, Note 98). This letter was dictated by Her Majesty The Queen a mere eleven days before she died. It was her last letter to Kitchener, and by the time it reached him, she had already passed away.

48 I.e. Major-General F.W. Kitchener – see Note 38 above.

49 Queen Victoria died on 22 January 1901, before this letter reached her.

50 Printed in this publication as document [22].

51 Kitchener is referring to the Boers' successes at Nooitgedacht (see Note 24 above) and Monument Hill, north of Belfast in the Eastern Transvaal

(7 January 1901 – see Amery (ed.), op cit, V, pp. 123–5) and their unsuccessful attacks at Vryheid (see Note 40 above), Pan, Wonderfontein, Nooitgedacht and Wildfontein Stations (all in the Eastern Transvaal, 7 January 1901 – see Amery (ed.), op cit, V, pp. 124–6). See also Note 53 below.

52 Lieutenant-Colonel Charles Lambton (1857–1949). Previous service in the Sudan, 1898. Saw action in South Africa, 1899–1902: took part in Lord Methuen's advance, 1899; Lord Roberts' advance to Bloemfontein, 1900; in the Western Transvaal, 1900, and other Transvaal regions, 1900–1, and in the ORC, 1901–2. OC, 2nd Battalion, 5th (Northumberland) Fusiliers, 1900–2. Served 1914–15 in World War I, as Brigadier-General and OC of a brigade.

53 On 12 January 1901 General C.F. Beyers (see Biographical Notes) attacked the British between Johannesburg and Pretoria at Zuurfontein (now Kempton Park) and Kaalfontein, and crossed and blew up the railway line. G.D. Scholtz, *Generaal Christiaan Frederik Beyers 1869–1914*, p. 53; A.G. Oberholster (ed.), *Oorlogsdagboek van Jan F.E. Celliers 1899–1902*, p. 195.

54 Less than five weeks after the renewed Boer invasion of 15–16 December 1901, not many colonial Afrikaners had joined the Boer forces, but in due course some 3,000 rebelled and most of them stayed in the field until the cessation of hostilities.

55 From 8 to 25 January 1901 De Wet and his commandos were in the northwestern districts of the OFS, waiting for a suitable opportunity to move southwards and cross the Gariep into the Cape Colony. De Wet, op cit, p. 245.

56 Queen Victoria died at 18.20 on Tuesday 22 January 1901 at Osborne House on the Isle of Wight. Her last words were: 'What has been happening in South Africa these last few days?' She was laid to rest next to Prince Albert in the mausoleum at Frogmore, near Windsor Castle.

57 On Sunday 27 January 1901 an elaborate drive by five columns under the overall command of Lieutenant-General J.D.P. French was launched in the Eastern Transvaal, in an effort to drive the Boers from Pretoria south-eastwards against the Natal and Swaziland borders. The total British force had a strength of approximately 14,000 men with 58 field-guns and pom-poms. The drive lasted until 14 April 1901. The British estimated that they killed or wounded 362 Boers and captured 233, while 730 surrendered voluntarily, but this estimate is probably too high because it may have included several civilians. Not a single officer of note was captured. The British also captured eleven pieces of artillery, 2,300 wagons and carts, 272,000 rounds of rifle ammunition, more than 7,000 horses and mules, as well as large quantities of livestock. It is not certain exactly how many British soldiers were killed or wounded during the drive. Grant, op cit, IV, pp. 111–23; Amery (ed.), op cit, V, pp. 158–82.

58 From June 1900 to January 1901 Lieutenant-General N.G. Lyttelton (see Biographical Notes) was OC, 4th Division, responsible for safeguarding the railway line from Pretoria to Komatipoort. (Middelburg in the Eastern Transvaal has to be distinguished from Middelburg in the Midlands of the Cape Colony.)

59 On 25 January 1901 a council of war meeting of Free State forces took place at Doornberg, near Ventersburg. De Wet, Steyn, other members of the government, and about 3,000 burghers were present. Strategy was discussed, including a renewed effort to invade the Cape Colony, and Steyn was re-elected as State President. Scholtz, op cit, pp. 326–8.

60 Johannes Jacobus Morgendaal, a burgher from Kroonstad who laid down his arms (i.e. was a handsupper) in mid–1900 and became a volunteer peace emissary, was captured near Kroonstad roundabout 31 December 1900, when he was on his way to see De Wet. He was brought before a Boer court martial near Heilbron in the Northern ORC (6 January 1901), but the case was referred to a higher court. Three days later, when a British patrol approached De Wet's laager and the Boers had to inspan hastily, Morgendaal (realizing that rescue might be near) refused an order by Commandant C.C. Froneman to assist with the harnessing of a vehicle. Froneman lost his temper and lashed out at Morgendaal with his sjambok, but the prisoner plucked it out of his hands. De Wet, seeing what had happened, shouted at Froneman to shoot Morgendaal, which Froneman did, seriously wounding the prisoner. Morgendaal died on 19 January 1901. Grundlingh, op cit, pp. 101–4.

61 H.G. (not H.C.) Dixon – see Biographical Notes.

62 I.e. Major-General Coleridge Grove (1839–1920), who served in Egypt (1882) and in the Sudan (1884–5), and who was Private Secretary to three successive Secretaries of State for War, namely Henry Campbell-Bannerman, W.H. Smith and Edward Stanhope. He was Military Secretary at the War Office, May 1896–May 1901.

63 In December 1900 and January 1901, Lord Methuen ensured that the garrisons in the sprawling Griqualand West received the necessary supplies. Several minor clashes with Boer guerrilla units took place. Amery (ed.), op cit, V, p. 116.

64 See Part 1, Note 53.

65 See TNA reference PRO 30/57/22/Y14.

66 On 1 February 1901 De Wet and his commando arrived unopposed in the Free State town of Dewetsdorp (named after De Wet's father). Scholtz, op cit, p. 335.

67 See Note 57 above.

68 On his way south to invade the Cape Colony (1st, unsuccessful attempt), De Wet and his approximately 1,500 men besieged and defeated the British garrison at Dewetsdorp, 21–23 November 1900. The British force of about 480 men was under the command of Major W.G. Massy, RA. Fourteen

British soldiers were killed; the rest (including 82 wounded) were taken prisoner. The two British artillery pieces were also captured. It is unknown how many casualties there were on the Boer side. Scholtz, op cit, pp. 294–7; Amery (ed.), op cit, V, pp. 28–32.

69 See *Return of Buildings burnt in each Month from June, 1900, to January, 1901 including Farm Buildings, Mills, Cottages and Hovels* (Cd. 892).

70 Written slanted in top left-hand corner of the first page of the letter.

71 On 26 January 1901 De Wet, accompanied by President Steyn, other members of the Free State government-in-the-field, and about 2,000 burghers left Doornberg, between Ventersburg and Senekal in the ORC, trekked southwards and on 10 February entered the Cape Colony by crossing the Gariep at Sanddrif, between Norvalspont and Petrusville. Seventeen British columns (about 14,000 soldiers) pursued him, in what became known as the third drive against De Wet (or great De Wet hunt). Kitchener deemed the situation to be so serious that he rushed down from Pretoria and took charge of the operation on 16 February. De Wet was driven westwards, but on the banks of an impassable Brak River (and with the nearest British column only about 16 km behind him), the Boer commander decided on 19 February to turn back to the ORC. He side-stepped his pursuers, linked up with Hertzog's retreating commando on 27 February, and the next day both commandos crossed back over the Gariep into the ORC. De Wet's trek had lasted 43 days and he covered a distance of approximately 1,300 km. Scholtz, op cit, pp. 321–70; Amery (ed.), op cit, V, pp. 131–57.

72 I.e. the commandos of Hertzog and Kritzinger, albeit that Kritzinger only fell back to the ORC on 29 April 1901, and returned to the Cape Colony some three weeks later.

73 At De Aar, i.e. in the Cape Colony, to take over the overall command of the drive against De Wet. See Note 71 above.

74 Kitchener's letter of 25 January 1901 to Roberts is printed in this publication as document [31]. For Kitchener's letter to Brodrick, see TNA reference PRO 30/57/22/Y18.

75 General Arthur Power Palmer (1840–1904) was C-in-C, India, 1900–2, and was succeeded by Kitchener. He showed high administrative capacity in selecting regiments and commanders for the war in South Africa. Palmer saw service in the suppression of the Indian Mutiny (1857–8), on the North-Western Frontier in India (1863–4), in the Abyssinian Expedition (1868), Duffla Expedition (1874–5), in Achin (with Dutch forces, 1876–7), Afghanistan (1878–80), Suakim Expedition (1885), raid on Thakul (1885), in the Burma Expedition (1892–3) and in the Tirah Campaign (1897–8). Before becoming C-in-C, India, he was GOC, Punjab frontier force, 1898–1900.

76 General William Stephen Alexander Lockhart (1841–1900) was C-in-C, India, 1898–1900. He previously saw service in the Bhootan Expedition

(1864–6), Abyssinia (1867–8), Hazara Expedition (1868), Achin (with Dutch forces, 1875–7), Afghanistan (1879–80), Burma (1885–7), 1st and 2nd Miranzai Expeditions (1891), Isazai Expedition (1892), Waziristan Expedition (1894–5) and on the North-Western Frontier in India (1897–8).

77 I.e. Lord (George Nathaniel) Curzon (1859–1925) who was Viceroy of India from 1898–1905. Previously Conservative MP, 1886–98; Under-Secretary for India, 1891–2; for Foreign Affairs, 1892–8. Later Lord Privy Seal, 1915–16; President of the Air Board, 1916; Lord President of the Council and member of the War Cabinet, 1916–19; Secretary of State for Foreign Affairs, 1919–22. Earl, 1911; Marquis, 1921.

78 Middelburg in Transvaal.

79 No such letter could be found in the appropriate letter-book (see NAM. 1971-01-23-122-1), albeit that it has to be kept in mind that not all Roberts' letters were copied into the letter-books. There are copies of Roberts' letters to Kitchener, dated 25 January 1901 and 8 February 1901.

80 See document [38]. On 28 February 1901 Kitchener and General Louis Botha, Commandant-General of the Transvaal (see Biographical Notes), met for peace negotiations at the Eastern Transvaal town of Middelburg. Each commander put forward his government's conditions for the cessation of hostilities. Kitchener then drafted the proposed peace terms, which were then modified by Sir Alfred Milner and by the British government, and subsequently rejected by Botha on 16 March 1901. Kitchener regarded Milner's refusal to grant amnesty to the Cape rebels as the main reason for the breakdown of the talks, but it is possible that even if that condition had been met, the Boers would at that stage still have opted to continue with their struggle. Steyn, De Wet and most of the Free Staters, as well as many Transvaalers, were not prepared to accept the loss of their independence. S. du Preez, 'Vredespogings gedurende die Anglo-Boereoorlog tot Maart 1901', pp. 157–209; Amery (ed.), op cit, V, pp. 183–93; *South Africa. Papers relating to Negotiations between Commandant Louis Botha and Lord Kitchener* (Cd. 528); *South Africa. Further Papers relating to Negotiations between Commandant Louis Botha and Lord Kitchener* (Cd. 663).

81 For French's elaborate drive in the Eastern Transvaal, see Note 57 above. The reference to Botha's escape refers to his attack on a British camp at Lake Chrissie on 6 February 1901. See, for example, Amery (ed.), op cit, V, pp. 167–9.

82 See Note 71 above.

83 Colonel (later Major-General) Thomas Edward Verner (1845–1931) previously served in Afghanistan (1878–80) and in the Sudan (1898). Staff Officer, South Africa, 1901–2. Retired, OC troops in Rhodesia, 1902.

84 I.e. enteric (typhoid).

85 Middelburg in Transvaal.

86 See Note 80 above.

87 I.e. as Administrator of the ORC and the Transvaal Colony. Milner was appointed in that capacity on 8 October 1900, but it only became effective when Roberts left for England. On 21 June 1901 Milner became Governor of the Transvaal Colony, and two days later also of the ORC. *DSAB*, III, p. 615.

88 Nicolaas Jacobus de Wet (1873–1960), jurist, administrator, and politician. Studied law at the University of Cambridge, receiving his LL.B. in 1895, and winning the Chancellor's gold medal. Practised as an advocate in the Transvaal. General Louis Botha's Military Secretary, 1900–2. Interpreter during the peace negotiations, 1902. Represented Middelburg West in the Transvaal Legislative Assembly, 1907–10 (Het Volk Party). MP, Union of SA, 1913–20 (South African Party: Wakkerstroom 1913–15; Potchefstroom, 1915–20). Senator, 1920–9. Minister of Justice, 1913–24. Judge, Transvaal bench, 1932–7; Appeal Court Judge, 1937–9; Chief Justice of SA, 1939–45.

89 The question of political rights for blacks was also later discussed at the peace negotiations of May 1902, and it was once again decided (and agreed upon by both sides) that a decision with regard to political rights for blacks should be postponed until the Transvaal and ORC regained some form of self-government. In practice black, coloured and Asian South Africans only received equal political rights with their white counterparts in 1994.

90 See Note 60 above.

91 The British government was prepared to provide £1,000,000 to pay off republican debt. See Du Preez, op cit, pp. 186–92.

92 There is also a manuscript copy in the Milner Papers at the Bodleian Library (Oxford) – also available on microfilm no 175. There are a few typographical differences between the holograph and the manuscript copy, and the latter portion of the 3rd paragraph is not in the manuscript copy. For the purpose of this publication, the holograph kept by the Brenthurst Library has been used.

93 Milner left Cape Town for Johannesburg on 28 February 1901 to take up his duties as Administrator of the two new colonies. He insisted that Kitchener meet him in Bloemfontein so that they could discuss the Middelburg proposals before transmitting them to London. When they met on 3 March, Kitchener pleaded with Milner to allow amnesty for the rebels, but Milner was adamant they had to be treated as traitors. On 6 March Kitchener received the amended proposals from Joseph Chamberlain, for transmission to Botha. The amendments included the fact that rebels would be subject to courts-martial; repatriation of Boer POWs would take place 'as soon as practical'; future self-government for the ORC and Transvaal Colony was a 'privilege' and was phrased in vaguer terms; the £1,000,000 payment was re-termed as 'an act of grace' and was heavily qualified; assistance to farmers would be given in the form of a repayable loan and would be subject to the recipient swearing an oath of allegiance to King Edward VII; Dutch would

only be allowed in schools when requested by parents, and black people would receive franchise similar to that in the Cape Colony. S.J. du Preez, 'Vredespogings gedurende die Anglo-Boereoorlog tot Maart 1901', pp. 186–92.

94 See TNA reference PRO 30/57/22/Y21.

95 Colonel William Henry Birkbeck (1863–1929) saw action in the North-Western Cape Colony, 1901–2. Previously he took part in the Hazara Expedition (1888) and the Chin-Lushai Expedition (1889–90). Later he was attached to the Japanese 3rd Army, Manchuria (1905), Commandant of the Cavalry School, Netheravon (1906–11) and Director of Remounts, Army HQ (1912–20).

96 See *South Africa Despatches. Despatch by Lord Kitchener, dated 8th March, 1901, relative to Military Operations in South Africa* (Cd. 522).

97 During the British operations in the Eastern Transvaal during the first few months of 1901, the hospital ship *Orcana* was sent to Delagoa Bay (also known as Lourenço Marques, and today as Maputo), and wounded and ill soldiers were sent to it across the Portuguese border. Amery (ed.), op cit, VI, p. 518.

98 Surgeon-General William Deane Wilson (1843–1921) went out to South Africa in 1899 (with General Buller) as Principal Medical Officer, and stayed in the war zone in that capacity for the duration of the conflict.

99 The administration of the internment camps was partially handed over to civilian control in February 1901, but it was not until November 1901 that all responsibilities for the administration of the camps were handed over to civilians; and only after Joseph Chamberlain intervened and ordered Alfred Milner to do so. Information supplied by Rev. Dr Stowell Kessler.

100 See Note 80 above.

101 Not in PRO 30/57/22/Y30 at TNA.

102 See Note 57 above.

103 In practice De Wet did not attempt another incursion into the Cape Colony, but operated in the ORC until the cessation of hostilities.

104 Colonel Robert Fulke Noel Clarke (born 1853). Previous service in the Sudan, 1884–5. Principal Ordnance Officer, South Africa, from the outbreak of the war in 1899 until he was invalided home in April 1901.

105 Lieutenant-Colonel George Radley Hobbs (1853–1907). Previous service in the Anglo-Zulu War, 1879. Chief Ordnance Officer, Cape Colony Lines of Communications, 1899–1901.

106 Colonel Henry Walter Barrett (1857–1949), Chief Ordnance Officer, South Africa, 1900–1. Previous service in Anglo-Zulu War, 1879.

107 Major Robert Whyte Melville Jackson (born 1860) had no previous war service. Took part in Lord Methuen's advance, 1899; operations in the ORC, 1900, and in the Cape Colony, 1901–2. COO, Bloemfontein, 1900; and later COO, Lines of Communications; COO, Base Depots, Cape Colony, and COO, Cape Colony.

108 According to a note at the end of the typed copy, the letter was translated from the original Dutch by Lieutenant-Colonel A.E. Dalzell.

109 Both the British and the Boers used black and coloured persons in the war. The Hague Convention (1899) did not address the question of using black or coloured people in a war that was primarily fought between whites.

110 Hamilton John Goold-Adams (1858–1920), Deputy Administrator (1901–2) and Lieutenant-Governor of the ORC (1902–7), and Governor of the OFS (1907–10). As an Army officer he served in Bechuanaland (1884–5) and in Matabeleland (1893). Resident Commissioner, Barotseland (1896–7) and of Bechuanaland (1897–1901). Later he was British High Commissioner in Cyprus (1911–14) and Governor of Queensland, Australia (1915–20). See also E.M. Main and A. Wessels (eds), 'Letters: Lord Milner to Hamilton John Goold-Adams, 1901–1905', *Christiaan de Wet Annals* 5, October 1978, pp. 107–56 and C. Headlam (ed.), *The Milner Papers*, II, p. 237.

111 Also published in Main and Wessels (eds), op cit, pp. 124–5.

112 In 1901 there was an outbreak of bubonic plague in Cape Town. It was introduced into SA in 1899 in rat-infested fodder that was imported by the British military authorities from India and South America, where the plague was raging at that stage. The largest outbreaks occurred in Cape Town, Port Elizabeth, East London, Durban and Johannesburg, 1900–5. A total of 1,694 cases were reported, of whom 947 died. Later there were also outbreaks in SA in 1914 and 1938. *SESA*, 4, p. 379 and 8, p. 588. See also N. Janisch, *Report and Proceedings with Annexures, of the Cape Peninsula Advisory Board, Appointed to Advise the Government on Matters connected with the Suppression of Bubonic Plague 1901.*

113 The internment camp for whites in Port Elizabeth was established in November 1900, and broken up in November 1902. Only two adults and twelve children under the age of fifteen died in the camp. For more on the Port Elizabeth camp see, for example, J.J. Roodt, 'Die Port Elizabethse Konsentrasiekamp, 1899–1902'.

114 I.e. Lord Curzon – see Note 77 above.

115 There are two main types of horse-sickness in South Africa: glanders (brought to the country by horses imported from overseas) and (South) African horse-sickness (caused by gnats, usually during the rainy season). See also *Royal Commission on the War in South Africa. Appendices to the Minutes of Evidence taken before the Royal Commission on the War in South Africa* (Cd. 1792), pp. 10–12, Appendix 6: Report on the Army Veterinary Department in South Africa.

116 Brigadier-General H.C.O. Plumer (see Biographical Notes) left Pretoria on 26 March 1901 with approximately 1,300 mounted troops, a small detachment of RE, eight field-guns and a pom-pom for operations in the Northern Transvaal. They occupied Pietersburg (today Polokwane) on Easter Monday, 8 April. Amery (ed.), op cit, V, pp. 201, 203.

117 Ten columns under the overall command of Lieutenant-General N.G. Lyttelton (see Biographical Notes) took part in a drive in the South-Eastern ORC, 10–20 March 1901. Only about 70 Boers and a few horses were captured. Amery (ed.), op cit, V, p. 234.

118 I.e. Major-General R.S.S. Baden-Powell's South African Constabulary (SAC). In October 1900 Roberts ordered the formation of the SAC, with Baden-Powell as its GOC. The original purpose of the SAC was to operate as a police force in the former Boer republics to maintain law and order. Posts were erected for the SAC, and in due course these posts became part of the elaborate blockhouse system. By January 1902 the SAC had approximately 10,000 members. G. Tylden, *The Armed Forces of South Africa*, p. 164; National Archives of South Africa (Pretoria), Microfilm M673: Report on the South African Constabulary.

119 Lieutenant-General Henry Brackenbury (1837–1914), Director-General of Ordnance (1899–1902). Previously he saw action in the suppression of the Indian Mutiny (1857–8), Franco-Prussion War (1870–1), Ashanti (1873–4), Anglo–Zulu War (1879) and in the Sudan (1884–5). He was Director of Military Intelligence, War Office (1886–91), Military Member of the Viceroy's Council, India (1891–6) and President of the Ordnance Board (1896–9).

120 See Note 80 above.

121 A. Hodges, *Lord Kitchener*, pp. 146–7, quotes a large portion of this letter and at this point mentions 'two or three thousand rebels', which is probably the number of Cape rebels who took up arms during the second Boer invasion of the Cape Colony, December 1900–May 1902. However, the previous drafts of this letter of Kitchener to Brodrick (see TNA reference PRO 30/57/2/Y34 and TNA reference PRO 30/57/22/Y34) clearly refer to between 200 and 300 Cape rebels. Kitchener either thought there were indeed so few rebels left, or he was downplaying the figures to get Brodrick (and probably also the Chancellor of the Exchequer) to support his request for changes in the British peace proposals. (The assistance of Mr John L. Carr from TNA, who double-checked the documents, is gratefully acknowledged.)

122 See Note 121 above.

123 Michael Edward Hicks Beach (1837–1916) was Chancellor of the Exchequer, 1885–6 and 1895–1902. He was Conservative MP for Gloucester (East), 1864–85 and for Bristol (West), 1885–1906; Parliamentary Secretary to the Poor Law Board, 1868; Under Secretary of State for Home Affairs, 1868; Chief Secretary for Ireland, 1874–8 and 1886–7; Secretary of State for Colonies, 1877–80; President of the Board of Trade, 1888–92. Viscount St Aldwyn, 1906; Earl of Aldwyn, 1915.

124 Approximately 16,000 Australians (including 40 women) – in six contingents – left from October 1899 to April 1902 to serve in South Africa. Some 600 of them died, half from disease. (See, for example, the section written by

C. Willcox in P.B. Boyden, A.J. Guy and M. Harding (eds), *'Ashes and Blood'. The British Army in South Africa 1795–1914*, pp. 107–10, as well as R.L. Wallace, *The Australians at the Boer War*, passim.) A total of 6,495 New Zealanders saw service in South Africa (plus at least 30 nurses, and twenty teachers taught Boer children in internment camps) – 228 died, most from disease. (See, for example, the section written by I. McGibbon in Boyden, Guy and Harding (eds), op cit, pp. 110–13, as well as J. Crawford and E. Ellis, *To Fight for the Empire. An Illustrated History of New Zealand and the South African War, 1899–1902*, passim.)

125 See Note 24 above for the events at Nooitgedacht, 13 December 1900.
126 See Note 68 above for the events at Dewetsdorp, 21–23 November 1900.
127 The Military Compensation Board (1901–3) dealt with a great variety of claims. See the Archives of the Military Compensation Board 1901–1903, kept in the National Archives, Pretoria.
128 Colonel Hugh Pentland Shekleton (1860–1938) commanded a column in the Western Transvaal, 1900–1. Previously he served in the Sudan (1897–8) and later took part in the Dongola Expedition (1906) and in World War I (1914–18).
129 In practice De Wet did not attempt another invasion.

Part 3
April to December 1901
Introduction

1 For more on the use (and abuse) of horses and mules during the war see, for example, F.J. van der Merwe, *Horses of the Anglo Boer War / Perde van die Anglo-Boereoorlog*; *Proceedings of a Court of Enquiry held at St. Stephen's House, Westminster, S.W. on the Administration of the Army Remount Department since January 1899, by Order of the Commander in Chief dated 20th February 1902* (Cd. 993); *Reports by Officers Appointed by the Commander-in-Chief to Inquire into the Working of the Remount Department Abroad* (Cd. 995); *Army Remounts. Digest of Evidence taken before the Court of Enquiry on the Administration of the Army Remount Department*; H. Sessions, *Two Years with Remount Commissions*.

2 As far as the British blockhouse system is concerned see, for example, J. Hattingh and A. Wessels, *Britse Fortifikasies in die Anglo-Boereoorlog (1899–1902)*, p. 19 et seq.; L.S. Amery (ed.), *The Times History of the War in South Africa 1899–1902*, V, pp. 396–412.

3 See, for example, A. Wessels (ed.), 'Die Oorlogsherinneringe van kommandant Jacob Petrus Neser', *Christiaan de Wet Annals* 7, pp. 86–8.

4 As far as the death of Esau is concerned see, for example, B. Nasson, *Abraham Esau's War. A Black South African War in the Cape 1899–1902*, passim; K. Schoeman, 'Die Dood van Abraham Esau. Ooggetuieberigte uit

die besette Calvinia, 1901', *Quarterly Bulletin of the South African Library* 40(2), December 1985, pp. 56–66.

5 See, for example, L.M. Fourie, 'Die Militêre Loopbaan van Manie Maritz tot aan die Einde van die Anglo-Boereoorlog', pp. 118–20.

6 As far as the conviction and execution of rebels are concerned see, for example, J.H. Snyman, 'Rebelle-verhoor in Kaapland gedurende die Tweede Vryheidsoorlog met spesiale Verwysing na die Militêre Howe (1899–1902)', *Archives Year Book for South African History* 25, 1962, pp. 1–73; G. Jordaan, *Hoe zij stierven. Mededelingen aangaande het Einde dergenen, aan wie gedurende de Oorlog 1899–1902, in de Kaap-Kolonie het Doodvonnis Voltrokken is*, passim; G. Jooste and A. Oosthuizen, *So het hulle Gesterf. Gedenkboek van Teregstellings van Kaapse Rebelle en Republikeinse Burgers tydens die Anglo-Boereoorlog 1899–1902*, passim; D. Judd and K. Surridge, *The Boer War*, pp. 232–6.

7 The most definitive study to date with regard to the role played by former republican burghers in the British ranks is A.M. Grundlingh, *Die "Hendsoppers" en "Joiners". Die Rasionaal en Verskynsel van Verraad*. See also J.P. Brits (ed.), *Diary of a National Scout. P.J. du Toit 1900–1902*.

8 The most definitive study to date with regard to the effect the war had on South Africa's civilian population, is S.B. Spies, *Methods of Barbarism? Roberts and Kitchener and Civilians in the Boer Republics January 1900 – May 1902*. For black internment camps, see S.V. Kessler, 'The Black Concentration Camps of the South African War 1899–1902'. For internment camps in general see, for example, F. Pretorius (ed.), *Scorched Earth*; A.C. Martin, *The Concentration Camps 1900–1902. Facts, Figures and Fables*; J.C. Otto, *Die Konsentrasiekampe*. For case studies of particular internment camps see, for example, A.U. Wohlberg, 'The Merebank Concentration Camp in Durban, 1901–1902'; J.J. Roodt, 'Die Port Elizabethse Konsentrasiekamp, 1899–1902'; A.W.G. Raath and R.M. Louw, *Die Konsentrasiekamp te Bethulie gedurende die Anglo-Boereoorlog 1899–1902*; A.W.G. Raath and R.M. Louw, *Die Konsentrasiekamp te Springfontein gedurende die Anglo-Boereoorlog 1899–1902*; A.W.G. Raath and R.M. Louw, *Die Konsentrasiekamp te Vredefordweg gedurende die Anglo-Boereoorlog 1899–1902*; A.W.G. Raath, R.M. Louw and D. Olivier, *Die Konsentrasiekamp te Bloemfontein gedurende die Anglo-Boereoorlog 1899–1902*.

9 P.A. Pyper, 'Generaal J.C. Smuts en die Tweede Vryheidsoorlog (1899–1902)', pp. 64–114.

10 D.M. Moore, *General Louis Botha's Second Expedition to Natal during the Anglo-Boer War September – October 1901*, pp. 14–102; Amery (ed.), op cit, V, pp. 334–59; M.H. Grant, *History of the War in South Africa 1899–1902*, IV, pp. 216–22.

11 Amery (ed.), op cit, V, pp. 365–76; Grant, op cit, IV, pp. 306–15.

12 See, for example, NAM. 1971-01-23-122-1-85: Roberts – Kitchener, 13 July 1902 (letter); published in A. Wessels (ed.), *Lord Roberts and the War in South Africa 1899–1902*, pp. 187–8.

13 For more on Kitchener's relationship with the press see, for example, Judd and Surridge, op cit, pp. 251–6; J. Beaumont, 'The British Press and Censorship during the South African War 1899–1902', *South African Historical Journal* 41, November 1999, pp. 280–8.

14 For the role played by Hobhouse during and after the war see, for example, R. van Reenen (ed.), *Emily Hobhouse. Boer War Letters.*

15 M.G. Fawcett, *What I Remember*, pp. 153–74; *Report on the Concentration Camps in South Africa by the Committee of Ladies appointed by the Secretary of State for War, containing Reports on the Camps in Natal, the Orange River Colony, and the Transvaal* (Cd. 893), passim.

16 *South Africa. Correspondence relating to the Prolongation of Hostilities in South Africa* (Cd. 732), p. 6. The proclamation was issued on 7 August 1901, but was dated 6 August 1901.

17 *DSAB*, II, p. 285; W.S. Churchill, *Ian Hamilton's March*, passim; I. Hamilton (A. Farrar-Hockley, ed.), *The Commander*, pp. 101, 103; *DNB, 1941–1950*, pp. 347–8; I.B.M. Hamilton, *The Happy Warrior. A Life of General Sir Ian Hamilton G.C.B., G.C.M.G., D.S.O.*, pp. 41–6, 179–86; I. Hamilton, *Listening for the Drums*, pp. 130–46; P. Magnus, *Kitchener. Portrait of an Imperialist*, p. 180.

18 See Wessels (ed.), *Lord Roberts . . .*, pp. 206–9, 211–25, 228–38, 241–4, 250–6, 258–61, 264–5.

19 A. McLeod and F. Pretorius, 'M.T. Steyn se Ervaring van die Anglo-Boereoorlog vanuit 'n Sielkundige Perspektief', *Historia* 47(1), May 2002, pp. 33–55. According to this study, Steyn's muscle disorder can be described as a psycho-physiological disorder, the result of years of abnormal stress.

20 J.E. Rabie, *Generaal C.R. de Wet se Krygsleiding by Sannaspos en Groenkop*, pp. 31–59; Amery (ed.), op cit, V, pp. 431–44; W.L. von R. Scholtz, 'Generaal C.R. de Wet as Veldheer', pp. 407–15.

April to December 1901

1 On 26 and 27 March 1901, Generals C.R. de Wet and L. Botha met near the Klip River in the Vrede district, ORC. Botha gave feedback on the Middelburg peace negotiations (see Part 2, Note 80). W.L. von R. Scholtz, 'Generaal Christiaan de Wet as Veldheer', p. 372.

2 On Sunday 14 April 1901, when Lieutenant-General J.D.P. French's elaborate drive in the South-Eastern Transvaal ended (see Part 2, Note 57), Lord Kitchener launched another big drive, this time in the North-Eastern Transvaal. While Brigadier-General H.C.O. Plumer marched south from Pietersburg (today Polokwane), four columns under the overall command of Major-General Bindon Blood marched northwards from the Delagoa Bay railway line, and another two columns moved northwards and eastwards from Lydenburg. All in all approximately 11,000 soldiers with 31 artillery

pieces took part in the drive, which ended on 1 May 1901. The British claimed to have captured 1,100 burghers, but this probably included many civilians. They also captured four destroyed guns (including the British 4.7-inch naval gun lost at Helvetia – see Part 2, Note 39), two pom-poms, two machine-guns, 540 rifles, 247 horses, 611 wagons and carts, a large quantity of livestock and some rifle ammunition. L.S. Amery (ed.), *The Times History of the War in South Africa 1899–1902*, V, pp. 206–8.

3 By April 1901 the Boers had very few artillery pieces left – most had been blown up because they were too cumbersome to take along or because no ammunition was left. This included pom-poms, i.e. large Maxim-Nordenfeldt or Vickers-Maxim belt-fed machine guns of 37-mm calibre firing 1-lb (0.454 kg) explosive rounds with a range of up to 3,500 m. Their nickname "pom-pom" is derived from the peculiar sound they made when fired. The Transvaal bought 25 of these guns from Britain. Because of the success the Boers achieved with their pom-poms, the British Army acquired 57 similar guns for use in South Africa. (J.H. Breytenbach, *Die Geskiedenis van die Tweede Vryheidsoorlog in Suid-Afrika, 1899–1902*, I, pp. 87–9, 96–7; Amery (ed.), op cit, VI, pp. 476, 489–90; D.D. Hall, 'Guns in South Africa 1899–1902', *Military History Journal* 2(2), December 1971, p. 43.) As far as rifles are concerned, it should be noted that by the beginning of 1901 many Boers had, *inter alia* because of a shortage of ammunition, discarded their Mauser rifles for captured British Lee-Metford or Lee-Enfield rifles. See in general R. Bester, *Boer Rifles and Carbines of the Anglo-Boer War*.

4 Either Kitchener's letters of 7 March and 15 March, or 15 March and 22 March 1901 to Brodrick. All these letters are printed in this publication – see documents [39], [40] and [44].

5 Sir Alfred Milner arrived in London on 24 May 1901 for a period of leave, but also to silence the growing choir of protest about the way in which the British were conducting the war in South Africa. While in Britain he was made a viscount, and would henceforth be known as Lord Milner of St James's and of Cape Town. In the meantime Kitchener acted as High Commissioner in South Africa. Milner arrived back in South Africa on 27 August 1901. *DSAB*, III, p. 615.

6 In practice Major-General L.J. Oliphant (see Biographical Notes) did in fact go to South Africa in 1901. From time to time there was also talk of Lord Roberts perhaps returning to South Africa to relieve Kitchener, but in practice, of course, that did not happen.

7 Probably Major-General Barrington Bulkley Douglas Campbell (born 1845).

8 Lieutenant-General N.G. Lyttelton (see Biographical Notes) left South Africa mid-April 1901 to go on leave in Britain, and returned in September 1901, to become GOC, Natal.

9 For conditions in the camps see, for example, A.W.G. Raath, R.M. Louw and D. Olivier, *Die Konsentrasiekamp te Bloemfontein gedurende die Anglo-Boereoorlog, 1899–1902*; A.W.G. Raath, *Die Boervrou, 1899–1902*,

1: *Moederleed*; J.C. Otto, *Die Konsentrasiekampe*; A.C. Martin, *The Concentration Camps 1900–1902. Facts, Figures and Fables*.

10 By January 1901, 15,182 Boers had been captured, and by the end of the war a total of 12,954 Transvaalers and 12,358 Free Staters, plus 160 foreign volunteers and 7,587 Cape and Natal rebels – a grand total of 33,059, while 13,780 Transvaalers and 8,318 Free Staters gave themselves up voluntarily (total: 22,098). Of the POWs, more than 25,000 were sent to POW camps overseas, namely to the five islands of Bermuda, to India, to Ceylon (today Sri Lanka) and to St Helena. D. Hall, *The Hall Handbook of the Anglo-Boer War 1899–1902*, p. 187.

11 Should be spelt 'congé', i.e. leave or discharge.

12 Brodrick regarded this letter as so important (see first paragraph, document [56]) that he had portions of it typed for the Cabinet.

13 Brigadier-General H.C.O. Plumer occupied Pietersburg (today Polokwane) on 8 April 1901. Amery (ed.), op cit, V, p. 203.

14 Colonel W.P. Pulteney captured Roossenekal on Monday 22 April 1901, where he accepted the surrender of the magistrate and 60 burghers. Amery (ed.), op cit, V, p. 214.

15 In the consulted sources there is no reference to any major troop movements on 28 April 1901 or of any new drive that was launched on that day. However, on 29 April Lieutenant-General H.M.L. Rundle (see Biographical Notes) started off from Bethlehem in the Eastern ORC on an expedition against Boers in the Brandwater Basin, and on 1 May Lord Methuen launched an operation in the Western Transvaal. Amery (ed.), op cit, V, pp. 231–3, 240–1. See also Note 20 below.

16 Schomberg MacDonnell (1861–1915), 5th son of the 5th Earl of Antrim. Principal Private Secretary of Lord Salisbury, 1888–1902. Served in the Office of Works, 1902–12. Mortally wounded, Flanders, World War I, and died on 23 November 1915. Kitchener addressed him in his letters as Rom.

17 Georg Alfred Brand (1875–1922) was the son of the former OFS President J.H. Brand. Fought in Natal, 1899–1900. Invaded the Cape Colony with Hertzog, 1900–1 (see also Part 2, Notes 22 and 23). As Assistant Chief Commandant, fought in ORC, 1901–2. Joined the newly-formed Union Defence Forces, 1912. Retired as a Lieutenant-General, 1922.

18 On 1 May 1901 four columns, under the overall command of Lord Methuen, started an operation to clear the Lichtenburg-Ventersdorp-Klerkdorp triangle of Boers. The drive ended on 6 May without a single Boer being killed or captured; only a deserted field-gun was captured. Amery (ed.), op cit, V, pp. 231–3.

19 Lieutenant-Colonel H.M. Grenfell launched a drive against the Zoutpansberg commando and reached Louis Trichardt (today Makhado) on 9 May 1901. Amery (ed.), op cit, V, pp. 328–9.

20 On 7 May 1901 Major-General E.L. Elliot (see Biographical Notes) started a drive in the North-Eastern ORC, with five columns under his overall

command: two acted as stopper groups on the Vaal River; the other three moved from the Villiers-Frankfort-Tafelkop line in the direction of Vrede, near the Natal border. Botha's Pan was reached on 19 May, without having achieved much. Amery (ed.), op cit, V, pp. 287–8.

21 Lieutenant-General H.M.L. Rundle (see Biographical Notes) tried to clear the Brandwater Basin of the remaining approximately 700 Boers, but left by the end of May 1901, having captured only one burgher, killed a few, and destroyed some supplies. His expedition to Bothaville came to little. Amery (ed.), op cit, V, pp. 240–1, 286.

22 Major-General C.E. Knox (see Biographical Notes) was at this stage in command of the Central District in the ORC, and from time to time launched drives against the Boer commandos who operated in that area. Amery (ed.), op cit, V, p. 238.

23 Major-General B.M. Hamilton (see Biographical Notes) was at this stage in command of the Southern District in the ORC, and launched operations on both sides of the main railway line. Amery (ed.), op cit, V, p. 286.

24 See *South Africa Despatches. Despatch by General Lord Kitchener, 8th May, 1901, relative to Military Operations in South Africa* (Cd. 605).

25 See *South Africa Despatches. Despatch by General Lord Kitchener, 8th March, 1901, relative to Military Operations in South Africa* (Cd. 522).

26 See Note 5 above.

27 This letter is published in CAB 37/57/54. The published version differs in some instances from the holograph in punctuation and the use of capital letters, paragraphs and abbreviations. For the purpose of this publication, the original text is reproduced in transcribed but unedited form.

28 Lieutenant-Colonel William Riddell Birdwood (1865–1951). Previous service in Black Mountain Expedition, 1891; Tirah Expedition, 1897. He went to SA as a 'Special Service' officer in November 1899 and saw action in Natal, 1899–1900 (wounded). DAAG to Kitchener, 1900–2. Served under Kitchener in India, first as his Assistant Military Secretary, 1902–4, and then as his Military Secretary, 1905–9. GOC, Australian and New Zealand Army Corps, 1914–18 (saw action in Dardanelles Campaign, and in France). GOC-in-C, Northern Army in India, 1920–4; C-in-C of the Army in India, 1925–30. General, 1917; Field Marshal, 1925; 1st Baron of Anzac and Totnes, 1938.

29 Lieutenant-Colonel Henry Pottinger Young. Previous service in Afghanistan, 1879. As censor at Kitchener's HQ he was criticized for the way in which he handled censorship. When C.F. Moberly Bell (at that time manager of *The Times*, London) complained to Mr St John Brodrick (Secretary of State for War) that private letters had been opened by Young, the latter was replaced. See also J. Beaumont, 'The British Press and Censorship during the South African War 1899–1902', *South African Historical Journal* 41, November 1999, pp. 284–7.

30 In an effort to defend the Cape Colony, a home guard consisting of the District Mounted Troops (DMTs) and Town Guards was established. By

May 1901 the home guard was about 20,000 strong, of whom about two thirds were DMTs.

31 Major George Duff Baker (born 1860) had no previous war service. In South Africa he was in the field 1899–1901, for example taking part in operations in the Transvaal, 1900; ORC, 1900, and Cape Colony, 1900–1; Commandant, Naauwpoort, De Aar and Kimberley, 1901.

32 Major Fitzgerald Wintour (1860–1949). Previous service in Egypt, 1882; Sudan, 1884–6; North-Western Frontier, India, 1897. Served in South Africa, 1899–1901. Lieutenant-Colonel, 1904; Colonel, 1908. During World War I he commanded a brigade in France, 1914–15. Retired as a Major-General, 1918.

33 This paragraph of Kitchener's letter to Roberts was published by Brodrick and circulated, together with other communications received from Kitchener. In its published form the paragraph differs from the original as far as punctuation and spelling is concerned, for example 'Khudu Jauta' is printed as 'Khadu Jaunta'. According to G. Arthur, *Life of Lord Kitchener*, II, p. 34 (where it is printed as '*khadu jaunta*') it means 'very uncertain', but in the version published by Brodrick, its meaning is indicated in a note as 'is very certain'! According to Rev. Dr A.S. Erasmus of Bethlehem (Free State, South Africa), *jaunt* is, inter alia, an archaic English word meaning 'difficult, tiresome trip or journey', and *khud* is a Persian word meaning 'ravine' or 'precipice'. The suffix *a* at *jaunta* and the suffix *u* at *khudu* have no functional value or meaning, but are typical of 19th century flashy style. So, the expression used by Kitchener should have been spelt as *khud jaunt*, and it means (in the context of his letter) '(will be) very difficult'. According to B. Farwell, *Eminent Victorian Soldiers. Seekers of Glory*, p. 339, Kitchener could speak five languages fluently, and according to the *DNB, 1912–1921*, p. 307, he acquired a sound knowledge of the Arabian language while working for the Palestine Exploration Fund in the 1870s. P. Ziegler, *Omdurman*, p. 193, confirms that Kitchener could speak Arabic fluently.

34 The translation is not in the Roberts Papers at the NAM. Of course, Colonel Henry Seymour Rawlinson (see Biographical Notes) was not captured.

35 Kitchener's previous letter to Brodrick was written on 9 May 1901 (see document [51]), but could not have reached Brodrick by 18 May 1901. In Kitchener's letter to Brodrick dated 19 April 1901 there are many references to the Cape Colony – see TNA reference PRO 30/57/22/Y44–45.

36 On 10–11 May 1901 Louis Botha, Jannie Smuts, other senior Transvaal officers and members of the Transvaal government-in-the-field met for a council of war meeting on the farm De Emigratie, south-east of Ermelo. Without consulting the OFS government, they decided to renew peace negotiations, but would first contact Paul Kruger, in self-imposed exile in Europe. Kitchener made available a telegraphic connection, and Smuts acted as go-between. P.G. Cloete, *The Anglo-Boer War. A Chronology*, p. 238. See also Note 77 below.

37 Francis William Reitz (1844–1934), M.P., Cape Colony, 1872–3; first Chief Justice, OFS, 1875–88; President, OFS, 1889–95 (resigned for reasons of health); Secretary of State, Transvaal, 1898–1902, and as such signed the acts of peace, 31 May 1902, notwithstanding the fact that earlier that day he spoke out against accepting the British terms. As a private citizen he declined to take the oath of allegiance to Great Britain, and went abroad as an exile. Union of SA Senator, 1910–29. Also known as a pioneer Afrikaans poet. *DSAB*, II, pp. 577–85.

38 Marthinus Wessel Pretorius (1819–1901), fought against the Zulu at Ncome (Blood) River, 1838; President of the Transvaal, 1857–71, and of the OFS, 1859–63. Member of triumvirate that led Transvaalers in revolt against Britain, 1880–1 (after the British annexation of 1877). In 1901, Kitchener delegated the aged former President to speak to General Louis Botha about the possibility to end the war. Not long after the Middelburg peace negotiations, Pretorius died on 19 May 1901 of pneumonia after being interrogated by British soldiers on the cold night of 16 May. *DSAB*, I, pp. 648–54; S.J. du Preez, 'Vredespogings gedurende die Anglo-Boereoorlog tot Maart 1901', pp. 158–60.

39 Annie Botha – see Part 1, Note 61. After the British captured Pretoria, she stayed on in the town. By the beginning of 1901 she was very worried about her husband, and asked the British authorities for a pass to visit him. Initially they said that she would receive the necessary permission, on condition that she would speak to him about the possibility of ending the war, a request that she rejected. However, in due course she still received a pass, albeit that she was asked to tell her husband that Kitchener would like to meet him. That she did, and brought back a letter from Botha to Kitchener, in which he indicated that he was prepared to speak to the C-in-C.

40 Colonel E.B. Appelbe (see Biographical Notes) succeeded Colonel R.F.N. Clarke as Principal Ordnance Officer in South Africa when the latter was invalided home in April 1901. Amery (ed.), op cit, V, p. 456.

41 This last sentence is underlined in red on the holograph – probably not by Kitchener or Brodrick.

42 For the outbreak of bubonic plague at the Cape, see Part 2, Note 112.

43 See Note 36 above and Note 77 below.

44 See Part 2, Note 39 for more information on the battle at Helvetia, 29 December 1900.

45 A passenger ship of the Union Castle Lines. The *Tantallon Castle* went aground on Robben Island in Table Bay on 7 May 1901. The ship could not be freed and had to be abandoned. Information supplied by Mr P. du Toit, Cape Town.

46 Edward George Villiers Stanley, 17th Earl of Derby (1865–1948). Conservative MP, West Houghton Division, Lancashire, 1892–1906. Chief press censor, Cape Town, 1899–1900. Colonel and Private Secretary to Lord Roberts, 1900. Financial Secretary, 1900–3; Postmaster-General, 1903–5.

Raised five battalions of King's Regiment, 1914; Director of Recruiting, 1915–16; Under-Secretary of State for War, 1916; Secretary of State for War, 1916–18 and 1922–4; Ambassador, Paris, 1918–20.

47 Printed in this publication as document [49].

48 Director-General of Ordnance.

49 Inspector-General of Fortifications.

50 There is a possibility that this could be Major Harry Roderick Bottomley (born 1871) who served in South Africa for the duration of the war.

51 See Note 36 above.

52 On Wednesday 29 May 1901 General J.C.G. Kemp (see Biographical Notes) and a commando of approximately 500 burghers attacked Brigadier-General H.G. Dixon (see Biographical Notes), who had about 1,200 soldiers with seven pieces of artillery and a pom-pom under his command, at Vlakfontein (the present-day Derby) between Ventersdorp and Rustenburg in the Western Transvaal. After a heavy battle the Boers fell back. The British lost at least 49 killed and 129 wounded. Boer casualties are uncertain, but at least seven were killed and two of an unknown number of wounded succumbed later. Amery (ed.), op cit, V, pp. 281–4; M.H. Grant, *History of the War in South Africa 1899–1902*, IV, pp. 184–8; J.C.G. Kemp, *Vir Vryheid en Reg*, pp. 391–6.

53 See Note 77 below.

54 Could be Commandant Abraham Malan (died 1910), the son-in-law and adjutant of General Piet Joubert (who until his death in 1900 was C-in-C of the Transvaal's forces). Later, Malan fought under General Christiaan Beyers, and established the Afrikaner Cavallerie Corps.

55 President Kruger's cabled reply said that the Boers should not surrender. See Note 77 below.

56 Major-General William George Knox (1847–1916). Previous service in Abyssinia, 1867–8; Ashanti, 1873–4; Russo-Turkish War, 1877–8 (observer on Turkish side); Afghanistan, 1878–9; Anglo-Zulu War, 1879; war against Sekhukhune, Transvaal, 1879; Transvaal War of Independence, 1880–1. Saw action in Natal, 1899–1900 (including siege of Ladysmith). GOC, 23rd Brigade, ORC, 1900–2.

57 Could be Friedrich von Lindequist.

58 See Note 52 above.

59 See Note 23 above.

60 See Note 20 above. Elliot then turned about and his troops converged on Witkoppies, and by the end of May his force united again at Vrede. From there he moved to Kroonstad. En route, one of Elliot's contingents engaged a Boer force at Grenspan (6 June 1901) and drove them off. Amery (ed.), op cit, V, pp. 288–9.

61 Not the better-known Joseph James Cheere Emmett (1866–1933), brother of Louis Botha's wife, Annie (see Part 1, Note 62 and Note 39 above), who was only taken prisoner on 13 March 1902, but another of Annie's brothers. Unfortunately no additional information about him could be traced.

62 Before and after the Waterval council of war meeting (see Note 77 below), both the Transvaal and OFS governments-in-the-field were harassed by several British columns. Amery (ed.), op cit, vol. V, p. 300.

63 Pietpotgietersrust, since 1902 known as Potgietersrus, and since 2002 as Mokopane.

64 At the beginning of June 1900, six men who had earlier taken the Oath of Neutrality, left Pretoria illegally to rejoin the commandos. At Pietersburg (today Polokwane) station, they encountered a police patrol. A shoot-out took place and three of the men were taken into custody, namely P.R. Krause, N.T. Venter, and a Delport. They were taken back to Pretoria and during a one-day trial on 10 June, all three were found guilty of breeching an oath, the illegal possession of fire-arms, and attempted murder, and consequently condemned to death. Delport was pardoned because he was still very young (and sent to a POW camp), but Krause and Venter were executed by firing-squad in the Pretoria prison on 11 June 1901. G. Jooste and A. Oosthuizen, *So het hulle Gesterf. Gedenkboek van Teregstellings van Kaapse Rebelle en Republikeinse Burgers tydens die Anglo-Boereoorlog 1899–1902*, pp. 216–17.

65 Major-General John Grenfell Maxwell (1859–1929), Military Governor of Pretoria, 1900–2. Previous service in Egypt, 1882; Egypt and Sudan, 1884–5 and 1886–9; Dongola, 1896; Sudan 1898. Governor of Nubia (1896–8) and of Omdurman (1898–9). GOC, 14th Brigade, ORC and Transvaal, 1900. After the war he was GOC, Egypt, 1908–12 and 1914–15; GOC, Ireland, 1916; C-in-C, Northern Command, 1916–19. General, 1919.

66 General P.H. Kritzinger (see Biographical Notes) invaded the Cape Colony for a second time, 19 May–14 August 1901. Quite a number of Cape Afrikaners joined his force as rebels. At one stage (2 June) he occupied Jamestown in the Eastern Cape.

67 In the course of the war 435 Cape rebels were condemned to death, but only 44 were executed. G. Jordaan, *Hoe zij Stierven. Medelingen aangaande het Einde dergenen, aan wie gedurende de Oorlog 1899–1902, in de Kaap-Kolonie het Doodvonnis Voltrekken is*; J.H. Snyman, 'Rebelle-verhoor in Kaapland gedurende die Tweede Vryheidsoorlog met spesiale Verwysing na die Militêre Howe, 1899–1902', *Archives Year Book for South African History* 25, 1962; Jooste and Oosthuizen, op cit, passim.

68 The date is difficult to decipher. It could be 25 or 26 May, but it should be 25 May, in which case the letter is printed in this publication as document [56].

69 See Note 66 above.

70 Leander Starr Jameson (1853–1917) qualified as a medical doctor in London and in 1878 settled in Kimberley. He became Cecil John Rhodes' Private Secretary in 1886, Chief Magistrate of Mashonaland (in the present-day Zimbabwe) in 1891, and in 1895 also Resident Commissioner of that part of Bechuanaland bordering on the Transvaal. On 29 December

1895 Jameson led 510 policemen and volunteers (with three field-guns and eight maxims) into the Transvaal in an attempt to overthrow the government, but the Jameson raiders were defeated and forced to surrender on the farm Vlakfontein (adjacent to the farm Doornkop which is usually, incorrectly, indicated as the place of the surrender), near Krugersdorp, on 2 January 1896. See, for example, *The Jameson Raid. A Centennial Retrospect* and W.J. du Plooy, 'Die Militêre Voorbereidings en Verloop van die Jameson-inval'.

71 Although a few Afrikaners entained hopes of a united South Africa under Afrikaner rule, the Boers had no intention of conquering the Cape Colony and Natal. Their military strategy was defensive. See, for example, A. Wessels, 'Afrikaners at War' in J. Gooch (ed.), *The Boer War. Image, Experience, Direction*, pp. 82–5 and A. Wessels, 'Die Boere se strategie aan die begin van die Anglo-Boereoorlog', *Tydskrif vir Geesteswetenskappe* 39(3&4), September & December 1999, pp. 227–42.

72 The Afrikaner population of the Transvaal numbered about 148,000 in 1899, and about 71,00 in the OFS, for a total of 229,000 (Wessels, op cit, in Gooch (ed.), op cit, p. 73). In June 1901 there were approximately 85,000 Afrikaners in internment camps (Cloete, op cit, p. 343), and at least approximately 30,000 burghers had either been captured or had surrendered voluntarily (see Note 10 above); i.e. Kichener's estimate on the Boer population in captivity is correct.

73 Although the original manuscript clearly refers to W. Chamberlain, J. (Joseph) Chamberlain is probably meant.

74 On 12 June 1901 an Australian force of approximately 350 men under the command of Major C.J.N. Morris (and part of Colonel S.B. Beatson's force) was camped at Wilmansrust, between Middelburg and Ermelo in the Eastern Transvaal. At about 19.30 approximately 120 Boers, under the command of General C.H. Muller, stormed and overran the camp. Fifteen British soldiers were killed and 42 wounded (most of them taken prisoner, together with most of the unwounded men) and the Boers also captured two pom-poms. Boer casualties were apparently few in number. The Boers released their POWs before moving on. Amery (ed.), op cit, V, pp. 294–6; Grant, op cit, IV, pp. 203–4.

75 Latin: It is my fault; I am to blame.

76 Colonel Henry Timson Lukin (1860–1925) was awarded the DSO in May 1900. At the beginning of 1901 he received a second DSO, which at the end of the war was changed to a CMG. He previously saw service in the Anglo-Zulu War (1879), in Basotholand (1881) and in the Langeberg Campaign (1897). OC, Cape Mounted Riflemen Artillery Troop, North-Eastern Cape Colony (1899–1900), OFS (1900) and Cape Colony (1901–2). Brigadier-General, 1912. IG, SA Union Defence Forces, 1912–14. In World War I he served in German South-West Africa (1914–15), Egypt (1916) and France (1916–18). Major-General, 1916.

77 On Thursday 20 June 1901 the governments of the Transvaal and OFS, and their military leaders, met at Waterval, near Standerton in the Transvaal. Those present included Steyn, Schalk Burger (Acting President of the Transvaal), Botha, De la Rey, Smuts, De Wet and Hertzog. In answer to the Transvaalers' telegram of 10 May to President Kruger (see Note 36 above), the Transvaal President sent back a telegram in which he urged his people to continue the struggle. Steyn seriously admonished the Transvaalers for the unilateral decisions they took on 10 May. Those present at Waterval decided to continue the struggle and issued a proclamation to that effect, in which they also stated that they would not accept any peace conditions that did not guarantee their independence and did not safeguard the interests of the rebels. It was also decided that Smuts would invade the Cape Colony to relieve the pressure on the republics. Cloete, op cit, p. 245.

78 Helen Harris was a Quaker and the wife of Professor Rendel Harris of Cambridge, England. She was sent out by the Quakers and pro-Boer women in England to investigate conditions in the internment camps, 1901. Lord Kitchener gave her permission to visit some of the camps. T. van Rensburg (ed.), *Camp Diary of Henrietta E.C. Armstrong. Experiences of a Boer Nurse in the Irene Concentration Camp, 6 April – 11 October 1901*, p. 100 (Note 127).

79 See in general the book of A.M. Davey, *The Pro-Boers 1877–1902*.

80 On 17 December 1900 a Peace Committee was formed, at a meeting in Belfast, Eastern Transvaal, where Meyer de Kock was the chairman. De Kock was elected secretary of the committee and on 21 December 1900 they held a meeting of surrendered Boers in Pretoria, urging those who were still in the field that in the light of the fact that further resistance was hopeless, they should also surrender. Kitchener was present and delivered a sympathetic address. Peace emissaries visited various commandos in an effort to convince the Boers that it was in their own interest to surrender, but in most instances they were regarded as cowards and traitors, and accordingly fined or imprisoned (kept in custody by the commandos). De Kock, who had ridden into General Ben Viljoen's commando (see Biographical Notes) on 22 January 1901, was tried, sentenced to death for high treason, and shot on 12 February 1901. Amery (ed.), op cit, V, pp. 92–3; A.M. Grundlingh, *Die "Hendsoppers" en "Joiners". Die Rasionaal en Verskynsel van Verraad*, pp. 84–6, 95–6.

81 Edward Cardwell (1813–86) was MP, 1842–74; Secretary to the Treasury, 1845–6; President of the Board of Trade, 1852–5; Secretary of State for Ireland, 1859–61; Secretary of State for the Colonies, 1864–6; Secretary of State for War, 1868–74. He introduced short service and the Army Reserve, and abolished commissions by purchase. Viscount, 1874.

82 See *South Africa Despatches. Despatch by General Lord Kitchener, 8ᵗʰ July 1901, relative to Military Operations in South Africa* (Cd. 695).

83 An extract of this letter was published in C. Headlam (ed.), *The Milner Papers*, II, p. 258.

84 These square brackets seem to have been added to the original text by an unidentified person.

85 I.e. the first words of the Song of Simeon in Luke 2 verse 29, namely to declare oneself willing or delighted to depart from life or from some occupation; also the first words of one of the Prayer Book hymns.

86 I.e. Milner's so-called Kindergarten, consisting of young men who served on his personal staff, in the administrations of the Transvaal and ORC, and in the Inter-Colonial Council. These included men like John Buchan, Lionel Curtis, Patrick Duncan and W.L. Hichens. These young civil servants had all studied at Oxford, rendered outstanding service in SA, and had a lasting influence on the history of the country. See, for example, Amery (ed.), op cit, VI, pp. 147–8; *SESA*, 7, p. 420.

87 The Duke and Duchess of Cornwall and York visited South Africa from 13–23 August 1901 as part of their world tour which lasted for eight months and covered some 80,000 km – the longest and probably the most expensive of its kind ever undertaken by members of the Royal Family. The Duke (George Frederick Ernest Albert, 1865–1936) ascended the throne as King George V (1910–36), and his wife (Victoria Mary Augusta Louise Olga Pauline Claudine Agnes, 1867–1953) was henceforth known as Queen Mary. The Royal couple arrived in Durban (from Australia) on 13 August 1901, where they spent four hours before going to Pietermaritzburg where they spent the whole of 14 August (see Note 112 below), and returned to Durban the next day, i.e. 15 August. That same day (14 August) they inspected the Princess Christian Hospital Train (see Part 1, Note 98) in Durban, before departing on board their ship, the *Ophir*, having been in Natal for a hectic 53 hours. They arrived in Simon's Town on 18 August, and proceeded to Cape Town by train the next day, where they received a rousing welcome. The Royal couple embarked at Simon's Town on 23 August, for Canada. During their visit to South Africa they received many valuable gifts, including a parcel of 700 diamonds, weighing 261.5 carats, then worth £14,000 (and 100 years later about £400,000). Cloete, op cit, pp. 259–260; P. Buckner, 'The Royal Tour of 1901 and the Construction of an Imperial Identity in South Africa', *South African Historical Journal* 41, November 1999, pp. 324–48. See also Notes 112 and 116 below.

88 In the light of the fact that between July 1901 and the end of the war many Boers were killed or (especially) taken prisoner or surrendered voluntarily, and yet at the end still had about 21,000 in the field, this number (13,000) supplied by Kitchener on 5 July 1901, is a gross underestimate. According to Amery (ed.), op cit, V, p. 332, there were still about 35,000 Boers in the field by September 1901. A figure of about 30,000 for the period July–September 1901 will probably be nearer to the correct number.

89 Major-General A.S. Wynne (see Biographical Notes) was GOC, Cape Colony, April–December 1901.

90 Sir Walter Hely-Hutchinson (see Biographical Notes) was Governor of the Cape Colony, March 1901–May 1910.

91 See Note 82 above.

92 Lieutenant-Colonel Richard Boileau Gaisford (1854–1924) previously served in the Transvaal War of Independence (1880–1), and in Burma (1886–7). He served throughout the Anglo-Boer War, for example in Natal (1899); took part in Lord Roberts' advance to Bloemfontein, and to Pretoria (1900); AAG, HQ (1900–2). AQMG, Scottish Command, 1908–11. Inspector of Infantry, with temporary rank of Brigadier-General, 1914–16; as Honorary Brigadier-General, served in France, 1917.

93 At the Waterval meeting (see Note 77 above) it was decided that De la Rey had to prepare a well-equipped commando (to be led by Smuts) to invade the Cape Colony. Smuts invaded the Cape Colony on 4 September 1901 (see Note 130 below).

94 This paragraph was written (probably as a postscript) slanted in the top left-hand corner of the first page of the letter.

95 Mr De Waal, not De Vaal. Nicolaas Frederic de Waal (1853–1932) was born in the Netherlands, but emigrated to South Africa in 1880, and in due course settled in Middelburg, Cape Colony, where he took over the local newspaper. De Waal identified himself with the political aspirations of the Afrikaner, and in 1887 he joined the Afrikanerbond. (The Afrikanerbond was a Cape Colony political organisation, 1880–1911. Before and during the war the Bond campaigned for peace, and it played a role in ensuring that the rebellion did not get out of hand. However, a few Bond members did rebel. See, for example, T.R.H. Davenport, *The Afrikaner Bond. The History of a South African Political Party, 1880–1911*.) De Waal was the Bond's Assistant Secretary, 1890–8; member of the Disciplinary Committee, 1889–98 and 1910–11; member for Colesberg in the Cape Legislative Assembly, 1898–1910. During the Anglo-Boer War, De Waal campaigned to end the rebellion in the Cape Colony. As Mayor of Middelburg, he received Joseph Chamberlain in February 1903. De Waal was later Colonial Secretary, Cape Colony, 1908–10; Administrator, Cape Colony, 1910–25. Knighted, 1911. *DSAB*, II, pp. 189–90; *So Onthou Ons Hulle / Middelburg Pays Homage*, pp. 10–11.

96 On the night of 10–11 July 1901 Steyn and most members of the OFS government were sleeping in the town of Reitz (having occupied it when Colonel H. de B. de Lisle departed) when a British force under the command of Brigadier-General R.G. Broadwood entered. Steyn and seven others succeeded in escaping, thanks to his valet, a coloured man by the name of Ruiter. The other members of the OFS government, as well as senior officers (a total of 29 persons) were taken prisoner, and a large volume of documents captured, including correspondence between Steyn and the Transvaal government, in which the latter's pessimistic view of affairs was reflected – the propaganda value of which was exploited to the full by the

British. *DSAB*, II, p. 711; Amery (ed.), op cit, V, p. 301; Grant, op cit, IV, pp. 247–9; N.J. van der Merwe, *Marthinus Theunis Steyn.'n Lewensbeskrywing*, II, pp. 20–4. For translations of some of the captured documents, see *South Africa. Further Correspondence relating to Affairs in South Africa* (Cd. 903), pp. 54–7.

97 This letter of Smuts to Steyn could not be traced and is, according to L. Scholtz, *Waarom die Boere die Oorlog Verloor het*, pp. 167, 196, indeed lost.

98 Gordon A. Fraser, one of those taken prisoner on the night of 10–11 July 1901 in Reitz. See Note 96 above.

99 See Part 2, Note 60.

100 Colonel James Latimer Crawshay St Clair (1850–1940) took part in the Anglo-Zulu War, 1879. Deputy Judge-Advocate, South Africa, 1899–1907.

101 Major-General William Freeman Kelly (1847–1914) previously saw action in the North-Western Frontier Campaign, India, 1876; Egypt, 1882–4; Sudan, 1885. In South Africa he served as Assistant Military Secretary, 1888; DAAG, 1888; AAG, 1890. Then he was DAG, Ireland, 1894–1900. Back in South Africa he served as AG to the Field Force, January 1900–October 1902, and for example took part in advance to Bloemfontein, and to Pretoria, 1900. Acting Chief of Staff, for a short time, 1900.

102 The portion underlined is underlined in red in the holograph – probably not by Kitchener or Brodrick.

103 Dr Kendal Mathew St John Franks (1851–1920), Irish surgeon who came to the Cape Colony in 1896, and settled in Johannesburg in 1897. Member of Roberts' staff (one of five consulting surgeons) and accompanied Roberts in South Africa, January–December 1900. Returned to England with Roberts, but was back in South Africa in 1901, once again as consulting surgeon for the British forces. At Kitchener's request he undertook an inspection tour of all the internment camps. After the war he continued to do sterling work as a surgeon in Johannesburg. *DSAB*, V, pp. 277–8. See also E. van Heyningen, 'British doctors versus Boer women: clash of medical cultures' in F. Pretorius (ed.), *Scorched Earth*, pp. 178–97, as well as the following report which contain some of Franks' views: *Reports etc. on the Working of the Refugee Camps in the Transvaal, Orange River Colony, Cape Colony and Natal* (Cd. 819) and *Report on the Concentration Camps in South Africa by the Committee of Ladies appointed by the Secretary of State for War, containing Reports on the Camps in Natal, the Orange River Colony, and the Transvaal* (Cd. 893).

104 I.e. Henry Edward McCallum (see Biographical Notes), who succeeded Walter Francis Hely-Hutchinson (see Biographical Notes) on 12 May 1901 as Governor of Natal, after Hely-Hutchinson, in March 1901, succeeded Milner as Governor of the Cape Colony.

105 Kitchener was Acting High Commissioner in the place of Milner who was in England on leave. See also Note 5 above.

106 On 7 August 1901 Kitchener issued a proclamation in which it was stated that all Boer officers and members of the ('former') Boer governments who did not surrender by 15 September 1901, would be permanently banished from South Africa. (*Correspondence relating to the Prolongation of Hostilities in South Africa* (Cd. 732), pp. 6–7.) The proclamation had very little if any effect, to a large extent backfired, made the Boers more resolute to continue their struggle, and was mockingly referred to by the Boers as Kitchener's 'paper bomb'. On 15 August 1901 President Steyn reacted in some detail to the proclamation, reiterating the Boers' determination to continue the struggle. Cloete, op cit, pp. 258–9; M.C.E. van Schoor (ed.), *'n Bittereinder aan die Woord. Geskrifte en Toesprake van Marthinus Theunis Steyn*, pp. 187–94.

107 Major-General H.J.T. Hildyard (see Biographical Notes) left South Africa in September 1901 on leave to England, and in 1903 he became Director of Military Education. It is not clear what he did in the period in between.

108 Lieutenant-General H.M.L. Rundle (see Biographical Notes) only gave up his command of the Harrismith district on 19 February 1902. Amery (ed.), op cit, V, p. 486.

109 Major-General A.H. Paget (see Biographical Notes) did not return to South Africa.

110 Major-General L.J. Oliphant (see Biographical Notes) arrived in South Africa towards the end of 1901, while Major-General B.B.D. Campbell (see Note 7 above) and Major-General I.R. Jones (see Biographical Notes) stayed on until 1902.

111 Lieutenant-Colonel John George, Marquis of Tullibardine (1871–1942) previously saw service in the Sudan, 1898.

112 The Duke and Duchess of Cornwall and York arrived in Durban on 13 August 1901 – see Note 87 above, and document [67]. In Pietermaritzburg, on 14 August, the Duke presented eight Victoria Crosses and several Distinguished Service Orders to imperial and colonial troops before a crowd of more than 10,000 people in the municipal park. Buckner, op cit, pp. 334–5.

113 Brodrick's wife, Hilda Charteris, died on 1 August 1901. In 1903 he married Madeleine Carlyle.

114 The postscript is written slanted in the top left-hand corner of the first page of the letter.

115 Major-General E.L. Elliot (see Biographical Notes) was in charge of a drive in the Western ORC. The drive ended on 10 August 1901 on the Modder River. Seventeen Boers were killed or wounded and 259 captured, as well as 814 vehicles, 186,000 sheep and 21, 000 cattle. Cloete, op cit, p. 258.

116 In Durban approximately 50,000 people of all races welcomed the Royal couple on their arrival (13 August 1901), and in Pietermaritzburg some 10,000 people attended a medal parade (14 August). See Buckner, op cit, pp. 333–5, and Notes 87 and 112 above.

117 Eight, according to Buckner, op cit, p. 335.

118 See Note 106 above.

119 See Part 1, Note 99.

120 I.e. Princess Alexandra Caroline Mary Charlotte Louise Julia (1844–1925) – eldest daughter of Prince Christian of Schleswig-Holstein-Sonderburg-Glücksburg (from 1863 King of Denmark) – who married Edward on 10 March 1863.

121 King Edward's elder sister, Victoria Adelaide Mary Louise (born 1840), died on 5 August 1901. She married Prince Friedrich Wilhelm of Prussia in 1888. He reigned as Friedrich III for less than three months before he died in 1888. They had eight children, including the later Emperor Wilhelm II of Germany.

122 Colonel Malcolm Orme Little (1857–1931) previously served in Afghanistan, 1878–80. Saw action on the Kimberley front, 1899–1900. OC, 9th Lancers, 1899–1900. Took part in Roberts' advance to Bloemfontein, and Pretoria, 1900. GOC, 3rd Cavalry Brigade, South-Western Transvaal, 1900 (wounded). Took part in anti-guerrilla operations, ORC and Transvaal, 1900–2. Served in World War I, 1914–18.

123 Colonel Edward Joshua Cooper (1858–1945) previously served in Egypt, 1882 and 1884–5. Saw action on Kimberley front, 1899–1900; Cape Colony, 1901–2 (twice seriously wounded during the war). Served in World War I, 1914–18.

124 Major-General John George Dartnell (1838–1913) served in the suppression of the Indian Mutiny, 1857–8; Bhootan Expedition, 1865; Anglo-Zulu War, 1879; Transvaal War of Independence, 1880–1. Fought in Natal (including defence of Ladysmith), 1899–1900. Then commanded the Natal Volunteers, and the Imperial Light Horse Brigade, 1900–1. He resigned his command in December 1901.

125 The drive, which took place from 18 August to 6 September 1901, was a failure. See, for example, Amery (ed.), op cit, V, pp. 322–4.

126 W.F. Hely-Hutchinson (see Biographical Notes) succeeded Milner as Governor of the Cape Colony in March 1901.

127 The outbreak of the war led to serious political divisions in the Cape Colony, with one portion of the population and their political representatives giving unconditional support to the British war effort, while others in various degrees had sympathy with the Boers. W.P. Schreiner's ministry and their supporters tried to avert war and wanted the Cape to stay neutral; former premier Sir Gordon Sprigg (see Biographical Notes) and his followers supported the British policy. The first Boer invasion and subsequent rebellion, 1899–1900, aggravated circumstances. The question of how to deal with the rebels brought matters to a head; Schreiner's cabinet was split on the issue and he resigned on 13 June 1900. Milner requested Sprigg to form a new government. The second Boer invasion, 1900–2, led to renewed crises, mainly concerning martial law and the abolition of the Cape

constitution. These problems continued after the cessation of hostilities. See, for example, C.J.S. Strydom, 'Die Kaapkolonie, 1899–1902: Skadevergoeding en die Rebelle in Ere herstel'.

128 See *South Africa Despatches. Despatches by General Lord Kitchener, dated 8th August, 8th September, and 8th October, 1901, relative to Military Operations in South Africa, including a Supplementary Despatch, dated 18th October, on the Actions at Itala Mount, Fort Prospect, and Moedwil* (Cd. 820).

129 See Note 125 above.

130 General J.C. Smuts (see Biographical Notes) left the Gatsrand, Western Transvaal, on 1 August 1901, and started moving southwards in the direction of the Cape Colony. In the ORC he side-stepped several British columns and in the early hours of 4 September 1901 he crossed the Gariep at Kibadrif into the Herschel district, North-Eastern Cape Colony. P.A. Pyper, 'Generaal J.C. Smuts en die Tweede Vryheidsoorlog (1899–1902)', p. 69 and T. & D. Shearing, *General Smuts and his Long Ride*, pp. 23–37. See also Note 146 below.

131 Probably Cd. 528 and Cd. 663 referred to in Part 2, Note 80.

132 I.e. deadline for Boer leaders to surrender – see Note 106 above.

133 Kitchener's brother, Major-General F.W. Kitchener (see Part 2, Note 38) and Colonel W.P. Campbell (see Note 134 below) left Wonderboom Station on 8 August 1901 and marched southwards towards Ermelo.

134 Colonel William Pitcairn Campbell (1856–1933) previously served in the Sudan, 1884–5. Saw action in South Africa, 1899–1902, for example as OC, 1st Battalion, King's Royal Rifles (KRR), and a mobile column in the Eastern Transvaal. GOC, Southern Command (1914–16) and Western Command (1916–18).

135 On Tuesday 10 September 1901, Colonel G.E. Benson (see Biographical Notes and Note 166 below), operating from Carolina, surprised several groups of Boers and also surprised and attacked a Boer laager at Pullen's Hope, near Carolina. He captured a total of approximately 50 Boers on that day, as well as cattle. Amery (ed.), op cit, V, p. 331; Grant, op cit, IV, p. 304.

136 Could be Lieutenant Johannes Lodewicus Malan (born 1873), Transvaal State Artillery. Took part in the suppression of the Jameson Raid, 1896 (see Note 70 above). Saw action in Anglo-Boer War, 1899–1902. Captured, March 1902, and sent to St Helena POW camp.

137 The internment camp for whites in Middelburg (Transvaal) was established in February 1901, and by July 1901 there were 7,751 inmates. At least 1,314 Boer civilians (including at least 1,142 children), and perhaps as many as 1,621 Boer civilians (including 1,343 children) died in the camp. The camp was broken up in January 1903. G. & E. van der Westhuizen, *Gids tot die Anglo-Boereoorlog in die Oos-Transvaal / Guide to the Anglo Boer War in the Eastern Transvaal*, pp. 188–9.

138 Henry Thurnburn Montague Bell (1873–1949), foreign correspondent of *The Times* (London), 1895–1906, including war correspondent, South

Africa, 1900–2. Editor, *North China Daily News and Herald*, Shanghai, 1906–11; managing director and editor-in-chief, *The Near East and India*, 1916–35.

139 Botha left the Eastern Transvaal on 7 September 1901 with a commando of approximately 1,000 men and moved southwards in the direction of the Natal border. At Blood River Poort he defeated a British force (17 September; see Note 145 below) and then divided his commando in two. One section attacked a British post at Itala (26 September), just inside the Natal border (see Note 149 below), while the other section launched an attack on Fort Prospect (26 September), east of Itala (see Note 157 below). Both attacks were beaten off, and Botha fell back to the Eastern Transvaal. D.M. Moore, *General Louis Botha's Second Expedition to Natal during the Anglo–Boer War September–October 1901*, pp. 14–102; Amery (ed.), op cit, V, pp. 334–59.

140 I.e. Sir Gordon Sprigg – see Biographical Notes.

141 Two Dutch Reformed Church ministers of the Cape Colony, Rev. C. Murray of Graaff-Reinet and Rev. J.F. Botha of Richmond, travelled to the ORC. They first visited President M.T. Steyn in the Lindley district and asked him to order the withdrawal of Boer forces from the Cape Colony, but the OFS President refused. They then travelled to De Wet, but he was also not prepared to withdraw forces from the Cape Colony; as a matter of fact, he told them that he would send even more commandos across the Gariep to invade the British territory. Scholtz, op cit, pp. 380–1.

142 Probably Kitchener's despatch of 8 September 1901 – see Cd. 820 referred to in Note 128 above.

143 Not in PRO 30/57/22 at TNA.

144 General Petrus Johannes Liebenberg (1857–1950) fought in several wars against black tribes in the Transvaal, and took part in the Transvaal War of Independence, 1880–1. Fought on the Kimberley front, 1899; invaded the North-Western Cape Colony, 1900; fought in the Western Transvaal, 1900–2.

145 Lieutenant-Colonel Hubert de la Poer Gough (1870–1963) previously saw service in Tirah, 1897–8. Saw action in Natal, 1899–1900; took part in anti-guerrilla operations, 1901–2. On 17 September 1901 his force of about 1,200 men was severely defeated by Botha at Blood River Poort, between Utrecht and Vryheid. The British lost at least twenty killed and 241 (including at least 24 wounded) taken prisoner. Three British artillery pieces were also captured. The Boers lost one man killed and three wounded. (See also Note 139 above.) After the war Gough was OC, 16th Lancers (1907–11); GOC, 3rd Cavalry Brigade (1914), 2nd Cavalry and 7th Cavalry Division (1915), I Corps (1916) and 5th Army (1916–18). General, 1922. Moore, op cit, pp. 24–35.

146 On 17 September 1901 Smuts surprised a squadron of 17th Lancers at Modderfontein near Tarkastad in the Eastern Cape. The British lost 38

killed or died of wounds and more than 100 taken prisoner (including about 50 of them wounded), as well as a machine-gun and a field-gun captured. When another squadron of 17th Lancers arrived on the scene, the Boers fled, leaving behind the prisoners and destroying the machine-gun and field-gun. The Boers only lost one man killed and five or six wounded, of whom three were soon captured by the British. Amery (ed.), op cit, V, pp. 388–9; Grant, op cit, IV, pp. 275–6; W. Hancock and J. van der Poel (eds), *Selections from the Smuts Papers*, I, pp. 417, 433; O.J.O. Ferreira (ed.), *Memoirs of Ben Bouwer as written by P.J. le Riche*, pp. 159–63.

147 On 19 September 1901 the commando of General G.A. Brand (see Note 17 above) crossed from south to north the fortified line stretching from Bloemfontein to Thaba 'Nchu, and at Slangfontein, near Sannaspos, surprised a farm-burning column of some 200 MI and SAC (with two field-guns). The British column was sent out from Boesman's Kop by Major-General C. Tucker (who was stationed in Bloemfontein). All the British soldiers, more than 200 horses and both the field-guns were captured, as well as a large quantity of ammunition. Amery (ed.), op cit, V, pp. 385–7.

148 James Rose Innes (1855–1942), MP, Cape Colony, 1883–1902. Attorney-General, Cape Colony, June 1900–February 1902. Opponents of the war criticized Innes for being too harsh on them (he sent two editors to jail for libel), but he was opposed to martial law and tried (without success) to soften its impact; and he opposed all efforts to suspend the Cape constitution. Judge-President, Supreme Court, Transvaal, April 1902–May 1910; Appeal Court Judge, Union of SA, May 1910–September 1914; Chief Justice, Union of SA, September 1914–February 1927. *DSAB*, II, pp. 328–32.

149 One portion of Botha's invasion force, about 1,400 men under the command of General Christiaan (Chris) Botha, attacked a British post at Itala, south of Babanango and just inside Natal, just past midnight on 26 September 1901. The British garrison (about 300 men with two field-guns under the command of Major A.J. Chapman) beat off the attack that lasted all day. The British lost 22 killed and 59 wounded and the Boers fifteen killed and 40 wounded – five or six of the latter died soon afterwards. Amery (ed.), op cit, V, pp. 344–8; Moore, op cit, pp. 46–66. See also Note 139 above.

150 Major Affleck Alexander Fraser (born 1855), 2nd in command of the 1st Battalion Bedforshire Regiment. He had no previous war service. Served in South Africa, 1899–1901, retiring when he was Commandant of the Thaba 'Nchu District.

151 In the night of 19–20 September 1901 General P.H. Kritzinger and about 70 men surprised 100 of Lovat's Scouts, commanded by Lieutenant-Colonel the Honourable A.D. Murray, in their camp at Quaggafontein, in the Zastron district, ORC. The British lost about 50 killed (including Murray and his brother) and wounded, and most of the others taken prisoner, as well as their whole camp and field-gun captured. The Boers retired again soon

afterwards, leaving behind most of the booty. Amery (ed.), op cit, V, p. 387; Grant, op cit, IV, pp. 288–9.

152 This is clearly a gross exaggeration by Kitchener.

153 Kritzinger invaded the Cape Colony for a third time on the night of 15–16 December 1901, but was seriously wounded and captured on 16 December 1901.

154 On Monday 8 October 1901 martial law was extended to all the Cape Colony's ports, and henceforth included the districts of Cape Town, Wynberg, Simon's Town, Port Elizabeth and East London. Cloete, op cit, p. 270.

155 See Note 139 above.

156 See Note 149 above.

157 In the early hours of 26 September 1901 General J.J.C. Emmett (see Note 61 above) and about 150 men attacked the British garrison (about 80 soldiers with one machine-gun under Captain C.A. Rowley) at Fort Prospect, approximately 15 km east of Itala (see Note 149 above), but were twice beaten back. The Boers' losses are uncertain: they acknowledged one burgher killed and two wounded, but according to Amery, they had 30–40 casualties. The defenders only lost one killed and eight wounded. Moore, op cit, pp. 67–74; Amery (ed.), op cit, V, pp. 349–50.

158 *Jeppe's Map of the Transvaal or South African Republic and Surrounding Territories*, researched and compiled by Friedrich (Fred, Fredrick) Heinrich Jeppe (1834–1898) and his son, Carl F.W. Jeppe (1870–1900; killed at the battle of Spioenkop on 24 January). Fred Jeppe was born in Germany, but in due course settled in the Transvaal, where he initially worked as a merchant. Postmaster-General of the Transvaal, 1868–75. In the meantime he gradually developed into the most important cartographer of the Transvaal. At the time of his death he was preparing a 1:476,000 cadastral map of the Transvaal. When the Anglo-Boer War broke out, the map had just been printed by Wurster, Randegger and Co. in Winterthur, Switzerland. Despite precautions, a copy of the map reached the British War Office, and when Lord Roberts landed at Cape Town, his Chief of Military Intelligence, Colonel G.F.R. Henderson, came across several hundred copies of the map in the Cape Town post office. The map was subsequently used as basis for British military maps of the Transvaal. *DSAB*, II, pp. 338–9; E.C. Liebenberg, 'Die Topografiese Kartering van Suid-Afrika, 1879–1972: 'n Histories-geografiese Ontleding', p. 173.

159 Sybella (Isabella, Is(s)ie) Margaretha Krige (1870–1954) married J.C. Smuts (see Biographical Notes) in 1897. They had nine children, of whom two sons and four daughters survived infancy. *DSAB*, IV, pp. 585–6.

160 Rachel Isabella (Tibbie) Fraser (1865–1955) married M.T. Steyn (see Biographical Notes) in 1887. They had five children: one son and four daughters. Mrs Steyn and her children left Bloemfontein with the President

shortly before the British occupation (13 March 1900) and accompanied the OFS government-in-the-field until the end of July 1900, when they stayed behind in Fouriesburg, and where they were placed under house arrest by the British forces. They were later transferred to Bloemfontein, where they stayed (as virtual prisoners) until the cessation of hostilities. After the war she played an important role in the reconstruction of the ORC and in the Afrikaner culture. See, for example, E. Truter, *Tibbie. Rachel Isabella Steyn, 1865–1955. Haar Lewe was Haar Boodskap.*

161 Rinderpest, the contagious virus desease of cattle, was introduced to SA from Asia via North and Central Africa. In 1896–7 a great epidemic ravaged cattle in South Africa, with 1896 being the worst year. See, for example, *South African Republic. Report on the International Rinderpest Congress, held at Pretoria from the 2ⁿᵈ to the 13ᵗʰ August 1897* (Pretoria, 1898).

162 Colonel Robert George Kekewich (1854–1914) previously served in Malaysia (1875–6) and in the Sudan (1884–5 and 1888). GOC, Kimberley, during siege, 1899–1900; commander of a mobile column, Western Transvaal, 1900–2. On 30 September 1901 Kekewich (with about 900 men, three field-guns and a pom-pom) was camped on the banks of the Selons River, between Zeerust and Rustenburg in the Western Transvaal, when he was attacked by De la Rey and at least 200 men. The British repulsed the attack with a loss of at least 56 killed and 131 wounded. The Boers captured more than 300 horses and lost at least nine killed, 33 wounded and three (including one of the wounded) taken prisoner. Grant, op cit, IV, pp. 293–7; J.F. Naudé, *Vechten en Vluchten van Beyers en Kemp "Bôkant" De Wet*, pp. 292–8; Amery (ed.), op cit, V, pp. 377–83.

163 In practice Boer commandos operated in the whole of the arid Western Cape Colony (including the Calvinia district) until the cessation of hostilities. See, for example, A. Wessels (ed.), 'The Anglo-Boer War Diary of Major H.S. Jeudwine' in A. Wessels (editor-in-chief), *Egodokumente. Persoonlike Ervaringe uit die Anglo-Boereoorlog 1899–1902*, pp. 58–87.

164 On 15 October 1901 Commandant J.L. van Deventer overwhelmed and captured 157 men of the Somerset East District Mounted Troops (DMT) at Doornbosch, near Somerset East. Amery (ed.), op cit, V, p. 395. As far as the DMTs are concerned, see also Note 30 above.

165 I.e. the despatch of 8 October 1901 – see Cd. 820 referred to in Note 128 above.

166 During the afternoon of 30 October 1901 Louis Botha and about 1,200 men launched an attack against Colonel G.E. Benson (see Biographical Notes) and his approximately 2,000 men, four artillery pieces and two pom-poms, at Bakenlaagte. Benson was on his way from Middelburg to Bethal in the Eastern Transvaal. The Boers captured the British positions on Gun Hill, but did not follow up their success by attacking the British laager at Nooitgedacht. The British lost at least 66 killed, 165 wounded (Benson being among those mortally wounded – he died the next day) and 120

captured, as well as two of the artillery pieces. Boer casualties were less than 100. Amery (ed.), op cit, V, pp. 364–76; Grant, op cit, IV, pp. 305–15.

167 On 25 October 1901 Brigadier-General M.F. Rimington and Colonel H.S. Rawlinson (with about 2,000 men and eight guns) approached the laager of Louis Botha and the Transvaal government-in-the-field at Schimmelhoek, 32 km east of Ermelo, when they stumbled on General Chris Botha and his 300 men. The ensuing fighting alerted Louis Botha and his companions, and they were able to escape, albeit that Botha left behind a bag of correspondence. Four Boers were taken prisoner. Amery (ed.), op cit, V, pp. 362–4.

168 General Jacobus Daniël Opperman (1861–1902) previously fought against Zibhephu (1884). He fought in Natal (1899–1900) and in the Eastern Transvaal (1900–2), and took part in Botha's Natal invasion attempt (1901). He was killed in action at Bankkop on 4 January 1902.

169 From 6–12 November 1901 a concentric drive took place in the North-Eastern ORC, in the area between Winburg, Heilbron, Standerton (in Transvaal) and Harrismith, with fourteen columns (a total of some 15,000 soldiers) moving in circles towards Paardehoek, between Frankfort and Reitz, where the Boers were supposed to be trapped. In the course of the drive 34 Boers were killed and wounded, and 86 captured, several farms were burnt, about 10,000 head of cattle captured, and about 200 wagons captured, but by the time the columns reached Paardehoek, there were no burghers in the trap. Amery (ed.), op cit, V, pp. 414–17.

170 I.e. Major-General F.W. Kitchener – see Part 2, Note 38.

171 See Note 52 above.

172 Lieutenant-General I.S.M. Hamilton (see Biographical Notes) was appointed as Kitchener's Chief of Staff on 7 November 1901, and he joined Kitchener in Pretoria on 29 November 1901.

173 As far as Kitchener's relationship with the press is concerned see, for example, J. Beaumont, 'The British Press and Censorship during the South African War 1899–1902', *South African Historical Journal* 41, November 1899, pp. 283–8.

174 Emily Hobhouse (1860–1926), British pacifist, philanthropist and humanitarian, visited South Africa 1900–1 and 1901 (see next Note), in an effort to alleviate the plight of the civilians in the internment camps, and also in 1903, 1905–8 and 1913. Her ashes were brought to South Africa and buried in the Women's Memorial, Bloemfontein. See, for example, R. van Reenen (ed.), *Emily Hobhouse. Boer War Letters*.

175 On 27 October 1901 Hobhouse arrived in Cape Town on board the SS *Avondale Castle* but the British authorities refused her permission to land. On 31 October she was physically carried off the ship and transferred to the *Roslin Castle* for deportation back to England, under martial law regulations. The next day, on board the ship, she wrote letters to Kitchener and Milner, accusing them, inter alia, of brutality. Van Reenen (ed.), op cit, pp. 139–51.

176 See Part 2, Note 115.

177 Towards the end of 1901 the British War Office asked Canada to raise a mounted unit, the 2ⁿᵈ Canadian Mounted Rifles (901 officers and men), commanded by Lieutenant-Colonel Thomas Evans. They arrived in SA in March 1902. C. Miller, *Painting the Map Red. Canada and the South African War, 1899–1902*, pp. 381, 391–413.

178 See Note 103 above.

179 I.e. thrash with a sjambok (horsewhip).

180 The Boer citizen armies lacked formal military training, and discipline was always bound to be a problem. From the outbreak of the war, many burghers tended to join commandos if and when they wished to do so, and stayed away if they wished. De Wet, op cit, pp. 13–14, 78, 85, 207–9, 351.

181 See Note 153 above.

182 In practice De la Rey did not invade the Cape Colony.

183 Captain the Honourable H. Lambton (Royal Navy), OC of the cruiser HMS *Powerful*. He commanded two 4.7-inch and four 12-pdr guns from his ships that were mounted on wheels and taken to Ladysmith to defend the town against the Boers, 1899–1900. Amery (ed.), op cit, II, pp. 213–14.

184 Captain Crowe (Royal Navy), the British Consul-General in Lourenço Marques, organised an intelligence branch in Delagoa Bay.

185 I.e. a form of horse-sickness – see Part 2, Note 115.

186 For statistics on horses used by the British, see Part 2, Note 17. The Boers took to the field more than 50,000 horses in October 1899, and they were replaced several times during the war. Their net wastage probably exceeded 100,000, but no accurate figures are available. D. Hall, *The Hall Handbook of the Anglo-Boer War 1899–1902*, p. 233.

187 Not in TNA reference PRO 30/57/22.

188 William George Granville Venables Vernon Harcourt (1827–1904), British statesman. Liberal MP for Oxford, 1868–80; for Derby, 1880–95, and for West Monmouth, 1895–1904. Solicitor-General, 1873; Home Secretary, 1880–5; Chancellor of the Exchequer, 1886, 1892–5. In 1901 he denounced the British conduct of the war in South Africa as unjust.

189 In March 1902 Kitchener said that there were 7,114 blacks and 2,939 coloureds in an armed capacity in British service. However, almost right from the start of hostilities, the British armed an ever-increasing number of blacks and coloureds. By the cessation of hostilities approximately 25,000 of them were used as blockhouse guards, and at least 25,000 others were employed as members of, for example, the flying columns. A further approximately 70,000 blacks and coloureds were employed in a non-combatant capacity, for example as servants and drivers. A. Wessels, *Die Militêre Rol van Swart Mense, Bruin Mense en Indiërs tydens die Anglo-Boereoorlog (1899–1902)*, pp. 9–20; P. Warwick, *Black People and the South African War, 1899–1902*, pp. 4–5.

190 See Note 153 above.

191 Hamilton wrote fairly long letters to Roberts – about every seven to ten days, November 1901–June 1902. These letters offer comments on the conduct of Kitchener and other officers in the field, and were an important source of information for the C-in-C at the War Office. Typescript copies of the letters are kept by the Liddell Hart Centre for Military Archives, London (see the Ian Hamilton Papers). Some of Hamilton's letters are published in A. Wessels (ed.), *Lord Roberts and the War in South Africa 1899–1902* (Army Records Society Volume 17), pp. 202–9, 211–25, 228–38, 241–4, 250–6, 258–61, 264–5. See also documents [88], [95], [105], [107] and [110] in this Kitchener volume.

192 I.e. Lieutenant-General Thomas Kelly-Kenny (see Biographical Notes) who succeeded General Evelyn Wood (see Biographical Notes) as AG in October 1901. Kelly-Kenny served as AG until 1904.

193 Lieutenant-Colonel James William Dunlop (1854–1923), RA, previously served in Afghanistan, 1879–80, and in the Burmese Expedition, 1886–7. Lieutenant-Colonel, 1900. He served in South Africa, 1901–2, taking part in operations in the Transvaal, ORC and Cape Colony; OC of a mobile column, December 1901–May 1902. Colonel, 1904. Later served in World War I, 1914–18.

194 The Bethlehem-Harrismith blockhouse line was completed in January 1902. See fold-out map in Amery (ed.), op cit, V, opposite p. 412.

195 16 November 1901. See document [80] in this publication.

196 The column was in fact at that stage not commanded in practice by Lieutenant-Colonel R.B. Firman (see Biographical Notes), but temporarily by Major F.A. Williams. Firman went on leave in the second week of December 1901.

197 In the early hours of Christmas Day, Wednesday 25 December 1901, De Wet attacked, surprised and overwhelmed a British force on top of Groenkop (henceforth also known as 'Krismiskop', i.e. Christmas Hill) on the farm Tweefontein, near the present-day Kestell in the Eastern ORC. At least 57 British soldiers were killed (including Major F.A. Williams, the temporary OC), 84 wounded and more than 200 (including most of the wounded) captured (and the bodies of 25 blacks were also found in the camp). The Boers, who also captured a large quantity of arms, ammunition and stores, lost fourteen killed and 30 wounded. J.E. Rabie, *Generaal C.R. de Wet se Krygsleiding by Sannaspos en Groenkop*, pp. 31–59; W.L. von R. Scholtz, 'Generaal Christiaan de Wet as Veldheer', pp. 407–15; Amery (ed.), op cit, V, pp. 431–44.

198 There were two main prisoner of war (POW) camps on the island of St Helena: Deadwood (approximately 3,200 POWs) and Broadbottom (approximately 2,300 POWs). The most high-ranking POW on the island was Gen. P.A. Cronjé (see Biographical Notes) who, together with his wife (see Part 1, Note 28), stayed in a house outside the POW camps, with an armed guard keeping watch. A third, smaller camp, known as Deadwood

No 2, or the 'Jam Camp', was established for those POWs who had sworn either an oath of neutrality or an oath of allegiance to Britain, and for whom it was no longer safe to stay in the bigger camps. POWs who tried to escape or who were rebellious, were sent to High Knoll Fort, a penal camp. In Jamestown there was a parole camp and, also in Jamestown, there was a Royal Army Medical Corps hospital camp. Information supplied by Ms Elria Wessels, War Museum, Bloemfontein. See also, for example, S.P.R. Oosthuizen, ' Die Beheer, Behandeling en Lewe van die Krygsgevangenes gedurende die Anglo-Boereoorlog, 1899–1902', pp. 146, 151–4.

199 Not in PRO 30/57/22 at TNA.

Part 4
January to April 1902
Introduction

1 P.G. Cloete, *The Anglo-Boer War. A Chronology*, p. 299.

2 L.S. Amery (ed.), *The Times History of the War in South Africa 1899–1902*, V, pp. 475–81; J. Hattingh and A. Wessels, *Britse Fortifikasies in die Anglo-Boereoorlog (1899–1902)*, pp. 115–16; Cloete, op cit, pp. 300–1; M.H. Grant, *History of the War in South Africa 1899–1902*, IV, pp. 401–4, J.W. Yardley, *With the Inniskilling Dragoons. The Record of a Cavalry Regiment during the Boer War, 1899–1902*, pp. 321–3.

3 Amery (ed.), op cit, V, pp. 481–91; Hattingh and Wessels, op cit, pp. 116–17; Cloete, op cit, pp. 303–4, 306–7; Yardley, op cit, pp. 324–7; J.D. Kestell, *Through Shot and Flame*, pp. 252–60; *South Africa Despatches. Despatch by General Lord Kitchener, dated 8th March, 1902, relative to Military Operations in South Africa* (Cd. 970), pp. 6–8.

4 Amery (ed.), op cit, V, pp. 491–4; Hattingh and Wessels, op cit, p. 118; Cloete, op cit, p. 311.

5 Amery (ed.), op cit, V, pp. 545–56; Hattingh and Wessels, op cit, pp. 118–19; Cloete, op cit, pp. 311–13, 317; Yardley, op cit, pp. 332–3; Grant, op cit, IV, pp. 479–80.

6 Amery (ed.), op cit, V, pp. 578–9; Hattingh and Wessels, op cit, p. 119.

7 R.D. McDonald, *In the Skaduwee van die Dood*, pp. 68–8; A. de Wet *et al.*, *Die Buren in der Kapkolonie im Kriege mit England*, pp. 121–6.

8 For the role played by Smuts in the latter months of the war see, for example, P. Burke, *The Siege of O'okiep (Guerrilla Campaign in the Anglo-Boer War)*, passim; Amery (ed.), op cit, V, pp. 550–3.

9 Amery (ed.), op cit, V, pp. 497–9; Grant, op cit, IV, pp. 410–15; J.F. Naudé, *Vechten en Vluchten van Beyers en Kemp "Bôkant" De Wet*, pp. 323–6.

10 Amery (ed.), op cit, V, pp. 501–8; Grant, op cit, IV, pp. 416–21; Naudé, op cit, pp. 327–36; *South Africa. Report from Lieut.-General Lord Methuen on the Action that took place near Tweebosch on 7th March, 1902* (Cd. 967), passim.

11 P. Magnus, *Kitchener. Portrait of an Imperialist*, p. 185.

12 Grant, op cit, IV, pp. 494–8; Amery (ed.), op cit, V, pp. 519–24; Naudé, op cit, pp. 345–9.

13 Amery (ed.), op cit, V, pp. 525, 531–7; Grant, op cit, IV, pp. 499–504; Naudé, op cit, pp. 352–4.

January to April 1902

1 I.e. the Williams incident – see Part 3, Notes 196 and 197.

2 The Boer attack started just after 02.00 on Christmas Day, 1901. See also Part 3, Note 197.

3 The summit of the hill could have been well defended, but in practice the British defensive positions left much to be desired. J.E. Rabie, *Generaal C.R. de Wet se Krygsleiding by Sannaspos en Groenkop*, p. 48.

4 Not in PRO 30/57/22 at TNA.

5 In practice General Christiaan de Wet left his commando in the hands of General Michael Prinsloo, went off to meet President M.T. Steyn at Leeuwkuil (10 January 1902), and then visited the Bethlehem, Kroonstad and Heilbron commandos.

6 Words and sentences in longhand that are *additions* to the typed manuscript, are printed in *italics*.

7 This note is written slanted in the left-hand top corner of p. 1 of the letter. It is not clear what exactly Lord Roberts had to do with the letter's (non-) delivery to Mr Brodrick.

8 Sybil Brodrick (died 1934) was a daughter of Mr St John Brodrick and his first wife, Hilda Charteris. See also Part 3, Note 113.

9 'as a rule' typed but scratched out and replaced by an undecipherable word in longhand.

10 See the New Model Drives referred to in Notes 27 and 35 below.

11 The National Scouts (first raised in 1901) were surrendered burghers of the Transvaal who voluntarily joined the British Army against their former comrades, and were consequently referred to by the Boers as joiners, and regarded as traitors. There were a total of approximately 1,500 National Scouts, plus about 450 ORC Volunteers. Furthermore, many other burghers served in various capacities in the British Army in SA. On 1 June 1902, a total of 5,464 Afrikaners were in British service. They were primarily deployed in their home districts where their knowledge of local conditions was of great help to the British forces. After the war the joiners were ostracised by the Afrikaner community, but Louis Botha worked towards reconciliation, which was achieved to some extent by 1910, when the Union of SA was established. A.M. Grundlingh, *Die "Hendsoppers" en "Joiners". Die Rasionaal en Verskynsel van Verraad*.

12 A reference to the Anglo-Zulu War (1879). Although some Boers might have been glad that the British subjugated the Zulus, others would have felt uneasy now that they had imperialistic British and no longer Zulu neighbours.

13 The coronation of Edward VII would have taken place on 26 June 1902, but because of the King's illness, it had to be postponed two days before the event. The King was eventually crowned on 9 August 1902, and a parade of colonial troops took place on 12 August 1902. In the consulted sources there is no indication that National Scouts took part in the coronation procession.

14 George Wyndham (1863–1913). Conservative MP for Dover, 1889–1913; Under-Secretary of State for War, 1898–1900; Chief Secretary for Ireland, 1900–5.

15 The greater portion of this letter to Brodrick, from the 5th paragraph ('Steyn and De Wet, our two ...') to the end of 2nd last paragraph before the postscripts ('I do not think that anyone can.') is quoted in Hamilton's letter of 20 January 1902 to Winston Churchill. See Churchill College Archives (Cambridge), Churchill Papers, CHAR 1/34/5-14.

16 See Part 2, Note 17.

17 See, for example, the correspondence in the BL, Oriental and India Office Collections, Lord George Francis Hamilton Papers, MSS Eur F 123/48.

18 See Note 11 above.

19 Commandant Stephanus Gerhardus Vilonel (1865–1918), OC of the Senekal commando, served in Natal, 1899–1900; took part in unsuccessful efforts to relieve General P.A. Cronjé at Paardeberg (see Part 1, Note 22) and to stop Lord Roberts' advance to Bloemfontein, 1900. He was relieved of his command in March 1900 when he refused to limit his amount of transport, and not long afterwards he surrendered voluntarily. He returned to the Boers as a peace emissary, believing that he could induce others to surrender, but he was taken prisoner by the Boers, found guilty of treason and kept in custody with the commandos, until he was freed when General Marthinus Prinsloo surrendered in the Brandwater Basin, July 1900. He became a leading figure in the ORC Volunteers. Grundlingh, op cit, pp. 251–7; Amery (ed.), op cit, III, pp. 480, 574, 577 and IV, pp. 30, 311, 339–40, 514.

20 General Daniël Jacobus Elardus Erasmus (1845–1914) previously fought in the Second OFS-Basotho War (1865), the Transvaal War of Independence (1880–1) and in wars against black tribes in the Transvaal (1894–8). Member of the Transvaal Volksraad, 1881–6. During the Anglo-Boer War he fought in Natal (1899–1900) and in the South-Eastern Transvaal (1900–2). He was captured on 3 January 1902. MP, Transvaal, 1907–10.

21 John Charles Ardagh (1840–1907) came to South Africa in December 1901 as a member of a commission that was appointed to investigate the claims for compensation by neutral subjects whom the British military authorities had deported from South Africa. He returned to England in March 1902, but was once again in South Africa from August 1902 as a member of the

Judicial Commission on Revision of Martial Law Sentences. Before the war he saw active military service in Egypt (1882) and in the Sudan (1884–6). He was Private Secretary to Lord Lansdowne (Viceroy of India), 1888–94; Commandant, School of Military Engineering, Chatham, 1894–6; Director of Military Intelligence, War Office, 1896–1901; and after the Anglo-Boer War he was Director of the Suez Canal, 1903–7.

22 Brigadier-General James Redmond Patrick Gordon (born 1860). Previous service in Afghanistan, 1880; Transvaal War of Independence, 1880–1; Bechuanaland Expedition, 1884–5; Burma, 1887; Expedition against the Jebus, Lagos, 1892; Ashanti, 1895–6. GOC, 3rd Cavalry Brigade, 1900–2: took part in Roberts' advance to Bloemfontein, to Pretoria, and eastwards along Delagoa Bay railway. GOC, 1st Cavalry Brigade, 1900–2: operations in the Transvaal and ORC.

23 General B.J. Viljoen (see Biographical Notes) was taken prisoner near Lydenburg in the Eastern Transvaal on 25 January 1902. He was sent to a POW camp on St Helena, where he wrote *My Reminiscences of the Anglo-Boer War*. Viljoen's conversation of about 30 minutes with Kitchener took place in Pretoria during the first week of February 1902. Ibid, p. 278.

24 See Part 2, Note 60.

25 Colonel Ludwig von Estorff (1859–1943) fought against the Herero in German South-West Africa (today Namibia), 1894–5, and suppressed the Swartbooi Hottentots revolt, 1897. Acting OC, colonial forces, German East Africa (today Tanzania), 1900–1. In the second quarter of 1901 he was transferred to German South-West Africa. En route he landed in Durban, visited the 1899–1900 battlefields near Ladysmith, travelled to Pretoria to visit Kitchener, who allowed him to visit the operational area as well as internment camps. In May 1901 he travelled via Cape Town to Swakopmund to become Acting OC, colonial forces, German South-West Africa. He was also Acting Governor, 1902–3. At the end of 1902 he signed an agreement with Boers who wanted to settle in the colony, allowing them to establish their own church congregation, and erect schools where their children could be taught in Dutch. The German government did not agree with Von Estorff's sympathetic policy towards the Boers and ordered him to cancel the agreement, but he refused, asked to be relieved of his command, and returned to Germany in 1903. However, in 1904 he was back in German South-West Africa, suppressed the Herero Revolt (1904), and fought against the Bondelswarts and Morenga (1905–6). OC, colonial forces, German South-West Africa, 1907–8, 1909–10. Served in World War I, 1914–18. Lieutenant-General, 1918. Governor, Königsberg (East Prussia), 1919–20. *DSAB*, IV, pp. 751–2.

26 See Part 2, Note 80.

27 The first New Model Drive lasted from 5–8 February 1902. A total of about 17,000 British troops took part, and about 300 blockhouses were also involved. A line of some 90 km was formed by some 9,000 troops, with the

Frankfort-Heilbron-Wolwehoek blockhouse line forming the northern flank, and the Bethlehem-Lindley-Kroonstad line the southern flank. The idea was to move westwards, sweeping the area clean of commandos, and pushing them against the Kroonstad railway line, which was also a blockhouse line, now manned by additional troops, and with four armoured trains patrolling the line. The drive, which was deemed to be relatively successful by the British, led to 286 Boers being killed, wounded or captured. However, De Wet and many others escaped, with De Wet and Steyn breaking unobserved through the Kroonstad-Lindley blockhouse line in the early hours of 7 February. L.S. Amery (ed.), *The Times History of the War in South Africa 1899–1902*, V, pp. 475–81; J.W. Yardley, *With the Inniskilling Dragoons. The Record of a Cavalry Regiment during the Boer War, 1899–1902*, pp. 321–3; M.H. Grant, *History of the War in South Africa 1899–1902*, IV, pp. 401–4.

28 The totals were apparently written in at a later stage, namely: 14.800 riding horses 1.050 Artillery [horses].

29 According to D. Hall, *The Hall Handbook of the Anglo-Boer War 1899–1902*, p. 237, no horses were imported from Russia.

30 A total of at least 23,028 horses were imported from Australasia. Ibid.

31 The British Army imported 106,658 horses (as well as 80,524 mules and donkeys) from the United States of America, while 3,220 horses (and 1,000 mules and donkeys) bought for the British South Africa Company in the USA were also used during the war. Ibid.

32 A total of 14,621 horses were imported from Canada. Ibid.

33 See Note 27 above.

34 The 4th Battalion of the Rifle Brigade (R.B.) sailed from England middle December 1901, and after arriving in SA took part in the closing operations in the ORC. J. Stirling, *Our Regiments in South Africa 1899–1902. Their Record, based on the Despatches*, p. 390.

35 The second New Model Drive lasted from 13–27 February 1902. A total of about 30,000 British troops took part. The area to be swept stretched from the Frankfort-Heilbron-Wolwehoek blockhouse line in the north to the Bethlehem-Lindley-Kroonstad line in the south. Once again, blockhouses played an important role in the overall plan. De Wet and Steyn managed to escape, but the Boers lost about 50 killed, and the British took 778 POWs, and also captured about 25,000 head of cattle, 2,000 horses and 200 wagons and carts. Amery (ed.), op cit, V, pp. 481–91; Yardley, op cit, pp. 325–7; J.D. Kestell, *Through Shot and Flame*, pp. 252–60; *South Africa Despatches. Despatch by General Lord Kitchener, dated 8th March, 1902, relative to Military Operations in South Africa* (Cd. 970), pp. 6–8.

36 Lieutenant-Colonel Lewis Munro (1859–1927) saw action in South Africa, 1899–1902, for example in the Ladysmith relief operations, 1899–1900. Later took part in Aden Hinterland Expedition (1902), and World War I (1914–18): first as Assistant to Major-General in Charge of Administration and AQMG, Eastern Command, and subsequently in Air Ministry.

37 Major (later Colonel) Alexander Sprot (1853–1929) previously saw action in Afghanistan, 1878–80. During the Anglo-Boer War he took part, for example, in operations on the Colesberg front, 1899–1900; in Roberts' advance to Bloemfontein, and to Pretoria, 1900; advance eastwards along Delagoa Bay railway line, 1900; anti-guerrilla operations in the Transvaal, ORC and Cape Colony, 1900–2. Later he served in World War I, 1914–18.

38 Colonel Augustus William Morris (1845–1906) previously served in the Anglo-Zulu War, 1879 and in the Transvaal War of Independence, 1880–1 (severely wounded at Amajuba). Served in South Africa, 1899–1902: first as AAG, 1899; Commandant, Durban, 1900; Assistant Inspector-General, Lines of Communication, 1900–2, and also in command of the Eastern Cape Districts.

39 Colonel (later Major-General) James Willcocks (1857–1926) previously served in Afghanistan, 1878–80; the Mahsood Wuzeeree Expedition, 1881; Sudan, 1885; Burma, 1885–9; the Chin-Lushai Expedition, 1889–90; the Expedition to Manipur, 1891; North-Western Frontier, India, 1897–8; West Africa, 1897–8, 1900. Employed on special service in South Africa, 1902. Took part in Zakka Khel Expedition, 1906; World War I, 1914–15. Governor of Burma, 1917–22.

40 On Wednesday 12 February 1902 the 28th Company MI (about 320 men under Major Dowell) was ambushed at Klip River, in the Transvaal, by about 250 Boers under Generals H.A. Alberts and J.N.H. Grobler. The British lost ten killed and about 50 wounded.

41 Commandant Wynand J. Viljoen (born 1872), younger brother of Ben Viljoen. As a member of the Johannesburg Police, he fought in the Eastern and North-Eastern Transvaal, 1900–2. One of the Transvaal delegates at the Vereeniging peace conference, May 1902, where he voted in favour of the peace proposals.

42 General Christiaan ('Chris') Hendrik Muller (1865–1945) took part in the suppression of the Jameson Raid (1896) and in the campaign against Mphephu (1898). During the Anglo-Boer War he served in Natal (1899–1900) and in the Eastern Transvaal (1900–2), since October 1900 as Commandant of the Boksburg Commando (under the overall command of General B.J. Viljoen), and after December 1900 as Assistant Combat General. After Viljoen's capture on 25 January 1902, Muller was appointed Assistant Commandant-General. (Muller's fame rested primarily on the success he achieved on 12 June 1901 when he defeated an Australian force of some 350 men at Wilmansrust, between Middelburg and Ermelo. Most of the Australians were captured.) In 1914–15 Muller rebelled against Louis Botha's government, was wounded, captured and sentenced to a term in prison. MP, Union of SA, 1920–6. *DSAB*, II, pp. 501–2; Amery (ed.), op cit, V, pp. 294–6; Grant, op cit, IV, pp. 203–4.

43 In practice, De Wet did not attempt another invasion of the Cape Colony.

44 'to death' inserted in red ink on holograph and initialed by Brodrick: 'St J B'. General P.H. Kritzinger (see Biographical Notes) was seriously wounded and captured on 16 December 1901, shortly after he invaded the Cape Colony for a third time. After spending a few weeks in hospital at Naauwpoort, he was transferred to the prison in Graaff-Reinet, where he was brought to trial on 7 March on charges of murder (re the death of six blacks on various dates and at various places) and train-wrecking. Influential newspapers in Britian and the USA took up the cudgels on his behalf, and on 6 April 1902 he was acquitted. He then became an ordinary POW. *DSAB*, III, p. 484.

45 Commandant Gideon Jacobus Scheepers (1878–1902), Transvaal State Artillery, saw action on the Kimberley front, 1899–1900; in the OFS, under De Wet, 1900; invaded the Cape Colony, 15–16 December 1900; formed his own commando and operated in the Cape Colony, 1901; fell seriously ill and was captured by the British, 10 October 1901; convicted of murder, etc. and executed, Graaff-Reinet, 18 January 1902.

46 As early as 13 August 1900, General J.H. de la Rey (see Biographical Notes) ordered the execution of armed blacks captured on republican soil. On 13 June 1901 General P.H. Kritzinger issued a proclamation at Stormberg in the North-Eastern Cape Colony, giving his burghers permission to summarily execute any black or coloured person (armed or unarmed) caught in British service. Blacks and coloureds who, on their own initiative, supplied the British forces with information, could also be shot. On 13 July 1901 Kritzinger repeated this controversial proclamation. These proclamations 'legalized' what the Boers and Cape rebels had in any case been doing since the second Boer invasion of the Cape Colony in December 1900, but it also gave Kitchener an excuse to arm more blacks and coloureds, so that they could defend themselves, and serve the British cause. F. Pretorius, 'Boer attitudes to Africans in wartime' in D. Lowry (ed.), *The South African War Reappraised*, pp. 105, 108–9, 119 (Note 23). In practice, Kritzinger was tried, inter alia for war crimes, but acquitted.

47 Kitchener is referring to the following battles:
   (1) In the Western Transvaal, Lieutenant-Colonel W.C. Anderson, OC of the 5th Battalion IY, escorted a convoy (sent by Lieutenant-Colonel S.B. von Donop from Wolmaransstad to Klerksdorp to get supplies) with about 700 men when, at 05.00 on Tuesday 25 February 1902, it was attacked between Yzerspruit and Jagdspruit by about 1,000 Boers under the command of Generals De la Rey and J.C.G. Kemp. The British lost their convoy, a large amount of ammunition, two field-guns, a pom-pom, at least 33 killed, 129 wounded (most of them taken prisoner), and about 240 unwounded soldiers captured. The Boers lost at least twelve killed and 31 wounded, of whom three died later. Grant, op cit, IV, pp. 410–15; Amery (ed.), op cit, V, pp. 497–9; J.F. Naudé, *Vechten en Vluchten van Beyers en Kemp "Bôkant" De Wet*, pp. 323–6.

(2) At about 05.00 on Friday 7 March 1902 De la Rey, assisted by Kemp and General J.G. Celliers, and about 750 men, attacked Lord Methuen's column (about 1,300 strong) near De Klipdrift in the Western Transvaal. Methuen was trekking from Tweebosch in the direction of Lichtenburg, co-operating with Colonel R.G. Kekewich and Lieutenant-Colonel H.M. Grenfell in an effort to corner De la Rey. British losses amounted to at least 68 killed, 121 wounded, and more than 800 POWs, as well as four field-guns, two pom-poms, and about 100 wagons and carts captured. The Boers lost at least eight killed and 26 wounded. Methuen was among those wounded and taken prisoner. Amid calls of protest from several Boers, De la Rey magnanimously decided to set Methuen free as soon as the latter's wound had been attended to. Accompanied by a doctor and a few others, Methuen was sent to Klerksdorp. Soon after his departure, pressure was exercised on De la Rey to reverse his decision. Messengers overtook Methuen's company, and they were taken to Gestoptefontein. At a meeting held on 9 March, De la Rey more or less convinced the burghers that it would be in the interest of the Boer cause to set Methuen free. Methuen finally reached Klerksdorp on 13 March and fully recovered. Grant, op cit, IV, pp. 416–21; Amery (ed.), op cit, V, pp. 501–8; Naudé, op cit, pp. 327–36; *South Africa. Report from Lieut.-General Lord Methuen on the Action that took place near Tweebosh on 7th March, 1902* (Cd. 967).

48 Lieutenant-Colonel William Campbell Anderson (1869–1926), who was OC, 5th Battalion, IY, operated in the Western Transvaal 1910–12; defeated at Yzerspruit/Jagdspruit (see Note 47(1) above).

49 The seven paragraphs that follow have been published. (See TNA reference PRO 30/57/22/Y3(a).) Typographically the published paragraphs differ somewhat from the holograph.

50 Both the Cape boys (from the Western Cape) and Bastards (from Namaqualand and Bushmanland in the North-Western Cape) were regarded as "coloureds"; i.e. people of mixed race.

51 Strict racial segregation was maintained as to sleeping arrangements in the blockhouse lines. Blacks and coloured were used both in and between the blockhouses, with a total of at least 25,000 serving in this capacity. J. Hattingh and A. Wessels, *Britse Fortifikasies in the Anglo-Boereoorlog (1899–1902)*, p. 93.

52 I.e. the Herschel district in the North-Eastern Cape Colony.

53 Many more blacks were armed by the British than Kitchener is suggesting here. See also Part 3, Note 189, as well as document [99].

54 Not included in the consulted collection.

55 Abraham Esau (1864–1901) was a respected figure in the 'coloured' community of Calvinia in the North-Western Cape Colony. He was a carpenter, blacksmith and haulier, and an ardent devotee of the British imperial presence in South Africa. He and a band of spies supplied

information to the British forces, 1900–1. Arrested by the Boers after they occupied Calvinia, January 1901; tortured and murdered, 5 February 1901.

56 Cecil John Rhodes (see Biographical Notes) died in his cottage at Muizenberg, near Cape Town, on 26 March 1902.

57 According to P. Magnus, *Kitchener. Portrait of an Imperialist*, p. 185, Kitchener was so upset when he heard what had happened to Methuen's column that he stayed in bed without food for 36 hours.

58 Without consulting with the Free State's President M.T. Steyn, the Transvaal's Acting State President, General S.W. Burger, requested safe conduct from the British military authorities to confer with Kitchener, and with the OFS government-in-the-field. Cloete, op cit, pp. 312–13. See also Part 5, Note 2.

59 It is clear that Brodrick sensed that there was something amiss with the official and private information on the employment of blacks in an armed capacity by the British. See also document [93] and Part 3, Note 189.

60 See Note 47(1) above for more on the British defeat at Yzerspruit/ Jagdspruit on 25 February 1902. Lieutenant-Colonel Stanley Brenton von Donop (1860–1941) saw action in the Western Transvaal, 1901–2. Later Director of Artillery, 1911–13; Master General of Ordnance, 1913–16; CO, Humber Garrison, 1917–20.

Part 5
April and May 1902
Introduction

1 S.J. du Preez, 'Die Vrede van Vereeniging', pp. 170–232; *DSAB*, II, p. 712; J.D. Kestell and D.E. van Velden, *The Peace Negotiations between the Governments of the South African Republic and the Orange Free State, and the Representatives of the British Government, which Terminated in the Peace Concluded at Vereeniging on the 31st May, 1902*, pp. 1–45.

2 Du Preez, op cit, pp. 233–340; Kestell and Van Velden, op cit, pp. 46–201.

3 P.G. Cloete, *The Anglo-Boer War. A Chronology*, p. 344.

4 J. Laband, 'Zulus and the War' in J. Gooch (ed.), *The Boer War. Direction, Experience and Image*, pp. 123–4.

April and May 1902

1 Easter Sunday.

2 On 17 March 1902 President M.T. Steyn and General C.R. de Wet arrived at General J.H. de la Rey's laager at Zendelingsfontein, between Klerksdorp and Wolmaransstad in the Western Transvaal. On 21 March the Transvaal government-in-the-field left Witnek, east of Rust de Winter (i.e. north of Pretoria and half-way to Warmbad, today Bela-Bela), and, without

319

consulting with the OFS government, requested safe conduct from the British (which was granted) to confer with the OFS government about peace talks. The next day the Transvaal government entered the British lines at Balmoral, and on 23 March they arrived in Pretoria en route to Kroonstad. From Kroonstad the Transvaal's Acting President, General S.W. Burger, sent a letter to Steyn, informing him about the negotiations that were about to take place. Steyn was furious that he was not consulted earlier, but with the proposed negotiations a *fait accompli*, and in an effort to preserve a united republican front, he had no other option but to support the Transvaal government's actions. P.G. Cloete, *The Anglo-Boer War. A Chronology*, pp. 311–13; S.J. du Preez, 'Die Vrede van Vereeniging', pp. 171–3.

3 Possibly a reference to the unsuccessful revolts in Poland in 1830, 1846 and/or 1863 against tsarist oppression.

4 I.e. his victory at Tweebosch/De Klipdrift, 7 March 1902 – See Part 4, Note 47(2).

5 On 24–25 March 1902 the British concentrated approximately 16,000 troops (fifteen columns) for a one-day umbrella-like drive against De la Rey's commandos. De la Rey (accompanied by Steyn) and his commandos slipped through the British columns, and the net result of the drive was only eight Boers killed and 165 taken prisoner. The British also recaptured three of their own field-guns, two pom-poms, about 100 wagons and carts, 1,700 horses and cattle. L.S. Amery (ed.), *The Times History of the War in South Africa 1899–1902*, V, pp. 512–17; M.H. Grant, *History of the War in South Africa 1899–1902*, IV, pp. 492–3; J.G. Naudé, *Vechten en Vluchten van Beyers en Kemp "Bôkant" De Wet*, pp. 341–4.

6 See, for example, his speech of 14 June 1901 at a dinner given by the National Reform Union, when he asked: 'When is a war not a war? When it is carried on by methods of barbarism in South Africa' – and his speech in the House of Commons on 16 January 1902, when he attacked the British government for the way the British Army conducted the war in South Africa. Cloete, op cit, pp. 244, 294.

7 See TNA reference PRO 30/57/22/Y132.

8 Probably Captain T.P. Milne-Home, who had no previous war service. Served in South Africa, 1899–1902.

9 See Part 4, Note 47. As far as court martialling officers who suffered defeats are concerned, see also Lieutenant-General I.S.M. Hamilton's views (written from South Africa in a letter to Lord Roberts, 18 May 1902) published in A. Wessels (ed.), *Lord Roberts and the War in South Africa 1899–1902*, pp. 250–6.

10 On Wednesday 9 April 1902 the republican governments met at Klerksdorp in the Western Transvaal to discuss the possibility of entering into peace negotiations with the British government. Amongst the ten-man Transvaal delegation were Acting President S.W. Burger, State Secretary F.W. Reitz and Generals L. Botha and J.H. de la Rey, and in the seven-man OFS

delegation were President M.T. Steyn and Generals C.R. de Wet and J.B.M. Hertzog. When the meeting ended on 11 April, it was decided to negotiate for peace under, amongst others, the following conditions: some retention of republican independence; the Uitlander franchise question had to be settled; Dutch and English were to receive equal status in schools, and there had to be bilateral amnesty. These proposals were presented to Kitchener in Pretoria on 12 April. Du Preez, 'Die Vrede van Vereeniging', pp. 173–90.

11 Not in PRO 30/57/22 at TNA.

12 On Sunday 12 April 1902 a Boer delegation handed Kitchener a document with their proposals for the basis of peace negotiations. An astonished Kitchener asked whether they in fact wanted to keep their independence, and Steyn answered in the affirmative. The Boers pointed out that according to the constitutions of the republics, they could not make decisions that would undo the independence of their countries. The people (i.e. the voters, albeit only white males) would have to be consulted. It was impractical to test all the voters, and consequently it was decided that the commandos would elect 30 delegates each for the Transvaal and the OFS, who would then meet at Vereeniging on 15 May to discuss the peace proposals. Du Preez, op cit, pp. 191–9.

13 In practice the Transvaal obtained self-government (i.e. responsible government) in 1906 and the ORC in 1907.

14 Steyn studied Law at the University of London, was admitted to the Inner Temple in January 1880 and called to the bar in November 1882. In December 1883 he was admitted as an advocate in Cape Town, and then moved to Bloemfontein in the OFS where he built up a large legal practice. *DSAB*, II, p. 708.

15 At the beginning of 1902, after spending almost two years in the field, President M.T. Steyn's health showed signs of serious deterioration. Steyn's vision and muscle problems were probably the result of a psycho-physiological disorder, brought about by the stress he suffered shortly before and during the war. A. McLeod and F. Pretorius, 'M.T. Steyn se Ervaring van die Anglo-Boereoorlog vanuit 'n Sielkundige Perspektief', *Historia* 47(1), May 2002, pp. 33–55; *DSAB*, II, p. 712.

16 Probably Lieutenant-Colonel Andrew Baird, who previously served in Bechuanaland, 1884–5; Zululand, 1888; Chitral, 1895. Served in South Africa, 1899–1902: Natal, 1899–1900; Transvaal, 1900; ORC, 1900–2.

17 Probably Lieutenant A.M. McKee, who had no previous war service, but who served throughout the Anglo-Boer War.

18 Major Edward Humphrey Manisty Leggett (1871–1947), who had no previous war service. Served on HQ Staff in South Africa, 1899–1902: Cape Colony, 1899–1900; OFS/ORC and Transvaal, 1900–2. After the war, Director of Burgher Land Settlement, and of Transvaal Burgher Camps, 1902–5. Member of the Legislative Council of British East Africa, 1908–9.

Attached to Belgian War Office, 1914–18. Chairman, East African Section, London Chamber of Commerce, 1919–30.

19 See the Middelburg (Transvaal) peace talks, February–March 1900, referred to in Part 2, Note 80.

20 See document [96].

21 The meeting on 12 April 1902 between Kitchener and the representatives of the republican governments, was continued with meetings between the above-mentioned on 13 April, 14 April (also attended by Lord Milner), and also on 15, 16 and 17 April. On the last day the British representatives decided to allow a national convention of 30 delegates from each republic to meet at Vereeniging to decide whether or not to continue the war. The British also undertook not to attack as from 11 May those commandos whose COs were attending the peace conference, on condition that those commandos stayed within their designated operational areas. On 18 April the republican delegation departed from Pretoria to consult with the commandos and to elect the delegates that would be sent to Vereeniging. Cloete, op cit, pp. 321–3.

22 Abraham Fischer (1850–1913) was a prominent OFS lawyer and advocate. Member of the OFS Volksraad, 1879–96, and of the OFS Executive Council, 1896–1900. Member of Boer Deputation that visited the Netherlands (April 1900), the USA (May–June 1900) and France, Germany and Russia (July–August 1900) in an effort to procure foreign arbitration in the war in South Africa, without achieving any success. He returned to South Africa in 1903. Prime Minister of the OFS, 1907–10; Minister of Lands (1910–13), and also of the Interior (1912–13) in the first Union of SA cabinet. One of his grandsons, Abraham (Bram) Fischer, became a prominent member of the SA Communist Party, played a significant role in the struggle against apartheid, and defended Nelson Mandela in the Rivonia Trial, 1963, before being sent to prison himself in 1966. *DSAB*, I, pp. 290–2 and V, pp. 263–4; S. Clingman, *Bram Fischer. Afrikaner Revolutionary*, passim.

23 Dr Wilhelm Johannes Leyds (1859–1940), Dutch-born (in Java) Transvaal State Attorney, 1884–8; State Secretary, 1888–98; Ambassador Extraordinary and Minister Plenipotentiary in Europe, 1898–1902. During the war he played an important role in mobilizing sympathy and support in Europe for the Boer cause, although material support was very limited. After the war he published several history books and source publications about the Transvaal. Although Leyds was accused in some quarters of inciting war, these allegations are unfounded. *DSAB*, III, pp. 516–20; L.E. van Niekerk, *Kruger se Regterhand. 'n Biografie van dr. W.J. Leyds*, passim.

24 See Note 15 above. Steyn resigned for reasons of health as State President of the OFS on 30 May 1902, and De Wet, as Acting State President, had to sign the 'acts of peace' on 31 May. After the war Steyn went to Europe for medical treatment in the Netherlands, Switzerland, Germany and France.

Although he never fully recovered, Steyn was fit enough to return to South Africa at the beginning of 1905. *DSAB*, II, p. 713.

25 I.e. the first day of the meeting of the delegates at Vereeniging on Thursday 15 May 1902, to discuss the possible cessation of hostilities.

26 Probably Kitchener's despatch dated 8 April 1902 (see Cd. 984).

27 Could be Major Roger Henry Massie (1869–1927), or even Captain John Harmon Massie (1872–1914) or Colonel William George Massy (1857–1941).

28 On Thursday 15 May 1902, 60 Boer delegates met in a tent at Vereeniging to decide whether they must (and can) continue the struggle or not. Their meeting, and the negotiations in between with the British authorities, continued until 31 May. For the minutes of the meetings, see J.D. Kestell and D.E. van Velden, *The Peace Negotiations between the Governments of the South African Republic and the Orange Free State, and the Representatives of the British Government, which terminated in the Peace concluded at Vereeniging on the 31ˢᵗ May, 1902*. See also Note 33 below.

29 I.e. Sir Gordon Sprigg – see also Biographical Notes.

30 I.e. take up the post of C-in-C, India.

31 'les défauts de ses qualités' – has qualities that are a disadvantage.

32 I.e. too bad.

33 See Kestell and Van Velden, op cit, passim. The minutes were kept by Rev. Dr John Daniel Kestell (1854–1941), a prominent leader in the Dutch Reformed Church and cultural leader, and Dirk Eliza van Velden (1869–1933), secretary of legislative bodies and Provincial Secretary of the Transvaal. The minutes were originally published in Dutch in 1909, and then translated by Van Velden for the English version that was first published in 1912.

34 From 31 May–5 June 1899 Sir Alfred Milner and President Paul Kruger met in the OFS capital, Bloemfontein, in an effort to avert war, albeit that questions can be asked about Milner's sincerity in that regard. The conference was arranged through the initiative of President M.T. Steyn (OFS) and W.P. Schreiner (Premier, Cape Colony). The chairman of the conference was A. Fischer (see Note 22 above). No agreement was reached, and the war broke out four months later.

35 Major-General C. Tucker (see Biographical Notes) was 64 when he married Ellen (Nelly) Mary O'Connell, only daughter of Sir Maurice O'Connell, on 19 April 1902. From his previous marriage (1865) to Matilda Frederica Hayler (died 1897), he had two sons and a daughter. *DSAB*, V, p. 783; information supplied by Dr Mark Curthoys.

36 I.e. (hanging) in the air.

37 Lieutenant-General I.S.M. Hamilton led approximately 17,000 British troops in the last drive in the Western Transvaal, 7–11 May 1902. The idea was to drive the Boer commandos westward against the Vryburg-Mafikeng railway line and its blockhouses (manned by some 4,000 soldiers). The

British also used six armoured trains. The Boers lost only one man killed, but 363 taken prisoner, in addition to 326 horses, 95 mules, 20 donkeys, about 3,600 head of cattle, 13,000 sheep, 175 wagons and 61 carts captured. Grant, op cit, IV, pp. 506–9; Amery (ed.), op cit, V, pp. 579–81; National Archives of South Africa (Pretoria), microfilm M.672: Staff Diary, Colonel Rawlinson's force, entry of 12 May 1902.

38 It was General J.C. Smuts' 32nd birthday on 24 May 1902. See also Biographical Notes.

39 This second day refers to the second day of the battle of Diamond Hill/Donkerhoek, east of Pretoria (11–12 June 1900) – the only battle where all the officers mentioned in the description that follows (i.e. Botha, De la Rey, Tobias Smuts, French, De Lisle and Pole-Carew, as well as Ian Hamilton) were present, albeit on both sides of the forces involved in the battle. Botha had some 6,000 men with 23 guns under his command at Diamond Hill, while Lord Roberts attacked the Boer defensive positions with 14,000 soldiers, after a bombardment with 70 guns. The British were unable to outflank the Boer positions, but their superiority in men and guns led to the Boers' withdrawal in the course of the night of 12–13 June 1900. The British lost at least 28 killed and wounded, and the Boers approximately 30 killed and wounded. Amery (ed.), op cit, IV, pp. 269–96; *History of the War in South Africa 1899–1902*, III, pp. 204–25; A.E. Breytenbach, 'Die Slag by Donkerhoek, 11–12 Junie 1900', passim; H.F. Nel, 'Die Slag van Donkerhoek 11–12 Junie 1900', *Militaria* 15(1), 1985, pp. 52–8 and 15(2), 1985, pp. 17–30.

40 General Tobias Smuts (1861–1916) previously served in wars against several black chieftains in Transvaal (Modjaji, 1890–1; Mmalelôlo, 1894; Magoeba, 1895; Mphephu, 1897–8). Member of Transvaal Volksraad, 1899. Saw action in Natal, 1899–1900: first as Assistant Commandant of the Ermelo commando; later as Combat General. As Assistant Commandant-General he commanded the Transvaal forces in the OFS, attempting to check Lord Roberts' advance, 1900; then fought in the Transvaal, 1900–2. Deprived of his rank in August 1901 because, contrary to orders, he burned down Bremersdorp in Swaziland; fought to the end as an ordinary burgher. MP, 1910–16.

41 On 15 December 1899 General Redvers Buller, who at that stage had more than 21,000 soldiers with 46 guns and eighteen machine-guns under his command at Chieveley, launched an attack against General Louis Botha's force of about 3,000 burghers, a howitzer, three field-guns and a pom-pom which had taken up positions along an extended front just north of the Thukela (Tugela) River. The attack, which was preceded by an artillery bombardment, was unsuccessful in all the sectors, and Buller ordered a withdrawal. He lost about 150 killed, 750 wounded and 250 missing (most of them became POWs), as well as ten field-guns. Boer losses amounted to only seven killed, one drowned and 30 wounded, of whom one later died.

C.J. Barnard, *Generaal Louis Botha op die Natalse front, 1899–1900*, pp. 46–71; H.A. Mocke, 'Die slag van Colenso, 15 Desember 1899', passim; J.H. Breytenbach, *Die Geskiedenis van die Tweede Vryheidsoorlog in Suid-Afrika 1899–1902*, II, pp. 226–332; J.F. Maurice (ed.), *History of the War in South Africa 1899–1902*, I, pp. 351–75; Amery (ed.), op cit, II, pp. 421–67.

42 On 6 January 1900 the Boers launched attacks against the British positions at Wagon Hill and Caesar's Camp (together also known as Platrand) in an effort to capture Ladysmith. In one of the bloodiest battles of the war, the Boers were eventually beaten back. They lost at least 56 killed and 125 wounded; the British at least 150 killed and 250 wounded. The Platrand area fell under Hamilton's command. As far as the battle is concerned see, for example, Breytenbach, op cit, III, pp. 10–61; Maurice (ed.), op cit, II, pp. 555–70; Amery (ed.), op cit, III, pp. 176–205.

43 A Boer force of not more than 8,200 burghers, with five field-guns and five pom-poms, entrenched themselves at the foot of Magersfontein and adjoining hills over a front of about 7 km. Lord Methuen, ordered to relieve the besieged Kimberley, had under his command about 15,000 troops, 33 guns and sixteen machine-guns. On 9 and 10 December 1899 he subjected the hills to the heaviest British bombardment since the siege of Sebastopol during the Crimean War (1854–6), but the shells flew over the entrenched Boers and only three were wounded. On 11 December the British frontal attack was repulsed. The British lost at least 288 killed, 700 wounded and 100 missing; the Boers 71 killed and 184 wounded. G.R. Duxbury, *The Battle of Magersfontein 11th December 1899* (2nd ed.), passim; Breytenbach, op cit, II, pp. 96–183; Maurice (ed.), op cit, I, pp. 304–31; Amery (ed.), op cit, II, pp. 383–420.

Epilogue
31 May 1902 and Beyond
Introduction

1 As far as Kitchener's role during the peace negotiations are concerned see, for example, A. Hodges, *Lord Kitchener*, pp. 149–53; G. Arthur, *Life of Lord Kitchener*, II, pp. 70–104; C.R. Ballard, *Kitchener*, pp. 164–6; E.S. Grew et al., *Field-Marshal Lord Kitchener. His Life and Work for the Empire*, II, pp. 190–206.

2 S.J. du Preez, 'Die Vrede van Vereeniging', pp. 341–401; J.D. Kestell and D.E. van Velden, *The Peace Negotiations between the Governments of the South African Republic and the Orange Free State, and the Representatives of the British Government, which Terminated in the Peace Concluded at Vereeniging on the 31st May, 1902*, pp. 201–8.

3 L.S. Amery (ed.), *The Times History of the War in South Africa 1899–1902*, VII, pp. 24–5.

4 T. van Rensburg (ed.), *Vir Vaderland, Vryheid en Eer. Oorlogsherinneringe van Wilhelm Mangold 1899–1902*, p. 356 (Notes 17–19); D. Hall, *The Hall Handbook of the Anglo-Boer War 1899–1902*, p. 187.

5 T. Pakenham, *The Boer War*, p. 572.

6 V.G. Kiernan, *European Empires from Conquest to Collapse, 1815–1960*, pp. 140–1.

7 See, for example, J. Pollock, *Kitchener. The Road to Omdurman*, p. 214; H.W. Nevinson, *Changes and Chances*, pp. 322–3.

8 Pollock, op cit, pp. 216–7; *Hart's Annual Army List, Militia List, and Imperial Yeomanry List, for 1906*, p. 4; Hodges, op cit, pp. 156–7. See also NAM, Birdwood Papers, 1967-07-19-269: Mr St John Brodrick–Lord Kitchener, 4.6.1902 (telegram); NAM, 1996-07-14: *Official Programme of the Home-coming of General Viscount Kitchener of Khartoum, G.C.B. July 12th, 1902*.

9 For Kitchener's evidence, see *Royal Commission on the War in South Africa. Minutes of Evidence taken before the Royal Commission on the war in South Africa*, I (Cd. 1790), pp. 7–13.

10 *DSAB*, II, p. 368; *DNB, 1912–1921*, pp. 311–13; Hodges, pp. 162–298; P. Magnus, *Kitchener. Portrait of an Imperialist*, pp. 192–359; G.H. Cassar, *Kitchener: Architect of Victory*, pp. 15, 138–476; Ballard, op cit, pp. 133–305; P. Simkins, *Kitchener's Army. The Raising of the New Armies 1914–16*, passim; V.W. Germains, *The Kitchener Armies. The Story of a National Achievement*, passim; H. le Bas (ed.), *The Lord Kitchener Memorial Book*, passim; Arthur, op cit, II, pp. 122–346 and III, pp. 1–349.

11 *DNB, 1912–1921*, p. 313; Hodges, op cit, pp. 304–5; Magnus, op cit, pp. 359–60; P. Trew, *The Boer War Generals*, pp. 132–3; Cassar, op cit, pp. 476–80; Ballard, op cit, pp. 308–10; Arthur, op cit, III, pp. 349–55. See also D. McCormick, *The Mystery of Lord Kitchener's Death*, passim, as well as exhibits in the Stromness Museum, Orkney Islands.

31 May 1902 and Beyond

1 Henry Spenser Wilkinson (1853–1937), military historian and journalist. Leader-writer and special correspondent, *Manchester Guardian* (1882–92) and *Morning Post* (1895–1914). Chichele Professor of Military History, Oxford, 1909–23. His many books include the influential *The Brain of an Army* (1890) and *The Brain of the Navy* (1895).

2 After discussing their options on 15–16 May 1902, the Boer delegates at Vereeniging sent a commission of five members (Generals J.C. Smuts, L. Botha, J.H. de la Rey, C.R. de Wet and J.B.M. Hertzog) to Pretoria, where from 19 to 28 May the 'acts of peace' (or rather the conditions under which the Boers would surrender) were hammered out in tough negotiations with Lord Milner and Lord Kitchener. From 29 May the Boer commission

was back at Vereeniging where the final British peace proposals were discussed in heated debates. The Boers had to accept the proposals no later than midnight on 31 May. The 'acts of peace' contained ten clauses, for example that all burghers had to lay down their arms and recognise the British monarch as their legitimate sovereign; Dutch would be taught in Transvaal and ORC schools, and would (if necessary) be used in courts of law; representative government (followed by self-government) would be granted as soon as circumstances permitted; the question of whether black people should be given political rights would not be discussed before the introduction of self-government, and the British government would make available £3,000,000 for the reconstruction and development of the two former republics. On the afternoon of 31 May these proposals were accepted by the Boer delegates by 54 votes to six. Members of both republican governments then travelled by train to Pretoria where, at 23.05 in the dining-hall of Melrose House, Kitchener's HQ, the 'acts of peace' were signed by all parties. J.D. Kestell and D.E. van Velden, *The Peace Negotiations between the Governments of the South African Republic and the Orange Free State, and the Representatives of the British Government, which terminated in the Peace concluded at Vereeniging on the 31ˢᵗ May, 1902*, pp. 46–208.

3 Ian Hamilton, then a Colonel, was General G.S. White's AAG in Natal. He led the infantry attack at Elandslaagte, 21 October 1899. A Boer force of 800 men with two field-guns under General J.H.M. Kock occupied Elandslaagte Station, 16 km north-east of Ladysmith. White sent 3,500 men and eighteen field-guns under Major-General J.D.P. French to dislodge the Boers. The overconfident Boers were dealt a shattering blow, and apparently lost 38 killed, 113 wounded (including many taken POW) and 185 unwounded POWs. General Kock was mortally wounded. Many German and Dutch volunteers were among the casualties. The British lost 50 dead and 213 wounded. For bravely leading and rallying his men from the front, French recommended Hamilton for the Victoria Cross, and he would probably have received it, had it not been considered inadvisable to set a precedent by conferring Britain's highest military award on an officer in the position of a Brigadier. J.H. Breytenbach, *Die Geskiedenis van die Tweede Vryheidsoorlog in Suid-Afrika, 1899–1902*, I, pp. 237–63; J.F. Maurice (ed.), *History of the War in South Africa 1899–1902*, I, pp. 157–71; L.S. Amery (ed.), *The Times History of the War in South Africa 1899–1902*, II, pp. 175–95.

4 Ian Hamilton assumed command in the Western Transvaal on 8 April 1902. At about 07.15 on 11 April some 800 Boers under the command of Ferdinandus Jacobus Potgieter (1857–1902), Commandant of the Wolmaransstad commando, charged (across open veldt) the columns of Von Donop and Grenfell at Rooiwal. The British forces totalled about 3,000 men with six guns. The attack was beaten back, the Boers losing at least 43 killed (including Potgieter), more than 50 wounded (of whom 40 were taken

prisoner), while 36 unwounded prisoners were taken. The British lost about twelve killed and 74 wounded. When Hamilton arrived at the scene of the atttack he ordered a general pursuit. Later Rawlinson's columns also joined in the pursuit, but the Boers got away. The British recaptured two of their own field-guns and a pom-pom they lost at Tweebosch/De Klipdrift. M.H. Grant, *History of the War in South Africa 1899–1902*, IV, pp. 499–504; Amery (ed.), op cit, V, pp. 525, 531–7; J.G. Naudé, *Vechten en Vluchten van Beyers en Kemp "Bôkant" De Wet*, pp. 352–4.

5 Not in the consulted document collection. For the drive, see Part 5, Note 37.

6 See *South Africa. Despatch by General Lord Kitchener, dated 1st June, 1902, relative to Military Operations in South Africa* (Cd. 986). However, this was not Kitchener's final despatch from South Africa – see *South Africa. Despatch by General Lord Kitchener, dated 23rd June, 1902, relative to Military Operations in South Africa* (Cd. 988).

7 Lieutenant-Colonel Hubert Ion Wetherall Hamilton (1861–1914) previously saw action in Burma (1886–8) and in the Sudan (1897–9). Served in South Africa (1899–1902), for example as DAAG and AAG, Army HQ (1900), and as Military Secretary to Lord Kitchener (1900–2). After the war he was Kitchener's Military Secretary in India, 1902–5. OC, 7th Brigade, 1906–8; Major-General on General Staff, Mediterranean Command, 1908–9; GOC, North Midland Division, 1911–14. Killed in action, World War I.

8 Pandeli Thomas (Tom) Ralli (1845–1928), a wealthy financier and hospitable bachelor, was a member of the Anglo-Greek community in London, and the son of one of the founders of the Greek firm of Ralli Brothers. Liberal MP, Bridport, 1875–80. Kitchener met him for the first time in Cyprus, 1880. He usually stayed with Ralli at 17 Belgrave Square when in London, for example for six weeks in 1899 before his return to the Sudan (from where he then went to SA), and again after the Anglo-Boer War, before going to India. Ralli looked after Kitchener's money matters. P. Magnus, *Kitchener. Portrait of an Imperialist*, pp. 41, 76, 143, 189, 238, 266; A. Hodges, *Lord Kitchener*, pp. 77, 117–18, 157.

9 The Alldeutscher Verband (Pan-Germanic League) was set up by Prof. Ernst Hasse in 1894, with as its main aim the development of German nationalist consciousness, especially among those German-speaking people who lived outside the borders of Germany. Adolf Hitler and his Nazis were influenced by the Pan-Germanic League and in due course they put in practice many of the League's ideals, eventually plunging the world in war in 1939. After Germany's defeat in 1945 at the end of World War II, Pan-Germanism's influence has diminished.

10 See Part 2, Note 88.

11 After the delegates at Vereeniging voted overwhelmingly in favour of accepting the peace proposals, they gathered once again and decided that Botha, De la Rey and De Wet (i.e. the most successful and best-known Boer generals) had to go to Europe in an effort to raise money for the Boer

civilians left destitute by the war. The generals were accompanied by W.J.C. Brebner (who acted as their secretary) and Rev. J.D. Kestell (who accompanied De Wet's commando as field preacher during the war and kept minutes during the peace negotiations), departed from Cape Town on 30 July 1902 and sailed via Funchal (Madeira, 12 August) to Southampton (16 August). In London they met King Edward VII. From 19–30 August the generals were in the Netherlands, and from 31 August–8 September back in London. From 9 September–21 October they were once again on the Continent, visiting the Netherlands, Belgium, Paris and Berlin. Everywhere the generals went they were received with great enthusiasm, but European governments were not at all eager to grant them interviews, and they were only able to collect £116,000. On 22 October they were back in London. Botha and De la Rey departed from Southampton back to South Africa on 13 December 1902. De Wet returned earlier, and the other two generals would also not have stayed that long, but Botha became ill. G.T.W. Omond, *The Boers in Europe. A Sidelight on History*, p. 93 et seq.

12 Captain Victor Reginald Brooke (1873–1914) served in South Africa, 1899–1900 (Lord Methuen's advance; and advance to Bloemfontein) and 1901–2 (Lieutenant-General Ian Hamilton's staff officer; operations in Transvaal). Military Secretary to Viceroy, India, from 1907. Killed in action, World War I.

13 In the letter to Churchill the two last-quoted paragraphs have been scratched out, probably by Churchill after reading that they are not really applicable.

14 Could not be traced.

15 On Sunday 8 June 1902 a religious service was held in Church Square, in the centre of Pretoria. Afterwards, Kitchener mounted a dais and called for three cheers for the King, and then the troops and civilian onlookers spontaneously cheered Kitchener. Hodges, op cit, p. 154.

16 At the cessation of hostilities, some 21,000 Boers were still in the field, while there were 5,464 joiners in British service. A.M. Grundling, *Die "Hendsoppers" and "Joiners". Die Rasionaal en Verskynsel van Verraad*, p. 167.

17 For services rendered during the war, Kitchener was promoted to full General, made a Viscount, received the Order of Merit, as well as several other honours, and the British Parliament voted to give him a grant of £50,000. *DSAB*, II, p. 368; E.S. Grew *et al., Field-Marshal Lord Kitchener. His Life and Work for the Empire*, II, pp. 207–28; G. Arthur, *Life of Lord Kitchener*, II, pp. 109–11.

18 Written slanted in the top left-hand side of the first page.

19 See Note 15 above.

20 See Note 17 above.

21 When Kitchener left South Africa for Britain on 23 June 1902, Lieutenant-General N.G. Lyttelton (see Biographical Notes) took over as GOC, SA until 1904.

22 See document [109].

23 See also the typed copy of this letter in TNA reference PRO 30/57/17/S25, which differs slightly from the holograph's punctuation and the use of capital letters.

24 See Note 21 above.

25 I.e. Major-General F.W. Kitchener – see Part 2, Note 38.

26 See Note 16 above.

27 Kitchener departed from Cape Town on Monday 23 June 1902 on board the *Orotava*. He arrived in Southampton on 12 July 1902.

28 Kitchener delivered the speech at a South African banquet, held in the Guildhall, London, on 31 July 1902, when he was presented with a sword of honour from the Corporation of Cape Town. P. Magnus, *Kitchener. Portrait of an Imperialist*, pp. 189–90 quotes a portion of the speech, albeit in edited form. In this publication, the original speech, as amended, is published.

29 The above-mentioned information is written on the title page of the original document.

30 Amendments are printed in *italics* in this publication. When a word originally typed was deleted, it is as far as possible indicated by [deleted], usually followed by the amendment(s) in *italics*.

31 Sir Joseph Dimsdale was the Lord Mayor of London in 1901. "Lord Mayors of London. Chronological Order", <http://www.steeljam.dircon.co.uk/lordmayorchrono.htm>.

32 Sir William Thorne was the Mayor of Cape Town from 12 September 1901 to 22 September 1904. J.R. Shorten, *Cape Town*, p. 152.

33 This section was rewritten on the back of the first page of the original document, and the original typed section scratched out.

Biographical Notes

Other persons mentioned in the transcripts are identified in the Notes.

Appelbe, Edward Benjamin (1855–1935). Previous service in Anglo-Zulu War, 1879; Transvaal War of Independence, 1880–1; Sudan, 1884–5. Served in Anglo-Boer War, 1899–1902: first as Chief Ordnance Officer Lines of Communication, then as Chief Ordnance Officer Natal, and finally as Principal Ordnance Officer South Africa. Colonel, 1900. Served as Brigadier-General, World War I, 1914–18.

Armstrong, Oliver Carleton (1859–1932). Previous service in Burma, 1898. Served as Major in South Africa, 1900–2, first as Financial Assistant to the Military Governor, Pretoria; afterwards as Financial Advisor to Lord Kitchener. Colonel, 1907. Retired, 1909.

Babington, James Melville (1854–1936). Previous service in Bechuanaland, 1884–5. GOC, 1st Cavalry Brigade, Kimberley front, 1899–1900. Relieved of command, February 1900. Took part in anti-guerrilla operations, Transvaal, 1900–2. C-in-C, New Zealand Defence Forces, 1902–7; GOC, 23rd Division, 1914–18; GOC, XIVth Corps, 1918–19.

Baden-Powell, Robert Stephenson Smyth (1857–1941). Previous service in Zululand, 1888; Ashanti, 1895; Matabeleland, 1896. Defended Mafikeng for 217 days during Boer siege. Major-General, 1900. GOC a column in the Western Transvaal, 1900; raised and GOC, South African Constabulary, 1900–2. Lieutenant-General, 1907. GOC, Northumbrian Division of Territorials, 1908–10. Founder of the Boy Scouts, 1908; Sea Scouts, 1909; Girl Guides, 1910. 1st Baron Baden-Powell of Gillwell, 1929.

Balfour, Arthur James (1848–1930). Conservative MP for Hertford, 1874–85; Manchester East, 1885–1906; City of London, 1906–22. President Local Government Board, 1885–6; Secretary for Scotland, 1886–7; Chief Secretary for Ireland, 1887–91; First Lord of the Treasury, 1891–2 and 1895–1905; Prime Minister, 1902–5. First Lord of the Admiralty, 1915–16; Foreign Secretary, 1916–19; Lord President Council, 1919–22 and 1925–9. Earl, 1922.

Barton, Geoffry (1844–1922). Previous service in Ashanti, 1873–4; Anglo-Zulu War, 1879; Egypt, 1882; China, 1884–5; Suakim Expedition, 1885. Major-General, 1898. Saw action in Natal, 1899–1900; on Kimberley front, 1900; in the Western Transvaal, 1900–2.

Beatson, Stuart Brownlow (1854–1914). Previous service in Jowaki Expedition, 1877–8; Afghanistan, 1878–80; Egypt, 1882; India, 1897–8. OC of a mobile column, Transvaal and Cape Colony, 1901. Major-General, 1905.

Benson, George Elliot (1861–1901). Previous service in Sudan, 1884–5; Ashanti, 1895; Dongola, 1896. Lieutenant-Colonel, 1900; Colonel, 1901. Fought on Kimberley front, 1899–1900. Commanded a column in the Western Transvaal, and then in the Eastern Transvaal. Died of wounds sustained in clash with Louis Botha's commando at Bakenlaagte.

Beyers, Christiaan Frederik (1869–1914). Lawyer, and Boer General. Fought in Natal, 1899–1900; Eastern Transvaal, 1900; Western Transvaal, 1900; Northern Transvaal, 1901–2. General, 1900. MP and Speaker, Transvaal Legislative Assembly, 1907–10; MP, Union of SA, 1910–12. First C-in-C, Union (of SA) Defence Forces, 1912–14. Opposed SA's planned invasion of German South-West Africa, and resigned as C-in-C. Took part in rebellion against Louis Botha's government. Drowned in Vaal River while trying to flee from government forces.

Blood, Bindon (1842–1940). Previous service in Jowaki Expedition, 1877–8; Anglo-Zulu War, 1879; Afghanistan, 1880; Egypt, 1882. Major-General, 1898. GOC, Lines of Communications, Eastern Transvaal, April–October 1901. General, 1906.

Botha, Louis (1862–1919). Boer General. C-in-C, Transvaal forces, 1900–2. Defeated Buller at Colenso, Spioenkop and Vaalkrans. Resorted to guerrilla warfare, 1900, operating mainly in the South-Eastern Transvaal. First Prime Minister of the Union of SA, 1910–19.

Brabant, Edward Yewd (1839–1914). Previous service in 9th Frontier War, Cape Colony, 1877–8; Moorooi Campaign, 1879; Basotholand, 1880–1. Brigadier-General, 1900. Raised Brabant's Horse, 1900; commanded the Colonial Division, 1900. Major-General, 1902. MP, Cape Colony, 1873–8, 1884–1902, 1905–7. Commandant-General of the Cape Colonial Forces, 1902–5.

Brodrick, William St John Fremantle (1856–1942). Conservative MP for Surrey (West), 1880–5 and Surrey (South West or Guildford), 1885–1906; Financial Secretary to the War Office, 1886–92; Under-Secretary of State for War, 1895–8; Under-Secretary of State for Foreign Affairs, 1898–1900; Secretary of State for War, 1900–3; Secretary of State for India, 1903–5. 9th Viscount Midleton, 1907; Earl of Midleton, 1920.

Brook, Edmund Smith (1845–1910). Previous service in Anglo-Zulu War, 1879; war against Sekhukhune, 1879; Transvaal War of Independence, 1880–1; North-Western Frontier, India, 1897–8. Major-General, 1898. Took part in Anglo-Boer War in 1902, including GOC, Harrismith District.

Buller, Redvers Henry (1839–1908). Previous service in China, 1860; Red River Expedition, Canada, 1870; Ashanti, 1873; 9th Frontier War, Cape Colony, 1877–8, Anglo-Zulu War (VC), 1879; Egypt, 1882; Sudan, 1884–5. QMG, 1887–90; AG, 1890–7. Major-General, 1881; Lieutenant-General, 1891; General, 1896. C-in-C, British Forces in South Africa, 1899–1900.

Bullock, George Mackworth (1851–1926) had no previous active military service. OC, 2nd Devonshire Regiment, Natal, 1899. Captured at Colenso, 15 December 1899. Freed when British forces occupied Pretoria, 5 June 1900.

Operated in ORC and Transvaal, 1900–2. Served in Egypt, 1902–8. Major-General, 1905. Governor of Bermuda, 1912–17.

Burger, Schalk Willem (1852–1918). Boer General and politician. Previous service in Sekhukhuneland, 1876–7; campaign against Nyabêle, 1882–3; campaign against Mmalebôhô, 1893. Member of Transvaal Volksraad, 1886–1900; and of the Transvaal Executive Council, 1896–1902. General, 1899. Saw action in Natal, 1899–1900. Vice-President of the Transvaal, 1900; Acting State President of the Transvaal government-in-the-field, 1900–2. Senator of the Union of SA, 1913–18.

Campbell-Bannerman, Henry (1836–1908). Liberal MP for Stirling Burghs, 1868–1908; Financial Secretary to the War Office, 1871–4 and 1880–2; Parliamentary Secretary to the Admiralty, 1882–4; Chief Secretary for Ireland, 1884–5; Secretary of State for War, 1886 and 1892–5; Leader of the Liberal Party in the House of Commons, 1899–1908; Prime Minister, 1905–8.

Cecil, Robert Arthur Talbot Gascoyne, 3rd Marquis of Salisbury (1830–1903). Conservative MP for Stamford, 1853–68; Secretary of State for India, 1866–7 and 1874–8; for Foreign Affairs, 1878–80; Prime Minister (and Secretary of State for Foreign Affairs), 1885–92; Prime Minister, 1895–1902 (and Secretary of State for Foreign Affairs, 1895–1900; Lord Privy Seal, 1900–2).

Chamberlain, Joseph (1836–1914). Liberal MP for Birmingham, 1876–86 (Birmingham West, 1886); Liberal Unionist MP for Birmingham West, 1886–1914; President of the Board of Trade, 1880–5; President of the Local Government Board, 1886; Secretary of State for Colonies, 1895–1903.

Chesham, Charles Compton William Cavendish, 3rd Baron (1850–1907). Member of Imperial Yeomanry Committee, 1899–1900. Saw action in OFS and in the Transvaal, 1900; in the Western Transvaal, as OC 1st Yeomanry Brigade. IG, Imperial Yeomanry, South Africa, 1901–2.

Churchill, Winston Leonard Spencer (1874–1965). Previous service in Malakand, 1897; Tirah, 1898; Sudan, 1898. War correspondent of the *Morning Post* in South Africa, 1899–1900, and served in South African Light Horse, 1900. Conservative MP for Oldham, 1900–4; Liberal MP, 1904–6 for Oldham, for Manchester (North-West), 1906–8, for Dundee, 1908–22; Conservative MP for Essex (Epping), 1924–45, for Woodford, 1945–64. President of the Board of Trade, 1908–10; Secretary of State for Home Affairs, 1910–11; First Lord of the Admiralty, 1911–15 and 1939–40; Minister of Munitions, 1917–19; Secretary of State for War and Air, 1919–21; Secretary of State for the Colonies, 1921–2; Chancellor of the Exchequer, 1924–9; Prime Minister (and Minister of Defence), 1940–5 and 1951–5 (and Minister of Defence, 1951–2). Knighted, 1953.

Clements, Ralph Arthur Penrhyn (1855–1909). Previous service in Cape Colony, 1877–8; Anglo-Zulu War, 1879; Burma, 1885. ADC to Queen Victoria, 1896. GOC, 12th Infantry Brigade, 1899. Served on Colesberg front, in the OFS and in the Transvaal, 1899–1902. Major-General, 1904.

Cotton, Stapleton Lynch (born 1860). Previous service in Afghanistan, 1878–80; Burma, 1885–7. As a Major he saw action in South Africa. He was wounded and surrendered at Helvetia, 29 December 1900.

Crewe, Charles Preston (1858–1936). Previous service in 9th Frontier War, Cape Colony, 1878; Basotholand, 1880. Raised in 1899 and commanded the Border Horse, a Cape Colonial unit, 1899–1901; commanded a mobile column in the Western Transvaal, 1901. MP for Aliwal North, Cape Colony, 1902–10 (Colonial Secretary, 1904–7; Minister of Agriculture, 1907–8, and was also responsible for education, defence and the police); MP for East London, Cape Province, 1910–20. Brigadier-General, 1915. Commanded a brigade in the German East Africa Campaign, 1916.

Cronjé, Pieter (Piet) Arnoldus (1836–1911). Boer General. Previous service in Transvaal civil strife, 1863; 2nd OFS-Basotho War, 1865; Transvaal War of Independence, 1880–1; suppression of Jameson Raid, 1896. C-in-C, Kimberley front, 1899–1900; outmanoeuvred, and forced to surrender at Paardeberg, 27 February 1900. POW on St Helena, 1900–2.

Cunningham, George Glencairn (1862–1943). Previous service in Egypt, 1882; Sudan, 1884–5 and 1887–9; OC, Unyoro Expedition, Uganda, 1895 (wounded); Niger-Sudan Campaign, 1897. Acting AAG, 3rd Division, South Africa, and in command of a Brigade, 1900–2, saw action in the Eastern Transvaal, 1900; Western Transvaal, 1900–1; ORC, 1902. Brigadier-General Plymouth General Reserve, 1914–16; special employment, BEF, France, 1917; Base Commandant, Brest, 1918.

De la Rey, Jacobus (Koos) Herculaas (1874–1914). Boer General who fought on the Kimberley and Colesberg fronts, 1899–1900, and as a guerrilla commander in the Western Transvaal, 1900–2. Opposed South Africa's participation in World War I, and was accidentally killed while involved in the planning of resistance against Louis Botha's government.

De Lisle, Henry de Beauvoir (1864–1955). Previous service in Egypt, 1885–6. Commanded the 2nd Corps Mounted Infantry, 1899–1902. Saw action on Colesberg front, 1899; took part in Lord Roberts' advance to Bloemfontein, and to Pretoria, 1900; took part in anti-guerrilla operations right across war zone, 1900–2. OC, 1st Royal Dragoons, 1906–10. Served in World War I, 1914–18. Major-General, 1915; Lieutenant-General, 1919; General, 1926.

De Wet, Christiaan Rudolph (1854–1922). Boer General who master-minded the guerrilla tactics. Previously fought against the British at Amajuba, 1881. Joined 1899 as an ordinary burgher. Acting Commandant, 1899; Combat General, 1899; C-in-C, OFS forces, 1900–2. Opposed South Africa's participation in World War I, took part in rebellion against Louis Botha's government, and was captured. Jailed for high treason, 1915. Freed after six months.

Dixon, Henry Grey (1850–1933). Previous service in Afghanistan, 1878–80; Egypt 1888–9. Saw action in South Africa, primarily in the Western Transvaal, 1901–2. Brigadier-General, 1901. GOC, Cyprus, 1916–18.

Downe, Hugh Richard Dawnay, 8th Viscount (1844–1924). Previous service in Anglo-Zulu War, 1879. Served in South Africa as a Colonel, 1899–1902, as ADC to Lord Roberts. Brigadier-General, 1901.

Edward VII (1841–1910). Field Marshal, 1875. King of the United Kingdom of Great Britain and Ireland, and Emperor of India, 1901–10.

Elliot, Edward Locke (1850–1938). Previous service in Afghanistan, 1878–9; Burma, 1887–9; Dongola Expedition, 1896. IG of Cavalry, India, 1898–1901. As Major-General commanded several units in the Northern ORC and Western Transvaal, 1901–2. GOC, 8th Division, Indian Army, 1905–10.

Fetherstonhaugh, Richard Steele Rupert (1848–1932). Previous service in Anglo-Zulu War, 1879; Nile Expedition, 1888–9. GOC, 9th Brigade, Kimberley front, 1899–1900 (severely wounded). GOC, three columns in the Western Transvaal, 1901–2. Major-General, 1902.

Firman, Robert Bertram (1859–1936). Previous service in the Sudan, 1884–5; Burma, 1886–7. Saw action with the 11th Battalion Imperial Yeomanry in South Africa, 1899–1902, in ORC, 1901–2.

Forestier-Walker, Frederick William Edward (1844–1910). Previous service in Griqualand-East, 1875; 9th Frontier War, Cape Colony, 1877–8; Anglo-Zulu War, 1879; Bechuanaland, 1884–5. Major-General, 1887. GOC, Egypt, 1890–5. Lieutenant-General, 1895. GOC, Western District, England, 1895–9; GOC, Cape Colony, 1899–1901. General, 1902. Governor and C-in-C, Gibraltar, 1905–10.

French, John Denton Pinkstone (1852–1925). Previous service in the Sudan, 1884–5. Major-General, 1900. Fought in Natal, on Colesberg front, and in the OFS, Transvaal and Cape Colony, 1899–1902. CIGS, 1912–14; Field Marshal, 1913; C-in-C, BEF, 1914–15; C-in-C, Home Forces, 1916–18; Lord Lieutenant of Ireland, 1918–21. Knighted, 1900; Viscount, 1915; Earl of Ypres, 1922.

Girouard, Eduard Percy Cranwill (1867–1932). Joined the Royal Engineers in 1888. Director of the Sudan Railways, 1896–8; President of the Egyptian Railway Board, 1898–9; Director of Military Railways, South Africa, 1899–1902; Commissioner of Railways for the Transvaal and ORC, 1902–4; High Commissioner in Northern Nigeria, 1907–8; Governor and C-in-C of East Africa, 1909–12; Director-General of Munition Supply, 1915–17.

Grey, Raleigh (1860–1936). Took part in punitive expedition, Zululand, 1888; fought against the Matabeles in Southern Rhodesia (present-day Zimbabwe), 1893; took part in Jameson Raid, 1895–6 (spent five months in jail). As Colonel, commanded the 2nd Brigade, Rhodesian Field Force, 1899–1902, serving primarily in the Transvaal. Member of the Southern Rhodesian Legislative Council, 1899–1920. Resigned his commission in 1904 and settled in Southern Rhodesia. Managing Director of the Jumbo Gold Mining Company, Rhodesia Lands, and the Mayo Ranching Company.

Hamilton, Bruce Meade (1857–1936). Previous service in Afghanistan, 1880; Transvaal War of Independence, 1880–1; Burma, 1885; Ashanti, 1895; Benin,

1897. Saw action in Natal, 1899–1900. GOC, 21ˢᵗ Infantry Brigade, OFS and Transvaal, 1900–1; GOC several columns, across whole war zone, 1901–2. GOC, 2ⁿᵈ Division, 1ˢᵗ Army Corps, 1904–7. Lieutenant-General, 1907. C-in-C, Scottish Command, 1909–13; General, Army Command Home Defence, 1914–18.

Hamilton, Ian Standish Monteith ('Johnnie') (1853–1947). Previous service in Afghanistan, 1878–80; Transvaal War of Independence, 1880–1; Sudan, 1884–5; Burma, 1886–7; India, 1895. Major-General, 1899. Saw action in Natal (besieged in Ladysmith), 1899–1900; ORC and Transvaal, 1900. Lieutenant-General, 1900. Returned to UK, 1901, but back in South Africa as Kitchener's Chief of Staff, 1901–2 (and commanded mobile columns in the Western Transvaal, 1902). General, 1907. GOC, Southern Command, UK, 1905–9; AG, War Office, 1909–10; Mediterranean Command, 1910–14. Served in World War I, first as GOC, Central Force for the defence of the UK, 1914–15; then GOC, Gallipoli Expedition, 1915. Recalled, October 1915, and was not given another command. Accepted the sinecure of Lieutenant of the Tower of London, August 1918. GCMG, 1919. Lord Rector, Edinburgh University, 1932–5. Published several books (autobiographies, military studies and prose) and volumes of poetry.

Harris, George Robert Canning, 4ᵗʰ Baron (of Seringapatam and Mysore, and of Belmont, Kent) (1851–1932). Under-Secretary of State for India, 1885–6; for War, 1886–9. Governor of Bombay, 1890–5. AAG, Imperial Yeomanry in England, 1900; in South Africa, 1901. Best known as an outstanding cricketer who captained England, 1880 and 1884, and popularized the game on the Indian subcontinent.

Hart, Arthur Fitzroy (1844–1910). Previous service in Ashanti, 1873–4; Anglo-Zulu War, 1879; Egypt, 1882. GOC, 5ᵗʰ Infantry Brigade, Natal, 1899–1900. Saw action in the Transvaal, ORC and Northern Cape, 1900–2.

Hely-Hutchinson, Walter Francis (1849–1913). Lieutenant-Governor of Malta, 1884–9; Governor of the Windward Islands, 1889–93; of Natal and Zululand, 1893–1901; of the Cape Colony, 1901–10.

Hertzog, James Barry Munnik (1866–1942) studied Law in Cape Town and in the Netherlands. OFS judge, 1895–9. Legal advisor, Kimberley front, 1899–1900. Combat General, and shortly afterwards Assistant Chief Commandant, 1900–2, taking part in guerrilla operations in the ORC. Invaded Cape Colony, December 1900–February 1901. MP for Smithfield, OFS Legislative Assembly, 1907–10; MP for Smithfield, Union of SA Parliament, 1910–40. Minister of Justice, 1910–12 (and of Native Affairs, 1912). Champion of the Afrikaans language. Founded National Party (NP), 1914. Prime Minister, 1924–39. Founded United Party (which merged the NP and J.C. Smuts' South African Party), 1934.

Hildyard, Henry John Thornton (1846–1916). Previous service in Egypt, 1882. Saw action in Natal, 1899–1900; Transvaal, 1900–1. Director-General of

British Military Education, 1903–4; as Lieutenant-General, GOC-in-C, South Africa, 1905–8.

Hunter, Archibald (1856–1936). Previous service in Egypt, 1884–9; Sudan, 1896–8. Major-General, 1896. Besieged in Ladysmith, 1899–1900. Lieutenant-General, 1900. Forced Boers to surrender in Brandwater Basin, ORC, 1900. Invalided home, 1901. GOC, Scottish District, 1901–3; commanded the Western and later the Southern Army, India, 1903–8. General, 1905. Governor and C-in-C, Gibraltar, 1910–13; GOC, Aldershot, 1914–17. Conservative MP, Lancaster, 1918–22.

Jones, Inigo Richmund (1848–1914). Previous service in Egypt, 1885. OC, 1st (Guards) Brigade, 1900–2: took part in Lord Roberts' advance from Bloemfontein to Pretoria; GOC, Midlands, Cape Colony, 1901–2. GOC, Scots Guards, 1903–5.

Kelly-Kenny, Thomas (1840–1914). Previous service in China, 1860; Abyssinia, 1867–8. Major-General, 1896. Lieutenant-General, 1899. Took part in Lord Roberts' advance to Bloemfontein, 1900. GOC of all British forces in the ORC, 1900. Returned to UK with Lord Roberts. AG, 1901–4. General, 1905.

Kemp, Jan Christoffel Greyling (1872–1946). Previous service in Magato War, 1895; suppression of Jameson Raid, 1896. Saw action in Natal, 1899–1900; then mainly in the Western Transvaal, 1900–2. Combat General, 1901. One of six delegates (out of 60) who voted against the peace terms, 1902. Joined Union (of SA) Defence Forces in 1912. Rebelled against Louis Botha's government and trekked to German South-West Africa (today Namibia), 1914; after initial successes he surrendered, 1915, and was imprisoned, but released after serving just over a year. MP for Wolmaransstad, 1920–46. Minister of Agriculture, 1924–34; and of Lands, 1922–7.

Kitchener, Horatio Herbert, 1st Earl, of Khartoum, and Broome (1850–1916). Previous service in Franco-Prussian War, 1871 (as a volunteer on the side of the French); Egypt, 1882; Sudan, 1884–5. Governor-General of the Eastern Sudan and the Red Sea Littoral, 1886–8; AG of Egyptian Army, 1888–92; Sirdar of Egyptian Army, 1892–9. Major-General, 1896. Defeated Khalifa's Army at Omdurman, 1898. Governor-General of Sudan, 1898–9. Lord Roberts' Chief of Staff, South Africa, 1900; C-in-C, South Africa, 1900–2. General, 1902. C-in-C, India, 1902–9. Member of Committee of Imperial Defence, 1910. British Agent and Consul-General in Egypt, 1911–14. Secretary of State for War, 1914–16. Baron, 1898; Viscount, 1902; Field Marshal, 1909; Earl, 1914. Went down with HMS *Hampshire* off Orkney Islands en route to Russia.

Knox, Charles Edmond (1847–1938). Previous service in Bechuanaland, 1884–5. Saw action under Lord Roberts, 1900. Wounded at Paardeberg. Anti-guerrilla operations, ORC, 1900–2. Major-General, 1902.

Kritzinger, Pieter Hendrik (1870–1935). Saw action in Cape Colony, 1899–1900; fought under C.R. de Wet in OFS, 1900; invaded the Cape Colony on three occasions, 1900–1. General, 1901. Wounded and captured, 16 December 1901.

Kruger, Stephanus Johannes Paulus (Paul) (1825–1904). State President of the Transvaal, 1883–1902. Went to Europe in self-imposed exile, 1900. Died in Switzerland.

Long, Charles James (1849–1933). Previous service in Afghanistan, 1879–80; Sudan, 1897–8. Saw action in Natal, 1899–1900 (lost his guns and wounded at Colenso, 15 December 1899); took part in 2nd De Wet hunt, 1901. Inspector of Remounts, 1914.

Lyttelton, Neville Gerald (1845–1931). Previous service in suppression of Fenian Rebellion, Canada, 1866; Egypt, 1882; Sudan, 1898. Major-General, 1898. Saw action in Natal, 1899–1900; Transvaal and ORC, 1900–2. Lieutenant-General, 1901. GOC, Natal, 1901; C-in-C, South Africa, 1902–4; CGS, 1904–8. General, 1906. C-in-C, Ireland, 1908–12.

MacDonald, Hector Archibald (1853–1903). Previous service in Afghanistan, 1879–80; Transvaal War of Independence, 1880–1; Egypt, 1885 and 1896; Sudan, 1888–91 and 1896–8. Major-General, 1900. Commanded the Highland Brigade, 1900. Took part in the relief of Kimberley; Lord Roberts' march to Bloemfontein (wounded at Paardeberg). Anti-guerrilla operations, Cape Colony, 1900–1. Commanded Belgaum District, India, 1901–2. Committed suicide before allegations of homosexuality could be investigated by a court of inquiry.

Mackenzie, Colin John (1861–1956). Previous service in Egypt, 1882; Burma, 1886–8; Hazara, 1888; Hunza-Nagar and Gilgit, 1891; Waziristan, 1894–5; Sudan, 1898. Lord Roberts' Director of Field Intelligence since February 1900 (after Colonel G.F.R. Henderson was invalided home); Military Governor of Johannesburg, 1900. Served in World War I, 1914–18, GOC, 61st Division, 1916–18 (wounded).

Mahon, Bryan Thomas (1862–1930). Previous service in Egypt, 1896–7. Commanded the column that relieved Mafikeng, 1900. Operated in Eastern Transvaal, 1900. Governor of Kordofan, Egypt, 1901–4; commanded Belgaum District, India, 1904–9; Lucknow Division, 1909–13; GOC, 10th (Irish) Division, 1914. Took part in Gallipoli Campaign, 1915. C-in-C, Salonika Army, 1915–16; C-in-C, Ireland, 1916–18; military commander, Lille, 1918–19.

Marks, Samuel ('Sammy') (1843–1920) was a Lithuanian Jew who emigrated to England (c. 1859) and then to SA (1868), where he became involved in the diamond mining-industry, and later also in many other fields, including agriculture, forestry and a variety of industries, mainly in the Transvaal. He was a confidant of both Kruger and Rhodes, regarded the Anglo-Boer War as a grave mistake, and tried his best to bring about peace. He stayed on his farm east of Pretoria after the British occupation, worked tirelessly to ensure that neither the Boers nor the British damaged the mines, and spent large amounts of money in the support of civilians who were left destitute by the war. Senator, Union of SA, 1910–20.

McCallum, Henry Edward (1852–1919). Previous service in Perak Expedition, 1875–6; Malaya, 1891. Governor and C-in-C, Lagos, 1897; Governor, Natal, 1901–7, and of Ceylon, 1907–13.

Methuen, Lord – see Sanford, P.

Milner, Alfred (1854–1925). Under-Secretary for Finance in Egypt, 1890–2; Chairman, Board of Inland Revenue, 1892–4. Governor of the Cape Colony, 1897–1901; High Commissioner for South Africa, 1897–1905; Administrator of the Transvaal Colony and ORC, 1900–1; Governor of the Transvaal Colony and ORC, 1901–5; Member of War Cabinet, 1916–18; Secretary of State for War, 1918–19; Secretary of State for Colonies, 1919–21. Knighted, 1895; Baron, 1901; Viscount, 1902.

Morgan, Hill Godfrey (1862–1923). Previous service in the Sudan, 1896–8. Served in South Africa as Director of Supplies, Natal, 1899–1900; Director of Supplies, South Africa, 1900–2. Served in World War I, 1914–18. Temporary Brigadier-General, 1917.

Oliphant, Laurence James (1846–1914). Previous service in Sudan, 1885. Major-General, 1898. Commanded mobile columns, 1901–2. GOC, Home District, 1903–6; Northern Command, 1907–11.

Paget, Arthur Henry Fitzroy (1851–1928). Previous service in Ashanti, 1873; Sudan, 1885 and 1888–9; Burma, 1887–8. Saw action on Kimberley front, 1899–1900. Major-General, 1900. GOC, 20th Infantry Brigade, 1900–1. Operated in OFS and Transvaal. GOC, 1st Division, Aldershot, 1902–6. Lieutenant-General, 1906. GOC, Eastern Command, 1908–11; C-in-C, Ireland, 1911–14.

Plumer, Herbert Charles Onslow (1857–1932). Previous service in the Sudan, 1884. Assisted Colonel B.M. Mahon with the relief of Mafikeng, 1900. Then operated primarily in the Eastern Transvaal. Major-General, 1902. QMG, 1904–5; GOC, 5th Division, Ireland, 1906–9. Lieutenant-General, 1911. GOC, Northern Command, 1911–14; 5th Corps, 1915 and 2nd Army, 1915–17 and 1918; GOC, Italy, 1917–18. Baron Plumer, of Messines and Bilton, Yorkshire, 1919; Field Marshal, 1919. GOC, Army of the Rhine, 1918–19; Governor, Malta, 1919–24; High Commissioner, Palestine, 1925–8.

Pole-Carew, Reginald (1849–1924). Previous service in Afghanistan, 1879–80; Egypt, 1882; Burma, 1886–7. Major-General, 1899. On General Buller's staff, Natal, 1899, but transferred to Kimberley front as GOC, 9th Brigade, 1899–1900; GOC 1st (Guards) Brigade under Lord Roberts, 1900; Eastern Transvaal, 1900. Returned to UK. GOC, 8th Division, 3rd Army Corps, 1903–5. MP for the Bodmin electoral district, 1910–16.

Rawlinson, Henry Seymour (1864–1925). Previous service in Burma, 1887–8; Sudan, 1898. Besieged in Ladysmith, 1899–1900; AAG on Lord Roberts' Staff, 1900; operated against guerrillas, 1901–2. Major-General, 1909. Commanded 4th Division, 1914; 7th Division and 3rd Cavalry Division, 1914; GOC, IV Corps, 1914–15; 1st and 4th Armies, 1915–19. Knighted 1914; Lieutenant-General, 1916; General, 1917; Baron, 1919. GOC, Aldershot, 1919–20; C-in-C, India, 1920–5.

Rhodes, Cecil John (1853–1902). First came to South Africa in 1870. MP for Barkly West, Cape Colony, 1877–1902. Instrumental in the British occupation of Bechuanaland (today Botswana) and Southern Rhodesia (Zimbabwe). Made a fortune out of the diamond-fields of Kimberley and the Witwatersrand goldmines. Prime Minister, Cape Colony, 1890–6. Besieged in Kimberley, 1899–1900.

Rimington, Michael Frederic (1858–1928). Previous service in Bechuanaland, 1884–5; Zululand, 1888. Founder and commander of a volunteer intelligence unit called Rimington's Guides, or Scouts, 1899. Saw action on the Kimberley front, 1899–1900; in the OFS and Transvaal, 1900–2. Inspector of Cavalry, India, 1902.

Roberts, Ada Stewart Edwina (1875–1955). Fourth (and second surviving) daughter of Lord Roberts. Married Colonel (later Brigadier-General) Henry Frederick Elliot Lewen, 1913. One son, Frederic Roberts Alexander; killed in action, 1940.

Roberts, Aileen Mary (1870–1944). Elder surviving daughter of Lord Roberts. Never married.

Roberts, Frederick (Fred) Sleigh, 1st Earl, of Kandahar, Pretoria, and Waterford (1832–1914). Previous service in suppression of Indian Mutiny (VC), 1857–8; Ambeyla Expedition, 1863; Abyssinia, 1867–8; Lushai Expedition, 1871–2; Afghanistan, 1878–80; Burma, 1886–7. Major-General, 1878; Lieutenant-General, 1883; General, 1885; Field Marshal, 1895. QMG, India, 1875–8; C-in-C, Madras Army, 1881–5; C-in-C, India, 1885–93; C-in-C, Ireland, 1895–9; C-in-C, South Africa, 1899–1900; C-in-C, British Army, 1901–4. Baron, of Kandahar, 1892; Earl, of Pretoria, and Waterford, 1901.

Roberts, Nora Henrietta (née Bews) (died 1920). Wife of Lord Roberts. Married 1859. They had six children, three of whom died in infancy. Those who reached adulthood were Aileen Mary, Frederick Sherston (mortally wounded, Colenso, 15 December 1899), and Ada Stewart Edwina.

Rundle, Henry Macleod Leslie (1856–1934). Previous service in Anglo-Zulu War, 1879; Transvaal War of Independence, 1880–1; Egypt, 1882; Sudan, 1884–5, 1885–7 and 1889–98. Major-General, 1896. AG, Egypt, 1896–8. GOC, 8th Division, 1900–2. Operated in OFS, 1900–2. GOC, 5th Division, 1902–3. Lieutenant-General, 1905. General, 1909. Governor and C-in-C, Malta, 1909–15; C-in-C, Central Force, 1915–16.

Salisbury, Lord – see Cecil, R.A.T.G.

Sanford, Paul, 3rd Baron Methuen of Corsham (1845–1932). Previous service in Gold Coast, 1873; Ashanti, 1874; Egypt, 1882; Bechuanaland, 1884–8. GOC, Home District, 1892–7. GOC, 1st Division. Defeated at Magersfontein, 1899; captured at Tweebosch/De Klipdrift, 1902 (released soon afterwards). GOC, Eastern Command, 1903–8; GOC, South Africa, 1908–12, and Governor of Natal, 1910. Field Marshal, 1911. Governor and C-in-C, Malta, 1915–19.

Schleswig-Holstein, Christian Victor Albert Ernst Anton, Prince of (1867–1900). Eldest son of Princess Helena (later also known as Princess Christian), Queen Victoria's third daughter. Previous service in Hazara Expedition, 1891; Miranzai Expedition, 1891; Isazai Expedition, 1892; Ashanti, 1895–6; Sudan,

1898. Major, 1896. Saw action in Natal, 1899–1900; Transvaal, 1900. Died of typhoid.

Settle, Henry Hamilton (1847–1923). Previous service in the Sudan, 1884–5 and 1888–9; at Takar, 1891. Co-ordinated anti-rebellion operations in the North-Western Cape Colony, 1900; anti-commando operations in the ORC and Transvaal, 1900; and Cape Colony, 1900–2. GOC, Cape Colony, 1902–3; Portsmouth Defences, 1905–8. Lieutenant-General, 1908.

Smith-Dorrien, Horace Lockwood (1858–1930). Previous service in Anglo-Zulu War, 1879; Egypt and Sudan, 1882 and 1884–5; Chitral, 1895; Tirah, 1897–8; Sudan, 1898. Commanded the 19th Brigade in South Africa, 1899–1900. Fought at Paardeberg; took part in advance to Bloemfontein, and to Pretoria, 1900; column commander, 1900–1. Major-General, 1901. AG, India, 1901–3; GOC, 4th Division, Quetta, 1903–7; GOC at Aldershot, 1907–12; Southern Command, 1912–14; II Corps and 2nd Army, 1914–15; East Africa, 1915–16; Governor of Gibraltar, 1918–23.

Smuts, Jan ('Jannie') Christiaan (or Christian) (1870–1950). Boer General. State Attorney of the Transvaal, 1898–1902. Saw action in Transvaal, 1900–1; Cape Colony, 1901–2. Colonial Secretary and Minister of Education in the Transvaal, 1907–10. Played key role in the formation of the Union of SA, 1910. MP, Union of SA, 1910–48; Minister of Defence, 1910–19 and 1939–48; of the Interior, 1910–12; of Finance, 1912–15; of Native Affairs, 1919–24; of Justice, 1933–9; of Foreign Affairs, 1939–48. Prime Minister, 1919–24 and 1939–48; Member of British War Cabinet, 1917–19. Created the Royal Air Force as an independent service, 1918. Field Marshal in the British Army, 1941.

Solomon, Richard Prince (1850–1913). MP, Cape Colony, 1887–8. Attorney-General of the Cape Colony, 1898–1900. Accepted Milner's invitation to assist with the reconstruction of the Transvaal. Legal advisor of the Transvaal administration and of Lord Kitchener, 1901–2. Attorney-General of the Transvaal, 1902–6. Agent-General for the Transvaal in London, 1907–10. Union of SA's 1st High Commissioner in London, 1910–13.

Spens, James (1853–1934). Previous service in Afghanistan, 1879–80. Commanded the 85th King's Light Infantry, 1899–1900; the 19th Brigade, 1900; and a mobile column, Transvaal, 1901–2. GOC, 12th (Eastern) Division, 1914–15; GOC, Australian Training Depot, 1915; GOC, Cairo District, 1915–16.

Sprigg, John Gordon (1830–1913). Came to the Cape Colony from England in 1858. MP, Cape Colony, 1869–1904. Premier, 1878–81, 1886–90, 1896–8 and 1900–4.

Steyn, Marthinus Theunis (1857–1916). Studied Law in the Netherlands and in England (admitted to the Inner Temple, 1880; called to the bar, 1882). Attorney-General of the OFS, 1889; judge, 1889–96. President of the OFS, 1896–1902. Treated for ill health in Europe, 1902–5. Although still plagued by ill health, he played an important role in the reconstruction process after the war, and in the unification of SA.

Ternan, Trevor Patrick Breffney (1860–1949). Previous service in Afghanistan, 1880–1; Egypt, 1882; Sudan, 1884–5; Unyoro Expedition, Uganda, 1895; OC, operations against King Mwanga, Uganda, 1897; suppression of mutiny, Uganda, 1898–9 (wounded). Acting Commissioner and Consul-General, British East Africa, 1900. Commanded punitive expedition against Ogaden Somalis, 1900–1. Served in South Africa, 1901–2, commanded a mobile column, North-Western ORC, 1902. AAG, Southern District, Portsmouth, 1903; AAG, South Africa, 1903–5; GOC, Standerton District, Transvaal, 1906–7; served in World War I, 1914–18.

Tucker, Charles (1838–1935). Previous service during Bhootan Expedition, 1865; at Perak, 1875; in Sekhukhuneland, 1878; Anglo-Zulu War, 1879. Major-General, 1893. Commanded the 7th Division in South Africa, 1900. Took part in relief of Kimberley and advance to Bloemfontein, and to Pretoria, 1900. Defended lines of communication in ORC, 1900–1; commanded several mobile columns, 1901–2. Lieutenant-General, 1902. C-in-C, Scottish District, 1903–5.

Victor, Prince Christian – *see* Schleswig-Holstein, C.V.A.E.A.

Victoria (1819–1901). Queen of the United Kingdom of Great Britain and Ireland, 1837–1901, and Empress of India, 1877–1901. Entirely approved of the policy of Lord Salisbury's government towards the Transvaal, especially as formulated and applied by Joseph Chamberlain. She keenly followed events in South Africa, and showed a sincere and constant interest in the welfare of her soldiers.

Viljoen, Benjamin ('Ben') Johannes (1868–1917). Boer General who saw action in several of the wars against black tribes in the Transvaal, and in the suppression of the Jameson Raid, 1896. As Commandant of the Johannesburg commando he fought in Natal, 1899–1900, and as Combat General in Transvaal, 1900–2. On 25 January 1902 he was ambushed and taken prisoner near Lydenburg in the Eastern Transvaal, taken to Durban, and then by ship via Cape Town to a POW camp on St Helena. After the war he went to Europe, then to Mexico (where, in 1911, he helped to overthrow Porfirio Díaz), and eventually settled in the USA, where he died.

Willson, Mildmay Willson (1847–1912). Previous service in the Sudan, 1884–5. As Major-General the GOC, military district to the west of Johannesburg, 1901–2; commanded mobile columns in that area, 1902.

Wilson, Guy Douglas Arthur Fleetwood (1850–1940). Civil servant who served in a great variety of capacities, e.g. in the War Office as Secretary to Special Committee on Army Reorganisation, 1887; as private secretary of several prominent politicians, e.g. Mr Edward Stanhope, 1888–92, and Mr Henry Campbell-Bannerman, 1892–3. Financial Advisor to Lord Kitchener, South Africa, 1901. Later, inter alia, Director-General of Army Finance, 1904–8; Finance Member of the Supreme Council of India, 1908–13.

Wolseley, Garnet Joseph, 1st Viscount of Cairo and Wolseley (1833–1913). Previous service in 2nd Burma War, 1852–3; Crimean War, 1854–6;

suppression of Indian Mutiny, 1857–8; China, 1860; Red River Expedition, Canada, 1870; Ashanti, 1873–4; Anglo-Zulu War, 1879; Egypt, 1882; Sudan, 1884–5. QMG, War Office, 1881–2; AG, 1882–90; C-in-C, Ireland, 1890–5; C-in-C, British Army, 1895–1900. Major-General, 1874; Lieutenant-General, 1878; General, 1882; Viscount, 1885; Field Marshal, 1894.

Wood, Henry Evelyn (1838–1919). Previous service in the Crimean War, 1854–6; suppression of Indian Mutiny (VC), 1857–8; Ashanti, 1873; 9th Frontier War, Cape Colony, 1877–8; Anglo-Zulu War, 1879; Transvaal War of Independence, 1880–1; Egypt, 1882. QMG, 1893–7; AG, 1897–1901. Major-General, 1882; Lieutenant-General, 1891; General, 1893; Field Marshal, 1903. GOC, 2nd Army Corps, Salisbury, 1901–5.

Wools-Sampson, Aubrey (1856–1924). Previous service in Sekhukhuneland, 1878; Anglo-Zulu War, 1879; Transvaal War of Independence, 1880–1. A founder member of the Imperial Light Horse and an outstanding intelligence officer. Saw action in Natal, 1899–1900; Transvaal, 1900–2. Helped in suppressing the Bambatha Rebellion, Natal, 1906. Progressive MP for Parktown, Transvaal Legislative Assembly, 1907–10; Unionist MP for Braamfontein, Union of SA Parliament, 1910–15.

Wynne, Arthur Singleton (1846–1936). Previous service in Jowaki Expedition, 1877–8; Afghanistan, 1878–9; Transvaal War of Independence, 1880–1; Sudan, 1884–5. Saw action in South Africa, 1899–1901 (wounded): on General Buller's Staff in Natal, 1899–1900; GOC, Cape Colony, 1901.

Bibliography

A select list of the sources, manuscript and printed, used in this book. All books published in London unless otherwise stated.

Manuscript Sources

André Wessels Private Document Collection, Bloemfontein
G.F.R. Henderson (file)

Bodleian Library, Oxford
Milner Papers

British Library Manuscript Room, London
Arnold-Forster Papers
Balfour Papers
Campbell-Bannerman Papers
Hutton Papers
Lansdowne Papers
Midleton Papers
Paget Papers
War Office Papers

Churchill Archives Centre, Cambridge
Esher Papers
Winston Churchill Papers

Devon Record Office, Exeter
Buller Papers, 2065

Gloucestershire Record Office, Gloucester
Sir Michael Hicks Beach Papers, D2455

House of Lords Record Office, London
Lloyd George Papers, A/9/2
Stanley Papers, ST/12/3

Hove Central Library
Wolseley Papers

Imperial War Museum, London
Esher Papers, 70/8
General Sir Horace Smith-Dorrien Papers, 87/47

Killie Campbell Africana Library, Durban
Various documents

Liddell Hart Centre for Military Archives, London
Ian Hamilton Papers, 1/1, 2/1, 2/3-5, 3/1, 3/2/5, 4/2/8, 7/10/12, 17/6

The National Archives (formerly known as the Public Record Office), Kew
Kitchener Papers, PRO 30/57/16-25
Roberts Papers, WO 93/41, 105/5-40, 108/306
St John Brodrick Papers, PRO 30/67/6
War Office Papers, WO32/7958

National Archives of South Africa, Pretoria
K.G. 737-8, 743, 760-1, 854, 927
Microfilm Collection, M672-3, M722, M727, M812-16, M2939, M3140
P.A. Nierstrasz, Der süd-afrikanische Krieg, 1899–1902 (typed manuscript)
Photocopy Collection, FK 1894–1911
Roberts Papers, 60 volumes

National Army Museum, London
Birdwood Papers, 1967-07-19
G.F. Gorringe Papers, 1982-12-18
Lord Rawlinson Papers, 1952-01-33
Marker Papers, 1968-03-4-4
Maxwell Papers, 1978-07-25
R.G. Broadwood Papers, 1975-08-34
Roberts Papers, 1955-04-64-60, 1971-01-23, 1983-10-156
S.L. Barry Papers, 1968-07-186
Spenser Wilkinson Papers, 1990-11-42

Public Record Office of Northern Ireland, Belfast
Papers of Schomberg MacDonnell, Louisa Countess of Antrim and the Stuart Family of Dalness

The Royal Archives, Windsor
King Edward VII Papers
Queen Victoria Papers

Scottish Record Office, Edinburgh
General Register House
    Major-General Dundonald Papers, vols GD 233/124/1-4; 233/128-9; 233/130/1; 233/131; 233/135; 233/142/2; 233/143/1; 233/145-6; 233/162/2; 233/157/1-2; 233/177/111

West Register House
    Duke of Hamilton Papers (GD 406), vol.1819
    Furgusson of Kilkerran Papers, (NRA(S) 3572) /12/27

South African National Museum of Military History, Johannesburg
    J.D.P. French, Boer War Diary, 9th November 1899–17th March 1900 (manuscript)

The Sudan Archive, University of Durham
    Rundle Papers, 231/1, 231/3

Published Papers

Beckett, I.F.W. (ed.), *The Army and the Curragh Incident, 1914* (Army Records Society Vol. 2, 1986).

Buckle, G.E. (ed.), *The Letters of Queen Victoria*, 3rd Series: *A Selection from Her Majesty's Correspondence and Journal between the Years 1886 and 1901*, Vol. III: *1896–1901* (1932).

Guy, A.J. *et al.* (eds), *Military Miscellany I. Papers from the Seven Years War, the First and Second Sikh Wars and the First World War* (Army Records Society Vol. 12, Stroud, 1996).

Hancock, W.K. and Van der Poel, J. (eds), *Selections from the Smuts Papers* (vol.1, Cambridge, 1966).

Headlam, C. (ed.), *The Milner Papers* (2 vols, 1931–3).

Robson, B. (ed.), *Roberts in India. The Military Papers of Field Marshal Lord Roberts 1876–1893* (Army Records Society Vol. 9, Stroud, 1993).

Wessels, A. (ed.), *Lord Roberts and the War in South Africa 1899–1902* (Army Records Society Vol. 17, Stroud, 2000).

—— (ed.-in-chief), *Egodokumente. Persoonlike Ervaringe uit die Anglo-Boereoorlog 1899–1902* (Bloemfontein, 1993).

Official Publications

Army. Correspondence between Field-Marshal Lord Roberts, Commanding-in-Chief, South African Field Force, and Acting Commandant-General Louis Botha, dated 12th, 13th, 14th and 15th June, 1900 (Cd. 461, 1901).

——. *Findings of a Court of Enquiry held at Barberton on 25th September, 1900, to Investigate the Circumstances under which Lieutenant-Colonel B.E. Spragge, D.S.O., XIIIth Bn. Imperial Yeomanry, and Others, became Prisoners of War* (Cd. 470, 1901).

——. *Proclamations Issued by Field-Marshal Lord Roberts in South Africa* (Cd. 426, 1900).

——. *Remounts. Digest of Evidence taken before the Court of Enquiry on the Administration of the Army Remount Department* (1902).

——. *Report by Lieut.-General Sir H.E. Colvile, K.C.M.G., C.B., on the Operations of the Ninth Division at Paardeberg* (Cd. 520, 1901).

——. *Return of Military Forces in South Africa 1899–1902* (Cd. 990, 1902).

Correspondence relating to the Prolongation of Hostilities in South Africa (Cd. 732, 1901).

Correspondence relative to the Treatment of Natives by the Boers (Cd. 821, 1901).

Correspondence with the Netherlands Government regarding the War in South Africa (Cd. 906, 1902).

Further Correspondence relative to the Treatment of Natives by the Boers (Cd. 822, 1901 and Cd. 888, 1902).

Hart's Annual Army List, Militia List, and Imperial Yeomanry List, for 1906 (1906; reproduction edition, 1995).

Janisch, N., *Report and Proceedings with Annexures, of the Cape Peninsula Advisory Board, Appointed to Advise the Government on Matters Connected with the Suppression of Bubonic Plague* (S.l., 1901).

Kestell, J.D. and Van Velden, D.E., *The Peace Negotiations between the Governments of the South African Republic and the Orange Free State, and the Representatives of the British Government, which terminated in the Peace concluded at Vereeniging on the 31st May, 1902* (1912).

List of Casualties in the Army in South Africa, from 1st January, 1902, to the 31st May, 1902 (S.l., s.a.).

List of Officers of the Royal Regiment of Artillery from June, 1862, to June, 1914, with Appendices II (New edition, Sheffield, 1914).

Notulen der Verrichtingen van den HEd. Volksraad van den Oranje Vrijstaat in zijne Gewone Jaarlijkse Zitting aanvangende op Maandag, den 5den April 1897 (Bloemfontein, 1897).

The Official Army List for the Quarter Ending 21st December 1899 (s.a.).

Papers relating to the Administration of Martial Law in South Africa (Cd. 981, 1902).

Proceedings of a Court of Enquiry i.e. Enquiry held at St. Stephen's House, Westminster, S.W., on the Administration of the Army Remount Department since January 1899, by Order of the Commander in Chief dated 20th February 1902 (Cd. 993, 1902).

Report of His Majesty's Commissioners Appointed to Inquire into the Military Preparations and other Matters connected with the War in South Africa (Cd. 1789, 1903).

Report on the Concentration Camps in South Africa by the Committee of Ladies appointed by the Secretary of State for War, containing Reports on the Camps in Natal, the Orange River Colony, and the Transvaal (Cd. 893, 1902).

Reports by Officers Appointed by the Commander-in-Chief to Inquire into the Working of the Remount Department Abroad (Cd. 995, 1902).

Reports etc. on the Working of the Refugee Camps in the Transvaal, Orange River Colony, Cape Colony and Natal (Cd. 819, 1901).

Return of Buildings burnt in each Month from June, 1900, to January, 1901 including Farm Buildings, Mills, Cottages and Hovels (Cd. 524, 1901).

Return of Military Forces in South Africa, 1899–1902 (Cd. 892, 1902).

Royal Commission on South African Hospitals. Appendix to Minutes of Evidence taken before the Royal Commission Appointed to Consider and Report upon the Care and Treatment of the Sick and Wounded during the South African Campaign (Cd. 455, 1901).

——. *Minutes of Evidence taken before the Royal Commission Appointed to Consider and Report upon the Care and Treatment of the Sick and Wounded during the South African Campaign* (Cd. 454, 1901).

——. *Report of the Royal Commission Appointed to Consider and Report upon the Care and Treatment of the Sick and Wounded during the South African Campaign* (Cd. 453, 1901).

Royal Commission on the War in South Africa. Appendices to the Minutes of Evidence taken before the Royal Commission on the War in South Africa (Cd. 1792, 1903).

——. *Minutes of Evidence taken before the Royal Commission on the War in South Africa* (2 vols, Cd. 1790 and Cd. 1791, 1903).

Rules for the Guidance of Press Censors in South Africa (Pretoria, 1901).

Secret. South African War, 1899–1902. Telegrams relating to Censorship, Prisoners of War, &c., &c. (s.a.).

South Africa. Correspondence, &c. between the Commander-in-Chief in South Africa and the Boer Commanders so far as it Effects the Destruction of Property (Cd. 582, 1901).

——. *Correspondence respecting Terms of Surrender of the Boer Forces in the Field* (Cd. 1096, 1902).

——. *Further Correspondence relating to Affairs in South Africa* (Cd. 43, Cd. 261 and Cd. 420, 1900; and Cd. 903, 1902).

——. *Further Papers relating to Negotiations between Commandant Louis Botha and Lord Kitchener* (Cd. 663, 1901).

——. *Letter from Commandant Louis Botha to Lord Kitchener, dated 13th February, 1901* (Cd. 546, 1901).

——. *Papers relating to Negotiations between Commandant Louis Botha and Lord Kitchener* (Cd. 528, 1901).

——. *Proclamation issued by Lord Kitchener, as Administrator of the Transvaal, on 1st July, 1901, respecting Payments under Contracts to Purchase or Lease Land or Mining Rights, &c., entered into Prior to the War* (Cd. 781, 1901).

348

——. *Report from Lieut.-General Lord Methuen on the Action that took place near Tweebosch on 7ᵗʰ March 1902* (Cd. 967, 1902).

——. *Return of Buildings burnt in Each Month from June 1900, to January, 1901, including Farm Buildings, Mills, Cottages and Hovels* (Cd. 524, s.a.).

——. *Return of Farm Buildings, &c., in Cape Colony and Natal destroyed by the Boers* (Cd. 979, 1902).

——. *Revised Reprint of the Principal Army Orders and Cape Colony District Orders from the Outbreak of Hostilities to the End of July, 1901 with the Principal Head Quarters' Circular Memos, for 1900 and 1901 (for Reference)* (Cape Town, s.a.).

——. *Telegrams concerning the Siege of Ladysmith* (Cd. 987, 1902).

South Africa Despatches. Despatch by General Lord Kitchener, dated 8ᵗʰ April, 1902, relative to Military Operations in South Africa (Cd. 984, 1902).

——. *Despatch by General Lord Kitchener, dated 8ᵗʰ December, 1901, relative to Military Operations in South Africa* (Cd. 824, 1901).

——. *Despatch by General Lord Kitchener, dated 8ᵗʰ February, 1902, relative to Military Operations in South Africa* (Cd. 965, 1902).

——. *Despatch by General Lord Kitchener, dated 8ᵗʰ January, 1902, relative to Military Operations in South Africa* (Cd. 890,1902).

——. *Despatch by General Lord Kitchener, dated 8ᵗʰ July, 1901, relative to Military Operations in South Africa* (Cd. 695, 1901).

——. *Despatch by General Lord Kitchener, dated 1ˢᵗ June, 1902, relative to Military Operations in South Africa* (Cd. 986, 1902).

——. *Despatch by General Lord Kitchener, dated 8ᵗʰ March, 1901, relative to Military Operations in South Africa* (Cd. 522, 1901).

——. *Despatch by General Lord Kitchener, dated 8ᵗʰ March, 1902, relative to Military Operations in South Africa* (Cd. 970, 1902).

——. *Despatch by General Lord Kitchener, dated 8ᵗʰ May, 1901, relative to Military Operations in South Africa* (Cd. 605, 1901).

——. *Despatch by General Lord Kitchener, dated 8ᵗʰ November, 1901, relative to Military Operations in South Africa* (Cd. 823, 1901).

——. *Despatches by General Lord Kitchener, dated 8ᵗʰ August, 8ᵗʰ September, and 8ᵗʰ October, 1901, relative to Military Operations in South Africa, including a Supplementary Despatch, dated 18ᵗʰ October, on the Actions at Itala Mount, Fort Prospect, and Moedwil* (Cd. 820, 1901).

South African Despatches, Vol. I (Cd. 457, 1901).

——, *Vol. II. Natal Field Army* (Cd. 458, 1901).

——, *Vol. I. From 1ˢᵗ November 1899 to 1ˢᵗ August 1900* (S.l., s.a.).

South African Field Force. Republication of the Principal Circulars issued during 1900. Army Headquarters, Pretoria, January, 1901 (Pretoria, 1901).

South African War, 1899–1902. Confidential Telegrams. 12ᵗʰ October 1899 to 1ˢᵗ October 1902 (S.l., s.a.).

——, *1899–1900. Vol. I. Home and Oversea Correspondence by Field-Marshal Lord Roberts K.P., G.C.B., V.C., &c., &c., from 12ᵗʰ December, 1899, to 4ᵗʰ June, 1900* (S.l., s.a.).

——, *1899–1900. Vol. II. Home and Oversea Correspondence of Field-Marshal Lord Roberts K.P., G.C.B., V.C., &c., &c., from 5th June to 5th September, 1900* (S.l., s.a.).

——, *1899–1901. Vol. III. Home and Oversea Correspondence of Field-Marshal Lord Roberts K.P., G.C.B., V.C., &c., &c., from 5th September, 1900, to 1st January, 1901* (S.l., s.a.).

——, *Vols I. to VI. Telegrams and Letters sent by Field-Marshal Lord Roberts K.P., G.C.B., V.C. &c. From 23rd December 1899 to 26th December 1900* (S.l., s.a.).

——, *1900. Field-Marshal Lord Roberts, K.P., &c. 1. – Proclamations. 2. – Army Orders (1901).*

Staats-almanak voor de Zuid-Afrikaanse Republiek 1899 (Pretoria, 1898).

Statistics of the Refugee Camps (Cd. 1161, 1902).

Works of Reference

Barker, B.J., *A Concise Dictionary of the Boer War* (Cape Town, 1999).

Boer War Services of Military Officers of the British and Colonial Armies, Imperial Yeomanry, Mounted Infantry, Local Units &cc 1899–1902 including Earlier Services (1998).

Bruce, G., *Harbottle's Dictionary of Battles* (2nd ed., 1979).

Burke's Genealogical and Heraldic History of the Peerage, Baronetage and Knightage (99th edition, 1949).

Cloete, P.G., *The Anglo-Boer War. A Chronology* (Pretoria, 2000).

The Dictionary of National Biography (*DNB*, 29 vols, 1967–81).

Dictionary of South African Biography (*DSAB*, 5 vols, Cape Town, Durban and Pretoria, 1968–87).

Dooner, M.G., *The "Last Post": being a Roll of All Officers (Naval, Military or Colonial) who gave their Lives for their Queen, King and Country, in the South African War, 1899–1902* (s.a.).

Hall, D., *The Hall Handbook of the Anglo-Boer War 1899–1902* (Pietermaritzburg, 1999).

Hazlehurst, C. and Woodland, C. (compilers), *A Guide to the Papers of British Cabinet Ministers 1900–1951* (1974).

Hepworth, P., *Archives and Manuscripts in Libraries* (2nd ed., 1964).

Malan, J., *Die Boere-offisiere van die Tweede Vryheidsoorlog, 1899–1902* (Pretoria, 1990).

Sandler, S. (ed.), *Ground Warfare. An International Encyclopedia* (3 vols, Santa Barbara, 2002).

Standard Encyclopaedia of Southern Africa (*SESA*, 12 vols, Cape Town, 1970–76).

Uys, I., *South African Military Who's Who 1452–1992* (Germiston, 1992).

Van Schoor, M.C.E. (ed.) and Steyn, E. and Prophet, J. (compilers), *A Bibliography of the Anglo-Boer War 1899–1902 / 'n Bibliografie van die Anglo-Boereoorlog 1899–1902* (Bloemfontein, 1999).

Watt, S., *In Memoriam. Roll of Honour Imperial Forces. Anglo-Boer War 1899–1902* (Pietermaritzburg, 2000).

Wessels, A., *Suid-Afrikaanse Verhandelinge en Proefskrifte oor die Geskiedenis van die Anglo-Boereoorlog. 'n Bronnestudie* (Pretoria, 1987).

Who was Who 1897–1960 (5 vols, 1935–67).

Biographies, Autobiographies, Published Diaries and Other Memoirs

Adye, J., *Soldiers and Others I have known* (1925).

Aitken, W.F., *Lord Kitchener of Khartoum* (1901).

Arthur, G., *Life of Lord Kitchener* (3 vols, 1920).

Ballard, C.R., *Kitchener (s.a.)*.

Brits, J.P. (ed.), *Diary of a National Scout. P.J. du Toit 1900–1902* (Pretoria, 1902).

Brodrick, W. St J.F., *Records and Reactions, 1856–1939* (1939).

Brooke-Hunt, V., *Lord Roberts. A Biography* (1900).

Cairnes, W.E., *Lord Roberts as a Soldier in Peace and War. A Biography* (1901).

Cassar, G.H., *Kitchener. Architect of Victory* (1977).

Churchill, W.S., *London to Ladysmith via Pretoria* (1900).

Clingman, S., *Bram Fischer: Afrikaner Revolutionary* (1998).

Cobban, J.M., *The Life and Deeds of Earl Roberts* (4 vols, Edinburgh and London, 1901).

Colvile, H.E., *The Work of the Ninth Division in South Africa 1900* (1901).

Comaroff, J.L. (ed.), *The Boer War Diary of Sol T. Plaatje, an African at Mafeking* (1973).

Curruthers, J., *Wildlife and Warfare. The Life of James Stevenson-Hamilton* (Pietermaritzburg, 2001).

De Watteville, H., *Lord Roberts* (1938).

De Wet, C.R., *Three Years War (October 1899–June 1902)* (1902).

Engelenburg, F.V., *General Louis Botha* (1929).

Esher, R., *The Tragedy of Lord Kitchener* (1921).

Farwell, B., *Eminent Victorian Soldiers. Seekers of Glory* (Harmondsworth, 1986).

Fawcett, M.G., *What I Remember* (1925).

Ferreira, O.J.O. (ed.), *Memoirs of Ben Bouwer as written by P.J. le Riche* (Pretoria, 1980).

Forrest, G., *The Life of Lord Roberts, K.G., V.C.* (1914).

French, G., *The Life of Field-Marshal Sir John French, First Earl of Ypres* (1931).

Grew, E.S. *et al.*, *Field-Marshal Lord Kitchener. His Life and Work for the Empire* (3 vols, 1917 (I), s.a. (II, III)).

Groser, H.G., *Field-Marshal Lord Roberts* (1900).

Hackwood, F.W. *The Life of Lord Kitchener (s.a.)*.

Hamilton, G., *Parliamentary Reminiscences and Reflections 1886–1906* (1922).

Hamilton, I., *Listening for the Drums* (1944).

Hamilton, I. (A. Farrar-Hockley, ed.), *The Commander* (1957).

Hamilton, I.B.M., *The Happy Warrior. A Life of General Sir Ian Hamilton G.C.B., G.C.M.G., D.S.O.* (1966).

Hancock, W.K., *Smuts* (vol. 1, Cambridge, 1962).

Hodges, A., *Lord Kitchener* (1936).

James, D., *Lord Roberts* (1954).

Kellett, R., *The King's Shilling. The Life and Times of Lord Kitchener of Khartoum* (1984).

Kestell, J.D., *Through Shot and Flame* (Johannesburg, 1976).

Le Bas, H. (ed.), *The Lord Kitchener Memorial Book* (*s.a.*).

Lehman, J.H., *All Sir Garnet. A Life of Field-Marshal Lord Wolseley* (1964).

Lennox, A.G. (ed.), *The Diary of Lord Bertie of Thame 1914–1918* (vol. I, 1924).

Lyttelton, N., *Eighty Years* (1927).

Mackenzie, D.A., *Lord Kitchener. The Story of His Life and Work* (1916).

Magnus, P., *Kitchener. Portrait of an Imperialist* (1961).

Maritz, S.G., *My Lewe en Strewe* (Pretoria, 1939).

McCormick, D., *The Mystery of Lord Kitchener's Death* (1959).

Meintjes, J., *Sword in the Sand. The Life and Death of Gideon Scheepers* (Cape Town, 1969).

Melville, C.H., *Life of General the Right Hon. Sir Redvers Buller* (2 vols, 1923).

Miller, S.M., *Lord Methuen and the British Army. Failure and Redemption in South Africa* (1999).

Newton, Lord, *Lord Lansdowne. A Biography* (1929).

Oberholster, A.G. (ed.), *Oorlogsdagboek van Jan F.E. Cilliers 1899–1902* (Pretoria, 1978).

Parker, B. (ed.), *Famous British Generals* (1951).

Pollock, J., *Kitchener. The Road to Omdurman* (1998).

Power, F. (pseud. for A.V. Freeman), *The Kitchener Mystery* (*s.a.*).

Preller, G.S., *Scheepers se Dagboek en die Stryd in Kaapland (1 Okt. 1901–18 Jan. 1902)* (Cape Town, 1938).

Protheroe, E., *Lord Kitchener* (3rd edition, 1920).

Reckitt, B.N., *The Lindley Affair. A Diary of the Boer War* (Hull, 1972).

Reitz, D., *Commando. A Boer Journal of the Boer War* (1929).

Royle, T., *The Kitchener Enigma* (1985).

Rye, J.B. and Groser, H.G., *Kitchener in His own Words* (1917).

Scholtz, G.D., *Generaal Christiaan Frederik Beyers 1869–1914* (Johannesburg, 1941).

Smit, A.P. and Maré, L. (eds), *Die Beleg van Mafeking. Dagboek van Abraham Stafleu* (Pretoria, 1985).

Smithers, A.J., *The Fighting Nation. Lord Kitchener and his Armies* (1994).

Truter, E., *Tibbie. Rachel Isabella Steyn, 1865–1955. Haar Lewe was Haar Boodskap* (Cape Town, 1977).

Van der Merwe, N.J., *Marthinus Theunis Steyn. 'n Lewensbeskrywing* (2 vols, Cape Town, 1921).

Van Niekerk, L.E., *Kruger se Regterhand. 'n Biografie van dr. W.J. Leyds* (Pretoria, 1985).

Van Reenen, R. (ed.), *Emily Hobhouse. Boer War Letters* (Cape Town, 1999).

Van Rensburg, T. (ed.), *Camp Diary of Henrietta E.C. Armstrong. Experiences of a Boer Nurse in the Irene Concentration Camp, 6 April–11 October 1901* (Pretoria, 1980).

—— (ed.), *Vir Vaderland, Vryheid en Eer. Oorlogsherinneringe van Wilhelm Mangold 1899–1902* (Pretoria, 1988).

Van Schoor, M.C.E. (ed.), *'n Bittereinder aan die Woord. Geskrifte en Toesprake van Marthinus Theunis Steyn* (Bloemfontein, 1997).

Viljoen, B., *My Reminiscences of the Anglo-Boer War* (1902).

Warner, P., *Kitchener. The Man behind the Legend* (1985).

Warren, H., *Christian Victor. The Story of a Young Soldier* (2nd ed., 1903).

Wessels, A. (ed.), *Anglo-Boer War Diary of Herbert Gwynne Howell* (Pretoria, 1986).

—— (ed.), 'Die Oorlogsherinneringe van kommandant Jacob Petrus Neser', *Christiaan de Wet Annals* 7 (*S.l.*, 1988).

Wheeler, H.F.B., *The Story of Lord Roberts* (1915).

Wilkinson-Latham, R.J., *Kitchener. An Illustrated Life of Field Marshal Lord Kitchener* (Aylesbury, 1973).

Secondary Works

Amery, L.S. (ed.), *The Times History of the War in South Africa 1899–1902* (7 vols, 1900–9).

Bakkes, C.M., *Die Britse Deurbraak aan die Benede-Tugela op Majubadag 1900* (Pretoria, 1973).

Barnard, C.J., *Generaal Louis Botha op die Natalse Front, 1899–1900* (Cape Town, 1970).

Bateman, P., *Generals of the Anglo-Boer War* (Cape Town, 1977).

Bester, R., *Boer Rifles and Carbines of the Anglo-Boer War* (Bloemfontein, 1994).

Bleszynski, N., *Shoot Straight, you Bastards! The Truth behind the Killing of 'Breaker' Morant* (Milsons Point, 2002).

Bond, B., *The Victorian Army and the Staff College* (1972).

Boyden, P.B., Guy, A.J. and Harding, M. (eds), *'Ashes and Blood'. The British Army in South Africa 1795–1914* (1999).

Breytenbach, J.H., *Die Geskiedenis van die Tweede Vryheidsoorlog in Suid-Afrika, 1899–1902* (6 vols, Pretoria, 1969–96).

—— and Ploeger, J., *Majuba Gedenkboek* (Roodepoort, 1980).

Burke, P., *The Siege of O'okiep (Guerrilla Campaign in the Anglo-Boer War)* (Bloemfontein, 1995).

Burleigh, B., *The Natal Campaign* (1900).

——, *Khartoum Campaign 1898 or the re-conquest of the Soudan* (1899).

——, *Sirdar and Khalifa or the re-conquest of the Soudan 1898* (1898).

Cammack, D., *The Rand at War 1899–1902. The Witwatersrand and the Anglo-Boer War* (1990).

Carver, M., *Britain's Army in the Twentieth Century* (1999).

——, *The National Army Museum Book of the Boer War* (1999).

Changuion, L., *Uncle Sam, Oom Paul en John Bull. Amerika en die Anglo-Boereoorlog 1899–1902* (Pretoria, 2001).

Churchill, W.S., *Ian Hamilton's March* (1900).

Crawford, J. and Ellis, E., *To Fight for the Empire. An Illustrated History of New Zealand and the South African War, 1899–1902* (Auckland, 1999).

Curtis, L., *With Milner in South Africa* (Oxford, 1951).

Das, M.H., *India under Morley and Minto. Politics behind Revolution, Repression and Reforms* (1964).

Davenport, T.R.H., *The Afrikaner Bond. The History of a South African Political Party, 1880–1911* (Cape Town, 1966).

Davey, A.M., *The Pro-Boers 1877–1902* (Cape Town, s.a.).

Davitt, M., *The Boer Fight for Freedom, from the Beginning of Hostilities to the Peace of Pretoria* (3rd ed., New York, 1902).

Dennis, P. and Grey, J. (eds), *The Boer War. Army Nation and Empire* (Canberra, 2000).

De Villiers, O.T., *Met De Wet en Steyn in het Veld. Avonturen, Ervaringen en Indrukken* (Amsterdam, 1903).

Devitt, N., *The Concentration Camps in South Africa during the Anglo-Boer War of 1899–1902* (Pietermaritzburg, 1941).

De Wet, A. *et al.*, *Die Buren in der Kapkolonie im Kriege mit England* (Munich, s.a.).

Doyle, A.C., *The Great Boer War* (1902).

Du Plessis, P.J., *Oomblikke van Spanning* (Cape Town, 1938).

Duxbury, G.R., *The Battle of Magersfontein 11th December 1899* (2nd ed., Johannesburg, 1979).

Evans, M.M., *The Boer War. South Africa 1899–1902* (Oxford, 1999).

Farwell, B., *Queen Victoria's Little Wars* (1973).

Ferreira, O.J.O. *Viva os Boers! Boeregeïnterneerdes in Portugal tydens die Anglo-Boereoorlog, 1899–1902* (Pretoria, 1994).

Finer, S.E., *The Man on Horseback. The Role of the Military in Politics* (1962).

Fortesque, J.W., *The Empire and the Army* (1928).

Fuller, J.F.C., *The Conduct of War 1789–1961. A Study of the Impact of the French, Industrial, and Russian Revolutions on War and its Conduct* (1961).

Fuller, J.F.C., *The Last of the Gentlemen's Wars* (1937).

Furgusson, T.G., *British Military Intelligence, 1870–1914. The Development of a Modern Intelligence Organization* (Frederick, 1984).

Gardner, B., *The Lion's Cage* (1969).

——, *Mafeking. A Victorian Legend* (1966).

Germains, V.W., *The Kitchener Armies. The Story of a National Achievement* (1930).

The German Official Account of the War in South Africa (2 vols, 1904–6).

Girouard, P., *History of the Railways during the War in South Africa* (Chatham, 1904).

Goldmann, C.S., *With General French and the Cavalry in South Africa* (1902).

Gooch, J., *The Plans of War. The General Staff and British Military Strategy, c.1900–1916* (1974).

—— (ed.), *The Boer War. Direction, Experience and Image* (2000).

Grant, M.H. and Maurice, J.F. (ed.), *History of the War in South Africa 1899–1902* (4 vols, 1906–10).

Greyling, P.J., *Pretoria en die Anglo-Boereoorlog. 'n Gids tot Geboue, Terreine, Grafte en Monumente / Pretoria and the Anglo-Boer War. A Guide of Buildings, Terrains, Graves and Monuments* (Pretoria, 2000).

Grinnell-Milne, D.W., *Baden-Powell at Mafeking* (1957).

Grundlingh, A.M., *Die "Hendsoppers" en "Joiners". Die Rasionaal en Verskynsel van Verraad* (Pretoria, 1979).

Haswell, J., *Citizen Armies* (1973).

Hamer, W.S., *The British Army. Civil-Military Relations 1885–1905* (Oxford, 1970).

Hattingh, J. and Wessels, A., *Britse Fortifikasies in die Anglo-Boereoorlog (1899–1902)* (Bloemfontein, 1997).

Hobhouse, E., *The Brunt of War and Where it Fell* (1902).

Iwan Müller, E.B., *Lord Milner and South Africa* (1902).

Jackson, T., *The Boer War* (1999).

The Jameson Raid. A Centennial Retrospective (Johannesburg, 1996).

Jooste, G. and Oosthuizen, A. *So het hulle Gesterf. Gedenkboek van Teregstellings van Kaapse Rebelle en Republikeinse Burgers tydens die Anglo-Boereoorlog 1899–1902* (Pretoria, 1998).

Jordaan, G., *Hoe zij Stierven. Mededelingen aangaande het Einde dergenen, aan wie gedurende de Oorlog 1899–1902, in de Kaap-Kolonie het Doodvonnis Voltrokken is* (Cape Town, 1917).

Judd, D. and Surridge, K., *The Boer War* (2002).

Kiernan, V.G., *European Armies from Conquest to Collapse, 1815–1960* (1982).

Knox, E.B., *Buller's Campaign with the Natal Field Force of 1900* (1900).

Kruger, R., *Good-bye Dolly Gray. A History of the Boer War* (1967).

Labuschagne, P., *Ghostriders of the Anglo-Boer War. The Role and Contribution of Agterryers* (Pretoria, 1999).

Lehman, J.H., *The First Boer War* (1972).

Le May, G.H.L., *British Supremacy in South Africa 1899–1907* (Oxford, 1965).

Liddell Hart, B.H., *Strategy. The Indirect Approach* (1967).

Lowry, D. (ed.), *The South African War Reappraised* (Manchester, 2000).

Luvaas, J., *The Education of an Army. British Military Thought, 1815–1940* (1965).

Marix-Evans, M., *The Boer War. South Africa 1899–1902* (Oxford, 1999).

Martin, A.C., *The Concentration Camps 1900–1902. Facts, Figures and Fables* (Cape Town, *s.a.*).

Marwick, A., *War and Social Change in the Twentieth Century. A Comparative Study of Britain, France, Germany, Russia and the United States* (Basingstoke, 1974).

Maydon, J.G., *French's Cavalry Campaign* (1902).

McDonald, R.D., *In die Skaduwee van die Dood* (Cape Town, 1943).

Meintjes, J., *Stormberg. A Lost Opportunity* (Cape Town, 1969).

Miller, C., *Painting the Map Red. Canada and the South African War, 1899–1902* (Montreal, 1993).

Moore, D.M., *General Botha's Second Expedition to Natal during the Anglo-Boer War, September–October 1901* (Cape Town, 1979).

Moseley, S.A., *With Kitchener in Cairo* (1917).

Nasson, B., *Abraham Esau's War. A Black South African War in the Cape 1899–1902* (African Studies Series 68, Cambridge, 1991).

——, *The South African War 1899–1902* (1999).

Naudé, J.F., *Vechten en Vluchten van Beyers en Kemp "Bôkant" De Wet* (Rotterdam, *s.a.*).

Nevinson, H.W., *Changes and Chances* (1923).

Omond, G.W.T., *The Boers in Europe. A Sidelight on History* (1903).

Otto, J.C., *Die Konsentrasiekampe* (Cape Town, 1954).

Pakenham, T., *The Boer War* (1979).

Pemberton, W.B., *Battles of the Boer War* (1964).

Pieterse, H.C.J., *Oorlogsavonture van genl. Wynand Malan* (Cape Town, 1946).

Ploeger, J., *Die Fortifikasie van Pretoria. Fort Klapperkop – Gister en Vandag* (Pretoria, 1968).

Preller, G.S., *Talana. Die Driegeneraalslag by Dundee met Lewenssketse van genl. Daniel Erasmus* (Kaapstad, 1942).

Pretorius, F., *The Great Escape of the Boer Pimpernel. Christiaan de Wet. The Making of a Legend* (Pietermaritzburg, 2001).

—— (ed.), *Scorched Earth* (Cape Town, 2001).

Raath, A.W.G., *Die Boervrou, 1899–1902, 1: Moederleed* (Nylstroom, 2002).

——, *The British Concentration Camps of the Anglo-Boer War 1899–1902: Reports on the Camps* (Bloemfontein, 1999).

—— and Louw, R.M., *Die Konsentrasiekamp te Bethulie gedurende die Anglo-Boereoorlog 1899–1902* (Bloemfontein, 1991).

——. *Die Konsentrasiekamp te Springfontein gedurende die Anglo-Boereoorlog 1899–1902* (Bloemfontein, 1991).

——. *Die Konsentrasiekamp te Vredefortweg gedurende die Anglo-Boereoorlog 1899–1902* (Bloemfontein, 1992).

—— and Olivier, D., *Die Konsentrasiekamp te Bloemfontein gedurende die Anglo-Boereoorlog 1899–1902* (Bloemfontein, 1993).

Rabie, J.E., *Generaal C.R. de Wet se Krygsleiding by Sannaspas en Groenkop* (Pretoria, 1980).

Ransford, O., *The Battle of Spion Kop* (1969).

Richardson, F.M., *Mars without Venus. A Study of Some Homosexual Generals* (Edinburgh, 1981).

Sampson, V. and Hamilton, I., *Anti-Commando* (1931).

Scholtz, G.D., *Die Oorsake van die Tweede Vryheidsoorlog 1899–1902* (2 vols, Johannesburg, 1948).

Scholtz, L., *Waarom die Boere die Oorlog Verloor het* (Pretoria, 1999).

Sessions, H., *Two Years with the Remount Commission* (1903).

Shearing, T. & D., *Commandant Gideon Scheepers and the Search for his Grave* (Sedgefield, 1999)

———, *Commandant Lötter and his Rebels* (Sedgefield, 1998).

———, *General Jan Smuts and his Long Ride* (Sedgefield, 2000).

Shorten, J.R., *Cape Town* (Cape Town, 1963).

Sibbald, R., *The War Correspondents. The Boer War* (Dover (USA), 1993).

Simkins, P., *Kitchener's Army. The Raising of the New Armies, 1914–16* (Manchester, 1988).

Sixsmith, E.K.G., *British Generalship in the Twentieth Century* (1970).

Smith, I.R., *The Origins of the South African War, 1899–1902* (1996).

——— (ed.), *The Siege of Mafeking* (2 vols, Johannesburg, 2001).

Smurthwaite, D., *The Boer War* (1999).

Spiers, E.M., *The Late Victorian Army, 1868–1902* (Manchester, 1992).

Spies, S.B., *Methods of Barbarism? Roberts and Kitchener and Civilians in the Boer Republics, January 1900–May 1902* (Cape Town, 1977).

Steevens, G.W., *With Kitchener to Khartum* (23rd ed., Edinburgh, 1901).

Stirling, J., *The Colonials in South Africa 1899–1902. Their Record, based on the Despatches* (1907).

———, *Our Regiments in South Africa 1899–1902. Their Record, based on the Despatches* (1907).

Strachan, H., *European Armies and the Conduct of War* (1993).

Strydom, C.J.S., *Kaapland en die Tweede Vryheidsoorlog* (Cape Town, 1943).

Surridge, K.T., *Managing the South African War, 1899–1902. Politicians v. Generals* (Woodbridge, 1998).

Symons, J., *Buller's Campaign* (1963).

Taylor, A.J.P. (ed.) and Mayer, S.L. (compiler), *History of World War I* (*S.l.*, 1978).

Theron, B., *Pretoria at War 1899–1900* (Pretoria, 2000).

Trew, P., *The Boer War Generals* (Johannesburg, 1999).

Tylden, G., *The Armed Forces of South Africa with an Appendix on the Commandos* (Johannesburg, 1954).

Vallentin, W., *Der Burenkrieg* (Leipzig, 1903).

Van der Bank, D.A. (compiler), *1899–1902. Slagvelde, Gedenktekens en Grafte van die Anglo-Boereoorlog in Bloemfontein en Omgewing / Battlefields, Monuments and Graves of the Anglo-Boer War in Bloemfontein and Vicinity* (Bloemfontein, 2001).

Van der Merwe, F.J., *Horses of the Anglo Boer War / Perde van die Anglo-Boereoorlog* (Kleinmond, [2000]).

Van der Westhuizen, G. & E., *Gids tot die Anglo-Boereoorlog in die Oos-Transvaal / Guide to the Anglo-Boer War in the Eastern Transvaal* (S.l., 2000).

Van Hartesveldt, R., *Boer War* (Stroud, 2000).

Wallace, R.L., *The Australians at the Boer War* (Canberra, 1976).

Warwick, P., *Black People and the South African War, 1899–1902* (Cambridge, 1983).

—— (ed.), *The South African War. The Anglo-Boer War, 1899–1902* (Harlow, 1980).

Wassermann, J. and Kearny, B. (eds), *A Warrior's Gateway. Durban and the Anglo-Boer War 1899–1902* (Pretoria, 2002).

Wessels, A., *Die Anglo-Boereoorlog 1899–1902. 'n Oorsig van die Militêre Verloop van die Stryd* (Bloemfontein, 1991).

——, *Die Militêre Rol van Swart Mense, Bruin Mense en Indiërs tydens die Anglo-Boereoorlog (1899–1902)* (Bloemfontein, 1998).

——, *The Phases of the Anglo-Boer War 1899–1902* (Bloemfontein, 1998).

Wessels, E., *They Fought on Foreign Soil* (Bloemfontein, 2001).

——, *Veldslae. Anglo-Boereoorlog 1899–1902* (Pretoria, 2002).

Wheeler, O., *The War Office Past and Present* (1914).

Williams, C., *Hushed Up: A Case for Inquiry into some Suppressed Facts concerning the Conduct of the War in South Africa* (1902).

Yardley, J.W., *With the Inniskilling Dragoons. The Record of a Cavalry Regiment during the Boer War, 1899–1902* (1904).

Ziegler, P., *Omdurman* (1973).

Articles

Adams, J., 'Was "K" Gay?', *History Today* 49(1), November 1999, pp. 26–7.

Botha, H.J., 'Die Moord op Derdepoort, 25 November 1899. Nie-Blankes in Oorlogsdiens', *Militaria* 1(2), 1969, pp. 3–98.

Beaumont, J., 'The British Press and Censorship during the South African War 1899–1902', *South African Historical Journal* 41, November 1999, pp. 267–89.

Benyon, J., 'The "Walkover" that wasn't: "Miscalculation" and the "Unnecessary" South African War', *South African Historical Journal* 41, November 1999, pp. 106–29.

Buckner, P., 'The Royal Tour of 1901 and the Construction of an Imperial Identity in South Africa', *South African Historical Journal* 41, November 1999, pp. 324–48.

Du Preez, S., 'Die Val van Pretoria', *Militaria* 5(3), 1975, pp. 22–39.

Evaldsson, A.-K. and Wessels, A., 'The Anglo-Boer War Centennial: A Critical Evaluation', *Journal for Contemporary History* 27(3), December 2002, pp. 125–44.

Gomm, N., 'Commandant P.H. Kritzinger in the Cape, December 1900 – December 1901', *Military History Journal* 1(7), December 1970, pp. 30–2, 34.

Hall, D.D., 'Guns in South Africa 1899–1902', *Military History Journal* 2(2), December 1971, pp. 41–5.

Hattingh, J. and Wessels, A., 'Life in the British Blockhouses during the Anglo-Boer War, 1899–1902', *South African Journal of Cultural History* 13(2), November 1999, pp. 39–55.

Jacobs, J., 'Die Britse Besetting van Pietersburg en die Operasies in Noordoos-Transvaal in April 1901', *Tydskrif vir Geesteswetenskappe* 39(3&4), September & December 1999, pp. 263–86.

Kessler, S.V., 'The Black and Coloured Concentration Camps of the Anglo-Boer War 1899–1902: Shifting the Paradigm from *Sole Martyrdom* to *Mutual Suffering*', *Historia* 44(1), May 1999, pp. 110–47.

Main, E.M. and Wessels, A. (eds), 'Letters: Lord Milner to Hamilton John Goold-Adams, 1901–1905', *Christiaan de Wet Annals* 5, October 1978, pp. 107–56.

McLeod, A., 'Generaals Christiaan de Wet en Jan Smuts: hoe hulle die Anglo-Boereoorlog Ervaar het', *Tydskrif vir Geesteswetenskappe* 39(3&4), September & December 1999, pp. 293–313.

—— and Pretorius, F., 'M.T. Steyn se Ervaring van die Anglo-Boereoorlog vanuit 'n Sielkundige Perspektief', *Historia* 47(1), May 2002, pp. 33–55.

Mongalo, B.E. and Du Pisani, J.A., 'Victims of a White Man's War: Blacks in Concentration Camps during the South African War (1899–1902)', *Historia* 44(1), May 1999, pp. 148–82.

Morton, R.F., 'Linchwe I and the Kgatla Campaign in the South African War, 1899–1902', *The Journal of African History* 26(2&3), 1985, pp. 169–90.

Nasson, W.R., 'Moving Lord Kitchener: Black Military Transport and Supply Work in the South African War, 1899–1902, with Particular Reference to the Cape Colony', *Journal of Southern African Studies* 11(1), October 1984, pp. 25–51.

Nel, H.F., 'Die Slag van Donkerhoek 11–12 Junie 1900', *Militaria* 15(1), 1985, pp. 52–8 and 15(2), 1985, pp. 17–30.

Potgieter, T.D., 'Nineteenth Century Technological Development and its Influence on the Anglo-Boer War, 1899–1902', *Journal for Contemporary History* 25(2), December 2000, pp. 116–35.

Pretorius, F., ' "Deze Vergadering . . . beschouwt, dat onder de Omstandigheden het Volk niet Gerechtvaardigd is, met den Oorlog voort te gaan . . ." 'n Ontleding van die Redes waarom die Boere-afgevaardigdes by Vereeniging op 31 Mei 1902 die Britse Vredesvoorwaardes aanvaar het', *Journal for Contemporary History* 27(2), May 2002, pp. 75–96.

Schoeman, K., 'Die Dood van Abraham Esau. Ooggetuieberigte uit die besette Calvinia, 1901', *Quarterly Bulletin of the South African Library* 40(2), December 1985, pp. 56–66.

Scholtz, L., 'Clausewitz, Mao Zedong en die Anglo-Boereoorlog', *Journal for Contemporary History* 25(2), December 2000, pp. 236–69.

Sixsmith, E.K.G., 'Kitchener and the Guerrillas in the Boer War', *The Army Quarterly and Defence Journal* 104(1), January 1974, pp. 203–14.

Smith, I.R., 'The Origins of the South African War (1899–1902). A Reappraisal', *South African Historical Journal* 22, November 1990, pp. 24–60.

Steytler, F.A., 'Bronnenavorsing in Groot-Brittanje, 1951–1954' *S.A. Argiefblad* 8, 1966, p. 31.

Truter, E.J.J., 'Die Rol van die Vrou in die Voortsetting van die Anglo-Boereoorlog met Spesiale Verwysing na die Oranje-Vrystaat', *Journal for Contemporary History* 25(2), December 2000, pp. 197–211.

Watt, S.A., 'The Anglo-Boer War: The Medical Arrangements and Implications thereof during the British Occupation of Bloemfontein: March–August 1900', *Military History Journal* 9(2), 1992, pp. 44–54.

Wessels, A., 'An Assessment of the British Military Strategy during the Anglo-Boer War up to "Black Week", December 1899', *Journal for Contemporary History* 27(2), May 2002, pp. 1–21.

——, 'An Assessment of the British Offensive during the Anglo-Boer War, 16 December 1899–10 February 1900', *Journal for Contemporary History* 25(2), December 2000, pp. 100–15.

——, 'Die Boere se Strategie aan die Begin van die Anglo-Boereoorlog', *Tydskrif vir Geesteswetenskappe* 39(3&4), September & December 1999, pp. 227–42.

——, 'Militêre Strategie tydens die Anglo-Boereoorlog (1899–1902): 'n Herwaardering na Verloop van 100 Jaar', *Historia* 47(1), May 2002, pp. 9–32.

——, 'Die Traumatiese Nalatenskap van die Anglo-Boereoorlog se Konsentrasiekampe', *Journal for Contemporary History* 26(2), December 2001, pp. 1–20.

—— (ed.), 'Irish Nationalists and South Africa, 1877–1902 (by J.L. McCracken)', *Christiaan de Wet Annals* 5, October 1978, pp. 157–84.

Wohlberg, A. and Wessels, A., 'The Interaction between the Merebank Concentration Camp and the City of Durban, 1901–1902', *New Contree* 48, 2000, pp. 86–102.

Wulfsohn, L., 'Elands River. A Siege which possibly Changed the Course of History in South Africa', *Military History Journal* 6(3), June 1984, pp. 106–8.

Theses

Bakkes, C.M., 'Die Militêre Situasie aan die Benede-Tugela op die Vooraand van die Britse Deurbraak by Pietershoogte (26 Februarie 1900)', M.A., University of Pretoria, 1966 (Published in *Archives Year Book for South African History* 30(1), 1967).

Basson, J.L., 'Die Slag van Paardeberg', unpublished M.A., University of Pretoria, 1972.

Botes, S.M., 'Van Residensie tot Presidensie: 'n Kultuurhistoriese Studie van Ampswonings in Bloemfontein, 1846–1900', unpublished M.A., University of Pretoria, 1993.

Botha, J.P., 'Die Beleg van Mafeking tydens die Anglo-Boereoorlog', unpublished D.Litt., University of South Africa, 1967.

Bothma, T., 'The Conciliation Movement in the Cape Colony during the Anglo-Boer War, 1899–1902', unpublished M.A., University of Cape Town, 1974.

Breytenbach, A.E., 'Die Slag by Donkerhoek, 11–12 Junie 1900', unpublished M.A., University of South Africa, 1980.

Buys, M.H., 'Militêre Regering in Transvaal, 1900–1902', unpublished D.Phil., University of Pretoria, 1973.

Cilliers, J.H., 'Die Slag van Spioenkop (24 Januarie 1900)', M.A., University of Pretoria, 1957 (Published in *Archives Year Book for South African History* 23(2), 1960).

Delport, P.J., 'Die Rol van genl. Marthinus Prinsloo gedurende die Tweede Vryheidsoorlog', unpublished M.A., University of the Orange Free State, 1973.

Du Plooy, W.J., 'Die Militêre Voorbereidings en Verloop van die Jameson-inval', unpublished M.A., University of Pretoria, 1959.

Du Preez, S.J., 'Vredespogings gedurende die Anglo-Boereoorlog tot Maart 1901', unpublished M.A., University of Pretoria, 1977.

——, 'Die Vrede van Vereeniging', unpublished D.Phil., University of Pretoria, 1986.

Fourie, L.M., 'Die Militêre Loopbaan van Manie Maritz tot aan die Einde van die Anglo-Boereoorlog', unpublished M.A., Potchefstroom University for Christian Higher Education, 1976.

Kessler, S.V., 'The Black Concentration Camps of the South African War 1899–1902', unpublished D.Phil., University of Cape Town, 2003.

Kruger, C.J.H., 'Militêre Bewind in die Oranje-Vrystaat, Maart, 1900–Januarie, 1901', unpublished M.A., University of Pretoria, 1958.

Liebenberg, E.C. 'Die Topografiese Kartering van Suid-Afrika, 1879–1972: 'n Histories-geografiese Ontleding', unpublished M.A., University of South Africa, 1973.

Maphalala, S.J., 'The participation of Zulus in the Anglo-Boer War', unpublished M.A., University of Zululand, 1979.

Mocke, H.A., 'Die Slag van Colenso. 15 Desember 1899', unpublished M.A., University of Pretoria, 1967.

Oosthuizen, J., 'Jacobus Hercules de la Rey en die Tweede Vryheidsoorlog', unpublished D.Litt., Potchefstroom University College, 1950.

Oosthuizen, S.P.R., 'Die Beheer, Behandeling en Lewe van die Krygsgevangenes gedurende die Anglo-Boereoorlog, 1899–1902', unpublished D.Phil., University of the Free State, 1975.

Pienaar, A.J., 'Christiaan Roedolf de Wet in die Anglo-Boereoorlog', unpublished M.A., Potchefstroom University for Christian Higher Education, 1975.

Pyper, P.A., 'Generaal J.C. Smuts en die Tweede Vryheidsoorlog (1899–1902)', unpublished M.A., Potchefstroom University for Christian Higher Education, 1960.

Roodt, J.J., 'Die Port Elizabethse Konsentrasiekamp, 1899–1902', unpublished M.A., University of Port Elizabeth, 1990.

Roos, J.C., 'Johannesburg en die Tweede Vryheidsoorlog Oktober 1899–Mei 1900', unpublished D.Litt. et Phil., University of South Africa, 1951.

Scholtz, W.L. von R., 'Generaal Christiaan de Wet as Veldheer', D.Litt., University of Leiden, 1978 (Published as *Generaal Christiaan de Wet as Veldheer*, Pretoria, 2003).

Schultz, B.G., 'Die Slag van Bergendal (Dalmanutha)', unpublished M.A., University of Pretoria, 1974.

Siwundhla, H.T., 'The participation of Non-Europeans in the Anglo-Boer War, 1899–1902', unpublished Ph.D., Claremont (USA), 1977.

Snyman, J.H., 'Die Afrikaner in Kaapland, 1899–1902', D.Litt., Potchefstroom University for Christian Higher Education, 1974 (Published in *Archives Year Book for South African History* 42(2), 1979).

——, 'Rebelle-verhoor in Kaapland gedurende die Tweede Vryheidsoorlog met spesiale Verwysing na die Militêre Howe, 1899–1902', M.A., University of South Africa, 1961 (Published in *Archives Year Book for South African History* 25, 1962).

Strydom, C.J.S., 'Die Kaapkolonie, 1899–1902: Skadevergoeding en die Rebelle in Ere herstel', unpublished Ph.D., University of Cape Town, 1932.

Terblanche, H.J., 'Die Beleg van Kimberley', unpublished M.A., Potchefstroom University for Christian Higher Education, 1973.

Van Vreden, C. de W., 'Pretoria en die Tweede Vryheidsoorlog, 11 Oktober 1899 – 5 Junie 1900', unpublished M.A., University of Pretoria, 1955.

Visser, G.R., 'Pres. M.T. Steyn in die Anglo-Boereoorlog', unpublished M.A., University of the Orange Free State, 1977.

Wessels, A., 'Die Britse Militêre Strategie tydens die Anglo-Boereoorlog tot en met die Buller-fase', unpublished D.Phil., University of the Orange Free State, 1986.

Wohlberg, A.U., 'The Merebank Concentration Camp in Durban, 1901–1902', unpublished M.A., University of the Free State, 2000.

Index

ARMY RECORDS SOCIETY
(FOUNDED 1984)

Members of the Society are entitled to purchase back volumes
at reduced prices.
Orders should be sent to the Hon. Treasurer, Army Records Society,
c/o National Army Museum,
Royal Hospital Road,
London SW3 4HT

The Society has already issued:

Vol. I:
The Military Correspondence of Field Marshal Sir Henry Wilson 1918–1922
Edited by Dr Keith Jeffery

Vol. II:
The Army and the Curragh Incident, 1914
Edited by Dr Ian F.W. Beckett

Vol. III:
The Napoleonic War Journal of Captain Thomas Henry Browne, 1807–1816
Edited by Roger Norman Buckley

Vol. IV:
An Eighteenth-Century Secretary at War.
The Papers of William, Viscount Barrington
Edited by Dr Tony Hayter

Vol. V:
The Military Correspondence of Field Marshal Sir William Robertson 1915–1918
Edited by David R. Woodward

Vol. VI:
Colonel Samuel Bagshawe and the Army of George II, 1731–1762
Edited by Dr Alan J. Guy

Vol. VII:
Montgomery and the Eighth Army
Edited by Stephen Brooks

Vol. VIII:
The British Army and Signals Intelligence during the First World War
Edited by John Ferris

Vol. IX:
Roberts in India
The Military Papers of Field Marshal Lord Roberts 1876–1893
Edited by Brian Robson

Vol. X:
Lord Chelmsford's Zululand Campaign 1878–1879
Edited by John P.C. Laband

Vol. XI:
Letters of a Victorian Army Officer: Edward Wellesley 1840–1854
Edited by Michael Carver

Vol XII:
Military Miscellany I
Papers from the Seven Years War, the Second Sikh War and the First World War
Editors: Alan J. Guy, R.N.W. Thomas and Gerard J. De Groot

Vol. XIII:
John Peebles' American War 1776–1782
Edited by Ira J. Gruber

Vol. XIV:
The Maratha War Papers of Arthur Wellesley
Edited by Anthony S. Bennell

Vol. XV:
The Letters of Lieutenant-Colonel Charles à Court Repington 1903–1918
Edited by A.J.A. Morris

Vol. XVI:
Sir Hugh Rose and the Central India Campaign 1858
Edited by Brian Robson

Vol. XVII:
Lord Roberts and the War in South Africa 1899–1902
Edited by André Wessels

373

Vol. XVIII:
The Journal of Corporal Todd 1745–1762
Edited by Andrew Cormack and Alan Jones

Vol. XIX:
Rawlinson in India
Edited by Marc Jacobsen

Vol. XX:
Amherst and the Conquest of Canada
Edited by Richard Middleton

Vol. XXI:
At Wellington's Right Hand:
The Letters of Lieutenant-Colonel Sir Alexander Gordon, 1808–1815
Edited by Rory Muir

Vol. XXII:
Allenby in Palestine:
The Middle East Correspondence of Field Marshal Viscount Allenby,
June 1917–October 1919
Edited by Matthew Hughes

Vol. XXIII:
Military Miscellany II
Manuscripts from Marlborough's Wars, the American War of Independence
and the Boer War
Edited by David G. Chandler in collaboration with Christopher L. Scott,
Marianne M. Gilchrist and Robin Jenkins

Vol. XXIV:
Romaine's Crimean War:
The Letters and Journal of William Govett Romaine
Edited by Colin Robins